. . . interpretive anthropology directly addresses the world in which we humans are. Conventional social science, in its search for underlying causes, explains away that world and in doing so alienates us from it and destroys its magic. When we are possessed, we do not exist within the category of psychological defense mechanisms. Instead, we are in the company of gods, who are all the more real for being human creations.

To reduce this world of contextual webs, of ghostly presences, to cause-and-effect language of conventional social science is to risk seriously misunderstanding our mode of being. (Richardson 1984, p. 275)

Exotic Deviance

Medicalizing Cultural Idioms—
From Strangeness to Illness

Dr. Robert E. Bartholomew

UNIVERSITY PRESS OF COLORADO

Published by the University Press of Colorado
5589 Arapahoe Avenue, Suite 206C
Boulder, Colorado 80303

The University Press of Colorado is a cooperative publishing enterprise supported, in part, by Adams State College, Colorado State University, Fort Lewis College, Mesa State College, Metropolitan State College of Denver, University of Colorado, University of Northern Colorado, University of Southern Colorado, and Western State College of Colorado.

The paper used in this publication meets the minimum requirements of the American National Standard for Information Sciences—Permanence of Paper for Printed Library Materials. ANSI Z39.48-1992

Library of Congress Cataloging-in-Publication Data

Bartholomew, Robert E.
    Exotic deviance: medicalizing cultural idioms—from strangeness to illness / Robert E. Bartholomew.
        p. cm.
    Includes bibliographical references and index.
    ISBN 0-87081-597-0 (c. : alk. paper) — ISBN 0-87081-598-9 (p. : alk. paper)
    1. Psychiatry, Transcultural. 2. Ethnopsychology. 3. Ethnocentrism. 4. Deviant behavior.
 5. Social control. 6. Hysteria, Epidemic. 7. Chorea, Epidemic. 8. Latah (Disease) 9. Koro (Disease) I. Title.

RC455.4.E8 B367 2000
616.85'8—dc21
                                                                              00-051878

Designed by Laura Furney
Typeset by Daniel Pratt

09 08 07 06 05 04 03 02 01 00   10 9 8 7 6 5 4 3 2 1

I dedicate this book to Peter Conrad and Joseph Schneider,
pioneers in the study of deviance and medicalization.
This study would not have been possible without the critical clarifying
comments of James Coughlan and Claudia Knapman
and the inspiration of Allan Patience.

Contents

Foreword

Over the past two decades a considerable literature has accumulated examining the medicalization of deviance in modern society. Social scientists and other researchers have investigated how a variety of forms of rule breaking, handled as sinful or criminal at another time, were defined as illness in our own age. Beyond constructing detailed cases of medicalization, analysts have examined its origins and consequences in society.

What is clear is that medical designations of deviance have become common in Western societies, framing problems like alcoholism, mental illness, anorexia, obesity, attention deficit disorder, battering, and any number of addictions (from drugs to gambling to sex). Although contracting funding may constrain treatment of medicalized problems, medicalization seems to be persisting in developed societies. At this point we know considerably less about medicalization in developing and non-Western societies. My experience in Indonesia left me with the impression that Western medical categories for behavior such as anorexia and attention deficit disorder are known among medical professionals but are not commonly applied. Our knowledge of medicalization in non-Western contexts is as yet rudimentary.

Robert Bartholomew makes a unique and important contribution to our explorations of medicalization. Using a social anthropological lens, he shows us again how history and culture can be great relativizers, rendering our contemporary realities more problematic. Basing his research on first-hand experience and an impressive command of the literature, Bartholomew extends the medicalization of deviance to non-Western societies. With great detail he questions psychiatric categories and challenges some long-standing anthropological and psychiatric conceptions. In particular, he investigates the empirical and intellectual underpinnings of three well-known "culture-bound syndromes" and finds much psychiatric thinking to be limited by Eurocentric and biomedical biases.

Unlike many other social scientists, Bartholomew takes a skeptical rather than a romantic stance as he reexamines the well-trodden terrains of *latah*, *koro*, and mass psychogenic illness. He is critical of the imposition of a Western psychiatric frame for troubles that can be seen as local "idioms." He argues persuasively against the misapplication of medical diagnoses to indigenous strange and enigmatic behaviors, viewing them in part as conceptual residues of the colonial era. Bartholomew's challenge to these "culture-bound syndromes" suggests that biomedical categories may restrict rather than further our understanding of these phenomena.

This book is a unique contribution to the medicalization literature in at least one other respect. The vast majority of medicalization studies trace the history of deviance designations from badness to sickness, elucidating the process by which a problem comes into medical jurisdiction. These studies generally bracket the question of whether a problem "really" is an illness or a disease, choosing to focus on the viability of the designations rather than the validity of the diagnosis. Bartholomew, in contrast, rather than tracing *latah*'s history as a psychiatric designation, actually endeavors to refute its standing as a medical category by examining both observational and published data on the disorder. This takes medicalization studies into relatively unchartered waters, at the same time offering fresh alternatives to the biomedical model.

This book presents us with important exemplars of the limitations of transcultural psychiatric categories and the perils of decontextualizing behaviors from their sociocultural sources. This provocative account is sure to be controversial in some circles, but it presents challenges not easily obviated by common understandings or biomedical assumptions.

—PETER CONRAD
Brandeis University

Preface

At different times and places, groups of people have engaged in seemingly bizarre behaviors for which labels of abnormal or mentally disturbed would seem appropriate. Men in parts of Asia continue to experience *koro* "epidemics," convinced that they are the victims of a contagious disease that causes their penises to shrink and eventually disappear. Those affected often take extreme measures such as placing clamps or string onto the organ or having family members hold the penis in relays until an appropriate treatment can be obtained. Occasionally, women are affected, believing their breasts or vaginas are being sucked into their bodies. Episodes can endure for weeks or months and affect thousands.

In the Southeast Asian nations of Malaysia and Indonesia, Western observers have noted a "strange peculiarity" among some inhabitants since the mid-nineteenth century. When startled, ordinarily shy, stolid elderly Malay women will suddenly swear profusely, mimic the gestures of others, and may be induced into "automatic obedience." During this latter state, "victims" of *latah* will do anything they are told: strip naked in public, slap themselves on the face, or crawl on the floor and growl like an animal. On rare occasions, men are affected.

History is replete with similar cases of seemingly aberrant behaviors. Between the eleventh and seventeenth centuries, Saint Vitus' dance swept across Europe, as tens of thousands of people lost all inhibition, participating in frenzied public orgies and wild dances lasting for days and even weeks. Some howled and screamed or asked to be tipped into the air, whereas others begged to be struck on their feet or whipped or made obscene gestures. In Italy this behavior was known as *tarantism,* as victims were believed to have been bitten by the tarantula spider, for which the only cure was thought to be frenetic dancing to certain music.

This study challenges psychological disturbance labels applied to latah, koro, and dancing mania and reappraises psychiatric pontifications as to their disorder status. Using historical case studies of the literature under scrutiny and ethnographic observation in the instance of latah, I shall demonstrate that pathological assessments of these three seemingly bizarre psychological disturbances are not supported by consistent biological or clinical findings of abnormality but exemplify what medical anthropologist Arthur Kleinman (1977) terms "category fallacies." They are based on faith, not science, and are socially designated deviance categories constructed within the Western social and cultural tradition by objectivist researchers seeking universalist, etiological causes of deviation, with norms, values, and worldviews that differ significantly from the participants. This is accomplished by utilizing an eclectic blend of interactionist, phenomenological, conflict, and feminist models that focus on various aspects of deviance creation and the social and cultural bases of deviance categorizing. By detailing the deviant's world and motivations, this theoretical approach explicates relationships between the deviant and stigmatizing agents of social control, emphasizing the significance of values, norms, culture, power, gender, context, and worldview in the social construction of illness.

Chapter 1 discusses the insidious, imperialistic nature of Western professional psychiatric theory and practice and its tendency to superimpose the relatively narrow constellation of Eurocentric norms onto "deviant" behaviors in non-Western cultures or distant historical eras by focusing on their "unusual" or "irrational" nature per se without adequate assessment of the participants' context and meaning. Emphasis is placed on Western ideological biases in constructing social problems and on medicine as an agent of social control, whereby certain unpopular, "strange," or unfamiliar behaviors are inappropriately labeled mental disorders and reified under the pretext of being discoveries within the apolitical, "neutral" domain of science. I shall label this process the medicalization of "exotic deviance"; that is, behaviors in non-Western cultures or distant historical periods receiving unsubstantiated illness or disorder designations using normality criteria embedded within Western medical ideology.

Chapters 2 through 5 consist of case studies illustrating the medicalization of "exotic deviance." I shall demonstrate that pathological assessments of the seemingly bizarre mental disorders of latah, koro, and Saint Vitus' dance are not supported by consistent biological or clinical findings of abnormality but are categories constructed within the Western social and cultural tradition by researchers with norms, values, and worldviews that differ significantly from those of the participants.

Despite the problem of misdiagnosing unfamiliar behaviors as mental disorders, there is a danger of "throwing out the baby with the bath water" by abandoning altogether the dominant Western medical-psychiatric model of psychological disturbance. This becomes evident in Chapter 6, where a fourth case study explores the appearance of "epidemic hysteria" in school settings. Although the uniformity of symptoms is remarkably consistent across cultures and time periods and clearly supports its status as a stress-induced medical syndrome, some antipsychiatrists and radical feminists champion the dubious and dangerous claim that few, if any, behaviors deserve the mental illness label.

In Chapter 7 it becomes clear that Western scientists must be more cognizant of the diversity of transcultural, transhistorical social realities, which often engender concepts of normality that differ radically from the narrow Western tradition. The realization that people apprehend and interpret the world within specific sociocultural contexts needs to be fully appreciated before reductive or value-laden judgments are imposed on those interpretations. Without adequate sociocultural sensitivity, scientists risk distorting the ethnographic record by reducing "foreign" behaviors to grandiose categories of the irrational or psychologically disturbed.

Acknowledgments

Portions of Chapters 2 and 3 first appeared in "Disease, Disorder, or Deception? Latah as Habit in a Malay Extended Family," *Journal of Nervous and Mental Disease* 182:331–338 (1994), and "Letter. The Idiom of Latah: Reply to Dr. Simons," *Journal of Nervous and Mental Disease* 183:184–185 (1995). Both are reproduced with permission of the Williams and Wilkins Company, 428 E. Preston Street, Baltimore, Maryland. Part of Chapter 2 first appeared in "Culture-Bound Syndromes as Fakery," *Skeptical Inquirer* 19(6):36–41 (1995). It is reproduced with permission from the Committee for the Scientific Investigation of Claims of the Paranormal, Box 703, Amherst, New York 14226-0703. Part of Chapter 3 first appeared in "The Medicalization of the Exotic: Latah as a Colonialism-Bound Syndrome," *Deviant Behavior* 18:47–75 (1997). It is reproduced with permission from Taylor and Francis. A portion of Chapter 4 first appeared in "The Medicalization of Exotic Deviance: A Sociological Perspective on Epidemic Koro," *Transcultural Psychiatry* 35(1):5–38 (1998). It is reproduced with permission of the Division of Social and Transcultural Psychiatry, Department of Psychiatry, McGill University, Montreal, Canada. Portions of Chapter 5 first appeared in "Dancing With Myths: The Misogynist Construction of Dancing Mania," *Feminism and Psychology* 8(2):173–183 (1998). It is reproduced with permission from Sage Publications. Also, "Tarantism, Dancing Mania, and Demonopathy: The Anthro-Political Aspects of 'Mass Psychogenic Illness,'" *Psychological Medicine* 24:281–306 (1994). It is reproduced with the permission of Cambridge

University Press. Part of Chapter 6 first appeared in R. E. Bartholomew and
F. Sirois, "Epidemic Hysteria in Schools: An International and Historical
Overview," *Educational Studies* 22(3):285–311 (1996). It is reproduced with
permission of Carfax Publishing, Oxfordshire, England.

EXOTIC DEVIANCE

1

Western Medical Imperialism
and the Politics of Psychiatric Classification

In showing the special character of what purports to be universal, sociology can contribute to public life—the visions of other realities, other ways of conceptualizing human actions, other possible ways of inventing human institutions (Joseph Gusfield 1980, p. ix).

Man . . . maker of tools, rules, and moral judgments (Philip K. Bock 1979, p. 261).

The "syndromes" of *latah* in Malayo-Indonesia, *koro* in Asia, and medieval European "dancing mania" are typified as exotic psychiatric disturbances. This study challenges these designations after examining their sociocultural context and meaning and argues that they have been unjustly given medical labels. Mislabeling has occurred because the general global mainstream medical profession has a Western or Eurocentric[1] bias that serves as an insidious instrument of social control through its unrivaled claim to possess superior health-related knowledge. This book examines the influence of imperialistic Western medical dominance in successfully defining as psychiatric disorders behaviors occurring in contemporary non-Western cultures (latah and koro) or in Western subcultures from the distant past (dancing mania). The objectivity and accuracy of Western medical ideology, especially in the contested field of psychiatry, are questioned. Simply put, scientists have biases too. The behaviors explored in this book are at such variance with present-day Eurocentric notions of normality, rationality, and reality that they are labeled as medical problems no "right-thinking" person could engage in at any place or time.

TAXONOMIES AS A SOCIAL PROCESS

Professional medical ideology is typified as an unproblematic culture and value-neutral enterprise that dispassionately applies universal scientific principles to explain, diagnose, and treat disease. However, classificatory schemes (taxonomies) do not exist as objective elements in nature awaiting description. Thomas Hunt Morgan (in Clark 1984, p. 23) writes that "the arrangement . . . into species, genera, families, etc., is only a scheme invented by man for purposes of classification. Thus there is no such thing in nature as a species, except as a concept of a group of forms more or less alike."

In discussing the tendency for mental health practitioners to construct and accept nosologies (disease classification systems) of disorder and disease that conspicuously reflect both the popular and professional zeitgeist (spirit of the times), a psychiatrist with extensive anthropological training, Arthur Kleinman (1988, p. 12), urges caution in accepting these schemes, given the historical tendency to reify them as part of everyday reality. He remarks that validating psychiatric diagnoses also entails "verification of the meaning of the observations in a given social system . . . [as] observation is inseparable from interpretation. Psychiatric diagnoses are not things, though they give name and scope to processes. . . . [They] derive from categories . . . [that] are outcomes of historical development, cultural influence, and political negotiation" (Kleinman 1988, p. 12). Hence, taxonomies are socially constructed in a subjective, value-laden process[2] that may reveal more about those imaginatively creating nosologies as opposed to persons exhibiting the behavior under study. For instance, it is no surprise that during the nineteenth century, white males of European heritage were placed at the pinnacle of the evolutionary hierarchy, as they had the political power to create such a scheme.

HUMAN DIVERSITY AND THE WESTERN MEDICAL MONOPOLY

Although scientific methods may be used to study a constellation of behavioral signs, identifying and labeling a particular conduct into dichotomies of normal/abnormal, moral/immoral, legal/illegal reflects the evaluators' norms, values, and beliefs concerning health at any time and place (Wing 1978, p. 16). It is therefore crucial to understand that the transcultural, transhistorical variation in norms, values, practices, and beliefs is dynamic, voluminous, and extreme.[3] Examples include cannibalism, head-hunting, and polyandry (having multiple husbands at one time) as established cultural traditions among certain peoples, whereas Western medicine has justified colonization, slavery, bloodletting, and phrenology (a theory that skull shape indicates intelligence) based on prevailing folk realities. This is a critical point, because it often appears that no one in their "right mind" would engage in what appears to be obviously sick, disordered, or immoral behavior.

Normality is not an objective given from which unproblematic behavioral assessments can be rendered independent of historical era, culture, subculture, or social group. Not surprisingly, many of the earliest challenges to narrow universalist conceptions of normality were from cultural anthropologists because of their familiarity and interaction with an array of behavior patterns that were accepted or institutionalized within their respective settings. For instance, Edward Sapir (1932, p. 230) noted the importance, especially for psychiatrists, of the wide variation and plasticity of normality across cultures as follows: "personalities are not conditioned by a generalized process of adjustment to the 'normal' but by the necessity of adjustment to the greatest possible variety of idea and action patterns according to the accidents of birth and biography." Ruth Benedict (1959 [1934], p. 276) observed that normality "within a very wide range is culturally defined," and therefore psychiatrists should resist using a set list of symptoms in determining abnormality but should instead examine how a certain constellation of behaviors aligns with the deep structural values, beliefs, and mores of the people in question. A. Irving Hallowell (1934, p. 2) emphasized having a detailed knowledge of a certain culture in its totality and being "aware of the normal range of individual behavior within the cultural pattern and likewise understanding what the people themselves consider to be extreme deviations from this norm." This new relativistic position, gaining momentum in the 1930s, reflected a growing sensitivity to understanding transcultural behaviors and mental disorders but was open to criticisms, such as statistical reductionism as "normal" was equated with ideas and actions that were popular. However, the significant realization these and other relativistic studies helped to foster is that the normality standards of one culture (especially the West) cannot be imposed on another culture without raising significant ethical and moral questions.

The ethnographic record of acceptable or institutionalized behaviors is indeed remarkable. It includes altruism, Nazism, and everything in between. In certain parts of Sulawesi, Indonesia, it is perfectly acceptable for close male friends to greet each other by grabbing and gently squeezing the others' testicles.[4] Based on a survey of 185 cultures, polygyny (having multiple wives simultaneously)—an arrestable offense in many contemporary Western countries—was allowed in 84 percent (Ford and Beach 1951, p. 108). Among the Banaro peoples of Papua New Guinea, a man is forbidden to have sex with his wife "until she has borne a child by a friend of his father" (Haralambos et al.

1996, p. 380). The Siriono of eastern Bolivia are one of several peoples for whom "parents may masturbate their own children" and "open self-masturbation of children is accepted and taken for granted" (Barnouw 1975, p. 284). Although typified as deviant in the modern West, fondling or playing with children's genitalia was common in medieval Europe (Archer 1985, p. 760). In medieval Italy and France, droit du seigneur (right of the lord) was reported to be a feudal right allowing a lord, if he so desired, to sleep with the bride of any of his vassals on her wedding night (Goetz 1986, p. 610). Bestiality or zoophilia (sex between a human and an animal), usually but not always by young males, is common in many cultures, such as young boys publicly fornicating with turkeys in parts of Brazil. When the famous Kinsey reports headed by biologist Alfred Kinsey were published in 1948 and 1953, a substantial number of U.S. males, especially from rural areas, admitted to having engaged in various types of sex acts with animals at least once (Kinsey, Pomeroy, and Martin 1948, pp. 667–678). A much smaller number of females admitted to achieving sexual stimulation with animals, usually vaginal licking by family pets such as dogs and cats (Kinsey et al. 1953, pp. 502–509). One hundred years from now, people may be appalled to learn that the custom of smoking tobacco was widely allowed throughout the twentieth century and was not illegal and punishable with lengthy prison terms. Silvano Arieti and Johannes M. Meth (1959, p. 560) note that "in the West, suicide is considered a sign of emotional disorder, in Japan it is normal for a samurai in certain circumstances. Among the islanders of Dobu (Melanesia), no sane woman leaves her cooking pots unguarded for fear of being poisoned. To us this behavior would indicate paranoia. Among the Papuans it is traditional for an uncle and nephew (mother's brother and son) to practice homosexuality. . . . It is not unusual for an Arapesh to marry simultaneously a mother and her daughter."

Richard Shweder (1984) provides more examples of social realities that are at extreme variance with Eurocentric traditions, noting that the Yiront Aborigines believe animal and green spirits are responsible for pregnancy, and on the Arabian Peninsula it is widely held that breast milk from pregnant women is poisonous. He continues:

> The Azande go in for oracular consultation. Posed a yes or no question, administered a modest dose of strychnine, the Azande oracle, a chicken, either lives or dies—yes or no. The oracle does not lie—or so the Azande believe.
>
> Killing people outside the clan is popular among the Gahuku-Gama—conduct worthy of commendation—unless the outsider happens to be a maternal kinsman. Scrupulous in avoiding uterine kin in battle, the moral

proscriptions of the Gahuku-Gama fail to generalize: other clansmen are "awarded points" for taking the head of your maternal relatives.

Other New Guinea groups go in for homosexuality in a big way. The "life force" of the tribe must be passed on by the males from generation to generation. Contained in semen, the life force gets passed on all right, orally, through fellatio between "uncles" and their young "nephews." (Shweder 1984, p. 29)

Cultural relativism is a theory of ethics or knowledge that holds that criteria for judging the behavior of other cultures are not static and absolute but are relative and vary according to circumstance. Shweder (1984, p. 49) notes that as few, if any, standards of universal conduct exist, for cultural relativists, to ask what is the proper way to classify the world or design a society "is like asking what is the proper food of man or what is the best language to speak." Indeed. Fried spiders are a delicacy in Cambodia, roast cockroach is relished in Angola, and Bengal tiger penis is enjoyed in China, whereas Indonesians eat sautéd rat, and mice are on the menu in India. Australian Aborigines eat ants, moths, and lizards; and in France, horse, sheep brains, and snails are considered delicious. Last but not least, in parts of Southeast Asia people dine at tables with a hole in the middle where the head of a live monkey is securely clamped, its skull is sliced off, and those gathered take great delight in immediately eating its still throbbing brains.

A survey of thousands of cross-cultural customs, manners, mores, and morals has been compiled by William Graham Sumner in his classic book, *Folkways* (1906). They include burning people alive to honor the gods Apollo and Diana in ancient Greece (p. 575). In Nuremberg, Germany, during the Middle Ages a popular carnival sport involved the "cat knight" who "fought with a cat hung around his own neck, which he must bite to death in order to be knighted" (p. 599). The West African Bondei strangle newborn infants if certain omens and portents are unfavorable, and the Malagassans of Madagascar "kill children who are born on unlucky days" (p. 317). Other examples include child marriages on the New Britain Islands (p. 382), widow burning in India (p. 388), and kissing, the latter regarded as a disgusting act in many societies—"They rub noses, or bite, or smell instead" (pp. 459–460). Historian Robert Darnton (1984) documents how medieval European carnivals commonly involved what was then considered a hilarious pastime—torturing animals, especially cats.

Crowds made bonfires . . . and threw into them . . . cats—cats tied up in bags, cats suspended from ropes, or cats burned at the stake. Parisians liked

to incinerate cats by the sackful . . . [others] preferred to chase a flaming cat
through the streets. . . . In the Metz region they burned a dozen cats at a
time in a basket on top of a bonfire. The ceremony took place with great
pomp in Metz itself, until it was abolished in 1765. . . . Although the
practice varied from place to place, the ingredients were everywhere the
same: *a feu de joie* (bonfire), cats, and an aura of [the] hilarious. (Darnton
1984, pp. 83, 85)

Ironically, ancient Egyptians worshiped cats, and killing them was punishable by death, whereas the Chinese neither worshiped nor feared them—
they ate them. That the world's peoples have a vast array of social realities is
an important realization in light of Western dominance over medical proce-
dures, technologies, and ideologies. This situation has significant implications
for social control by Western scientific elites in their medicalization of social
problems (Freidson 1970, 1988; Conrad 1979; Conrad and Schneider 1980),
as medical practitioners "often use illness metaphors when they are really
making social judgments" (Bates 1977, p. 21). One area of concern is the
bourgeois social agenda[5] and vested economic interests exclusive to medical
professionals per se.[6] Medical professionals often support the position of other
specialist elites in such areas as government, industry, and law to maintain
existing power structures, thus supporting the concerns expressed by radical
sociologist C. Wright Mills (1956) about the existence of a "power elite"
among top leaders. The most widely discussed uneasiness is over the historical tendency for scientific elites to unconsciously reify prevailing societal and
cultural norms and values as scientific "facts" (Rosen 1968; Szasz 1970;
Chamberlin and Gilman 1985; Pick 1989; Curra 1994, p. 6).

MEDICINE AS AN AGENT OF SOCIAL CONTROL

Sociologist Elliot Freidson's *Profession of Medicine* (1970) marked an ideological shift in medical sociology from the traditional concept of disease per
se to analyzing the socially constructed nature of medically defined illness
categories in relation to political interests and power structures (Armstrong
1996, p. 526). Jesse Pitts (1968, p. 391) remarks that "medicalization is one
of the most effective means of social control and . . . is destined increasingly
to become the main mode of *formal* social control."[7] The responsibility for
defining and treating social problems in most industrialized countries has
shifted from the almost exclusive domain of religion (sin) to jurisprudence
(crime) to medicine (sickness) (Zola 1972, p. 487; Conrad and Schneider
1980; Schneider and Conrad 1980; Turner 1987). Societies utilize "everyday
knowledge" that is commonly available and "formal knowledge" that is opaque,

unfamiliar, arcane, and inaccessible to all but a relatively small group of specialist professionals (Freidson 1988, pp. 2–3), at the pinnacle of which lies medical expertise (p. 112).[8] In most industrialized countries, Western medical ideology now transcends religious doctrine, and "neutral" scientific knowledge is relied on by courts and legislative bodies to formulate laws (Kosa 1970; Zola 1972, p. 502). Indeed, "high," "sacred" medical knowledge is an exercise of power capable of transcending ecclesiastical doctrine[9] and circumventing democracy. "People are not allowed to choose among a variety of alternatives because the issue is presented as a technical one that involves the necessary use of the 'one best method'" (Freidson 1988, p. 8). Classic contemporary examples include ideological debates between the church and state over the morality of abortion, birth control, and euthanasia and the increasing reliance on medical opinion in influencing legislation and public opinion, effectively usurping church authority.

In their influential approach to studying the medicalization of deviant behavior in Western society, especially in the United States, sociologists Peter Conrad and Joseph Schneider (1980) published *Deviance and Medicalization: From Badness to Sickness*. This seminal work draws on the labeling-interactionist tradition by utilizing a historical constructionist approach to analyze changes in mainstream deviance designations from being controlled by authorities in religious (moral) and legal (legislative) circles to the medical (scientific) domain; hence the subtitle of their book, *From Badness to Sickness*. This approach focuses on the history of social problems and how they change over time in response to claims-making groups, undermining realist conceptions of deviance as an objective condition awaiting discovery, by emphasizing the politics of constructing deviance designations. Conrad and Schneider (1980) present a five-stage sequential model "deviant" behaviors pass through in their redefinition as medical problems. These transformations are "collective achievements rather than inevitable products of the natural evolution of society or the progress of medicine" (p. xi). The stages are "(1) definition of behavior as deviant; (2) prospecting: medical discovery; (3) claims-making: medical and nonmedical interests; (4) legitimacy: securing medical turf; and (5) institutionalization of a medical deviance designation" (p. 266). I shall use a broadly similar theoretical approach in this study by emphasizing political and cultural influences that culminate in the medicalization of deviance designations in "exotic" behaviors in non-Western societies and cultures or among Western peoples in distant history; hence the subtitle of this study, *From Strangeness to Illness*.

Psychiatry is perhaps the most contentious branch of medicine (Bates 1977, p. ix; Lader 1977; Roach Anleu 1995, p. 148), and this situation shows no sign of abating (Micale 1994a, pp. 3, 26). Fundamental disagreement exists over the very concept of mental illness,[10] as most persons labeled mentally "ill" do not have a discernible cerebral disease that affects behavior[11] but are experiencing living difficulties. Hence, Edwin Fuller Torrey (1986, p. 2) contends that the term *client* is more appropriate than *patient* in describing such individuals.

Because of its subjective, arbitrary, political nature, Thomas Szasz (1974a, pp. xii–xiii) advocates abolishing the diagnostic term *mental illness* as pejorative because its employment legitimates the stigmatization of disapproved behaviors, noting that "inmates" of the first insane asylums were not only the "mad" but social undesirables: prostitutes, indigents, orphans, incurably sick, aged, lazy, and unmarried debauched girls (Szasz 1970, pp. 13–16, 1974a, p. x, 1979, p. 135). Szasz (1974a, p. 17) observes that just as physical illness involves the violation of certain physiological norms, "we call people mentally ill when their personal conduct violates certain ethical, political, and social norms." Although not denying the potential existence of mental illness, Szasz contends that very few "problems in living" can be clearly attributed to an organic cause, and thus the disease concept of mental illness is a myth that unduly elevates the status of psychiatrists to that of conventional medical practitioners.[12] Szasz is concerned with the ambiguous, dynamic, political processes involved in constructing mental disturbance nosologies, which are often influenced by the ability of special interest groups to effectively organize and lobby decisionmakers.

Although the concept of mental disorder varies transculturally and transhistorically, I shall employ the culturally and historically sensitive definition of Craig Little (1995, p. 106), who states that "in most times and places a person has been classified as mentally disordered when . . . [exhibiting] what seems to be uncontrolled, irrationally motivated behavior considered by most others to be sufficiently abnormal and irresponsible in its sociocultural context to require special treatment, isolation, or social control." Although this definition is imprecise, as it relies on an interpretation of a behavior, it attempts to account for the motivation of actions, its context, and its perception by others. It recognizes that the psychologically disordered "behave with unclear motives and, upon being judged irresponsible, require treatment or exclusion from everyday social situations in which their behavior is upsetting or potentially dangerous to others" (p. 106).

Social scientists in general, and especially psychiatrists, are particularly vulnerable to initiate iatrogenic illness,[13] as diagnoses rest almost exclusively on practitioner judgment with little recourse to physiological, anatomical, or genetic indicators. These scientists are especially prone to transmitting stereotypes based on their "social, ethical, and political milieu" (Illich 1976, p. 167; Fernando 1988, pp. 44–49). There are a plethora of historical and contemporary examples of the tendency for psychiatrists and other social scientists to reflect prevailing social and cultural norms in their practice of "objective" science. These include the incorporation of popular nineteenth- and early twentieth-century racist stereotypes of indigenous peoples, minority groups, and nonconformists to support so-called value-free scientific theories of degeneration, European intellectual superiority, and the genetic basis of behavior (Chamberlin and Gilman 1985; Castel 1985; Pick 1989; Fernando 1988, 1991). In parts of the southern United States during the mid-nineteenth century, rebellious Negro slaves who escaped plantation servitude were popularly believed to be suffering from a mental disease. At the time this position was widely rationalized on the grounds that slavery provided advantages to Negros over their "primitive" African existence, and their inferior psychological constitution was typified as ideally suited for bondage (Thomas and Sillen 1972). Many Caucasian scientists legitimized this folk portrayal of deviant runaway slaves with the medical label *drapetomania* (Proctor 1988). Fernando (1988) documents the upholding of this position in U.S. psychiatry, whereby slavery was viewed as a natural Negro condition and any deviation from which was associated with illness.[14] The support by many in the white-dominated psychiatric and medical professions for the continued enslavement of Negroes on plantations in the southern United States during the nineteenth century by diagnosing dissatisfied slaves as psychologically sick underscores the ambiguity of psychiatric diagnoses, their political nature, and the potential for popular social beliefs to become superimposed as "scientific" realities.

PSYCHIATRY'S POLITICAL AND CONTESTABLE NATURE[15]

In examining social problems and issues, it is important for investigators to give serious consideration to "the perspective that public definitions of public problems are the outcomes and continual objects of claims that interested groups put forth in public arenas" (Gusfield 1980, p. vi). For example, the politics of psychiatric diagnoses is evident in the first two editions of the DSM (APA 1952, 1968), which classified homosexuality as a mental disorder ("sexual orientation disturbance"). A campaign by the Sexual Preference Rights Movement, including disruptions of psychiatric conferences and public protests, prompted direct negotiations with the APA and removal of its disorder status after a reassessment of the gender preference literature and a subsequent unanimous vote by the APA board of trustees (Bayer 1981). In 1974 nearly 60 percent of 10,000 votes cast in an APA-member referendum to formally approve the change were in agreement, but in a separate survey of about 2,500 responding psychiatrists, nearly 70 percent opposed the change (Greenberg 1988).[16]

In 1985 a psychiatric committee responsible for revising DSM-III[17] proposed new disease categories for rapists ("paraphilic rapism") and masochistic behavior ("masochistic personality disorder"), prompting protests by some women's groups and mental health professionals. The concept of rape as an illness was in contradiction to the deviance literature, which views it in terms of "power, domination, and violence" (Little 1995, p. 58). This situation engendered concern over the potential claim of paraphilic rapism as a legal insanity defense, whereas masochistic personality disorder could unfairly stigmatize abusive relationship victims as antagonists, weakening abuser sanctions and increasing barriers to obtaining legal protection for the abused (Goleman 1985; Kutchins and Kirk 1989). As a result of the protests, threats of legal challenges, and subsequent interaction between members of the APA and various mental health and women's organizations, when DSM-III-R was published in 1987 rapism was deleted, and masochistic personality disorder was euphemistically renamed "self-defeating personality disorder." Both were placed in an appendix entitled "Proposed Diagnostic Categories Needing Further Study" (Kutchins and Kirk 1989, p. 98).[18] The handling of the classification of these "disorders" underscores political influences in composing a "scientific" document and the ambiguous, socially constructed nature of the categories.[19]

The role of mental health professionals in constructing the categories of "masochistic and self-defeating personality disorders" over the past 100 years typifies the caveats of scientists superimposing popular norms and beliefs as scientific facts. From the time Austrian physician, neurologist, and the founder of psychoanalysis Sigmund Freud (1856–1939) began treating the problem of female assault by their partners to the mid-1970s, the mental health community almost universally treated victims as a relatively small group of masochists, as psychoanalysts, psychotherapists, psychiatrists, and social workers typically focused on the victim's responsibility in "provoking" assaults and abuse (Caplan 1985; Davis 1987, p. 306; Kutchins and Kirk 1989, p. 91). Since the mid-1970s the problem of female assault has been recognized as significant, and the focus has been on the assailant. This is a classic example whereby popular nineteenth-century European cultural misconceptions regarding female behavior were dogmatically incorporated into mainstream psychiatry and social work, further legitimating its social reality. The fallacy of the female instigation of their batteries was common prior to the time Freud highlighted the "disorder." Consider this excerpt from Furneaux Jordan's *The Physical Constitution of Battered Wives* (1886, cited in Skultans 1975, pp. 237–238), a demonstrator in physiology at Queens's College in Birmingham, England:

I noticed that a very large proportion of the women who came into the hospital suffering from injuries inflicted by their husbands had . . . peculiarities . . . common to all of them. . . . I came slowly to see that the skin of the assaulted women was often clear, delicate, perhaps rosy. Their hair-growth was never heavy nor long, and the eyebrows were spare and refined. . . . The friends and neighbours usually let it be known that these unfortunate women . . . had sharp tongues . . . and an unfailing—unfailing by repetition—supply of irritating topics on which to exercise them.

Since psychiatry's inception as a formal profession, psychiatrists have used medical labels to control the treatment of deviant behaviors. For example, at the beginning of the nineteenth century, Christian revivalism in America grew in popularity, with adherents primarily from the lower socioeconomic classes, ethnic minorities, and females. Emotional zeal and ecstatic phenomena accompanying this movement were at variance with the rational linear model of human progress and were characterized by bourgeoisie[20] medicine as exemplifying "degeneration" because of the influence of the "maddening crowd." Congregants were portrayed as temporarily regressing to the unconscious mental level thought to typify "primitive" peoples, widely believed to be prone to emotional outbursts either as a result of inherent degeneracy or lack of integration with "superior" European civilization (Fernando 1991, p. 33). The nineteenth-century U.S. medical profession was almost exclusively composed of conservative Caucasian males of high socioeconomic status, adhering to a doctrine of rational scientism. Consequently, religious fervor was relabeled a medical problem, and emotional excitement associated with various deviant, unpopular, or unfamiliar religious groups was typified within mainstream psychiatry as "religious insanity" (Bainbridge 1984). This notion was promoted by prominent "psychiatrists and social scientists, accepted by the popular media . . . and enshrined by the census as the official position of the United States government" (Bainbridge 1984, p. 224). Consequently, various ritualized behaviors that were either learned and acted out or that would engender involuntary muscular spasms were marginalized as Shakers, Quakers, Leapers, Jumpers, Rollers, and Barkers. Many other examples exist of the pathologization of these and other religious "deviants" by Western scientists using mainstream Eurocentric criteria of normality and rationality (Bartholomew and O'Dea 1998).[21]

Contemporary Western medicine continues to transmit social and professional stereotypes as to what constitutes acceptable religious values and norms, using the ambiguously defined, pejorative, derogatory label *cult* to describe many nonconformist religious movements whose members are typified,

without scientific substantiation, as psychologically deviant, mentally ill, coerced, or "brainwashed" (Robbins 1980; Robbins and Anthony 1982). The
social and political influence of a relatively small number of U.S. scientific
elites in defining transcultural religious norms was evident as recently as the
1987 DSM-III-R. This "neutral" document was subsequently criticized within
the APA for propagating numerous negative, empirically unjustified stereotypes of many minority religious movements, their behavior and beliefs,
under the pretext of science. Examples include inappropriate innuendos concerning use of the words *cult, cultists, brainwashing, coercive persuasion,* and
thought reform and an association with mental illness (Levine 1989; Bohn and
Gutman 1989; Galanter 1989; Ungerleider and Wellisch 1989; Post 1992).[22]

The difference between a "cult" and acceptable religious beliefs and behaviors is often based on the number of followers and reflects changing diagnostic fashions and assumptions molded by the zeitgeist and professional
medical ideology. Jeremiah Gutman (1977, pp. 210–211) notes that when
certain practices appear strange or unpopular, "a religion becomes a cult;
proselytization becomes brainwashing; persuasion becomes propaganda; missionaries become subversive agents; retreats, monasteries, and convents become
prisons; holy ritual becomes bizarre conduct; religious observance becomes
aberrant behavior; devotion and meditation become psychopathic trances."

During the nineteenth century, the proliferation of one particular unpopular religious movement in the United States became the subject of fierce
controversy and opposition, precipitating widespread moral panic. According to David Bromley and Anson Shupe (1989, pp. 307–310), leaders were
erroneously typified as authoritarian and immoral, some female devotees were
characterized as sex slaves, there were initiatives to block the employment of
members, and rumors were rife that the group was in cahoots with Native
Americans in a scheme to violently overthrow the government. Protests erupted
into fatal riots in urban areas. Nevertheless, despite its earlier unpopularity
Roman Catholicism is now considered a mainstream religion in the United
States.

In numerous contemporary nonreligious instances collective deviance
exhibited by a particular group or social movement has been marginalized as
hysterical or sick, based solely on the assessments of these acts by scientists or
the lay public as at variance with those of mainstream Western-trained scientists who rendered such unsubstantiated judgments using ambiguous and
arbitrary criteria. One prominent example involves claims that the Nazi movement during the first half of the twentieth century was a form of mass psychopathology among the German people (Cartwright and Biddiss 1972), thereby
ignoring the literature on conformity dynamics and cultural context in shaping

Nazi beliefs (Kren 1978-1979; Asher 1979). Archivist Herbert Walther (1984, p. 14) notes that Hitler "had, by all accounts, a normal childhood and was loved by both parents. His education was equally unremarkable. There is nothing in the man's early life which would give any hint of the sort of man he was to become." He also states that until 1940, so beloved was Hitler in parts of Europe that he needed little security protection, frequently disregarding personal safety, and "would have made an easy target for any would-be sniper or assassin in the crowd" (p. 216).

Bartholomew (1990b) documents how the ambiguous criterion of "stress" has been used to explain the sudden appearance of "strange" behaviors attributed to irrational thought processes induced by individual or societal disequilibrium, dysfunction, or anomie, whereas other scientists (e.g., Gordon 1971; Clarke 1980, pp. 197–202) have taken the position of defining these "bizarre" behaviors as exemplifying mass psychopathology. In examining waves of claims and public discourse surrounding sightings of unidentified flying objects, Bartholomew deconstructs the popular notion of "flying saucer" witnesses as psychologically aberrant or mentally ill (Bartholomew 1989b, 1991b), documenting how this unsubstantiated position was reified by incredulous scientists who stigmatized witness claimants using the fantastic nature of the observational claims per se. Instead of viewing reports as examples of irrationality or disorder precipitated by rapid sociotechnological changes, Bartholomew shows how they are novel social realities given plausibility by rapid aeronautical advancements and accompanying mass media and science-fiction speculations that preceded their appearance. This emerging worldview altered perceptual orientations, allowing for the widespread redefinition of ambiguous, mundane, almost exclusively nocturnal aerial stimuli. These pathological interpretations have also obscured the symbolic significance of "flying saucers," which serves the unconscious resurrection of the power and function of omnipotent beings during a secular age (Bartholomew 1991b).[23]

THE MEDICALIZATION OF "EXOTIC" DEVIANCE

As a consequence of the contestable, subjective nature of psychiatric illness construction, much of what is presently classified as *mental illness* is neither mental nor illness but comprises unfamiliar, unapproved, or misunderstood conduct codes that are inappropriately labeled in medical terms (Voss 1979). The tendency for scientists to describe unpopular, seemingly irrational, immoral, or exotic symbol systems, subcultures, habits, and convictions with such terms as abnormality, disorder, disease, and maladaption is typically referred to as "the medicalization of deviance" (Conrad and Schneider 1980, p. xi). Most medicalization studies focus on social problems as they are designated in Western countries, which are often accepted in non-Western settings under the insidious guise of "neutral" science, which is dominated by unconscious Eurocentric conceptions of normality. This explains the cogency of Kleinman's (1977) warning that professional psychiatric categories are essentially Western constructions of normality, as they are products of Western theory and practice that are embedded with social and cultural assumptions typically viewed as unproblematic. Examples of Western medicalization include the application of disease or disorder classifications to alcoholism (Fingarette 1988), gambling (Rosecrance 1985), obesity (Schneider and Conrad 1980, p. 47), treating violence as a genetic or cerebral disorder (Conrad 1975, p. 12), and labeling adherents of unpopular or minority religious groups "brainwashed" cultists (Robbins and Anthony 1982).

Less known to Western sociologists are examples of medicalization uncovered by anthropologists in non-Western countries. One instance is the misinterpretation of melodramatic "suicide" swims on the tiny Western Pacific Island of Tikopia as a means of renegotiating life problems and elevating status—where female "victims" allow themselves to be caught and brought back to land (Littlewood and Lipsedge 1987, p. 292). A considerable body of evidence suggests that transient "madness" among various Papua New Guinea peoples entails calculated, theatrical demonstrations intended to derive material and social benefits (Clarke 1973). Anthropologists Michael Kenny (1978) and Raymond L. Lee (1981) consider exaggerated response to startle in Malayo-Indonesian latah to represent deliberate, culturally conditioned roles. Perhaps the best-documented example of medicalizing exotic rituals and unfamiliar belief systems is the mythical construction of *windigo* (psychotic cannibalism) in subarctic North American Algonquian Indians. Based on archival research and five years of fieldwork, Lou Marano (1982) found no reliable evidence for what was considered at the time to be a classic culture-bound disorder created when ethnographic data about the subarctic people were removed "from the context in which it is known, learned, and communicated" (Ridington 1988, p. 98).[24] Anthropologist Aihwa Ong (1987, 1988) shows how episodes of "mass hysteria" among Malay females undergoing rigid capitalist discipline in multinational factories in Malaysia are actually a form of "ritualized rebellion." By forcing native healers (*bomohs*) to rid the premises of evil spirits, these intermediaries are able to negotiate with management and change practices workers claim have offended the spirits. Lee and Susan Ackerman (1980) document a similar Malaysian negotiation idiom involving epidemic hysteria among Malay females experiencing strict Islamic discipline.[25] Other examples include Harry Eastwell's (1976, 1979) discussion of the social origins of "associative depressive illness" and pica consumption "epidemics" among certain

Northern Territory Aborigine clans in Australia. The former behavior appears to represent a culture-specific expression of bereavement that has received the erroneous culture-bound syndrome classification of *collective depressive psychosis.* The latter "abnormality" is explicable within the Aboriginal symbol system in which clay is viewed as pacifying and psychologically comforting (Bartholomew 1990b).

The near global reliance on "objective" Western medical knowledge can be regarded as a form of neocolonialism whereby Eurocentric values and norms are imparted transculturally. In this context Ivan Illich (1976) uses such terms as *medical colonization* (p. 8) and *diagnostic imperialism* (p. 76).[26] It is against this broad background that this study will challenge the validity of present-day mainstream medical designations of three culture-bound psychiatric "syndromes" by arguing that they are the creations of Western ideological imperialism. In demonstrating this point, I shall draw on a broad tradition of sociological theoretical analysis under the general heading of labeling and social interactionism. Before discussing the applicability of this approach, I shall locate this perspective as one of two broad, dichotomous orientations to studying deviance that rely on an incongruous set of assumptions regarding the origin and nature of deviance.

DIVERGENT DEVIANCE ORIENTATIONS:
OBJECTIVIST VERSUS SOCIALLY DESIGNATED DEVIANCE

Although deviance can be studied from various perspectives that involve different assumptions, methods, and definitions, researchers have utilized two broadly divergent theoretical traditions in their analysis and understanding. These approaches have been variously identified with such polemical descriptions as the old conception and new conception (Gibbs 1966), correction and appreciation (Matza 1969, p. 15), normative versus interpretive and establishment versus the new order (Hawkins and Tiedeman 1975, pp. v–vi), self-action and interaction (Trimble and Medicine 1976, pp. 162–175), consensus versus conflict (Akers 1977, p. 13), objectivist and subjectivist (Goode 1978), deterministic versus voluntaristic (Downes 1979, p. 1), positivist versus interactionist (Conrad and Schneider 1980, p. 1), social factist and definitional (Troyer and Markle 1982), emic versus etic (Marano 1982), Enlightenment and Romantic (Shweder 1984), traditional and modern (Thio 1988, p. 8), universalist and relativist (Bartholomew 1990b), and individualistic versus sociological (Roach Anleu 1995).

I have chosen to use the term *socially designated deviance,* as my analytical approach will involve an eclectic blend of interactionist, phenomenological, feminist, and conflict models. This will allow me to avoid using the interactionist model in the generic sense, which may invite disagreement as conflict and feminist structural features cannot be readily subsumed under interactionism. The term *deviance designation* is too limiting, as objectivist traditions account for deviance designations but do not recognize the social and cultural bases of their categorizing. My use of the term *objectivist* is more straightforward and intended to describe perspectives whose task it is to determine etiological causes of deviance that emanate from within the individual.

OBJECTIVIST PERSPECTIVES

Practitioners of objectivist models are also known as absolutists or realists who espouse positions typifying deviance as relatively unproblematic and real per se, in that persons exist in any given society who engage in deviations from consensual norms, the deviant can be objectively studied as an element in the natural sciences, and deviance is caused or determined by outside agents (Thio 1988, p. 15). The first identifiable objectivist perspective involved theological or supernatural explanations of deviance, attributing certain "wrong," "immoral," or "evil" acts to possession or influence by Otherworldly agents or, in the Judeo-Christian tradition, yielding to demonic temptation and hedonistic impulses inherent from original sin (Conrad and Schneider 1980, pp. 38–43; Roach Anleu 1995, pp. 2–3). Another early deterministic explanation for deviance was astrology, which became widespread in Europe during the sixteenth century when the movements of astronomical bodies were believed to influence brain function. From this movement words such as *lunacy* and *lunatic* to describe aberrant actions were derived from the Latin word *luna,* meaning "moon," and gained popular English-language usage (Barlow and Durand 1995, p. 15).

Four broad objectivist perspectives explaining deviance are utilized by contemporary researchers: medical, biological, psychological, and rational choice models. Medical explanations involve the disease concept in precipitating abnormal behavior. I have previously critiqued the medical model, noting the tendency to equate "deviant" or "abnormal" behavior with illness designations without clear supporting scientific substantiation but based on popular assumptions and folk beliefs. The existence of an illness component in most "mental illnesses" is a contentious issue among many contemporary psychiatrists who consider it to be an analogy or metaphor not meant to be taken literally for most diagnoses (Siegler and Osmond 1974, pp. 25–26; Fulcher 1975, pp. 78–79; Szasz 1987, pp. 136-140; Vatz and Weinberg 1994, p. 324). The incorporation of psychiatry as a branch of medicine was as much a practical and political as a scientific decision, as it strengthened the credibility and power of the professional psychiatric elite (Cochrane 1983, p. 145).[27]

A fundamental problematic with this approach is a reliance on ambiguous diagnostic criteria of an almost exclusively descriptive nature.[28] As a result, psychiatrists are especially prone to unconsciously use their position as agents of social control to support and reify popular cultural conceptions of what constitutes mental health and normality by medicalizing "deviant" behavior.

The conspicuous absence of objective criteria with which to assess the presence of mental illness or disorder is illustrated by an experiment in which David L. Rosenhan (1973) and seven colleagues epitomizing contemporary Western notions of mental health gained admission to separate mental hospitals representing different regions, funding levels and sources, and psychiatric approaches. Each pseudopatient presented with a single symptom, claiming to hear a voice in his or her head, and if admitted the "patients" were instructed to immediately act normal. With the exception of basic identifying information that could unveil their true identities (name, employment, and vocation), all other information about their life histories was accurate and freely offered. All were admitted and diagnosed with schizophrenia, with one exception (a diagnosis of "severe psychotic"). The subjects were institutionalized for an average of nineteen days, and all were discharged as having schizophrenia in remission. Throughout their stay, their unremarkable life histories were redefined as evidencing numerous examples of pathology. In a subsequent experiment, when incredulous staff from one mental hospital doubted these findings, it was agreed that one or more pseudopatients would seek admission over a designated three-month period, and the staff were forewarned. Although 41 of 193 patients were assessed, "with high confidence, to be pseudopatients by at least one member of the staff," no pseudopatients sought admission (Rosenhan 1973, p. 252). These now famous experiments by Rosenhan dramatically highlight the subjective nature of psychiatric diagnoses.

A second major objectivist deviance model involves biological theories,[29] which typically assume that certain persons are "born" deviant[30] and emphasize heredity, physiological anomalies, and body chemistry and remain controversial, either discredited or inconclusive. An early example is phrenology, developed and popularized by Franz Joseph Gall in the late eighteenth century on the assumption that skull contours corresponded with brain development and that it was possible to identify which persons were predisposed to criminal behavior by determining which parts of the brain were developed or underdeveloped by examining "bumps" on the head (Morris 1976, pp. 79–80). Italian physician and criminologist Cesare Lombroso (1911) developed a theory of atavism that gained prominence during the second half of the nineteenth and the early twentieth centuries, arguing that some criminals exemplified degeneration or regressive evolution to earlier primitive prehuman or animal-istic behavior patterns, resulting in difficulties in adjusting to modern social norms (Wolfgang 1972, p. 247). This was believed to be manifest in certain physical traits known as "stigmata," such as skull features corresponding to criminal types (e.g., a sloping forehead, a high brow, or an excess or absence of body hair) or facial characteristics in which beaklike noses were believed to be common among murderers and flat noses predominant among thieves.

Building on influential German psychiatrist Emil Kraepelin's (1883) con-viction that certain body typologies were indicative of a tendency toward mental disturbance (see Schafer 1976, p. 52), William Sheldon and colleagues (1949) have associated body types with temperament and personality, claim-ing that those with muscular physiques and large trunks (mesomorphs) are typically aggressive, adventurous, impulsive, and insensitive and thus possess delinquency-prone personalities. Their research has been widely criticized for exclusively involving boys at a juvenile delinquency detention facility and not considering such factors as ethnicity, social class, neighborhood, or family relations (Roach Anleu 1995, p. 7). Ironically, although Sheldon and colleagues (1940) disregarded phrenology as pseudoscience, their research has been labeled the "new Phrenology in which bumps on the buttocks take the place of bumps on the skull" (Washburn 1951, p. 561). Although subsequent somato-type studies by Sheldon Glueck and Elinor Glueck (1956, 1974) comparing delinquent versus nondelinquent boys have consistently found positive rela-tionships between delinquency and mesomorphy, it is improbable that it is a cause per se, just as mesomorphy does not cause one to become a rugby player but boys with athletic body types may have a higher probability of succeeding at rugby or delinquency (Little 1995, pp. 8–9).[31]

Genetic paradigms have been used to account for the possible inherit-ance of tendencies toward alcoholism (Catanzaro 1967), yet a specific gene predisposing individuals to chronic drinking has yet to be identified (Clinard and Meier 1995, p. 54). Even if one is located, it can account for only a small part of the complete explanation (Peele 1986), as sociocultural factors such as socioeconomic status, geographical region and residence, religious affiliation, racial and ethnic background, gender, and age can explain variations in alco-hol consumption among different groups (Thio 1988, pp. 378–383). Also, "social stress" and a lack of normative constraints against alcohol consump-tion correlate with significant increases in problem drinking (Linsky, Colby, and Straus 1986, 1987). In addition, some researchers contend that violent conduct is more prevalent in males possessing an extra Y chromosome (Jacobs et al. 1965; Hare and Connolly 1987). The distinguishing features of such individuals are an above-average height of 6 feet 3 inches, facial acne, slight mental retardation, and aggression. However, Werner Einstadter and Stuart Henry (1995, pp. 93–94) report that this theory is discredited by studies with opposite results, including carriers of an extra Y chromosome being more common in prison guards than inmates, more prevalent in less aggressive prisoners than aggressive ones, and more common in the general population. Further, social factors could also account for increased aggression, as unusually tall, mildly retarded males with a facial stigma may be ridiculed for their appearance and behavior and subsequently respond aggressively.

Another biological explanation is the chemical imbalance hypothesis of deviance, which includes attempts to associate female violence with premenstrual syndrome (Hall-Williams 1982; Chait 1986). However, plausible alternative explanations grounded in the social acquisition of behavior traits can account for the findings of objectivist theorists. In addition, Glenn D. Walters (1992) observes that early studies linking biology with deviance were poorly designed, whereas more recent, better-designed research has found little or no relationship between biology and deviant behavior. Following a century of inconclusive research, a general contemporary social science consensus holds that although biogenetic factors may exert some influence on behavior, it is of relatively little consequence when compared with social and environmental factors and the dynamic, relativistic nature of "deviance."[32]

Contemporary psychogenic deviance models constitute the third objectivist perspective, and they generally attempt to explain the formation of the hypothesized criminal, pathological, antisocial, or problem personality. The modern psychological tradition gained widespread professional acceptance during the mid-eighteenth century with the use of moral therapy[33] in which patients were treated with "normal" social interaction and exceptional care and compassion in serene surroundings. During this period mental disturbance was widely attributed to the effects of poor environmental conditions that were injurious to mental functioning. In the two centuries prior to the advent of moral therapy, persons designated as mentally disturbed were typically treated in pitiful lunatic asylums that resembled prisons or in actual prisons or poorhouses, and during the Middle Ages they were often executed.[34] Psychological theorists often administer personality inventories in an effort to identify certain behavioral types or traits and to highlight the significance of these personality correlates in differentiating deviants from conformists. Many psychologists contend that certain behavioral traits are inherent and that deviant personalities result from the interaction between fixed traits and adverse social conditions (Eysenck 1977; Eysenck and Gudjonsson 1989).

One branch of psychogenic theory involves psychoanalytical approaches that focus on the dynamics of processes and conflicts in the unconscious mind.[35] Pioneered by Sigmund Freud during the late nineteenth century, it examines the mental structure of personality and its distinct components (id, ego, and superego), which often clash; the concept of defense mechanisms; and psychosexual development, especially during the first five years when the personality is believed to be almost completely formed. Psychoanalysts typically assume that normal personalities form in a series of potentially overlapping developmental stages. Each stage reflects different needs, interests, and drives, especially of a sexual nature such as shifting aspects of sexual gratification beginning with oral fixations from birth until two years, anal preoccupations between ages one and three, followed by phallic preoccupations between ages three and five, and so on. Traumatic events such as family conflicts or physical, psychological, or sexual abuse can result in unresolved infantile conflicts and abnormal personality development, whereby a fixation on the oral stage may precipitate excessive eating in adulthood, for example.

Psychoanalytic theories have gradually diminished in popularity and credibility in recent decades. They are often criticized for being based on subjective, descriptive patient life histories that may have occurred years or decades earlier and that are open to a variety of interpretations by different psychoanalysts (Barlow and Durand 1995, p. 30). Psychoanalysts employ highly imaginative, speculative, abstract concepts (e.g., id, ego, superego, Oedipus complex, castration anxiety, and penis envy) that are empirically untestable (Thio 1988, p. 126). This ambiguity in identifying and diagnosing individual problems has resulted in the superimposition of practitioner value judgments that uphold popular notions, which in turn serve as a form of social and political control (Szasz 1974a, 1974b, 1990). Perhaps the most notorious example was the use of psychoanalysis in upholding various sexual mores during the late eighteenth and early nineteenth centuries, supporting the use of radical treatments for sexual deviants. Attempts to stop masturbators included castration, clitoridectomy, ovariotomy, circumcision, "insane" asylum incarceration, lobotomy, and a variety of contraptions placed around the waist (Hare 1962; Comfort 1967; Szasz 1970, pp. 180–206; 1990, pp. 20–21, 74–80). Such aggressive treatments were used to counteract masturbation, which was widely attributed to cause various physical and mental diseases: neurosis, insanity, consumption, digestive disorders, and poor eyesight. Carol Tavris (1993, p. 228) insightfully observes that "scientific efforts to categorize and label sexual disorders are, by definition, subjective decisions because they depend on criteria for sexual normalcy, which change with the times." The acceptance of psychoanalysis was enhanced during World Wars I and II, as it was used to reinforce coercive state policy in the United States (Szasz 1994, pp. 155–156).

Numerous examples in the annals of psychoanalytical history underscore its extremely subjective nature. For instance, Freud (1975 [1915], p. 200) analyzed the behavior of an adolescent male with a tendency to squeeze pimples by contending that it was "a substitute for masturbation. The cavity which then appears owing to his fault is the female genital, i.e., the fulfillment of the threat of castration." Other psychoanalysts have equated drug addiction with masturbation (Rado 1963). Although these interpretations may lack credibility in the eyes of contemporary observers, they were widely discussed and reified within the psychiatric community during the late eighteenth and early nineteenth centuries. The potential danger of such speculations is evidenced in a series of papers published by Freud in 1896 in which he argued that his hysterical female patients were exhibiting trauma from having been sexually molested by their fathers—an observation he recanted the following year (Siegler and Osmond 1974, p. 44).

Although psychologists have been unable to identify a consistent constellation of personality traits in deviants versus nondeviants (Bartholomew 1990b, p. 469; Clinard and Meier 1995, p. 662; Bartholomew and Sirois 1996), the elusive quest to locate a deviant or criminal personality continues, in part because "most people are reluctant to believe that rapists, serial murderers, child molesters, and those who commit hundreds of crimes during adolescence and early childhood have 'normal' personalities" (Bartol 1991, p. 38). Any psychological arguments are tautological in nature, employing circular reasoning (Lader 1977, p. 36; Roach Anleu 1995, p. 12; Clinard and Meier 1995, p. 62) whereby a particular behavior "is judged to be deviant and it is then used to infer a mental illness which is then designated as the explanatory cause of the original behavior" (Einstadter and Henry 1995, pp. 116–117). Although most psychological theorists place minimal emphasis on the influence of sociocultural interaction on personality traits, humans are meaning-oriented and significantly influenced by "social roles that are variable and socially determined and not static entities like so-called personality traits" (Clinard and Meier 1995, p. 62).

Rational choice models comprise the fourth perspective within the broad objectivist tradition of understanding deviance and typify human behavior as involving deliberate, calculated decisions whereby potential deviants choose particular actions after rationally weighing the costs and benefits. Early theorists, such as British philosopher Jeremy Bentham (1748–1832), viewed all behaviors as motivated by the inherent desire to maximize pleasure and minimize pain (Bentham 1789). Many of the world's criminal justice systems are based on a form of the rational choice model, assuming that persons defined as criminals or deviants possess a free will and choose their actions. Although some actions may appear "irrational" to outsiders unfamiliar with the decisionmaking rationale, of central importance is the rational logic of the deviant. Rational choice theory has been criticized for overemphasizing the role of free will and devaluating the conditions and meaning behind the decision to deviate. Also, what is logical and rational in one culture may be the opposite in another. Anthropologist Richard Shweder (1984, p. 28) questions the validity of a universalist social law and the view of history as a battleground between reason and science versus unreason and superstition:

> A central tenet of the romanticist [nonuniversalist] view holds that ideas and practices have their foundation in neither logic nor empirical science, that ideas and practices fall beyond the scope of deductive and inductive reason, that ideas and practices are neither rational nor irrational but rather *non*rational. . . .
>
> Thus, to ask which is superior, Islam or Christianity, an animistic world view or a mechanistic world view, a social order premised on individualism, equality, and monogamy or one premised on holism, hierarchy, and polygamy is like asking, "Which is the more valid mode of artistic expression, cubism or impressionism?" (italics in original)

SOCIALLY DESIGNATED DEVIANCE MODELS

The second broad deviance tradition focuses on the general theme of deviance designation. This approach encompasses, under an extremely expansive umbrella, an array of perspectives generally regarded as competing or mutually exclusive. However, each of these models overlaps on the key point of emphasizing that the deviance label is socially designated. The four major theoretical traditions that will comprise the analytical framework of this study are interactionist, phenomenological, feminist, and conflict models of deviance.

The first major stream under this category is the labeling-interactionist, symbolic-interactionist, or social-interactionist approach, and it is also variously referred to in general terms as the particularist, humanist, antipositivist, qualitative, and subjectivist position. The kindred theme of social-interactionist perspectives is a shift from narrow individual etiological causes of deviance to a relativist definition emphasizing its ambiguous, dynamic nature, the role of social controlling agents in creating and maintaining deviant labels (Rubington and Weinberg 1973, p. vii), and the consequence of such designations in fostering further deviations (Schur 1971, p. 27). Einstadter and Henry (1995, p. 213, citing Box 1971, p. 63) provide a cogent example of the dynamic and arbitrary demarcation separating deviants from nondeviants and the role of controlling agents.

The members of the jury were requested to complete claim forms for expenses they had incurred while fulfilling this civic duty. On filling these in, there was considerable discussion concerning which items could be inflated, such as mileage by car, and whether to risk the claim that by fulfilling their jury service they had lost their normal weekly wage. After payment had been made, there were comparative calculations on the amount of money that had been illegally obtained, or "spending money," as one of them called it. The money acquired in this fashion ranged from 3 ($6) to 25 ($50) pounds. No one condemned this practice or reported it to policemen on duty in the court; yet shortly before the same [jury] men had found an adolescent guilty of stealing items valued at 2 pounds 50p ($5), and had all morally condemned his behaviour by agreeing with the judge's sentencing of nine months in prison.

Sociologist Howard S. Becker (1963, p. 18) underscores the political and malleable quality of deviance, noting that "differences in the ability to make rules and apply them to other people are essentially power differentials . . . [as] groups whose special position gives them weapons and power are best able to enforce their rules." Although interactionists have been criticized for focusing almost exclusively on the powerless, "the study of deviance *is* the study of the powerless" (Plummer 1979, p. 109[36]), as the disempowered comprise the overwhelming portion of persons to whom the deviant label has been successfully applied (Becker 1963; Duster 1970; Conrad and Schneider 1980, p. 7; Clinard and Meier 1995, p. 125). From this perspective come a number of questions directed at the principal subject matter of this study, such as: What political advantage was gained in successfully labeling latah as a mimetic disorder within British-controlled colonial Malaya? Did such a label "scientifically" justify (under the guise of social Darwinism) colonial rule among a people deemed unfit for self-autonomy? Are victims of latah, koro, and epidemic hysteria comprised mostly of the powerless, without the potency to create, apply, or alter deviance designations made by others in power positions?

A second branch of related perspectives subsumed within the interactionist approach is generally known as phenomenological theory and includes such designations as new deviancy theory, creative sociology, existential sociology, social constructionism, social reaction theory, ethnomethodology, and the sociology of everyday life. Whereas mainstream interactionists emphasize audience reaction in creating deviance and the consequences of such labels on the "deviant," the phenomenological branch views sociological objectivity as unattainable, thereby focusing on common sense understandings and social realities of everyday life in an effort to apprehend the social actors' subjective

perceptions, which influence their behavior. Drawing on the work of Alfred
Schutz (1967 [1932]) and buoyed by the influential treatise of Peter Berger
and Thomas Luckmann (1971 [1966]), the phenomenological stream was
incorporated into the rapid proliferation of social-constructionist studies of
social life that began during the 1960s and continues to the present.[37] By
focusing on the subjective perceptions of the actors as the subject of study,
phenomenological approaches seek to describe "people's subjectivity (called
phenomenon) including their consciousness, perception, attitudes, feelings,
and opinions about deviance" (Thio 1988, p. 61[38]). Studies within this tradition include marijuana users (Matza 1969), a hermaphrodite (Garfinkel 1967),
suicides (Douglas 1972), and unidentified flying object witnesses (Miller 1985;
Bartholomew 1991b, 1993a; Bartholomew and Howard 1998).

Phenomenological theory can be used to emphasize social and cultural
folk realities held by the exhibitors of the culture-bound "syndromes" being
studied. For instance, what was the meaning of dancing in the vicinity of
religious shrines in Europe during the Middle Ages? Was the "dance mania"
really a form of hysteria that was spontaneous and uncontrollable as is typically asserted, or is there evidence of volition? What common sense social and
cultural understandings among "victims" of collective koro episodes might
foster an absolute belief that their genitalia is shrinking? Can anxiety precipitated by koro-related rumors actually cause discernible penile or breast shrinkage, further reinforcing local beliefs? What is the association between latah
and femininity, and "mass hysteria" and femininity, within Malayo-Indonesian cultures? What worldviews are held by Islamic Malay females in Malaysia
that render them disproportionately vulnerable to epidemic hysteria?

The broad interactionist position has been criticized as an ambiguous,
embryonic perspective (Gibbons and Jones 1975, p. 130; Hawkins and
Tiedeman 1975, p. 51) that is conceptually impoverished (Davis 1972), which
when taken to extreme assumes that people are essentially empty organisms
and that "deviance seems all societal response and no deviant stimulus" (Bordua
1967, p. 153). Further, although labeling can create deviance, it is not responsible for the deviance in the original instance (Akers 1977, p. 33). In addition, labeling theory overemphasizes disempowered groups to the neglect of
powerful deviants who are rarely the focus of study.

A third stream of theories that are distinct from symbolic interactionism
and phenomenological approaches but also focus on aspects of socially designated deviance are conflict models also referred to as critical, new, anarchist,
or radical criminology, political economy, left realism, and structuralist Marxist
theory. These theories agree with symbolic interactionists on the arbitrary
creation of deviance definitions and labels and the importance of studying

temporal changes but disagree on their origins. Conflict approaches view deviance construction as a class struggle between the interests of the powerful ruling class that maintains domination through its power to define deviation and disempowered victims. In differing from labeling perspectives, conflict models view deviance designation as emerging from ruling-class interests and motives (structures) as opposed to social interaction (Conrad and Schneider 1980, p. 21). Despite differences in the focus of study in deviance creation, Conrad and Schneider (1980, pp. 21–22) note that both interactionist and conflict approaches provide insights into "the development and change of deviance designations," as phenomenological models are sensitive to the socially constructed quality "of deviance designations—that they emerge from social interaction and that they are humanly constructed and hence can be humanly changed." Meanwhile, conflict models are sensitive to structural in-equalities in the "power to construct reality—that deviance designations may serve political interests and . . . are created usually through some type of social conflict. We call this conflict the politics of definition" (p. 22).

A fourth set of perspectives that examine socially designated deviance are feminist theories, which encompass various categories and subcategories, each addressing different aspects of female inequality. These interests are reflected in such headings as radical, liberal, socialist, Marxist, Third World, black,[39] cultural, aboriginal, postmodern, psychoanalytic, material, lesbian, and exis-tentialist feminism (Tong 1989; Smart 1990; Einstadter and Henry 1995, pp. 259–276). In a broad sense, feminist perspectives utilize "all means available . . . [in] uncovering the sources of sex and gender inequality," including cer-tain aspects of functionalism (Edwards 1988, p. 47). Feminist theories have been criticized on various grounds, including engaging in the same exclusion-ary bias as phallocentric perspectives. For instance, it has been argued that the experiences of black women are distinct from those of white women (e.g., socially, culturally, and economically) and that the latter have been generally insensitive to ethnic and racial differences among the female experiences and engage in racism and white sexism by "asserting white middle class experi-ence as normal, and designating black people's experience to the category of 'other'" (Ahluwalia 1991, p. 12). By focusing exclusively on male power struc-tures, white feminists typically neglect "the privilege that white women have over black men and also neglect to implicate white women in perpetuating racism and using violence against black people" (p. 12).

Although noting these criticisms, my interest is in the commonality of feminist theories and their utility in deconstructing as socially designated deviance gender aspects of the culture-bound "syndromes" under scrutiny. This approach can address such questions as why females are overrepresented as "victims" of latah, dancing mania, and mass conversion "hysteria" in schools, and what is the social positioning of "victims" in the societies in question. Why is severe latah predominantly found among postmenopausal females in socially marginal positions and within only certain ethnic groups? Why is koro a predominantly male "disorder"? What do these "disorders" symbolize in terms of gender-based power structures relative to internalized notions of masculinity and femininity? Do these "bizarre" behaviors serve a particular function for those affected? For instance, it has been postulated that psychological distress (in the form of individual and group "hysteria") may serve as a means of protest or negotiation for oppressed Malay female workers in multinational corporations operating in Malaysia (Ong 1988).

Feminist theories share with symbolic interactionists, phenomenologists, and neo-Marxists suspicions of the hidden political agendas, subconscious motives, prejudices, and stereotypes embedded within the psyche of researchers in their promotion and reification of prevailing societal attitudes and beliefs. An implicit agreement also exists in challenging the realist reductionist analysis of variables and contentions of being able to describe objective reality by separating the subject from the object to engage in a culture-, value-, class-, power-, and gender-neutral social science (see Turner and Killian 1987, p. 18). Hence, feminist-constructionist theorists are skeptical of variable analysis and its tendency to reflect dominant societal beliefs and mores, as "their experiences define what variables are significant for study, [and] what their indicators . . . [and] presumed relationships are" (Andersen 1987, p. 18). Positivist approaches are ill equipped to appreciate "the multiple interpretations of reality that we must begin to see if we are to include those who have previously been excluded . . . [and] too easily assume that there is a single interpretation of reality" (p. 18).

Normative theories comprise another constellation of perspectives that are sometimes used to understand socially designated deviance, although these theories will not be utilized in this study because of criticisms that will become evident. The unifying features of these models are (1) they synonymously treat deviance as a norm violation; (2) social control and deviance are nonproblematic, as they occur in reaction to rule breaking; (3) they seek to classify various forms of deviance; and (4) they attempt to understand various factors (e.g., social, cultural, economic, psychological) that motivate deviants to violate norms (Roach Anleu 1995, p. 20). Normative theorists include influential sociologists Emile Durkheim and Talcott Parsons. Both view deviance as normal and relative, varying across history and cultures in accordance with a particular consensus at a certain time and place. Normative theorists often differ in identifying the origins of deviance. For instance, Robert Merton

(1938) considered structural inequalities as the root cause of deviance, whereas for Parsons (1951) it was a dysfunctional state of disequilibrium within the social system.

Major problems exist in using consensus theories in the present study. For example, deviance and social control are considered nonproblematic. From a normative perspective, if one deviates from the consensus of a particular society, he or she may be labeled dysfunctional, abnormal, or ill. This process is especially evident in the history of Western psychiatric theory and practice, which is replete with examples of the formation of consensus on the abnormality status of various behaviors exhibited by certain minorities in Western society or behaviors in non-Western societies that are at variance with the consensual normality standard of the West. An example of the latter case is the popular pathological assessment of Nazism during World War II by both Western scientific elites and the lay public.

As a result of their nonproblematic, objectivist nature, normative/consensus theories share certain underlying realist assumptions that render them incompatible with the theoretical framework of the present study. These criticisms are articulated by sociologists Ralph Turner and Lewis Killian (1987, p. 18) who note the underlying assumption of this view:

> All imply [that] . . . given sufficient time, resources, and skill, social scientists will be able to identify and describe social reality and its laws. This description need not correspond to the image that the members themselves have of their society and its culture. Indeed, it probably will not because the expert—the social scientist—is held to be necessary for . . . construction of a valid, objective account.
>
> Social scientists with this . . . approach . . . seek laws of social change but assume that the roots of change are . . . in . . . the social order . . . not in the behavior of the members of the society. Such concepts as "cultural lag," "anomie," "dysfunction," and "structural strain" imply that social change, including collective behavior, comes about because something is not working correctly or normally in the culture, the social structure or the social system. For the advocates of this approach, the social scientist's goal is to describe this structure of social system accurately in order to . . . recognize malfunctions or disorders, explain what produces them, predict their consequences, and, if asked, prescribe remedies or policies to correct them.

Despite inadequacies, elements of the traditions of symbolic interactionism, phenomenology, new Marxist, and feminist perspectives can be fruitfully used as an eclectic montage of paradigms with the capacity to pose important questions about such factors as the origin, nature, and consequences of socially designated deviance. The present study will utilize a composite of these perspectives, which offer a multitude of theoretical approaches that focus on varying aspects of the creation of deviance and the social construction of meaning in the genesis and maintenance of three culture-bound "syndromes."

An important emphasis of the present study is the focus on historical, temporal aspects of deviance and deviance designations, which has been successfully used in the analysis of the U.S. temperance movement (Gusfield 1963), prostitution (Hobson 1987), mental disorder (Szasz 1970), and wife beating (Dobash and Dobash 1992). Applying natural history or sociohistorical approaches to studying the development of social problems is especially apposite to analyzing the process of the medicalization of deviance, as they emphasize "the dynamic role of claims-making groups in defining deviance and other social problems" (Rosecrance 1985, p. 275). Examining the temporal aspects of certain social problems can assist in illuminating their inconstant, dynamic, and political nature, potentially providing valuable insights into the sociocultural background, power, gender, and class structures within which public problems and issues are situated and debated. The use of these approaches is supported by Joseph Gusfield (1980, p. vi), who discusses their applicability within one particular tradition—social-constructionist analyses:

> History is, at least here, also a relativizing device. It gives distance and strangeness to what is otherwise seen as near and familiar. The medicalization of social problems . . . [is sometimes] not the culmination of a movement to find a solution to the problems but only another period in which one imputed reality is substituted for another.
>
> There is in this stance . . . a distancing of the observer from the observed. Those being analyzed—the members of the society, official agents, major spokesmen—are caught up in the Enlightenment view of history as evolution toward progress. Science is, in this formulation, outside of history—not itself a target of study. Those doing the analyzing—the sociologists themselves—are not so caught up. They will not give medicine and its claim to authority through science any special consideration or status. They take it as topic rather than resource.

THIS STUDY'S APPROACH

Historical approaches are well situated to highlight the shifting role of special interest groups in defining and successfully publicizing new deviance designations. A dramatic example of this process is the history of child abuse and subsequent medicalization of abusers. The first major public concern over abused children was raised in America during the 1870s when the Society for the Prevention of Cruelty to Animals interceded in a case involving a maltreated girl after unsuccessful attempts to convince church officials to intervene. This case prompted the formation of the New York Society for the Prevention of Cruelty to Children, which enjoyed only fleeting interest and support. Child abuse was "rediscovered" as a serious and widespread social problem following a series of sporadic studies beginning in 1888 and culminating in recognition within the medical community during the 1960s. The problem of physically abused children received widespread awareness almost exclusively by the actions of pediatric radiologists and not pediatricians after identifying similar limb breakage and fracture patterns in X rays (see Pfohl 1977; Conrad and Schneider 1980, pp. 161–169). Surprisingly, physicians in direct contact with the children had not sought to highlight the problem for various reasons: ignorance, disbelief, concern over potential legal liability for possible breach of medical confidentiality, and unwillingness to become engaged in the legal system (Pfohl 1977, p. 13). Radiologists, less concerned with violating patient confidentiality and only marginally part of the medical profession, were less inhibited than physicians in direct contact with the children to implicate parental involvement.[40] The radiologists' success enhanced their professional status within the medical community, in part because of their designating the problem as a syndrome whereby abusers required psychiatric rehabilitation for their "illness" (Pfohl 1977; Conrad and Schneider 1980).

This study deconstructs and analyzes culture-specific behavior patterns almost exclusively considered within mainstream psychiatry to represent local variants of universal psychological disturbances. For example, transcultural psychiatrists and medical anthropologists continue to debate the origin and nature of culture-bound syndromes, syndromes that consist of a constellation of signs and symptoms almost exclusively confined to specific cultural settings. These so-called ethno-specific disorders are typically conceptualized as local variants of universal disease or disorder categories colored by social and cultural influences. For instance, Malayo-Indonesian latah is typified as a variant of a universal startle-matching taxon (Simons 1985a, 1994, 1995, 1996), koro is perceived as part of a genital retraction taxon (Berrios and Morley 1984; Simons 1985b; Anderson 1990), and "epidemic" hysteria is viewed as a variant of somatoform disorders (Sirois 1974).

The concept of culture-bound syndromes was initially devised in 1951 by British-trained, Hong Kong–based ethnic Chinese psychiatrist Pow Meng Yap (1951) and was subsequently refined by him (1962, 1965, 1967). Since the mid-1970s a vigorous debate has developed, primarily among transcultural psychiatrists and psychologists and medical anthropologists and sociologists, as to the nature of what Yap (1951, p. 313) described as mental "diseases peculiar to certain cultures." One group of researchers supports Yap's original formulation, which is also the present consensual view within the scientific community—namely, that distinctive norms, values, and beliefs can precipitate psychiatric disorders that are confined to a particular culture or set of cultures and as such represent local variants of a universal biological potential. Advocates of this position are led by Ronald Simons and Charles Hughes (1985).

An alternative approach, which I advocate, is to conceptualize these "syndromes" as deviant social roles and worldviews. This is achieved by focusing on such factors as (1) the social and cultural patterning of episodes, (2) the political nature of deviance designations relative to whose interests are being served by such labels, and (3) the conspicuous gender aspects of those defined as deviant. For example, in the latter instance, why is it that observed and reported severe latah is almost exclusively confined to socially marginal, postmenopausal females within the Malayo-Indonesian cultural dynamic? Or why is "epidemic hysteria" in Malaysian schools almost exclusively confined to subordinate adolescent Islamic Malay females undergoing rigid religious and educational discipline?

One important focus of this study is on the social construction underlying the attachment of deviance labels to the culture-bound "syndromes" of collective koro, latah, and mass psychogenic illness. This is accomplished by examining these deviant behaviors and demonstrating that they are not reflections of individual or societal pathology per se but are rather actions governed by specific sociohistorical cultural rules and conduct codes that are "misinterpreted" in the Western literature as a result of the interests, motivations, and convictions of imperialistic Western socio-medico controlling agents in their creation of these pathological "illness" categories. Adhering to a relativistic definition of deviance, meaning-oriented approaches seek to explicate relationships between the deviant and stigmatizing agents of social control, emphasizing the significance of norms, values, context, culture, power, gender, and worldview in the social construction of illness.[41] This method involves detailing the deviant's world and underlying motivations.

In attempting to understand "foreign" actions in non-Western cultures, Shweder and Edmund Bourne (1984, p. 164) advocate a similar approach that involves focusing on their "objectives, premises, presuppositions, standards, knowledge, meanings . . . [in] so much detail that the ideas and conduct come to make sense given the 'context.'" The goal of contextual approaches is to obtain detailed information, especially involving non-Western cultures where behaviors are more likely to be unfamiliar or at variance with Eurocentric norms. In each case study in the following chapters, those defining deviance are Western-trained social scientists who without scientific substantiation superimpose biological, psychiatric, psychoanalytical, or psychological explanations to account for the appearance of the particular "syndrome" in question. Consequently, popular stereotypes, prejudices, assumptions, and folk realities as to the origin and nature of deviance among certain groups of non-European peoples, and among Europeans what I shall term the historical and female Other,[42] appeared and continue to appear under the guise of science. These erroneous illness labels are often imposed through structural power by way of colonialism. That these typifications continue to be propagated by Western imperialist psychiatry underlies the significance of this study.

Edward Said (1978, p. 43) states that Orientalists "promoted the difference between the familiar (Europe, the West, 'us') and the strange (the Orient, the East, 'them')." When Said and I refer to "the West," this is, of course, an oversimplification—but one that is useful for helping to broadly conceptualize differences between the Occident and Orient. Of course, culture is a dynamic that is constantly changing from within and through interaction with "outsiders." There is no such thing as a pure culture or entity such as "the West," just as there is no pure or even relatively uniform entity known as "the Orient." Inaccurate Western typifications of the Orient (and non-Western typifications of "the Occident") can become incorporated by these "others" as part of their own heritage, leading to the invention of culture.

The tendency for Western-trained psychiatrists to employ medical models designed to identify transcultural examples of universal mental disorders, to the neglect of thoroughly examining the sociocultural context of illness behaviors, is what Kleinman (1977) terms a "category fallacy." This process involves the dismissal of indigenous categories of disease, disorder, or abnormality on the grounds that they embody culture-specific folk schemes regarding the very concept of illness, its cause and treatment. Kleinman (1977, p. 4) cautions that culture not only shapes the illness experience; "it shapes the very way we conceive of illness." Although Western "scientific" illness categories are promoted as neutral, culture-free, and thus superior to "native" concepts, they insidiously superimpose Eurocentric cultural categories onto "deviant" behavior in non-Western settings. This imposition of Western-bound illness categories onto behavior from cultures with significantly different social realities, semantic networks, symbol systems, and emotional worldviews promotes "the erroneous belief that deviance can be studied in different societies independent of specific cultural norms and patterns of normative behavior"

(Kleinman 1977, p. 4). Although Kleinman (1988, p. 2) is convinced that certain categories of mental illness are universal, he is critical of the potential for Western diagnostic imperialism in such documents as DSM-IV, which can reify Western social realities, noting that "psychiatric concepts, research methodologies, and even data are embedded in social systems" (1988, p. 3).

The present study adds to the growing body of sociological literature that has appeared with increasing frequency since the early 1980s, which almost exclusively examines the medicalization of deviance in Western contexts. This study uniquely focuses on the inappropriate placement of illness or disorder labels onto non-Western societies, exposing the biomedical and Eurocentric biases of contemporary anthropological and psychiatric classification schemes in their creation of such "disorders" as latah, koro, and mass psychogenic illness.

Chapters 2–5 consist of case studies of illness behaviors labeled as culture- or history-specific examples of disease or disorder assumed to represent local variants of universal illness categories as they were conceptualized in the Western biomedical tradition. In challenging the validity of their classification as culture- or history-specific illness entities that are colored by social and cultural camouflage, I shall examine their context and meaning, the social and cultural patterning of episodes, and the historical circumstances under which they became defined as exemplifying psychological disturbance. In reassessing their illness status, I shall demonstrate that in most instances they are most appropriately interpreted as unique idioms of expression that reflect the human propensity for adapting to unique circumstances with creativity and imagination, which have been in turn inappropriately reduced to unitary Western categories of disease or disorder. The following case studies in the medicalization of exotic deviance underscore the need to provide detailed descriptions of the social and cultural context and meaning of seemingly strange behaviors, particularly in non-Western settings or Western subcultures, and to avoid exclusively basing evaluations of such behaviors on the "bizarre" or "sick" nature of the actions per se.

NOTES

1. Throughout this study I use the terms *Eurocentric* and *Western* with the knowledge that "the West" and Europe encompass a large land area containing diverse cultural traditions. When referring to "Europe" and "Western," I mean those holding Anglo-Saxon-Celtic attitudes and values that generally predominate in Europe and the Americas.

2. In recognizing that "scientific" realities are contestable, negotiable social constructions, Berger and Luckmann (1971 [1966]) redefined the orientational boundaries of the sociology of knowledge by focusing on phenomenological patterns, away from Karl Mannheim's traditional objectivist approach, which emphasizes apprehend-

ing penultimate reality. This is relevant to the deconstruction of culture-bound "syndromes," as it addresses not only "the empirical variety of knowledge in human societies" but "the processes by which *any* body of 'knowledge' comes to be socially established *as* reality" (p. 15; italics in original).

3. Throughout this study the words *transcultural* and *transhistorical* are meant to be applied in their broadest sense—that is, all cultures and eras of human history.

4. Sulawesi native Syamsul Lussa, now a prominent Indonesian Tourism Ministry official, conveyed this custom about his home village while a student at James Cook University in Queensland, Australia, during the early 1990s and was absolutely serious.

5. For instance, as physicians are generally recruited from upper socioeconomic levels, they may focus their research agendas on cardiovascular diseases that more directly affect members of their class while not emphasizing research topics that typically affect the lower class, such as the prevention and treatment of malnutrition-related health problems (see Zola 1972, p. 489). The medical community can also define what is a "significant" illness or disorder, with the potential to trivialize medical conditions found primarily in the lower classes and females.

6. The medical community has the power to create markets for its services by redefining social problems as disease (Lock 1988, p. 44). This power has also been referred to as the "medical industrial complex" (Edwards 1988, p. 149; Rodwin 1993, p. 407).

7. Italics in original.

8. Even within the health care system, the medical profession "dominates the health division of labour economically, politically, socially and intellectually" to the extent that it is exempt from "direction and evaluation by other health care occupations" (Willis 1983, p. 2).

9. Lapp (1965) describes scientific elites as "the new priesthood."

10. The scientific study of social problems is most commonly situated in the sociological domain and also reflects the investigators' norms and values. Herbert Blumer (1971, pp. 301–302) observed that social problems "are the result of a process of definition in which a given condition is picked out and identified as a social problem . . . [and] does not exist for a society unless it is recognized by that society to exist." Howard Becker (1963, p. 9) defined a deviant as "one to whom that label has successfully been applied." His study was significant for shifting the then common emphasis of deviance analysis away from etiological categories in nature to examining those people who evoke the deviant label (Kitsuse and Spector 1975). The theoretical focus is not on how the social structure generates deviance conditions "but how conditions come to be perceived and defined as social problems, how members generate definitions and constructions of conditions" (p. 586).

11. For example, cerebral diseases such as Alzheimer's disease or advanced syphilis, which can precipitate disordered thinking or behavior.

12. Although Szasz makes an important point, indeed one that is a fundamental tenet of this study, his position is extreme in arguing that very few mental deviations can appropriately be designated as an illness in a medical model sense. His contention that most behavior labeled as mental disorder cannot be substantiated with a medical label is dangerous and erroneous. For example, Szasz (1970, p. xxi) contends that women who

transgress particular laws or mores related to personal conduct that involves neglect of their newborn infants are labeled postpartum psychotics, when in fact they may have no verifiable mental illness but are exhibiting unconventional behaviors. This is misleading. Prior to the twentieth century and effective treatment of puerperal infections with antibiotics, the incidence of acute organic postpartum psychosis was high, calculated at 14 percent in one major study (Mayer-Gross, Slater, and Roth 1963, p. 331). Today, most postpartum psychosis cases receiving modern medical care are unrelated to infection and are clearly linked to various biological changes associated with childbirth that are exacerbated after onset by psychosocial stress (Brockington et al. 1988; Nyberg, Lindstrom, and Terenius 1988; Vinogradov and Csernansky 1990; Sandyk 1992; Kumar 1994; Bartholomew and Likely 1998). Kleinman (1988, p. 184) also criticizes the position of so-called antipsychiatrists as "dangerously irresponsible: mental illness is real." Another group of antipsychiatrists acknowledges that certain individuals become mentally disordered, but not necessarily in an illness sense, in response to stresses that occur after their unconventional behavior is stigmatized by the label of mental illness by agents reinforcing the morals of the prevailing social structure (e.g., Goffman 1961; Laing 1965; Scheff 1966).

13. *Iatrogenic* is a medical term referring to the unintentional elicitation of psychological or physical disorders or symptoms resulting from a physician's diagnosis, manner, or treatment (Simpson and Weiner 1989a, pp. 592–593).

14. Another "disease" of Negro slaves was *dysoesthesia oethiopeca* involving their "characteristic" propensity to destroy and disregard the property rights of others, including deliberately breaking tools while using them (Fernando 1988, p. 24).

15. Of course, much of medical practice and medical categorization also has strong social components (Atkinson 1995), with Julia Epstein (1995, p. 6) observing that medical practice has fostered a taken-for-granted notion "that we can establish an objectively defined delineation of the 'normal' with respect to the human body."

16. This change in the psychiatric status of homosexuality was first reflected in the seventh printing of the 1968 edition of DSM-II, which appeared in July 1974 (see pp. 6, 44).

17. DSM-I refers to *The Diagnostic and Statistical Manual of Mental Disorders,* which was first published in 1952. It was developed by the American Psychiatric Association Committee on Nomenclature and Statistics and published by the American Psychiatric Association. DSM-II was an updated version that was published in 1968, DSM-III appeared in 1980, DSM-III-R refers to a revised edition of DSM-III appearing in 1987, and DSM-IV was published in May 1994. The DSM series has become increasingly influential in diagnosing instances of apparent mental disorders, to become the most widely used medical and psychiatric diagnostic manual in the world at present. The widespread use of the DSM series by psychiatrists, psychologists, and social workers does not necessarily mean they believe it is a useful document. For example, a survey of clinical social workers in the United States by Kutchins and Kirk (1988) revealed widespread dissatisfaction with DSM, which was used primarily because of its importance in obtaining medical insurance reimbursement rather than for its scientific utility. One typical respondent found the manual "of absolutely no functional use except for insurance purposes. . . . Its organization bears little resemblance to the way the human

mind and psyche are organized. We just make a list of the DSM . . . diagnoses that are most frequently paid for and then . . . pick one that most nearly describes our client" (p. 219).

18. Despite this decision, "self-defeating personality disorder" was given an official diagnostic code number and a list of characteristic features, meaning "it could be used as a legitimate diagnosis" (Tavris 1993, p. 181).

19. In reacting to the decision to exclude "paraphilic rapism" and "masochistic personality disorder" from the official categories of mental disorders in DSM-III-R, Marshall Clinard and Robert Meier (1992, p, 356) remark that "it is difficult to conceive of a sound medical diagnosis being withdrawn when threatened with a lawsuit."

20. From the French word *bourgeois,* referring to a middle-class person. However, it is specifically used in the context of this passage to refer to the capitalist class, in the Marxist sense.

21. These behaviors were highly organized, institutionalized, and socially accepted within their particular subculture as a means of penance, worship, or divine favor. Medical historian George Rosen (1962) reports that those experiencing the condition of psychomotor agitation known as "the jerks," induced through prolonged dancing, singing, and zealous orations, were often considered divinely possessed. The "barking exercise" was viewed "as a means of chastisement for sins," as participants occasionally surrounded a tree while on all fours, barking and yelping in an effort to "tree the devil" (p. 35). It was subsequently considered an act of piety or a sign of divine favor. The rationale for walking naked in public was seen by Quakers as a form of truthfulness (p. 27).

22. Stephen Post (1992, p. 81) writes that "because psychiatry is powerful socially and politically, it should avoid the pretext of objectivity in controversial areas of nosology, and acknowledge that its interpretation of some phenomena may be reductionistic or erroneous."

23. Although labels of severe mental illness have been typically applied by scientists antecedent to inquiry to persons claiming to have had contact with extraterrestrials, a biographical analysis of 152 claimants by Bartholomew, Basterfield, and Howard (1991) revealed a history remarkably devoid of mental disturbance. In 132 cases, subjects were found to have a symptom pattern similar to that of the fantasy-prone personality (see Wilson and Barber 1981, 1983), a rich state of fantasy involvement that can develop in normal, healthy individuals as an adaptive response to such factors as social isolation and child abuse. Although claimants exhibit higher than normal incidence of psychopathological symptoms, Bartholomew and colleagues (1991) suggest that another subset of fantasizers might be otherwise well-adjusted, harnessing their creative capacities to lead productive personal and professional lives, as was typical of Wilson and Barber's (1981, 1983) normal fantasy-prone sample, as opposed to those whose fantasies invite derision and generally diminish the quality of life and societal status.

24. Marano (1982, p. 385) states that when "windigo psychosis" is viewed from the group psychodynamic perspective rather than as individual psychopathology, "the crucial question is not what causes a person to become a cannibalistic maniac, but under what circumstances a Northern Algonquian is likely to be accused of having become a cannibalistic maniac and run the risk of being executed as such." Marano argues that

those executed for going into a cannibalistic rampage were not experiencing a culture-bound variant of hysteria peculiar to Northern Algonquians but were victims of witch hunts or triage homicide.

25. However, it should be made clear that these epidemic hysteria episodes in Malaysian schools and factories are not regarded as idioms of purely social and culturalogical origins but as a combination of syndrome and ritual—a position I support.

26. Other writers use similar descriptions such as *medical imperialism* but limit their discussion solely to the economic exploitation of less technologically developed countries (see Taylor 1979, pp. 228–234), neglecting ideological imperialism, although these two concepts are interrelated, as ideological influence can precipitate economic dependence and vice versa.

27. Another significant reason for affiliating with medicine was the growing, unjustified assumption during the nineteenth century that a majority of the "insane" suffered from organic brain diseases (Garton 1988, p. 99). This belief was buoyed by discoveries such as paresis (paralysis or muscular weakening) in patients diagnosed as insane being precipitated by cerebral lesions resulting from syphilic infection (Bates 1977, p. 10; Micale 1994b, p. 126; Barlow and Durand 1995, p. 18).

28. Eminent British psychiatric historians Richard Hunter and Ida Macalpine's (1963, p. ix) acerbic critique of the then contemporary state of psychiatric practice remains salient today, noting that the history of psychiatry is a chronicle "of perennial problems, recurrent ideas, disputes and treatments, trailing in the wake of medicine and exhibiting paradoxically—as medicine did of old—a mixture of as many false facts as false theories." They also observed that

> Case-taking . . . which provides psychiatry's basic data, is inseparable from observer influence and error. There is not even an objective method of describing or communicating clinical findings without subjective interpretation and no exact and uniform terminology which conveys precisely the same to all. In consequence there is wide divergence of diagnosis, even of diagnoses, a steady flow of new terms and an ever-changing nomenclature, as well as a surfeit of hypotheses which tend to be presented as fact. Furthermore, etiology remains speculative, pathogenesis largely obscure, classifications predominantly symptomatic and hence arbitrary and possibly ephemeral; physical treatments are empirical and subject to fashion, and psychotherapies still only in their infancy and doctrinaire. (p. ix)

29. This paradigm overlaps with the medical model in that certain genetic traits or chemical imbalances are often defined as illnesses. Although the medical model is the subject of considerable criticism, it remains the dominant mainstream paradigm, whereas biological explanations are generally held to have little or no credibility. However, a central criticism of both perspectives is that they focus on the individual while downplaying the impact of the sociocultural context and base their theories on the hope "that eventually a biological or biochemical basis of the major disorders will be discovered" (Cochrane 1983, p. 3). Szasz is constantly reminding medico-biological determinists of this point. In discussing the lack of advances in biological psychiatry, Richard Vatz and Lee Weinberg (1994, p. 325) state that "the unfulfilled promises of the

discovery of neurobiological correlates specific to particular 'mental illnesses' constitute an irresolvable crisis for psychiatry."

30. This category also includes claims that behavioral anomalies acquired after birth are responsible for deviant actions, such as the attempt by psychiatrist Dorothy Lewis to associate homicide with head injury (see Thio 1988, p. 124). After studying fifteen convicted murderers, Lewis (1986) found that all had experienced serious head injuries prior to committing the killings. However, the sample size is small, and nonanalyzed sociocultural factors could plausibly account for the findings, as murderers have typically been subjected to earlier violence (Thio 1988, p. 124). In other words, having sustained an earlier head injury could be spuriously linked to being a murderer, whereas unexamined sociocultural factors could be the real determinant.

31. Donald Gibbons (1968, p. 134) extends this argument in speculating that delinquent subcultures may "recruit new members selectively, placing a premium upon agile, muscular boys" while excluding excessively obese "or overtly thin and sickly youngsters," as they have a lower probability of succeeding in the physically demanding lifestyle of the delinquent. "If so, this is a social process, not a biologically determined pattern of behaviour."

32. Although biogenetic theories of deviance remain controversial, strong recent evidence indicates that postpartum psychosis, which if undiagnosed or untreated often leads to a mother suddenly killing her newborn infant or herself, is precipitated by an inherited chemical imbalance (see Bartholomew and Likely 1998). These symptoms are transculturally specific and universally recognized as abnormal behavior.

33. This treatment was not related to morality per se, but the word *moral* during this period also referred to emotional or psychological aspects of human behavior. Moral treatment was first instituted in Paris, France, in 1793 by physician Phillippe Pinel.

34. There were rare exceptions, such as in ancient Greece, when certain forms of behavioral deviations such as epilepsy were considered desirable, sacred qualities.

35. This theory is highly complex, and for our purposes it will be necessary to produce only a brief overview and critique, especially as it is not central to this research.

36. Italics in original.

37. For a discussion of the origins and integration of phenomenological approaches within the interactionist tradition, refer to Einstadter and Henry (1995, pp. 197–226).

38. Italics in original.

39. *Black* is a generic term I shall use to refer to the skin description of all non-Caucasian females of color.

40. An influential publication responsible for the widespread contemporary awareness of physically abused children was the article by pediatrician C. Henry Kempe and colleagues (1962) in the *Journal of the American Medical Association*. As Gelles, quoted in Conrad and Schneider (1980, p. 164), notes: "The Kempe article made physicians and medical practitioners aware of the problem of child abuse, but none of this was new to other agencies, which had for years been trying to cope with the problem of abused children."

41. On the importance of examining cultural meanings to discern the intentions of "foreign" actors, Geertz (1973, p. 5) remarks that individuals are suspended in self-spun

webs of significance: "I take culture to be those webs, and the analysis of it to be therefore not an experimental science in search of law but an interpretive one in search of meaning. It is explication I am after, construing social expressions on their surface enigmatical."

42. Western females have been historically regarded as an "Other," a conceptualization explicitly supported by scientists during the nineteenth and early twentieth centuries, typifying females as physically, emotionally, and intellectually inferior to their male counterparts. In the section discussing the association between females and communicable hysteria, I shall demonstrate that this "Otherness" characterization continues in a subtle form within contemporary scientific studies. By "Western historical Other," I refer to the tendency of most present-day scientists to discuss historical behaviors among peoples of European ethnic origins (e.g., witch burnings, the Crusades) as if they belong to some distant, separate race of ancestors, with the implication that such "irrational" actions could not recur today among educated people on a mass scale (see Bullard 1994). This type of writing is evident in Chapter 5 on European dancing manias.

2

Disease, Disorder, or Deception:
Latah as Habit and Fraud in a Malay Extended Family

Oh what a tangled web we weave, When first we practice to deceive! (Sir Walter Scott, cited in John Bartlett 1992, p. 378).

Nearly all forms of deception are now accepted by the medical profession as a form of illness. Even where deception is recognised, as for instance in the confabulations of the Munchausen syndrome, this is attributed to previous mental trauma, or to some form of cultural disadvantage. The deceiver, always referred to as a patient, is said to be "disturbed"; he [or she] is regarded as a victim, not as a rogue (J. M. Naish 1979, pp. 139–140).

A Ph.D. . . . does not confer expertise in detecting trickery. Thus, they are just as vulnerable, if not more so, to the magic tricks of a [professed psychic Uri] Geller as are people who lack their scientific training (Terence Hines 1988, p. 92).

INTRODUCTION TO THE LATAH "DISORDER"

This chapter will review and reappraise the general contemporary psychiatric consensus that latah is a mental disease, disorder, or abnormality manifest in susceptible individuals and precipitated from the culture-specific exploitation of a neurophysiological potential to startle that exists in all humans (see Simons 1985c; Howard and Ford 1992). It is based on ethnographic observations and interviews following my marriage into a Malay extended family, with the general findings related to the latah literature.[1]

Latah is a stereotypic, chronic, conditioned behavioral response to a variety of external stimuli characterized by verbal mimicry (echolalia), mimicking of body movements (echopraxia), verbal profanity (coprolalia), mimicking the general actions of another (echomimia), "automatic obedience," and hypersuggestibility. Latah and latahlike behavior are reported in diverse cultural settings that span a disperse geographical spectrum: Siberia, Africa, Europe, Southeast Asia, Oceania, and North America (Yap 1952; Adams 1955; Simons 1985c). For each society affected, the presentation of characteristics varies slightly. Among the Japanese Ainu, it is most commonly precipitated by the sudden recognition of, stepping on, or imagining having seen or stepped on a snake (Arieti and Meth 1959; Langness 1967) or snakelike creature such as a caterpillar (Yap 1952). In the northeastern United States and Canada, some residents react to a sudden startle by typically jumping into the air, in addition to exhibiting classic latah elements: obeying commands; repeating sounds, words, or phrases; proclaimed temporary loss of control; and fear and resentment at being exploited through teasing (Beard 1880a).

Malaysian latah is of particular interest because it is relatively rare in other parts of the world except for the Malay Peninsula,[2] nearby Java and Borneo, and some surrounding islands where it is common in certain locations, although there is a consensus among researchers that its frequency is declining.[3] The word *latah*, occasionally spelled *lata* or *lattah*,[4] is of Malay origin, of unknown etymology, and apparently derived from the Malay words for ticklish, nervous, creeping, and love madness. Although the first known verifiable accounts were recorded in Batavia of the Netherlands Indies or the Dutch East Indies (now Jakarta, Indonesia) during the 1860s, an incident near Malacca, Malaya, in 1846 contained several characteristic features (Winzeler 1984, p. 79).[5] Yap (1952, p. 516) suggests that references in Malay literature to latah as a behavioral anomaly may date to the fourteenth century, but no known explicit accounts exist. Malaysian latah occurs primarily in those of Malay descent, especially in women over age forty. Occasionally observed in men and young children, it is extremely rare among Indian and Chinese citizens except for the Straits Chinese, who comprise a small group of migrants from China who settled in what is now Peninsular Malaysia prior to the European colonialization of the region.[6] It is also occasionally reported among interacting ethnic groups within the Malayo-Indonesian cultural dynamic; the Ambonese, Balinese, Batak, Bidayuh, Boyanese, Buginese, Iban, Madurese, Malanau, Nonya, Semai, Sundanese, Thai in central and southern Thailand, and transplanted Portuguese.

Latah symptoms range on a spectrum from mild to intermediate to serious, with increasing severity and duration as subjects grow older. W. Gilmore

Ellis (1897) and Pow Meng Yap (1952) identify two categories, A.R.D. Adams (1955) three, and H. A. O'Brien (1883) four. In its mild form, presentation is confined to the claimed involuntary utterance of incomprehensible sounds, meaningless or obscene words, and gesturing, up to a few seconds in duration. As cases progress in severity, an increased presence of mimicry and claims of amnesia during, and loss of consciousness following, episodes are seen. Subjects typically exhibit similar patterns of initiation and presentation. For instance, some may become latah only if they drop something unexpectedly or if suddenly poked in the ribs without warning—but under no other circumstances, no matter how pronounced the stimulus.[7] Subjects do not appear to vacillate from mild occurrences during one episode, severe the next, then return to mild. The typical pattern is for mild cases to suddenly exhibit pronounced symptoms of increasing duration and intensity if they progress to a severe condition. A general consensus within the latah literature indicates that cases described as "severe" or "serious" latah are those involving any form of mimicry or other claimed involuntary behaviors persisting for more than a few seconds and that can be extended for several minutes or longer through "teasing."[8] Considerable anecdotal evidence suggests that the onset of severe symptoms coincides with sexual conflict in the form of dreams (Van Loon 1928; Van Wulfften-Palthe 1933; Murphy 1976, p. 15), social trauma and depression (Yap 1952, pp. 536–537; Chiu, Tong, and Schmidt 1972, p. 159; Kenny 1978, p. 210).

Latah is most typically classified as a culture-bound psychiatric syndrome possessing psychotic, neurotic, or hysterical dimensions. It has been described as a psychosis (Langness 1967; Tan 1980, pp. 380, 384), paroxysmal neurosis (Fitzgerald 1923; Richards 1981, p. 183), nervous disease (Wilkinson, Coope, and Mohamed 1961, p. 156), self-hypnosis (Gimlette 1897; Galloway 1922), epidemic hysteria (Ormerod 1912), and atypical schizophrenia (Opler 1967, p. 133; Rosenthal 1970). It is commonly categorized as a form of individual hysteria (Ballard 1912; Pino and Wittermans 1963, p. 87; Schmidgall-Tellings and Stevens 1981, p. 187) induced by religious excitement (Simpson and Weiner 1989b, p. 676), being female (Echols and Shadily 1968, p. 216), or general stress (Kiev 1972, p. 75). Other researchers consider latah to represent learned behavior (Kessler 1977; Lee 1981; Kenny 1985), a genetic disorder (Swettenham 1963 [1895]), or a conditioned, involuntary neurophysiological response in susceptible individuals (Simons 1980, 1985c, 1987) that is exploited for social gain (Jenner 1990, 1991).

Confusing, unsubstantiated, often contradictory information continues to exist concerning latah. Langness (1967, p. 149) proclaims that it is "definitely psychotic." Eng-Seong Tan (1980, p. 380) remarks confidently that "the hysterical nature of the condition is inescapable," and in the *Dictionary of Medical Syndromes,* Sergio Magalini and Euclide Scrascia (1981, p. 477) contend that chronic latah "leads to automatic obedience and severe personality deterioration." Samuel Wilson (1940, p. 1632) asserts that latah is associated with compulsive tics, whereas Yap (1952, p. 524) states emphatically that "the latah reaction and compulsive tics are unrelated."

In this chapter I shall examine cases of latah in my wife's Malay extended family, suggesting that it is a fictitious disorder that has been socially constructed by Western-trained universalist scientists. Based on ethnographic data collected and a review of the latah literature, I will argue that family members have been erroneously classified as having a psychological disturbance. The latah cases in my wife's family are readily divisible into two broad categories: habitual (akin to Western swearing) and performance (the conscious exaggeration, in ritualized fashion, of sudden startle). Based on the meaning of latah in the family studied, I will conclude that latah among these family members is best understood as a cultural idiom that serves different functions for people at different points in the life stage.

SURVEY RESULTS OF LATAH IN MY WIFE'S FAMILY

The 115 family members surveyed may be classifiable as "mild" (N=33) and "severe" (N=4), according to classic textbook definitions of the condition, ranging from 16 to 70 years old. Of these 115 family members, 2 "severes" and 14 "milds" are deceased, and general features of their latah histories were garnered from family members.[9] None of the living subjects classified as mild consider themselves to be suffering from latah but do consider themselves to be exhibiting a response akin to swearing in Westerners. Mild cases can be further subdivided into two classes: those age 16 to approximately 40 years old, and those age 40 and upward. Those in the former category almost never respond with coprolalia, the most common being "*Oh! Mak engkau*" (Oh! Your mother), "*Yeah! Allah!*" (Yes! God!), and the meaningless nonsense phrase, "*Oh! Pocot!*" In those above age 40 coprolalia predominates, with the actual frequency and duration of responses appearing to remain steady. The most common are "*Oh! Puki Mak engkau*" (Oh! Your mother's cunt), "*Oh! Puki*" (Oh! Your cunt), "*Oh! Pantat Mak engkau*" (Oh! Your mother's cunt, pussy, or ass).[10] Other than the incidence of coprolalic content, the two categories are indistinguishable. The only severe case observed was that of Siti,[11] my wife's aunt.

THE CASE OF SITI

Siti is an indigenous Malay woman, age about 70 (she and her family members are unsure of her exact age), of low socioeconomic status, living in a small, isolated *kampong* (Malay village) about 10 kilometers from Malacca. She is a family outsider who married into the family, divorced, and remarried and conceived nine children by a second marriage (five female, four male), all but one of whom are still living. Latah was common among her aunts and sisters as she grew up and is common in her contemporary family, as all of her daughters exhibit mild features but her sons do not. Siti experienced mild symptoms ever since she can recall until a daughter fell sick and died during the week the daughter was to be married. Siti believes her daughter was hexed by a marriage rival.

Soon after her death, Siti's symptoms became severe. Not long afterward her husband died, and Siti found herself living with a son, whom she says does not pay her sufficient attention. Siti says she becomes occasionally deranged by talking nonsense because the deaths were a shock. Blaming latah on her unstable emotional situation, Siti states that during episodes she experiences total amnesia; words flow from her mouth uncontrollably and without thinking. She is unable to stop in the presence of people and needs to be left alone to calm down. During episodes she mimics virtually any gesture, phrase, or action of the person initiating the teasing. Siti says severe episodes may last the entire day if continually teased, after which she usually feels sleepy and losses her appetite. On a typical day she will latah several times depending on the number of startles. Usually alone during the day, Siti says she is briefly startled most commonly by the sudden sound or movement of chickens, cats, birds in flight, insects, and falling fruit. Since the death of her second husband and child, Siti has lived a dependent, lonely life, depressed and often consumed by thoughts of her deceased relatives. She has no television or radio.

I first observed Siti while attending my brother-in-law's wedding at which this timid, decrepit wizen-faced woman was intentionally startled by her elderly uncle, who walked near her and clapped his hands. She responded with a short vulgar phrase, stood up, lost all inhibition, and began following each of her teaser's commands and mimicking his every gesture. During the ensuing 10-minute episode, Siti was "made to" cry like a baby, perform *silat* (Malay self-defense or martial arts), dance vigorously, and partially disrobe, all to the obvious amusement of the entire wedding party who crowded around her inside the bride's parents' home. She would occasionally improvise gestures, such as lifting her sarong in a sexually suggestive manner, and utter the most vile words and phrases. Throughout the episode, after some outrageous display she would apologize immediately and profusely for her vulgarity, then launch unhesitatingly into another series of behaviors, apologizing over thirty times during this particular paroxysm. The next day at a crowded wedding reception at the groom's home, I was able to tease her into a similar, less dramatic episode by suddenly slapping my hands on the floor next to her. She responded with another 10-minute display, mimicking my every action, from dancing to slapping her face repeatedly. Other family members joined in the teasing.

A few days later I visited Siti at her residence in the presence of two relatives (my wife and my wife's mother). I startled her by melodramatically throwing crumpled paper onto the floor next to her. She responded with a short vulgar phrase ("Your mother's cunt"). Immediately thereafter I slapped my hands on the floor next to her, as I had done at the wedding, but there was no response. Next I slapped the floor, then my face—hard—but again no response. I was perplexed. Just a few days earlier in the presence of about sixty people, even minor startles would send her into prolonged episodes. On both occasions she was sitting on the floor next to me, and I executed the same sequence—startling her, slapping the floor, then my face. Subsequently, family elders explained emphatically that outside a large social gathering, "severes" never exhibit anything beyond "mild" symptoms, responding only with a word or phrase that is typically obscene. They also report that "teasers" are always close relatives—ensuring that the "victim" does not do anything too outrageous, such as being asked to stab someone with a knife.

Over the course of a month, I observed Siti teased into approximately 10-minute paroxysms at separate weddings where she sat in the main crowded room of the groom's house, despite claiming to dread being teased. If Siti genuinely fears teasing, she could simply inform family members to not engage in teasing or avoid wedding crowds or visit privately instead of prancing onto the theatrical equivalent of center stage. "If you suffer amnesia during 'attacks,' how can you apologize if you are unaware of your actions?" I later asked. She had no explanation. Although Siti would commonly drop and throw objects while latah, she was frequently allowed to cradle babies in her arms, never dropping a baby or behaving in a life-threatening manner.

Although claiming to dread teasing, Siti and onlookers seem to heartily enjoy the paroxysms. This denial of self-control is essential for the ensuing performance because it "sets the stage" for the subsequent transgression of Malay norms and affords the subject complete immunity from blame. What Malay latah subject, almost always an older woman, can be seen to willingly invite a condition where she temporarily loses control of her body, utters the most profound vulgarities, and exhibits lewd, sexually suggestive gestures? Siti's protestations are not vehement and are essentially perfunctory—as mothers, sons, and grandchildren would certainly not torment their elder loved ones, who are always treated with the utmost dignity and respect in Malayo-Indonesian culture. From this perspective, the latah startler unwittingly serves as a coach, orchestrating and dictating the transgressions. This ritual also allows for the release of individual expressions in that although the subject is required to perform the coach's choreography, the foul language and obscene body gestures are improvisations conducted entirely by the latah performer. The performance is almost always terminated by both physical and verbal cues that she is tired. Yet in this ritual of deception, although family members recognize the latah subject is not ill, they appear to genuinely believe the subjects have complete temporary control over their minds and are careful to keep knives and sharp objects away from them during episodes.

THE DUBIOUS HISTORY OF LATAH

Latah has been an enigmatic "syndrome" in that its classification has curiously eluded a number of competent researchers. Arieti and Meth (1959, p. 546) place it under "rare, unclassifiable, collective, and exotic psychotic syndromes." To date, all known published research has been by outsiders,[12] who note considerable difficulty in gathering detailed case histories from "severe" informants, as has Yap (1952, p. 537), despite fluency in the Malay language. Canadian anthropologist Michael Kenny (1985, p. 74) remarks that only a single case of latah has been observed and studied in sufficient context and depth to provide some insights into the processes involved. He is referring to a study by Australian sociologist Clive Kessler (1977), who in the course of examining the *main peteri*,[13] Malay spirit possession or seance, in the northern Malaysian state of Kelantan, inadvertently encountered a case of latah experienced by an elderly woman (pp. 313–316). Coincidentally, Kessler describes this woman as having a histrionic personality.

An exhibitionism explanation can account for: why "severe" latah is not considered an illness by participants and their families, the reluctance of informants to provide detailed information, observations that most subjects are described as clever (Fitzgerald 1923, p. 154; Murphy 1973, p. 46), and the conspicuous absence of any sign of mental abnormality outside of episodes (Swettenham 1963 [1895], p. 73; Freedman and Kaplan 1967, p. 1158; Murphy 1976, p. 13).[14] An exhibitionist model also explains its almost exclusive restriction to social subordinates—lower-class women and servants—and their conspicuous tendency to startle in the presence of higher-status peers (Geertz 1968, p. 96; Murphy 1973, p. 45, 1976; Kenny 1978, p. 213) as a means to gain attention and elevate their social position. In fact, some Malays contend that latah is "a type of malingering and that the victim is in complete control of his or her behavior" (Resner and Hartog 1970, p. 377).

It has been observed that "severe" subjects typically lead solitary and reclusive lives to avoid teasing (Langness 1967, p. 149). Yet it is equally plausible that these subjects become performers because they *are* lonely and desire attention. Previous observers have presented primarily anecdotal evidence that the onset of "severe" symptoms coincides with depression, financial dependence, and loneliness after the death of a close family member (Yap 1952, pp. 536–537; Chiu, Tong, and Schmidt 1972, p. 159; Kessler 1977, p. 313; Kenny 1978, p. 210). Kenny (1978, p. 217) argues that latah symbolizes the plight of such people and is a means of conveying to others that something is amiss. Siti matches this profile, exhibiting severe symptoms while depressed, unemployed, in social isolation, and dependent on her children for support. Researchers have focused their attention on the conditions that are likely to prompt latah, largely ignoring the circumstances under which oppressed, repressed, or depressed social subordinates are likely to feign or exaggerate for social benefit. It is notable that two other family members were in virtually the exact social situation after the death of their husbands. Both of these "mild" subjects experienced latah slightly longer than usual. They explained latah as an unconscious means of relieving emotional stress and perhaps an unconscious way of receiving attention.[15] Yet neither was able to become "severe."

It cannot be overemphasized that "severe" latahlike behavior is rare, even in Malayo-Indonesian culture.[16] A. C. Colson (1971, p. 96) identifies five cases in a Malay village of over 400 people; Gerald Resner and J. Hartog (1970, p. 376) state that traditional Malay villages usually have but one latah inhabitant; and Chiu and colleagues (1972) located only 69 cases from 13,219 East Malaysians surveyed.[17] One reason researchers downplay the obvious exhibitionistic features of "severe" cases is that reports indicate that latah once affected the majority, if not the entire population, of British Malaya and Dutch-ruled Indonesia (Clifford 1898, p. 195; Murphy 1976, p. 11). Some anthropologists reason that large numbers of inhabitants could not be feigning; therefore, it must possess some unconscious ritualistic or symbolic quality. Hence, although Yap (1952, p. 537) was convinced that latah is a mental disease of hysterical dimensions, he remarked that "it is often difficult to separate the genuine cases from those which are basically histrionic and exhibitionist in nature." Both Ari Kiev (1972, pp. 72–75) and H.B.M. Murphy (1976) also assume that this behavior characterizes its hysterical aspects and dissociative nature, especially as most "sufferers" are female. Tan (1980, p. 380) concurs, noting that "the hysterical nature of the condition is inescapable to the [trained] psychiatric observer. The condition invariably occurs in the presence of an audience, the behavior of the subject has a marked theatrical quality about it, often provoking spasms of laughter among the audience, and the subject pleads amnesia for her buffoonery when she comes out of her altered state of consciousness."

Upon closer scrutiny, the argument that "severe" latah cannot be fraud because of its pervasiveness dissolves. As "milds" do not consider themselves to be suffering from a disorder, when I explained to family members the common psychiatric definition of "mild" I was told that "everyone is a little latah." No known published or oral historical evidence indicates that "severe" cases were more common in previous centuries than they are today. Its habitual form persists in certain families, although it has no major social significance except as a prerequisite for performers to emulate and elaborate. Mild latahs simply respond to startle in a manner comparable to Western swearing. There is no exaggeration, mimicking, amnesia, or involuntary expression. Mild latah can be viewed as an infrequent habit formed almost exclusively by postpubescent females in certain Malay households with cultural traditions of such behavior. As it is considered a feminine trait typically associated with obedience, submissiveness, and the belief in an inherently weak mental constitution, or *semangat*,[18] most males do not engage in the habit, but if they do it is infrequent and typically denied.[19] The view of "mild" latah as habit is consistent with Murphy's (1976, p. 11) enigmatic observations that during the first half of the nineteenth century the condition was extremely rare in Malayo-Indonesia, by the 1890s it was reported on every street and was common among men, during the 1920s it was scarce, and today it has diminished in frequency in most locations and is almost exclusive to females.

THE MEDICALIZATION OF HABIT

The status of latah as a disorder is reminiscent of social scientists' mislabeling other habits and fashions as pathological. L. S. Penrose (1952) considered the yo-yo and crossword puzzle fads to be mild forms of herd-induced psychopathology. Charles Mackay (1852, pp. 623–624) discussed a common nineteenth-century social science view that the habitual use of certain words (in this case *flare* and *flare up* by Londoners to describe virtually any behavior) exemplified irrational crowd suggestibility. Child psychiatrist William Burnham (1924, pp. 337–338) makes a similar evaluation of the brief "craze" of tickling residents with feather dusters in Worcester, Massachusetts, during the early part of the twentieth century. Robert Markush (1973, p. 375) considers the worldwide proliferation of the cigarette smoking habit to be a variant of epidemic hysteria, and U.S. psychiatric pioneer Benjamin Rush (1962 [1812], p. 265) classified lying as a disease.

Psychiatrist Jack Jenner (1990, 1991) reports discovering evidence that latah is an abnormality of the human startle mechanism that varies with cultural conditioning. He treated a forty-year-old Dutch woman in Holland who would swear profusely, became abusive, and acted "oddly" upon being startled.

He claimed the subject had no Malayo-Indonesian cultural ties and was successfully treated with "flooding therapy," consisting of her husband and son startling her daily with unexpected noises and gestures as often as possible. Yet it is remarkably coincidental that the sole documented case of individual spontaneous "severe" latah in an otherwise normal person occurred in someone from a culture with a significant population of Malaysian and Indonesian descendants, both countries having been Dutch colonial outposts for centuries. In fact, the Netherlands only agreed to transfer sovereignty to Indonesia in 1949. Unanswered are such fundamental questions as to whether the woman had Malaysian or Indonesian companions—a possibility given their presence in Holland—or if she was previously aware of latah.

Jenner remarks that his patient startled several times daily for 20 years without seeking professional help. Only when her startling nearly resulted in a car accident did her husband seek psychiatric assistance for his wife. Jenner (1990, p. 195) states that the woman utilized her condition to obtain various secondary gains: avoiding housework, exercising influence in deciding holiday destinations, and serving as "her most effective weapon in marital conflicts." A fraud perspective is equally plausible and best conforms to historical and contemporary evidence. It can be argued that when flooding therapy commenced, the subject rebelled, intensifying malingering to demonstrate the ineffectiveness of treatment. However, when she realized the determination of her husband and psychiatrist to continue this strategy, symptoms suddenly ceased. As continuance of exaggerated startling would only elicit negative responses, the performances have never returned.

A habitual explanation is consistent with the "mild" reactions observed in my wife's family. Although both habitual and performance subjects report occasional episodes while alone, these appear confined to brief habitualized conditioned responses to sudden unexpected stimuli, possessing no social benefit. In terms of tension management, they may assist in relieving the stress of exposure to startling stimuli through the "flee or fight" reaction. In a similar vein, smokers often do smoke out of habit to relieve stress, commonly in social isolation. Yet the same smokers may use this habit to derive enhanced status among certain peer groups by appearing more adult. Furthermore, under extreme stress and conditioning, individuals can become chain smokers. Just as habitual latah is common in certain Malay households with such traditions, smoking predominates in children of parents who smoke by way of emulation. Both examples involve partially involuntary processes (nicotine craving, adrenalin reaction to startle), yet subjects appear under conscious control of the behavioral response. This is consistent with the apparent dramatic decline in the incidence of Malayan latah with colonization and subsequent Westernization. Many alternative means now exist for entering into Malay adulthood, such as smoking, drug use, and clothing fashions. Latah is in some ways comparable to Western swearing, predominantly found in males and correspondingly associated with masculinity and adulthood. Although some Western females swear, it is behavior typically considered "unbecoming of a lady,"[20] and like the distribution of latah, there are regional variations depending on social and cultural traditions. Latah in young habituals is viewed as cute, especially as they involve nonsense words or phrases. In older females the increased frequency of coprolalia allows for the transgression of ordinarily sanctioned verbal norms with impunity, proscriptions by which Malay males are less constrained.

WESTERN DOUBLE STANDARDS AND MEDICALIZING FRAUD

Kenny (1978, 1985) and Lee (1981) contend that "severe" latah subjects do not enter an altered state of consciousness but are engaging in a "performance," "role," and "theatre"—a culture-specific idiom expressing marginality while simultaneously reaffirming normative boundaries (Lee 1981). Never are the words *fraud* or *deception* used.[21] Yet numerous examples exist of feigning illness or abnormality in Western cultural settings: the Salem witch trials of 1692 (Gardner 1991), numerous spiritualist mediums (Hyman 1985; Kurtz 1985), and channelers associated with the contemporary New Age movement (Gardner, cited in Hines 1988, p. 29). Epidemic demon possession in medieval European nunneries often occurred in reaction to rigid Christian discipline, with oppressed nuns pursuing personal and political agendas by using various tactics: ventriloquism, magic tricks, self-inflicted scratches and bruises, fictitious rape accusations, purported clairvoyance, and feigned possession (Bartholomew 1994a). Often, social or political structures inadvertently encourage illness faking. I can recall several instances when student friends in Australia, ill-prepared for university exams, easily obtained medical certification from physicians indicating that they were sick to obtain postponements. Other prominent examples include nonrigorous medical examination for those seeking worker's compensation benefits, military discharge, or negligence awards from lawsuits. Yet this state of affairs does not justify medicalizing such deviant social roles as "military malingering syndrome," "pre-exam feigning disorder," or "compensation behavioral malady."

Anthropologists and psychiatrists tend to use different language in scrutinizing similar non-Western traditions. Whereas William Haviland (1987, p. 319) states that the functions of "faith healers and many other evangelists in their own [Western] society conform in every respect to our definition of the shaman" in non-Western traditions, Western faith healers are typically viewed as fraudulent (Randi 1986, 1987). However, place an exotic label on essentially the same behavior involving shaman in an exotic location and anthropologists emphasize the "symbolic" qualities. Yet there is also symbolism in fraud. Carlos Castaneda's fictional writings contain a seductive, naive adventuresome quality that was ideal for captivating popular U.S. culture during the 1960s and 1970s, blending psychedelic drug use, a belief in supernatural and paranormal powers, and mysticism (Hines 1988, p. 277). The "discovery" of a "stone age" Tasaday tribe in the Philippines during 1971 captured the imagination of the world largely because of its ultrapacifist symbolism, typified in the media as a community of "noble savages" living in unspoiled harmony, isolated from the decadence of twentieth-century civilization (Sponsel 1990). The Tasaday deception was subsequently uncovered by O. Iten (1986), who gained access to their restricted preserve and found the so-called lost tribe "living in houses, wearing Western clothing and saying they had faked the whole thing" (Willson 1989, p. 18). The conspiracy was apparently perpetrated by the government of Ferdinand Marcos to deceive the world for political and economic gain (Dumont 1988).

Social scientists loosely use such euphemistic terms as *malingering, histrionic, performance, role,* and *symbolic action* to describe attempts at achieving social benefit in the absence of organic illness. The issue is highly ambiguous and is yet to be addressed thoroughly. It is typically difficult and problematic to ascertain the extent of a person's involvement relative to unverifiable illness claims and whether the person is involved in subconscious, unconscious, partially conscious, or wholly conscious deception for personal gain or a variety thereof.[22] In this sense "severe" latah subjects can be viewed as engaging in a culture-bound idiom of deception couched in semilegitimizing scientific terms. Anthropologists have a tendency to emphasize, idolize, and glorify the exotic, especially when it appears in someone else's backyard (Keesing 1989; Bartholomew 1990b), whereas psychiatrists are often overly eager to place a convenient and unitary disorder or disease label on deviant, deceptive, and unconventional behavior worldwide. For example, there are clearly fraudulent aspects to most shamans, including ventriloquism, magic tricks, and the widespread practice of "the sucking cure" (Boas 1930; Barnouw 1973, pp. 233–240; Howells 1986, p. 132), but they are not typically viewed as frauds by anthropologists as they reportedly appear to believe they have some supernatural influence (Oliver 1981, p. 344). Yet when Westerners seek "the sucking cure" from native healers, the practitioners are labeled frauds whether they may actually believe they possess some special power or not, such as in the Philippines (see Nolen 1974 and Gardner 1984 for case studies).

If latah is a disorder, it is inconsistent with all known epidemiological patterns of mental disturbance. Conversely, the social patterning of latah symptoms is consistent with its local context and meaning. Furthermore, a feigning hypothesis for "severes" is not without historical precedent. Numerous examples of malingering are found within the social science literature—idioms that wax and wane in popularity and practicality, especially in "subordinate" females, depending upon the restrictive nature of the prevailing social structure. Severe latah is one more example.

SUMMARY

In this chapter I have raised several concerns regarding the contemporary typification of Malayo-Indonesian latah within the medical and psychiatric literature, where it is unproblematically characterized as a culture-specific mental illness or disorder manifested in susceptible individuals. For instance, no known unambiguously recorded cases exist of latah as a behavioral abnormality prior to the second half of the nineteenth century, despite a rich colonial literature on Malayo-Indonesian people and culture covering the centuries prior to that time. The initial Western diagnosis of latah is based solely on its "strangeness" to Western elites as described by scientists, politicians, and explorers from the British and Dutch colonial empires during the late nineteenth century. Latah "victims" have no identifiable biological abnormality, they do not seek patienthood, nor do their friends or relatives seek medical assistance for the condition. The medical-psychiatric model assumes that latah subjects are exhibiting a local variant of a universal startle reflex abnormality precipitated by elements of Malayo-Indonesian culture. This perspective assumes that latah subjects are engaging in an involuntary dissociative state that first appears in childhood or early adolescence in a "mild" form and increases in frequency, duration, and severity with age.

However, based on ethnographic observations and interviews with my wife's Malay extended family, who reside in several states across Malaysia, latah is not considered to be an abnormality either by affected or unaffected members but represents a personal idiosyncrasy or habit. By examining the local context and meaning of latah within this family, I have argued that latah is best understood as a local idiom utilized primarily by females for a variety of social functions depending on their age and situation. The vast majority of known/examined latah cases consist of the so-called mild variety, which involves the habit of exhibiting nonsense words in response to startle and is primarily confined to children and adolescents, who view it as "cute."[23] "Intermediate" subjects utilize this idiom to perpetrate minor transgressions of the Malayo-Indonesian conduct code with impunity, such as briefly swearing or suddenly lifting a sarong. "Severe" subjects are rare and occupy deviant social roles that represent symbolic performances as an expression of social marginality and distress—an idiom utilized almost exclusively at present by postmenopausal females. Latah is a multifunctional idiom that serves a variety of purposes—an idiom that has been taken literally by Western medical, economic, political, and intellectual elites without adequately considering its meaning to those affected.

In Chapter 3 contradictory aspects of the purported disorder status of latah will be discussed, based on a review of all known legal and historical accounts of this behavior pattern within the Malayo-Indonesia region. This includes evaluating claims that latah is an uncontrollable state of temporary dissociation and that "sufferers" occasionally inflict serious injury or death to bystanders. A social-interactionist approach is applied in examining the early history of latah and the scientific basis for claims by advocates of the medical-psychiatric model of latah causation. Drawing on information presented in Chapter 2, the following chapter focuses on the timing of the "discovery" of latah as a behavioral abnormality and the purpose that served colonial elites to label it a psychiatric disorder. The designation of latah as a psychological disturbance reinforced then existing evolutionary theory in which Malayo-Indonesians were considered mentally feeble in comparison to people of European descent. The successful placement of this label also justified colonial control of the people and the rich natural resources within the region. I will argue that the disorder status of latah was created exclusively by colonial elites who first recorded this unfamiliar conduct pattern, redefining what the local inhabitants had previously considered to be a peculiarity or idiom and not a psychological disturbance.

NOTES

1. On January 2, 1990, I married into an extended Malay family in which latah is prevalent. Over the proceeding 3½ years, I gained the confidence of family members. Although having no intention of studying latah, despite it landing literally at my doorstep, the more I observed and inquired, numerous contradictions became evident. This made it of potential interest from an epistemological perspective, especially in relation to the Western construction of "the Other." "Epistemology" refers to the branch of philosophy concerned with the theory and validity of human knowledge, including its origin, nature, and methods. The formal data (observations and taped interviews and conversations) were gathered between December 1992 and June 1993. Before this period, from January 1990, I did not live with the family continuously but interspersed my stay with overseas trips. I have observed severe episodes (each in the same individual) on five occasions and mild incidents hundreds of times, later quizzing "sufferers" about their episodes and questioning family members on their latah history. The interviews

were informal, typically tape recorded; allowed for potentially lengthy, open-ended responses; and consisted of asking each family member approached five questions: (1) Do you latah and, if yes, about how often—once per day, per week, per month, per year; (2) If you latah, when did it first begin? Describe your latah experiences as specifically as possible; (3) Do you believe latah subjects can control their behavior; (4) Have you ever heard of latah subjects causing injury to others; and (5) What does latah mean to you?

The family studied is based in several houses located between 5 and 20 kilometers from Malacca with singular family units in the states of Johore, Negeri Sembilan, Selangor, Kuala Lumpur Capital Territory, and Terengganu, Malaysia, as well as the nation-state of Singapore. My wife's great-grandfather hails from Bengkalis, Indonesia, immigrated to Muar, Malaya, in the late nineteenth century, where he met and married an indigenous Malay, moved to a Malay village outside Malacca, and raised a family near the turn of the twentieth century.

When part of this chapter originally appeared in the *Journal of Nervous and Mental Disease* (see Bartholomew 1994c, p. 331), I stated that "I will allow any University-affiliated researchers, regardless of their preconceived position on the topic, access to the family kinship schematic, including latah status, sex, family position, and symptomatology, and allow them to interview all family members." Unfortunately, the offer is no longer valid. This followed a serious illness my wife experienced on June 29, 1994, and the failure of relatives to seek conventional medical intervention, after which we fled to Singapore for treatment, losing most of our belongings including latah records. For a description of this incident, refer to Bartholomew and Likely (1998).

2. Michael Kenny (1985) argues persuasively that in the few, scantily documented groups where latahlike behavior is reported, it results from social and not biological influences. Although accepting the possibility of a universal startle reflex, he considers it irrelevant in the same sense that whereas almost all people are born with hands, "only some cultures have exploited the fact in requiring them to be shaken in formal greeting" (p. 74). Although Murphy (1976, p. 18) believes latah occurs in a variety of cultures, "usually we have only one or two reports and then the condition seems to disappear from view again. . . . Outside of Malaysia the reports on these transient states and the people who harbor them have usually been too slight to permit much deduction." As latah behavior is often dramatic and thus likely to elicit comments from both scientists and laypersons, the scarcity of accounts prior to the nineteenth century, when the illness category was first devised by Western medical practitioners, is a conundrum (Murphy 1973, p. 43).

3. The one exception is anthropologist Robert Winzeler (1995) of the University of Nevada at Las Vegas, who contends that latah remains common and may actually be increasing in frequency in the Malaysian states of Kelantan and Sarawak. For reasons that will become evident, I believe Winzeler's observations, which are based on lengthy fieldwork in both of these states, support my argument that latah is best understood as an idiom and thus is subject to waxing and waning popularity depending on the functions it fulfills.

4. It is typically spelled latah in Malaysia, lata in Indonesia, and lattah in the Dutch literature.

5. Logan (1849, p. 29) met a Malay man at his residence in Naning, near Malacca, who reacted in the following "peculiar" manner: "At first his manner was embarrassed and apparently dry, and his efforts to break through the restraint . . . were abrupt and grotesque. When we ascended into the verandah he blurted out his welcome again, jerked his head about, bent his body forward, and shifted his position every second. He was most delighted, he said, highly honoured, but oppressed with shame. His house was such a miserable hut, and he was such a poor, ignorant, vile person, mere dung in fact! . . . And so he continued vilifying himself, and accompanying each new expression of humility by a sudden and antic alteration of his attitude and position." Winzeler (1995, p. 141) believes the man was exhibiting Tourette's Syndrome.

6. This small, relatively cohesive group has communities in Malacca, Pinang, and Singapore. They have assimilated many Malay traditions over several generations after exposure to Malay culture and marriage to non-Muslim Malays. These include similar cuisine, mannerisms, language, dress, and various aspects of daily living. However, they typically retain Chinese religious and kinship ties. Males are referred to as *baba* and females, *nonya* or *nyonya* (Clammer 1983; Tan 1980, p. 379).

7. My wife, for instance, will latah only if *she* drops something unexpectedly or someone *behind her* suddenly drops something, whereas an aunt will latah only if someone else drops something either in front of or behind her.

8. Severe latah episodes will not endure for more than a few seconds unless a series of rapidly produced or startling gestures are presented and attract the attention of the latah subject. Teasers are persons who, once a latah paroxysm has been initiated, either intentionally or inadvertently will then deliberately exhibit gestures within the latah subject's perceptual field in an effort to continue the elicitation of latah symptoms. Teasing is only applicable to "severe" cases.

9. The features of these sixteen deceased people do not differ from those of the seventeen still alive when the survey was conducted.

10. The meaning of *pantat* varies within the Malay family under study and can mean cunt, pussy, or ass.

11. A pseudonym.

12. That is, non-Malays; with the exceptions of Malaysian anthropologist Raymond Lee (1981) and Indonesian psychiatrist Lilis Indriastuti (1995), all researchers have been outside the Malayo-Indonesian cultural dynamic.

13. "Play of the princess," typically used to heal the sick or reinvigorate the spiritually depleted.

14. Although Chiu and colleagues (1972, p. 157) were able to confirm four cases of mental illness out of fifty latah subjects who were psychiatrically examined, it was noted that thirteen exhibited symptoms "resembling psychiatric abnormality but these were considered to be insufficiently distinct or specific to warrant firm diagnosis."

15. They did not state this directly to me but told my Malay wife, whom they have known since birth. It is highly unlikely that they would make such an admission to anyone outside the family.

16. The four cases of "severe" latah in my wife's extended family, which I surveyed, are the highest percentage of "severe" latah in any contemporary Malaysian or Indonesian family I am aware of.

17. Although the vast majority of latah cases are said to be "mild," and Chiu and colleagues (1972) make no distinction between the severity of cases, the number of "severe" cases in this survey by Chiu and colleagues is likely to be minuscule.

18. This is an ambiguous, intangible concept referring to what many Malays consider to be a person's spirit, soul, or courage. A more detailed discussion of semangat appears in Chapter 6.

19. In a similar vein, smoking cigarettes was once considered a solely masculine trait in Western society, and women who smoked usually denied it.

20. Of course, this is a sexist stereotype brought about by the socialization of femininity and masculinity and represents what may be termed an ideal type.

21. Kenny (1985, p. 65) explicitly states his opinion that it is a form of malingering, substituting the word *performance* because of its neutrality as opposed to *reaction, syndrome,* or *latah,* "as it presupposes little about the meaning, cause, or psychopathological significance of its referent, while at the same time calling attention to the social nature of the display."

22. Malingering is a complex and contentious term typically defined as the conscious, volitional feigning or gross exaggeration of physical or psychological symptoms with the intent to obtain a specific outcome. The presence of malingering is notoriously difficult to verify. Common examples include avoiding work, schooling, military service, and criminal prosecution or using symptoms to receive financial compensation, sympathy, or attention (see Bluglass 1976; Meyerson 1989, p. 1396; Carson, Butcher, and Mineka 1996, p. 254).

23. Among very young children in the first few years of life, mild latah is best characterized as children's play-acting that imitates adult behavior, such as when children play school or play store. During the later childhood years, mild latah is more akin to an individual child imitating an adult swearing.

3

From Idiom to Illness:
The Western Construction of *Latah*

IDIOM . . . from *idios,* one's own, personal, private. . . . An expression
unique to a language, especially one whose sense is not predictable from the
meanings and arrangement of its elements, such as *kick the bucket,* a slang
term meaning "to die," which has nothing obviously to do with kicking or
buckets (Thomas McArthur 1992, p. 497).

This chapter reviews all known legal and historical accounts of Malayo-
Indonesian latah. There is neither a single firsthand eyewitness account of
a latah subject inflicting serious injury nor a recorded legal case describing
the perpetration of a violent act. Neither participants nor onlookers appear to
be distressed by paroxysms, nor do they seek patienthood, with supporting
ethnographic accounts suggesting that latah is a deviant social role. Claims
advanced in Chapter 2 that latah is a local variant of a universal startle disorder
shaped by cultural conditioning are critiqued. Based on an examination of the
history of latah, I shall argue that it is most appropriately described as a
uniquely Malayo-Indonesian idiom of expression erroneously conceptualized
as an illness or disorder by nineteenth-century colonialist medical practitioners. This supported the then popular notion of "the Other" in Orientalist
discourse[1] and to this day has served to reinforce Western imperialist exploitation in Southeast Asia. The medical designation of latah is an unsubstantiated, superficial attempt to impose a convenient, singular psychiatric rubric onto
an ethno-specific idiom without adequately examining its sociocultural context.

LATAH: A THEORETICAL OVERVIEW

Social, health, and medical scientists are divided as to whether latah is a disease (Yap 1952; Opler 1967; Rosenthal 1970, p. 98), a disorder (Simons 1985a, 1985c; Howard and Ford 1992), or a learned coping strategy signifying social distress (Kessler 1977; Lee 1981; Kenny 1985). However, the contemporary medical and psychiatric consensus holds that latah is a mental disorder or abnormality (Horne 1974; Friel 1982; Simons 1987; Thomas 1989) characterized by involuntary behavior or a temporary alteration of consciousness (Magalini and Scrascia 1981; Hensyl 1982; Kaplan and Sadock 1985; Walton, Beeson, and Scott 1986; Deva 1990) that should be incorporated into future editions of international disease classification schemes (Simons 1987). In DSM-IV latah is categorized under "dissociative trance disorder" (American Psychiatric Association 1994, p. 490), whereas the *ICD-10 Classification of Mental and Behavioural Disorders: Diagnostic Criteria for Research* (World Health Organization 1993, p. 180) lists two suggested classifications: "other specified neurotic disorders" and "other specified dissociative [conversion] disorders."[2]

From a sociocultural perspective, latah has various symbolic meanings. Among Malays it is believed to result from weakened *semangat,* a condition commonly attributed to psychological stress, shock, or illness. Latah is a physical and symbolic means of conveying this psychological situation to others. It can also symbolize femininity, as females are believed to possess weaker semangat than males. Correspondingly, latah is associated with Malay transvestitism (Kenny 1978, p. 224). Winzeler (1995) describes how latah in the northern Malaysian state of Kelantan has a multiplicity of symbolic meanings and social uses, including joking, satire, mockery, and subtle protest, noting that imitation and sexual humor are integral facets of Javanese theatre.[3] He suggests that latah is an appealing mode of expression because "it provides opportunities for amusing foolishness, aggressive teasing, and sexual humour for people among whom other forms of joking are rather restricted" (p. 97). Winzeler (1995) also observes that latah typically conveys masculinity in Kelantanese males practicing *silat,* as they may exhibit latah in reaction to startle in the form of sudden violent kicks or punches.

Kessler (1977, p. 313) analyzes the behavior of a Malay woman who began exhibiting latah with increasing chronicity after her husband died. A once competent manager of her household, she was suddenly living with, and dependent upon, a married daughter. Kessler argues that latah predominates among women as a culture-specific idiom of subordinates responding to stress associated with the transition to, or maintenance of, ambiguous social positions. Lee (1981) emphasizes sociocultural aspects of role reversal, viewing latah as an acceptable means of transgressing Malay conduct codes while simultaneously reaffirming normative boundaries. As such, and applying Victor Turner's (1969, 1974) theory of structure and antistructure, any changes in the presentation of the condition should reflect the changing Malay social structure. Hildred Geertz (1968) and Michael Kenny (1978) concur with this position, holding that latah represents an inversion of the Malayo-Indonesian conduct code that reflects the ambiguous, marginal social status of women, particularly those past menopause. Kenny (1978, p. 222) also argues that the appearance of Malayo-Indonesian latah is a purely symbolic role associated with such local concepts as witchcraft, childbirth, and shamanism, whereby social marginality and distress are often communicated through "a standard-ized cultural idiom."

Indonesian psychiatrist Lilis Indriastuti (1995) examines the life histories of two latah women who were dominated by relatives and oppressive hus-bands with no means of redress. In these cases she suggests that the cultural tradition of latah provides a convenient outlet for expressing frustrations in a socially acceptable manner. It is notable that neither subject sought treatment for her latah and received no psychiatric intervention for this behavior. Geertz (1968), Kessler (1977), Kenny (1978), Lee (1981), and Indriastuti (1995) view latah either primarily or exclusively as a symbolic performance or acting. This position is consistent with my sociological explanation, which assumes that subjects are not mentally disturbed or experiencing any abnormality of their startle mechanism but use the occasion of intentional or inadvertent startle or fright to engage in what are purely performances.

Another sociological explanation is offered by Bartholomew (1994c), as discussed in Chapter 2, based on my experience through marriage into a traditional Malay extended family. To briefly reiterate, upon observing several family members exhibiting latah, I surveyed latah-related information about relatives, in which 37 of 115 reported "symptoms." Based on observations and conversations with family members, including my latah wife, I concluded that "mild" cases—by far the most common form—are a culture-specific habit akin to Western swearing but without the obscenities. It is engaged in almost exclusively by children and adolescents, involves the use of nonsense words or phrases, is viewed as cute, and attracts limited attention. "Intermediate" sub-jects are between twenty and forty years old and utilize this idiom to exhibit verbal obscenities with impunity. I concluded that "severe" subjects are low in the power hierarchy and are *always* malingering.

Psychoanalytic perspectives are taken by Yap (1952) and Murphy (1976).

Yap (1952) considers latah to be a neurosis, or fear reaction, in susceptible individuals who react to fright-evoking stimuli by exhibiting ego disintegration. Murphy (1976, pp. 16–17) uses an eclectic approach in considering the influence of various contributing factors in Malayo-Indonesian culture—repressed sexual desires, child-rearing practices conducive to dissociation, the rewarding of hypersuggestibility and the encouragement of imitation—concluding that it is a culture-reflective variant of hysteria.

The leading neurophysiological proponent, Simons (1980, p. 196), argues that latah entails "culture specific exploitations of a neurophysically determined behavior potential." He considers Malaysian latah to be a local variation of a universal abnormality involving an exaggerated startle response. Although its regional appearance is related to cultural elaborations, which reflect unique meanings in susceptible individuals, it is primarily a neurological response to shocking or startling stimuli—hence the worldwide similarity of features. Simons contends that severe latahs act involuntarily and, once startled, typically enter a dissociative state. Utilizing this model to account for the claimed presence of amnesia and involition in most severe subjects, he also admits that a distinct category exists of severe cases who malinger, and he classifies them as "role latah."

Winzeler (1995, and personal communication, August 21, 1995) acknowledges the significance of performance or ritual in many subjects, but he concurs with Simons that a genuine syndrome exists involving startle and alterations of consciousness (1995, pp. 129–136). For instance, he notes that "in a few cases the interviews produced what I took to be nervous latah reactions that could not be helped" (1995, p. xiv). However, the existence of a neurophysiological abnormality has not been confirmed by any consistent abnormal medical or psychiatric findings. Simons does not advance his cause with his confrontational writing style and use of broad, sweeping statements. Although he has vehemently attacked my research and findings, this is to be expected, as I have argued that he has been embarrassingly duped by his informants on a topic on which he has established his career.

DISORDER OR DEVIANCE?

Unsubstantiated reports of episodes engendering social stigma, pain, suffering, injury, and death provide a major reason for designating latah a disorder.[4] I shall examine all known recorded latah cases, arguing that these assumptions are unfounded, in sharp contrast to the Malayo-Indonesian culture-bound dissociative syndrome of *amok*. I shall then critique dubious comparisons with latahlike behaviors in geographically disperse transcultural settings and highlight their colonialist origins.

A literature review was also conducted for legal cases involving latah. Surveys were made of the *Straits Law Journal and Reporter* (1888–1891), *Straits Settlements Law Reports* (1893–1915), *Digest of Cases 1808 to 1911 in the Straits Settlements Federated Malay States,* and the *Malaysian Law Journal* (1932–1995).[5] Topical headings searched include criminal law, criminal procedure, insanity, temporary insanity, automatism, and latah. Not a single case involving latah or latahlike behavior was located, supporting my suspicion of the mythological nature of latah.[6]

Latah is distinct from amok, another Malayo-Indonesian behavior pattern also characterized as a culture-bound dissociative disorder. Amok involves sudden, mass homicidal assault in subjects who have experienced personal indignity or outrage. In addition to hundreds of journalistic reports that have appeared in Malaysian newspapers,[7] numerous legal cases in Malaysian law journals involve amok runners.[8] Correspondingly, a voluminous historical and ethnographic literature describes in minute detail amok episodes in Malayo-Indonesia dating from the fifteenth century (Teoh 1972; Murphy 1973; Spores 1976, 1988). Most descriptions cite specific names, dates, and episode locations.

European scholars with intimate familiarity of the region have written extensively on Malayo-Indonesian culture, often citing episodes of amok and its frequency. In fact, many who have written on latah have also discussed amok (e.g., Ellis 1893; Van Brero 1896; Swettenham 1900; Gimlette 1901; Abraham 1912; Galloway 1924; Van Loon 1927). It is striking, therefore, that during the nineteenth century the identical legal system that prosecuted numerous amok cases and the same writers who discussed amok in great detail did not produce a single eyewitness account of "severe" latah subjects causing death or serious injury. All such cases of latah-related death or serious injury are anecdotal or secondhand. As "severe" latah was and remains more prevalent than amok, and it is a dramatic condition that can cause death or injury to bystanders as in the case of amok, the complete absence of firsthand reports is conspicuous. Various medical conditions that can precipitate involuntary reactions have been documented as resulting in death or serious bodily harm and have a corresponding legal and historical record. These include uncontrollable behaviors related to transient global amnesia, alcohol and drug ingestion, epileptic seizures, sleep states, and hypoglycemia (Fenwick 1990).

Adams (1955, p. 5) states that "acts of violence perpetrated during the actual latah state have been followed by a defence in the subsequent criminal proceedings that the defendant was not responsible for his action." Yet no reference citation or examples supporting this passage are provided. Adams's statement may have been influenced by District Surgeon William Fletcher

(1908, p. 254) of the Kuala Lumpur Mental Hospital, who claimed latah episodes in then Malaya were an everyday occurrence in some Pahang District courtrooms and common in Upper Perak yet fails to cite a single incident. Fletcher claimed a district officer had told him "that when he was holding court in some of the Pahang districts he has found it quite impossible to examine the witnesses as they could do nothing but imitate and repeat the questions put to them" (p. 254). However, it is conspicuous that most books detailing the histories of Pahang District and Upper Perak lack even passing references to latah, to say nothing about court-related cases in Malayan legal publications. J. McNair (1972 [1878], pp. 143, 202) makes two references to Perak natives "mimicking any movement made to them" yet does not mention death, injury, social offense, or court cases, whereas many pages are devoted to amok episodes involving specific names and places.

It is possible that Fletcher was repeating urban legends that may have circulated during the early twentieth century.[9] Present-day Malaysian urban legends about the propensity of latah subjects to cause death or injury and to be prosecuted abound (Bartholomew 1995a). F. J. Van Leent (1867) made similar claims for the judiciary involving latah in Batavia without citing a source or specific case. In fact, there should be many more of these cases, and one would expect a strict taboo prohibiting "severe" subjects from holding babies, chopping coconuts, cutting meat, sewing, and driving automobiles and motorbikes. The conspicuous absence of even a single credible firsthand incident of latah-induced automobile and motorbike accidents, sewing, chopping and cutting mishaps, and baby dropping seriously discredits claims that latah is an involuntary disorder.

Several writers have in passing questioned the quality of latah reports, especially nineteenth-century accounts (coincidentally the most spectacular and plentiful). For example, Yap (1952, p. 517) states that a description of a latah woman who imitated the vibrating tongue of a snake using her finger and was fatally bitten "was probably exaggerated." Kenny (1978, p. 227) places many latah reports in the category of "amusing stories about native peoples." Winzeler (1984, p. 83) remarks that two prominent early writers on the subject (British proconsuls Sir Hugh Clifford and Sir Frank Athelstana Swettenham) engaged in considerable literary embellishment, and Raymond Prince and Françoise Tcheng-Laroche (1987, p. 12) observe that many "sound like accounts exchanged over 'District Officers' evening dinner parties." None of these researchers have delved further into their suspicions, presumably in significant part because of references to the existence of reports of latah percipients inadvertently injuring others and being taken to court.

LATAH-RELATED DEATH AND SERIOUS INJURY

ETHNOGRAPHIC EVIDENCE

> A man should look for what is, and not for what he thinks should be (Albert Einstein, quoted in Michelmore 1962, p. 20).

The most comprehensive ethnographic fieldwork on latah has been conducted by Robert Winzeler and Ronald Simons, who have published their penultimate works on the subject (see Winzeler 1995; Simons 1996). In these books the authors present their best evidence for Malayo-Indonesian latah being an involuntary abnormality. Let us examine their evidence.

ROBERT WINZELER

Although Winzeler (1995) notes several cases of death reportedly caused by latah, he acknowledges that "they were all hearsay and may have even been folklore" (personal communication, August 21, 1995). For all of his latah-related fieldwork intermittent over a decade and thirty years of exposure to episodes, the best example of serious injury Winzeler can cite involves "a Chinese Latah woman in Kelantan who told of having driven a nail into her hand as a result of being deliberately startled and while I did not see it I did see the scar and I believed her" (personal communication, August 21, 1995). Even if this incident occurred, it is not dissimilar to what one might expect from ordinary startle. Winzeler (1995, and personal communication, August 21, 1995) reports interviewing over 100 "serious" cases, yet he does not include a single detailed case in his book.

My purpose in noting this glaring omission is not to suggest he does not have the interviews. My point is—look at the irony. After research spanning three decades, having written the definitive work on the subject, and having interviewed over 100 "serious" subjects, he cannot offer so much as a single detailed firsthand case study of a latah subject or a description involving death or serious injury. Given that these are "serious" cases, one would expect startles triggered by friends and relatives or inadvertently in the normal course of events—enough to provide detailed inclusion in his book. Because Winzeler's book is so rich in other aspects of latah, it is a conspicuous omission. What does this say about the "compelling" nature of latah?

RONALD SIMONS

Simons (1996, p. 189) reports obtaining twenty-three "systematically collected accounts" from Malaysian informants on latah, including five deaths, four injuries to bystanders, one self-injury, and eight other accounts describing

the dangers posed by latahs. Although suggesting that these examples are powerful evidence of involuntary matching (imitation) by latahs, Simons says that
"only one informant ever told me that he had actually seen a fatal encounter,
and his story was not convincing. All other accounts were at least secondhand" (p. 190). In fact, not one of the accounts presented by Simons is very
specific, convincing, or compelling. Simons concedes this and believes these
accounts should not be taken literally.

Let us examine these cases. Simons (1996) mentions five cases of latah-
related death. Three are so vague as to be limited to a single sentence each: (1)
"In another [account] a male *latah* who has been commanded to climb a
coconut tree and act in a reckless manner is stung by bees and falls to his
death" (p. 189); (2) "in a story I heard several times . . . a *latah* mother who
was watching the actions of a frog held her baby under the water whenever the
frog went under until it finally drowned" (p. 189); (3) "one Malay woman told
me . . . one *latah* killed a baby" (p. 188).

The two other cases of latah-induced death are more detailed. One incident involves a Malay midwife about age fifty named Mak Cik Esah bin
Daud, who was summoned at 1 A.M. by a man named Kassim from nearby
Kampung (village) Sri Langkan whose wife was having a difficult labor. When
they reached home, a large crowd had gathered, among whom was a latah
woman named Timah. Simons's informant continues:

> While Cik tensely performed her daily routine job, Timah saw the long
> umbilical cord, and, thinking it to be a snake, retreated in fear. The midwife
> followed suit, and they both began to strike out at each other. As it
> happened, the midwife was holding a knife and she stabbed Timah's
> abdomen. They exchanged cuts, stabbing each other and causing confu-
> sion and unnecessary bloodshed. Neither would give way. Finally, however,
> without knowing what she was doing, Timah stabbed herself and collapsed
> . . . [ending] with them killing each other. (1996, p. 189)

Where is Kampung Sri Langkan, what was the date, what kampung was the
midwife from, what was her house address and that of the woman giving
birth, and why are there no police reports, court records, journalistic accounts as
there have been for centuries in Malayo-Indonesian amok episodes (see
Bartholomew 1997a)? This report certainly rivals the drama of most amok cases.

The fifth case of a purported death caused by a latah has a distinct folkloric quality (as in the previous report). An informant in his seventies claims
he heard the following story as a boy: "When the British were here [govern-
ing] there was a court in Pengkalan Balak. Major Bawal was the judge. He was

responsible for sentencing. One time a *latah* was holding a knife when some-one came up from behind, startled her with a poke, and ordered 'Stab!' Right away she stabbed a man to death! When the victim died, she was arrested by the police." When the woman pleaded not guilty because of her involuntary latah condition, the judge had a plank studded with about ten nails, with the sharp points facing upward. The informant continues:

> The judge said, "Now we'll test whether you're a real *latah*." A policeman came up behind the *latah* and poked her in the ribs, and he shouted, "Slap those nails!" Right away the old lady slapped down on those nails, and blood began to gush from her hand. The judge had to agree. "Truly, this woman is a real *latah*. This old woman is not guilty; the guilty one is the person who poked her."
>
> So the woman who poked the *latah* was the one who was sentenced to be hanged. (Simons 1996, p. 167)

Although Simons does not tell us where Pengkalan Balak is, it is a village in Malacca, Malaysia. Where is the court record, press discussion, or discus-sion of this case in Malaysian law journals? One would think the decision to hang a woman who poked a latah would set a legal precedent. When I was a teacher training instructor in Shah Alam, Malaysia, a colleague told me an almost identical story, except it was said to have occurred ten or twenty years ago and he said he could recall reading of the case in the Malaysian press. Having searched the archives of the major Malaysian newspapers at the of-fices of the *New Straits Times* and the *Star,* I could locate no such story in files dating back to about 1960, suggesting a folkloric origin to this story.

The five cases Simons refers to involving injury or self-injury by a latah are either not described at all or vaguely discussed, and the discussion of these cases in Simons (1996) comprises just two sentences. "In one story a girl is disfigured when her *latah* father throws [boiling] water . . . into her face" (p. 189); "the seven tales one Malay woman told me [included] . . . two *latahs* [who] injured themselves, one seriously" (p. 188).

Although Simons does not accept at face value his twenty-three accounts of latahs causing death or injury or appearing to pose a threat, he says they are "powerful evidence of involuntary matching." He asks: "Why then are such stories so frequent in Malay accounts of *latah*? I think that it was largely because they make the point about the absolutely compelled nature of *latahs'* matching and obedience" (Simons 1996, p. 190). Simons also implies that genuine latah reactions involving violent startles can cause serious injury, strongly supporting its involuntary nature (see Simons 1985c, p. 77).

THE HISTORICAL EVIDENCE

> If you can't have an experiment, do the best you can with whatever data
> you can gather, but do be very skeptical of historical data and subject them
> to all the logical tests you can think of (Robert Hooke, quoted in Gaither
> and Cavazos-Gaither 1996, p. 57).

Several incidents, all involving "severe" subjects, suggest involition, as
their actions have only dire negative and apparently unintended, potentially
fatal consequences. It should be emphasized that these are the "best" and
most frequently cited cases. Such cases support Simons's contention of an
underlying biological etiology for those so-called severe subjects who are not
engaging in "role latah." Swettenham (1963 [1895], pp. 76–77) describes observing from afar a Malay police officer, continuously hurling mud at a nest of
bees or hornets, as the officer later explained that the exiting insects "appeared to be thrown at him, and he could not help imitating what he saw."
Swettenham implies that if he had not ordered men to rescue the officer, he
may have died. Swettenham also reports that a "severe" latah male complied
with a command to leap into a ferocious current (p. 75). The man reportedly
escaped drowning after swimming 200 yards to shore. Yet once such reports
are scrutinized, a similar pattern emerges—in no instance has a latah subject
engaging in a "paroxysm" been observed firsthand to injure himself/herself or
others. Even the earlier case of a Malay policeman said to be mimicking the
motion of hornets or bees transpired where "the path from the stockade to the
village was in sight of the stockade throughout its length" (p. 76), and hence
his unusual behavior was observed from the stockade and he was "rescued."

Five cases dramatically describe seemingly involuntary reactions on be-
half of latah subjects. The first two cases have implications as to the legal
responsibility of the instigator in allegedly initiating acts resulting in serious
personal injury or death. Clifford (1898, pp. 189–192) describes a Malay
male cook named Sat who, after being startled by a capsizing cooking pot he
was using, was purportedly teased into repeatedly placing his hand in the fire,
inflicting severe burns:

> A boy . . . in the cook-room with Sat, made an instinctive grab at the fallen
> rice-pot, and in an instant Sat's hand was in the fire, grasping the burning
> hot metal. He withdrew his flayed fingers . . . [but] the boy once more
> made a feint at the smoking rice-pot, and again Sat's fingers glued them-
> selves . . . to the scalding metal, and then returned aimlessly to his head. I
> do not know how many times this was repeated, but Sat's fingers were in a
> terribly lacerated condition when . . . some one chanced to enter the cook-
> room, and interfered to prevent the continuation of Sat's torture. (p. 191)

Although Clifford knows Sat, he was not a direct witness. Clifford acknowledges that Sat burned his hand, but the fact that it resulted from latah is conveyed secondhand at best. In fact, the only firsthand accounts available involve relatively minor transgressions of a mischievous nature—startling someone to jump into a river (Swettenham 1963 [1895]), tossing clean laundry through a window (O'Brien 1883), eating soap (Forbes 1885), passing flatus (Ellis 1897, p. 37). If latah is an involuntary mental disorder, it appears to be conspicuously selective.

Bartholomew (1995a) reports discussing "severe" latah with about 200 teachers from across Malaysia.[10] Many could recall reported accounts of maiming or death inflicted by "severe" subjects, yet none were able to supply specific details such as names, witnesses, dates, a specific location, or mass media citations. This pattern is consistent from the first recorded case of purported latah-induced death.

> I have met a man several times lately who is a very strong *latah* subject. He is cook on board a local steamer . . . [and one day a crew member] stood before him with a billet of wood in his arms, which he began nursing in the same way as the *latah* was nursing his baby. Presently he began tossing the billet up to the awning, and the cook tossed his child up also, time for time. At last, the sailor opened his hands wide apart and let the wood fall upon the deck, and the cook immediately spread out his hands away from the descending child, who never moved again after striking the boards. (O'Brien 1883, p. 150)

O'Brien's description is curious in that for such a spectacular incident it is a brief, ambiguous passage. Although he knows the perpetrator, he does not state whether he was present. But almost certainly if O'Brien had been, he would have provided more details—the name of the cook and ship, the date, whether the man was arrested, and attempts to resuscitate the child. Severe latah incidents of this kind could be expected to attract spectacular legal and media attention, yet no known accounts are given of this incident other than O'Brien's vague description. This episode occurred when Malaya was under British rule, and amok was afforded prominent legal and journalistic treatment.

Another report of involition is described by Adams (1955, p. 6, citing Fletcher 1938, p. 641) and involves two Malay male companions walking along a jungle path. One, after being startled, severed his friend's hand and was incarcerated:

> The two Malays, Daud and Amat, both latah, were walking together through the jungle, each carrying his parang [a large knife]. . . . A dead

branch suddenly fell . . . and Daud, startled by its fall and in imitation of it, flung himself to the ground. This, in turn, startled Amat, who, overcome by the impulse to imitate, threw himself down too and, as he fell, swung his right arm round with the parang in his hand, with the result that the heavy knife struck Daud on the wrist and cut off his hand. Amat was arrested and sent to gaol for six months.

This ambiguous description is reminiscent of "friend of a friend" folkloric accounts. Conspicuously absent is such rudimentary information as the date, time, location, full names of the perpetrator and victim, and where he was tried and incarcerated. Although a description of what was apparently this same incident appeared in Fletcher (1908) and is said to have transpired "years ago in Malacca," the men involved were listed as Amat and Kasim. Fletcher also mentions a Malay latah who was startled by a Sikh in the jungle, splitting his head, but provides no details (p. 255).

The question arises of whether a latah subject can be induced to perpetrate crime. At the Kuala Lumpur General Hospital, Fletcher (1908, p. 255) experimented with a "severe" Malay female latah patient under treatment for an unrelated breast sarcoma by suddenly commanding her to kill what she was told was a woman asleep in a bed wrapped in a blanket but that was actually a dummy: "Suddenly a large amputating knife was thrust into her hands and a command was shouted at her, 'Kill that woman and steal her jewellery.' J— rushed at the bed and with great force drove the knife into the blanket and the raincoat underneath. Hardly had she struck before she uttered a cry of remorse and threw herself back with a look of horror on her face. The command 'kill (patong)' was shouted at her and again she fell to hacking the raincoat with her knife." Fletcher's experiment can hardly be deemed scientific. Could the woman, a known "severe" latah, actually believe a prominent physician would credulously ask her to kill a fellow patient?

Two references involve Malays purportedly dying as a result of entering a latah state. Both are fleeting mentions of vague, secondhand stories that appear folkloric. The first incident is described by naturalist Henry Forbes (1885, p. 70): "Another case which came under my knowledge was more tragic in its results. This woman, startled by treading in a field on one of the most venomous snakes in Java, became so lata[11] that she vibrated her finger in imitation of the tongue of the reptile in front of its head, till the irritated snake struck her; and the poor creature [the woman] died within an hour." In a second reference to the death of a "severe" latah, Resner and Hartog (1970, p. 377), who conducted two years of fieldwork on mental disorders among Malays, noted that "some Malays consider *latah* dangerous because of reported cases of people in trance falling into a river and drowning while imitating the gesture of the provocateur."

SOCIAL EMBARRASSMENT AND LATAH

Three prominent cases involve purported involuntary social embarrassment to "severe" latahs. Conspicuously, unlike recorded claims of death or serious injury caused by "severe" subjects, these are firsthand accounts, the performance aspects of which are striking in terms of their obvious exhibitionist nature. The first report involves "teasing" a susceptible individual into publicly disrobing:

> A Malay woman, of respectable position and exceedingly respectable age, was introduced to me some time ago as a strong latah subject.
>
> I talked to her for at least ten minutes, without perceiving anything abnormal in her conduct or conversation. Suddenly her introducer threw off his coat. To my horror, my venerable guest sprang to her feet and tore off her *kabayah*.[12] My entreaties came too late to prevent her [from] continuing the same course with the rest of her garments, and in thirty seconds from her seizure the paroxysm seemed to be over.
>
> What struck me most in this unsavory performance was the woman's wild rage against the instigator of this outrage. She kept on calling him an abandoned pig, and imploring me to kill him, all the time that she was reducing herself to a state of nudity. (O'Brien 1883, p. 150)

Another episode is related by Forbes (1885, pp. 69–70), who mischievously flicked a caterpillar (abhorred by the natives) onto his Javanese servant's dress. Becoming "instantly lata, and throwing off all her clothing, she made off like a chased deer . . . repeating the word for caterpillar as she ran, until compelled by exhaustion to stop."

Twentieth-century latah cases involving explicit sexual exhibitionism are unrecorded in the Malaysian colonial literature. This contemporary modesty corresponds with unprecedented Western social influences such as the common present-day acceptance that public nudity among adults is generally viewed as inappropriate. Such changes in social values appear to have altered the content of latah performances. Summarizing his observations of Indonesian latah in the twentieth century, Nathan Kline (1963, p. 814) remarks that "if a female is told to pull up her sarong she will not do so."

In the third example involving social embarrassment, the stimulus for the elicitation of a 30-minute episode was a loud exclamation, after which the woman could be induced to follow any command:

The patient seemed quite normal and intelligent until she was startled by a
loud exclamation, when she sat [she] at once became completely latah. She
could now be induced by the verbal suggestion of anyone present,
supplemented by appropriate gestures, to laugh or cry, sing, dance or pray,
and to advance or retreat at will. For example, I told her to strike the
inspector of police who was sitting near me, and for whom she had the
greatest respect, whereupon she responded, "Strike, strike," and struck him
heavily in the chest several times. No other suggestion being at once
offered, she seemed to recover her senses instantaneously, as it were, and
carried her hands to her head, looking round with a perplexed expression.
Towards the close of this pitiable exhibition, which lasted about half an
hour, the patient was gradually robbed of her power of self-control and
command. She invariably repeated the suggestions offered to her, and not
only imitated grimaces, however absurd, but mimicked different qualities of
voice, and repeated strange English words with remarkable accuracy. On
being handed a box of matches and told to eat it, she had no hesitation in
commencing, and declared it delicious; but on the suggestion of another
person that it was pork, she threw the box away with an expression of great
disgust.[13] At last she was evidently becoming exhausted, and she asked for a
glass of water. Her pulse was a hundred and she was trembling. When she
had half finished the water, it was suddenly suggested to her that it
contained poison, and that she had better throw it away. She at once
dashed both glass and its contents on the floor. (Adams 1955, p. 4)

LATAHLIKE BEHAVIORS WORLDWIDE:
UNIVERSALISM VERSUS PARTICULARISM

Only after respected and influential psychiatrist George M. Beard[14] (1878,
1880a, 1880b) attracted worldwide attention when he reportedly located a
culture-specific variant of latah ("jumping") did scientists begin searching for
transcultural examples of latah (see Gilles de la Tourette 1884; Neale 1884;
Hammond 1884).[15] In the New England region of the northeastern United
States and the adjacent province of Quebec, Canada, small pockets of people,
especially in isolated communities and lumberjack camps, jump vigorously in
response to sudden startle. Jumping is especially prominent among residents
of French-Canadian heritage, hence Beard's famous description of them as
the "Jumping Frenchmen" of Maine. The association with latah is under-
standable, as some jumpers exhibit brief violent motions, "automatic obedience" to a forceful command, or the immediate repetition of a short phrase
addressed to them. However, sociocultural factors are important, as both

Reuben Rabinovitch (1965) and E. Charles Kunkle (1967) emphasize the influence of learned roles related to a game played in the region where jumpers are found. Kunkle (1967, p. 357) notes that this involved subjects who when startled were "expected to produce a formalized response of jumping violently, flailing out, and shouting angrily, often imitating the cry of a kicking horse." This "horseplay" was sometimes practiced by adults, especially in isolated communities and lumberjack camps, apparently representing a "socially conditioned reflex, reinforced by example and by repeated stimulation." In other words, jumping after startle is similar to a local cultural horseplay.

Soon after the publication of Beard's reports (1878, 1880a, 1880b), the jumpers gained international prominence, and the search began to locate global variants of this "peculiar abnormality." Within a few years, various "exotic" behaviors remotely resembling jumping or latah were categorized as identical. However, it is unlikely that the few similar reports of "latah" in widely separated geographical and cultural locations refer to kindred behaviors, as most supporting documentation is old, scattered, incomplete, and unconvincing (Murphy 1973, p. 42; Kenny 1978, p. 210, 1985, p. 64). One article translated from English into Russian erroneously identified the "Jumping Frenchmen of Maine" as gymnasts (Stevens 1965, p. 312)!

Behavior remarkably similar to Malaysian latah was reported in Southwest African Kaffirs by Andrew Gilmour (1902), the only known report from the region. However, a significant Malayo-Indonesian cultural presence exists in both South Africa and Southwest Africa,[16] with the Dutch colonial government importing slaves from their Batavian colonies during the seventeenth and eighteenth centuries (Molema 1963 [1920]; Wiedner 1962; Troup 1972). Further, claims that "Lapp panic" in Scandinavia and Russia is a variant of latah are challenged by Winzeler (1995, pp. 42–43, 49–50), who has examined the early ethnographic literature. He concludes that any association is dubious and appears to be grounded in superstition and folklore. Johannes Meth (1974, p. 727) remarks that *ramenajana*[17] in Madagascar is similar to Malayo-Indonesian latah when they are clearly unrelated (Bartholomew 1994a, p. 291). Both Aldo Castellani and A. J. Chalmers (1919) and Yap (1952) contend that the "dancing mania" and ecstatic religious phenomena are related to latah. This association is based on the unsubstantiated premise that all three are forms of hysteria (Bartholomew 1994a, 1994b). Although latah has been reported among the Burmese, such claims appear "limited to a single account published in 1940 by R. M. Still" (Winzeler 1995, p. 38).

Imu is a latahlike behavior among the Japanese Ainu,[18] where subjects typically retain "full memory" of their paroxysm (Yap 1952, p. 523), the exact opposite of Malayo-Indonesian latah. Imu can also involve reverse verbal and bodily mimesis, which is not reported among any other groups exhibiting latahlike behaviors. The Maine jumpers are often cited as the best unambiguous example of latah in a culture unrelated to Malayo-Indonesia, yet Meth (1974, p. 727) dismisses this association, as coprolalia is absent in Beard's cohort. Further, jumping almost always affects males and typically becomes prominent during childhood, whereas latah rarely, if ever, involves jumping, and "severe" cases are almost exclusive to socially marginal, postmenopausal females.[19]

Although the imitative behavior of *myriachit*[20] among paleo-Siberian groups is often cited as similar or identical to latah, an "epidemic" observed by Yankovsky (1885, p. 602, cited in Stevens 1965, p. 312) among fourteen soldiers at Novokievsky in 1876 is suggestive of a ritual or regional idiom.

> When I asked "what is the matter with you"—all of them jointly answered "what is the matter with you." Question: "What are you complaining of," etc. In answer to each question they jointly repeated the same question. The commanding officer of the company said that these people had eaten potato with hemp oil bought from a Korean. Having heard the word "oil," everybody in a different manner started repeating "oil, oil, oil." Neither requests nor orders could prevent these patients from repeating the words uttered by someone of us or some of them. . . .
>
> I was inclined to attribute everything to hemp oil but it was found out later that the Korean who had sold oil was a "miryasha" (suffering from Miryachit). Only those fourteen men who had seen him fell ill, the rest (perhaps three men) who had eaten oil but not seen the vendor remained healthy. Moreover, I myself ate the oil under suspicion, and it was eaten by other people but nothing happened to anyone.

Yankovsky met numerous individual cases, noting that initially the phenomenon is caused by the sight of a "miryasha," a pattern that is absent among the jumpers and Malayo-Indonesian latahs. The absence of any myriachit reports during the past several decades has handicapped attempts to understand the behavior.

HYPERSTARTLING, JUMPING, AND LATAH

The most prominent proponent for the contemporary widespread acceptance within the medical and psychiatric communities that latah is an illness, disorder, or abnormality is Simons (1980, 1985a, 1985b, 1985d, 1987), who believes latah subjects (except role latahs) comprise a small portion of the general population who are hyperstartlers. He considers this condition to be similar or identical to "startle neurosis" described by Frederick Thorne (1944), who identified exaggerated startles in approximately 1 in every 2,000 healthy male army recruits. J. Hardison (1980) also noted exaggerated jumplike startles in two "goosey" human subjects. Although hyperstartlers typically respond with coprolalia and echopraxia, their startles, although intense, are brief and, even in extreme cases, never persist for more than a few seconds. Further, coprolalia and echopraxia are features of normal startle (a universal reaction in humans) and can be conditioned, depending on the environment, appearing in extended form among hyperstartlers.[21] Although the recruits examined by Thorne (1944), Hardison's (1980) "goosey" individuals, and Simons's (1980) twelve subjects all exhibited similar jumplike startles, none exhibited unambiguous "command automatism."[22] M. H. Sainte-Hilaire and colleagues (1986), who studied eight jumpers in the region of Beauce, Quebec, were able to elicit brief "obedience" to forceful commands (e.g., jump, run, dance) in four cases. Such "obedience" may be entirely sociocultural responses related to their degree of conditioning to jumping, much as kicking like a horse in response to startle was a common socially conditioned behavior exhibited by Rabinovitch (1965) and his childhood companions.

It is not apparent that latah subjects are hyperstartlers or if the phenomenon is related to jumping. Significant differences exist between jumping and latah, with the latter of much longer duration and a far more elaborate response.[23] Hence, based on the "exaggerated suggestibility" of latahs, Kunkle (1967), who medically examined fifteen jumpers and the history of the phenomenon, concluded that it does not bear close resemblance to latah (or miryachit, for that matter). Further, no evidence indicates that jumpers enter altered states of consciousness, which is purported for latah because of the duration and complexity of responses in the latter.

In the jumpers of Maine, Beard (1880a) noted that this condition typically begins in childhood, whereas in Malayo-Indonesian children, latah virtually never occurs in "severe" form during childhood or adolescence. This difference occurs despite children in both societies playing at these behaviors (Rabinovitch 1965; Pfeiffer 1968; Sainte-Hilaire, Sainte-Hilaire, and Granger 1986; Bartholomew 1994c). Although a variety of startling stimuli are purported to elicit "the same range of effects" among hyperstartlers transculturally (Simons 1994, p. 341), Malaysian latah episodes often begin with no apparent startling stimulus or nonforceful stimuli such as a stare. Latah is much more prevalent than jumping, especially during the late eighteenth century when latah occurred on virtually every street (Clifford 1898, p. 195; Murphy 1976, p. 11) and not a single documented case of injury is known. Yet in the small population of jumpers, several have injured themselves or others (Beard 1880a, 1880b; Kunkle 1967, p. 356). Sainte-Hilaire and colleagues (1986,

p. 1269) cite the case of a man who "once jumped from a height of 10 feet after a sudden command." Some of Beard's subjects "very forcibly" struck each other, and one who was holding a knife quickly threw it when forcefully commanded. Of fifteen jumpers examined by Maine physician E. Charles Kunkle (1967, p. 356), eleven exhibited an involuntary "aggressive gesture or actual blow directed at the nearest bystander."

> One individual, when startled while dancing with his wife, struck her so forcefully as to knock her to the floor. In a few jumpers this violent response has led to moderate injury. Men with this propensity are sometimes known to their colleagues as "killer jumpers," although no death from such a cause has been described. Two men of the group emphasized the risk run by anyone who rouses them from sleep by firm touch or tap and recommended that the awakening stimulus be applied from the foot of the bed, beyond fist range.

Simons contends that hyperstartlers typically respond with potentially harmful actions, emphasizing the involition and violent nature of reactions. For instance, he quotes one informant as saying, "My mind went blank. When my body stopped trembling he again suddenly poked me in the ribs. I picked up a stick and hit him. I couldn't think" (Simons 1985c, p. 77).[24] In this instance the latah woman reacted without mimesis, bent down, picked up a stick, and struck her poker (an action that could ordinarily elicit serious social repercussions). This is also an elaborate response. What if this woman had been holding a baby or driving a car? Sudden unexpected events are common. Yet not one credible case of death or injury has occurred under any circumstances. The protests of latahs are perfunctory and necessary to maintain the idiom of deception. Jumpers are dangerous if they are holding a sharp object when startled, which is also true to a lesser extent of a normal startle response.

THE MEDICALIZATION OF DEVIANCE

Since the first Western descriptions of the previously unfamiliar behavior of latah, the theory of European racial superiority is evident in accounts. Its medicalization during the nineteenth century was not based on any rigorous scientific collection and analysis of data but on impressionistic observations and anecdotes based on stereotypes. The view of P.C.Z. Van Brero (1895, p. 537) is typical, noting that "mental feebleness" among Malayo-Indonesians "prevents them from becoming independent in thought and action, so that there is always a weak development of individuality." Even now, with the exception of exhibiting an episode, there is no known way to distinguish a latah subject from a "normal." This observation was noted a century ago, when Swettenham (1963 [1895], p. 73) remarked that "except when under influence [of latah], when actually showing the evidences of this strange peculiarity, latah people are undistinguishable from others." P. H. Manson-Bahr (1966, p. 576), in his textbook on tropical diseases, stated that apart from episodes, subjects "differ in no way from their neighbours."

Beginning in the late nineteenth century, technical and jargonistic terms began to appear in episode descriptions, reflecting and reinforcing the medical model of latah. These include the common usage of such specialized words as *coprolalia* and *coprophrasia* to describe verbal obscenity, *mimesis* (mimicry), *echolalia* for verbal mimicry, *echomimia* and *hyperimitation* (mimicking the general behavior of another), and *echopraxia, echopraxis,* or *echokinesis* (body mimicry). Severe subjects often claim fatigue and sleepiness, which typically results in the cessation of teasing.[25] Such behavior has been referred to as "catalepsy" (Gimlette and Thompson 1971 [1939]) and "somnambulism" (Yap 1952, p. 518). Attempts were also made by many colonial psychiatrists and physicians to change the local name for such behavioral displays from latah to existing, more legitimate scientific terminology by integrating latah into accepted Western categories of mental disturbance, the most prominent explanations being variations of hysteria (Adelman 1955; Linton 1956; Tan 1980), psychosis (Langness 1967; Rosenthal 1970), or neurosis (Van Loon 1924; MacNalty 1961, p. 813; Richards 1981). More novel medicalized, grandiloquent descriptions include "provoked imitative and impulsive myospasia" (Van Brero 1895), "abnormal reflex discharge" neurosis (Gimlette 1897), and "protopathic-instinctive phenomena" (Van Loon 1928).

If latah is a medical condition, its psychiatric epidemiology is unprecedented. It has typically been viewed as a mysterious, elusive "disorder" that almost defies classification. Richard Strong (1945) discusses it under a chapter on "Diseases of Rare Occurrence or of Doubtful Origin." Arieti and Meth (1959) use the title "Rare, Unclassifiable, Collective, and Exotic Psychotic Syndromes." "Sufferers" do not even consider themselves ill, which is the consensus of most Malays (O'Brien 1883; Yap 1952; Bartholomew 1994c). The then medical superintendent of the Singapore government's mental asylum, W. G. Ellis (1897), states that latah cases were never sent for psychiatric treatment, as they showed no propensity toward mental illness. Although latah remains firmly entrenched in contemporary psychiatric textbooks as a mental disorder, only one recorded case in the literature describes a latah subject seeking treatment for this condition (Jenner 1990, 1991). Even in this instance, it was the husband who forced his wife to seek treatment after using her illness status to obtain social gains over a period of 20 years.[26]

The historical presentation of latah and ethnographic descriptions of "severe" cases suggest that subjects are in complete control of their actions. Its only association with startle is to allow for the deflection of blame, and some "severe" cases initiate episodes with no apparent triggering event (Galloway 1922, p. 146; Yap 1952, p. 536). Latah was very common in Malaya at least since the late nineteenth century, with some Western observers contending that it affected the majority of the, if not the entire, population (Clifford 1898; Murphy 1976). Yet only a handful of cases are recorded involving latah-induced death, serious injury, or social offense, with the former two categories exclusively confined to anecdotal accounts, as noted in Chapter 2.

There is a discernible histrionic (Kenny 1978, p. 211) or performance (Lee 1981) character to the behavior of "severe" subjects to the point where they can be viewed as engaging in theatre and playacting for attention in order to violate ordinarily proscribed Malay norms with impunity. Although both "mild" and "severe" subjects report occasional episodes while alone, these may be viewed as habitualized conditioned responses to sudden unexpected stimuli and thus possessing no social benefit. Such responses are akin to swearing by Westerners when startled (Bartholomew 1994c). No more than two dozen "severe" cases have been reported in the literature. Firsthand accounts of "severe" subjects involve incidents described by onlookers and the percipient as humorous, entertaining, harmless. Consider this account by Swettenham (1963 [1895], p. 80). Although Simons would argue that this case exemplifies "role latah," the extent to which these brothers conduct their charade is remarkable and prompts the question, "Are all episodes role latah?"

> Every night, owing to the myriads of mosquitoes, a large bonfire was lit in the middle of the stockade, for only in the smoke of that fire was it possible to eat one's dinner. One night some Malays from the village had come in, and the police were trying to amuse them and forget their own miseries by dancing and singing round the fire. . . . Someone had introduced one of the Kasims, in his character of orang latah,[27] for the benefit of the strangers, and one of the men was inspired to fetch the roll of matting, and solemnly presenting it to Kasim the younger, said, "Kasim, here is your wife."
>
> Even now I do not forget the smile of beatitude and satisfaction with which Kasim Minor regarded that undesirable and figureless bundle. Breathing words in a low voice, almost sighing to himself, "Kasim, here is your wife," he embraced the matting with great fervour, constantly repeating "My wife! My wife!" Someone said, "Kiss her!" and he kissed her—repeatedly kissed her. Then by another inspiration (I do not say

whence), someone brought up the other Kasim, and introducing him to the other side of the roll of matting said, also very quietly, "Kasim, this is your wife!" and Kasim the elder accepted the providential appearance of his greatly desired spouse, and embraced her with no less fervour than his namesake and rival.

It was evident that neither intended to give up the lady to the other, and as each tried to monopolise her charms a struggle began between them to obtain complete possession, during which the audience, almost frantic with delight, urged the actors in this drama to manifest their affection to the lady of their choice. In the midst of this clamour the Kasims and their joint spouse fell down, and as they nearly rolled into the fire and seemed disinclined even then to abandon the lady, she was taken away and put back in her corner with the chairs.

LATAH AND THE "WILD MAN" IDIOM

Whereas the Malayo-Indonesian latah behavior pattern typically appears aggressive and potentially threatening to outsiders, their actions are ostentatious and metaphorical, explaining why it does not worry those exhibiting this behavior or their friends and relatives. In fact, friends and relatives typically deliberately initiate episodes at large social functions and allow children to observe "severe" subjects at the front of a crowd gathered to observe the display. The potential threat of violence and unpredictability temporarily elevates the subject's power and status while simultaneously communicating distress.

In this regard, "severe" latah parallels several related culture-specific idioms in the Papua New Guinea Highlands that are characterized by pseudoaggression, bluffing, and playacting ("wild man" episodes) and have been erroneously medicalized by outsiders unfamiliar with the local conduct code (Newman 1964; Clarke 1973). For example, a form of "wild man" behavior known as *negi-negi* among the Gururumba people of the Papua New Guinea Highlands has been viewed as theatre (Newman 1964). The "wild man" often brandishes a weapon and appears to enter a state of uncontrollable, destructive rage against people and property. When the episode concludes, claims of amnesia and spirit possession deflect the attribution of blame. This behavior is typically confined to young males who are socially or politically weak, grow impatient, and feel aggrieved by excessive dowry stipulations from relatives of the betrothed. Performances allow marriage compensation terms to be renegotiated, explaining the "disproportion between the injury threatened and actually inflicted" (Seligman 1928, in Littlewood and Lipsedge

1985, p. 119) and why natives appear inappropriately composed and casual during episodes, to the extent of overtly "hiding" weapons. Hence, Marie Reay (1965, p. 26) observes that among the Kuma, "wild man" episodes never result in death or serious injury, despite threatening behavior. P. L. Newman (1964, p. 7) states that people come from nearby villages just to watch the spectacle, and although "spectators are prone to keep their distance because of the potential danger," they "obviously enjoy the instances when the wild man turns on the group and chases one after another of them in erratic, and seemingly comic pursuit . . . the community can be regarded as an audience to a performance."

Imu among the Japanese Ainu can also be viewed along similar ritualistic lines. Like "severe" latah, it occurs primarily among repressed females who utilize this idiom as an opportunity to temporarily invert the social hierarchy (in which females are at the bottom) with impunity. Consider the social context in which imu occurs: "An Old Ainu woman was sent rolling down a bank of mud by a . . . man. In spite of this insult she did not offer a single word of protest nor any act in self-defence; her daily training in habitual submission was too strong. In another community two 'imu' patients who had been aroused to an attack fell upon the men surrounding them and showed their undisguised joy in having thrown one of these to the ground" (Uchimura 1935, p. 1273). In a society characterized by absolute female obedience, both mimesis and reverse mimesis can be interpreted as social protest, inverting the normal social order (see Lee 1981). The following example involves reverse mimesis:

> In some patients . . . instead of repeating what is said to them they answer
> with a direct opposite; instead of imitating movements they make one, the
> significance of which is exactly reverse; instead of obeying suggestions they
> act in a directly contrary manner. Thus, a reply to "one" will be "two"; . . . to
> "man," "kuruma" (a Japanese woman). When [shown] a closed fist the
> patient will extend her open hand and vice versa; if the observer bends, the
> patient will stand erect; if ordered to approach she will retire. (Uchimura
> 1935, p. 1273)

Emiko Ohnuki-Tierney (1985) has conducted extensive ethnographic fieldwork on imu, emphasizing the importance of understanding this behavior in terms of its local meaning and context.

Mimicking various movements and occasionally words of Europeans during their first contact with indigenous peoples has been observed on several occasions (Prince and Tcheng-Laroche 1987, p. 14). Its relevance to the latah debate is unclear, but it is certainly a social and not a pathological phenomenon that is unrelated to hyperstartling. An example of the idiomatic and nonneurophysiological aspects of latah is apparent in the case cited earlier of a Malay cook named Sat who was burned, purportedly during a paroxysm. Clifford had lived with Sat for a year prior to this episode, unaware of his condition. In the two months after Clifford's first observance of Sat's latah, it became increasingly frequent, reducing him to a "pitiable condition" (Clifford 1898, p. 192). Curiously, about this time several in Clifford's household began exhibiting latah, as "Sat seemed to cause them to lose the control which they had hitherto contrived to exercise over themselves." This pattern is inconsistent with hyperstartling, implying that latah is a social phenomenon elicited by exposure to other latah subjects.

If latah exists as an involuntary abnormality, numerous contemporary incidents should exist involving injury or death. The view of latah as a disorder cannot explain the almost exclusive confinement of reported "severe" episodes to large social gatherings and why they are able to maintain control in one setting and not the other (Bartholomew 1995a). It is also difficult to believe it is acceptable for "teasers" to instigate behavior purportedly embarrassing, degrading, and potentially life-threatening to loved ones. Not only can each of the claims for involitional behavior in some "severe" latah subjects be countered, but no corroborating evidence exists in the form of Western written historical accounts and legal cases.

Latah was conceptualized during the late nineteenth century by Western colonialist intellectuals adhering to the theory of social and racial evolution, which placed Europeans and European societies at the pinnacle of the biological and social evolutionary hierarchy. Subtle remnants of this antiquated perspective continued in the twentieth century. For instance, no rigorous systematic empirical evidence supports the contention that latah subjects possess diminished mental capabilities, such as weakly developed egos or low intelligence quotients (IQs). In fact, based on a review of the literature, an opposite claim can be made (Fitzgerald 1923; Murphy 1973; Simons 1987).

Near the turn of the nineteenth century, Gimlette (1897, p. 456) suggested that the disproportionately high number of latah cases among Malays stemmed from their likely "morbid proclivity toward imitativeness." D. J. Galloway (1922) postulated that the "primitive" Malay mind spent a significant amount of time daydreaming and that this "unconscious" state fostered a reflex or instinctive reaction, especially as most Malays had not received formal schooling. Yap's (1952) seminal study concluded that Malayan latah was fostered by the low level of cultural development and that subjects often possessed below-normal intelligence. He describes one informant as mentally dull, "with a dazed expression" (p. 536), whereas another was "a slow, stupid woman of rather elementary mentality, not easy to draw into conversation"

(p. 534). Yet Yap conducted interviews with his seven informants in Malay (not his native tongue) and characterized them as illiterate, lacking in formal schooling, and a challenge to communicate with, as he was a relative stranger. Local etiquette precluded the gathering of formal psychiatric histories (p. 534). P. Manson and P. Manson-Bahr (1972, p. 725) state, "All of the Malay races are very high strung and nervous . . . and there appears to be an heredi-tary tendency to the latah state in every Malay." Kiev (1972, p. 75) implies that latah is more common in technologically underdeveloped countries be-cause of a lack of sophistication and complex mental organization. Meth (1974, p. 727) remarks that typical sufferers were Malay women of "dull intelligence," and M. Sim (1981, p. 412) describes latahs as "usually female, simple and compliant." These differing observations of the interpretations of latah during the past 100 years by scientists, especially psychiatrists, illustrate their ten-dency to superimpose popular stereotypes about the psychological instability of "primitive" peoples and females by reifying latah as an abnormality and typically doing so with absolute certainty, despite the lack of thorough social and cultural descriptions of the context and meaning of latah.

Over a century and a half has elapsed since the first apparent Western recorded observation of the latah behavior pattern in 1846 (Logan 1849). Despite no means to differentiate between latah subjects and "normals" (out-side of paroxysms) and the lack of firsthand accounts supporting its involun-tary nature, the psychiatric model of latah continues to hold prominence within the medical community. If latah is a deviant social role utilized by marginals to gain attention and power by temporarily contravening local conduct codes with impunity, its rapid disappearance in recent decades corresponds to more liberal attitudes toward the West and an unprecedented proliferation in em-ployment and social opportunities for Malay women outside of the house-hold. Further, "severe" cases are rare and develop within a social context where children traditionally play at latah. Resner and Hartog (1970, p. 377) report that some Malays consider latah "a type of malingering and that the victim is in complete control of his or her behavior." Of course, performers cannot be expected to admit they are role-playing. Hence, they insist they do not suffer from a disorder. This characteristic feature of latah corresponds with the absence of any signs of mental abnormality apart from paroxysms (Van Wulfften-Palthe 1936, p. 525; Lehmann 1967; Murphy 1973; Bartholomew 1994c).

The case for latah being involuntary is inconsistent with firsthand obser-vations and court, historical, journalistic, and ethnographic records. Prince and Tcheng-Laroche (1987, p. 7) raise legitimate concerns regarding the over-zealous application of cultural relativity to culture-bound syndromes and the danger of drifting toward meaninglessness.

However, before committing latah to a DSM or an ICD-10 classification scheme, we must be wary of using excessive biological reductionism to perpetuate a psychiatric myth. The continuing adherence to medical models in explaining latah is a form of neocolonialism whereby performance is redefined as "hysteria," ritual mimicry is labeled "hypersuggestibility," shyness becomes "ego disintegration," obscenity is viewed as "sexual repression," erotic dreams become "sexual trauma" and "genital obsession," unfamiliar cultural tradition is reduced to "genetic trait," attention seeking becomes "histrionic," and technological underdevelopment and illiteracy are interpreted as "simplicity" and "below-average intelligence."

LATAH AS A PRODUCT OF ORIENTALIST DISCOURSE

During the nineteenth century, two divergent racist perspectives on the mental health of indigenous people predominated in psychiatry. The first view held that natives were "noble savages" who, in the absence of the degenerating influence of Western civilization, were virtually free of mental disturbance. A second position considered "savages" to be "mentally degenerate because they lacked Western culture" (Fernando 1991, p. 33). Despite the prominence of both views, scientific and scholarly discourse on latah almost exclusively utilizes this latter perspective, considering it a racial abnormality inherent in the Malay character (Clifford 1898, p. 195; Abraham 1912, p. 438). In keeping with the late nineteenth-century view that "primitive" people were lower on the evolutionary scale, Gimlette (1897, p. 457) compared latah with the "mimetic tendency of monkeys." The exhibition of coarse language and obscene gestures during paroxysms reflected the common nineteenth-century theory that primitive races were susceptible to instantaneous degeneration, unwilling prisoners of their genetic and environmental circumstances submitting to instinctive, vulgar impulses. Hence, upon "returning to their senses," they typically apologized for their temporary transgressions. This is clear in Clifford's (1898, p. 196) discussion of latah, where he notes that following a sudden startle a subject "will not only give a violent start, but will also shoot out some exceedingly coarse word, for which, in all probability, he will forthwith apologise." F.H.G. Van Loon (1931) argued that latah was prevalent among Malays and other "primitives" because of their lack of cerebral control in relation to highly civilized people.

When latah was first identified and labeled a mental disorder during the late nineteenth century in colonial Malayo-Indonesia, it was framed within the Western intellectual tradition of Orientalist discourse, viewed as a reflection of "the Other." The latah idiom was medicalized as a means of reinforcing Western intellectual supremacy. The sole basis for its present disorder status involves observations and anecdotes that portray it as exotic, bizarre, and abnormal.

The earliest known reference to latah as a behavioral disorder was by Van Leent (1867), and although prior to this time there are references to the word *latah,* no explicit descriptions exist of it as a malady or a peculiarity. The disorder designation was made by colonial psychiatrists adhering to the theory of European social and racial superiority, using descriptions of this "strange" and heretofore unfamiliar behavior. Because of the exhibitionist nature of many "severe" cases who would often sing, dance, or disrobe, it was widely assumed that subjects were histrionic and latah was a regional variant of individual hysteria.

Syed Hussain Alatas (1977) eloquently documents how popular and scientific Western literature during the eighteenth and nineteenth centuries portrays Malayo-Indonesian natives as indolent, immoral, backward, dull, physically inferior, and lacking a capacity for self-government and thus supporting colonial mastery. This was especially so during the nineteenth century when colonial domination of the region peaked "and capitalist exploitation required extensive control" (p. 70). The pathologization of latah, beginning in the mid-nineteenth century, supported the colonial capitalist exploitation by the Dutch in Indonesia and the British in Malaya by further justifying the necessity of Western rule. Orientalist discourse on the Malayo-Indonesian Other, which portrayed the "natives" as psychologically unfit for self-autonomy and in need of Western custodial guidance, was perpetuated through the "neutral" medium of scientism.

Surgeon John Gimlette (1897, p. 457) noted that during latah paroxysms in female Malays, their "servile portion of human nature is unconsciously displayed." A Dutch psychiatrist in Java, Van Brero (1895, p. 537), observed that Javanese natives "have a mental feebleness [latah] which prevents them from becoming independent in thought and action." Batavian psychiatrist and neurologist Van Loon (1927, p. 434) wrote that latah was a psychosis "inherent to the Malay peoples" that should be studied not only for scientific value but for "practical, economic reasons" (p. 434). Van Loon (1927, pp. 440–441) noted that Malay soldiers were prone to hypnoticlike suggestibility, whereas females were even more subject to "infantile-primitive" latah regressions, as the "inclination to imitation and to complete psychic surrender easily finds the opportunity to control . . . the 'stupified' woman." This view of women reflects the popular late nineteenth-century Darwinian view that females occupied an intermediate evolutionary position between adult men and male children (Paicheler 1988, p. 40).

Colonial writers deemed latah subjects capable of experiencing involuntary and potentially dangerous mimetic reactions and "automatic obedience." Although this usually occurred in response to sudden startle, numerous instances were precipitated with no stimulus. As effective government requires leadership and self-control and the mimetic portrayal made Malays ideal followers, copiers, and servants, they were justifiable candidates for colonial domination. Fletcher's (1908, p. 254) discussion of latah and crime implicitly suggests that under an "immoral" control, suggestible Malays "might be induced to kill or commit some other crime." Hence, logic dictated that if the British did not control the Malays and the Dutch did not control Indonesia, some other rival foreign power could, using the purportedly impressionable, mimetic, latah-prone Malays to support their ends.

Scientific theory was used to locate latah as a regional variation of hysteria-based afflictions that tend to affect "primitive" peoples globally. The hypocrisy of "neutral" scientific labeling of mental disorder is evident in the discussion and treatment of jumping. The sole Western variant of latah was jumping among a small group of lumberjacks living in rustic, isolated conditions in the U.S. state of Maine and the adjacent Canadian province of Quebec. As jumping was not required for colonial exploitation and occurred among those of European descent, following Beard's initial descriptions (Beard 1878, 1880a, 1880b) no further firsthand investigations transpired until incidental accounts by Harold Stevens (1965) and Kunkle (1967), who encountered it in their medical practices during the 1960s. Although Beard (1880a) attributed the condition to heredity and thought it was precipitated by habitual tickling, he described it as a fleeting trance persisting for only a second (p. 489) and never associated jumping with diminished mental capacity per se, suggesting that we are "all potential jumpers" (p. 488). Although during the 1880s Western observers commonly portrayed Malays as inherently nervous and prone to psychological instability and irrationality, Beard describes the Caucasian jumpers as physically and mentally robust: "One thing was certain, that these jumpers were not nervous; the phenomenon was not a symptom of neurasthenia, and in this it agreed with the servant-girl hysteria epidemic of the middle ages, with the jerkers and with the phenomenon of the 'holy rollers.' Psychologically, these jumpers were modest, quiet, retiring. . . . They were strong and capable of doing hard physical work, and some of them could read and write and were as intelligent as the class to which they belonged" (p. 489). Beard viewed jumping as akin to religious excitement, and he noted that jumpers were members of the Holy Rollers[28] and would engage in what he considered to be similar forms of primitive mental stimulation. This position reflects the nineteenth-century notion that religious excitement could induce mental disturbance. He also speculated that it was precipitated by temporary degeneration from exposure to a primitive environment. Conspicuously absent were discussions of racial heredity and diminished capacity to make rational judgments. Ironically, several firsthand instances of jumpers causing serious injury have been reported, but no confirmed instances exist of latah causing serious injury.

It is important for Western-trained social scientists to record the latah idiom to illustrate the ethnocentricity of superimposing Western-biased value judgments on its normality. Those who continue to classify latah in pathogenic terms distort "reality" with their narrow Eurocentric approaches. With this power monopolization comes the responsibility of sensitizing ourselves to the existence of radically different social realities that must be evaluated within the context of their unique social, cultural, and historical milieus. Should atypical culture-bound "syndromes" such as latah be placed under Western classification schemes when the clinical evidence to do so remains dubious? Kleinman's (1987, p. 51) remarks are particularly applicable (although he is referring to DSM-III, they remain equally applicable to the publication of DSM-IV in 1994):

> DSM-III is a symbol system, one that condenses core meanings and value orientations in American society, in American psychiatry, and in the current politics of the American Psychiatric Association. It is unacceptable that in non-Western societies, where more than 80 percent of the world's population resides, major categories of disorder have to be relegated to DSM-III's atypical affective disorder, atypical anxiety disorder, and many other atypical categories. The only thing "atypical" is the use of North American and European populations as the source of determining clinical types for a world in which they are a distinctive (albeit the most powerful) minority.

Western-trained scientists should listen more carefully to the voices of those most intimately familiar with latah and ponder the conspicuous absence of historical, legal, and ethnographic evidence for its existence as an involuntary mental abnormality. One more type of evidence remains to be undertaken—the monitoring of neurophysiological responses in those judged to be "severe" cases to determine the presence of atypical patterns. During the late nineteenth century, hysteria was the paramount concept in psychiatry, and it was logically assumed that reports of mimeticlike behaviors in disperse cultural settings were variants of a unitary hysterical condition. In fact, because of the involvement of imitation, hysteria was also referred to as "neuromimesis" (Inglis 1990, pp. 70–73). That latah continues to be labeled in pathological terms, often using dogmatic language, despite insufficient supporting evidence questions the adequacy of transcultural psychiatric theory while lending credence to the existence of a larger neoimperialist project.

Latah is a behavioral idiom that allows peoples from diverse ethnic groups subsumed within the Malayo-Indonesian cultural dynamic to express themselves in myriad ways: joking, satire, entertainment, protest, habit, in addition to accentuating feminine and masculine social traits, and to a multitude of personal crises typically associated with human fragility, especially but not necessarily as it relates to women.[29] As new meanings and uses for latah continue to appear, it will be interesting to observe what new idioms emerge. For this is the way humans continuously add to the ethnographic record. That dominant Western cultures continue to medicalize foreign deviant social roles to fit their Eurocentric classification schemes is also part of that record.

SUMMARY

This chapter has examined several conspicuous aspects of latah, which continues to be typified in the medical-psychiatric literature as an uncontrollable state of temporary dissociation that can precipitate serious injury or death. However, no firsthand observation of a latah subject inflicting serious injury or death exists, and there are no corresponding legal cases. I have surveyed the historical context of the successful placement of the label of latah as a behavioral abnormality, which conspicuously coincided with British and Dutch attempts to justify colonial rule in Southeast Asia. The medicalization of latah was an ideal example with which to illustrate the inferior, mimetic nature of the Malayo-Indonesian Others, portrayed as copiers who were good at following orders and in need of a disciplined colonial administration. During the entire period of colonial rule in Malayo-Indonesia, which lasted until Malaysia obtained formal independence in 1963, the most common scientific explanation for the appearance of latah was the racist notion of the inherently nervous nature of the "natives." The use of jargonistic medical and psychiatric terms further reinforced its illness or disorder status. This dubious label was successfully applied to "sufferers" as a "discovery" within the "neutral" discipline of science.

The initial classification of latah upon its "discovery" as a psychological disturbance during the late nineteenth century held that it was a regional variation of universal hysteria-based mental disorder precipitated by the exposure of "primitive," uncivilized peoples experiencing degeneration or evolutionary regression. Superficial comparisons were located with latahlike behaviors in geographically disperse transcultural settings without adequately assessing the social and cultural context and meaning of such behaviors. Parallels have also been drawn between latah and other "exotic" non-Western behaviors in "primitive" peoples that have been assessed to be idioms using detailed social, cultural, and contextual information on the participants. These include imu among the Japanese Ainu and "wild man" behavior in Papua New Guinea. Based on a historical examination of the literature, latah is most accurately described as a multifunctional idiom that has been "mistranslated" by Western scientists in their search for universal laws of disease or disorder to the relative exclusion of scrutinizing its local meaning and context.

In Chapter 4 I present another example where the meaning and context of human behavior have been ignored and the label of disease or disorder has been inappropriately invoked based solely on the "strange," implausible nature of the participants' beliefs per se. In that chapter "epidemics" of perceived genital shrinkage that occur periodically in certain cultures will be scrutinized, and claims by scientists that participants are experiencing sexual disturbances and body image disorder will be challenged.

NOTES

1. Throughout this study I shall refer to the term *Orientalism,* typically defined as any qualities, customs, and characteristics associated with the peoples of Asia, especially the Far East. The Far East typically refers to East Asian countries, especially China and Japan. The word *Orientalism* has many meanings. For instance, in the decade prior to the publication of Edward Said's influential book *Orientalism* (1978), it had a positive connotation in terms of studying various features of Oriental societies. Said's "orientalism" also includes the "Middle East" and all "Islamic" countries of this region. Throughout the present study Orientalism is used as an inclusive term to describe "the literary means of treating a stereotypical and mythic East through which European rule could be more readily asserted" as a way to gain insight "into the culture of imperialism, particularly in relation to British rule in South Asia" (MacKenzie 1995, p. xii).

2. Hereafter referred to as ICD-10, the tenth and most recent edition of the World Health Organization's counterpart to the American Psychiatric Association's DSM series. A discussion of mental disorders did not appear in the ICD series until ICD-6, published in 1948 under the title *Manual of the International Statistical Classification of Diseases, Injuries, and Causes of Death.* Criticisms over the inadequacy of ICD-6's new section on mental disorders prompted the creation of the DSM series (see DSM-II [1968], pp. vii–xx; DSM-IV [1994], pp. xv–xxv).

3. Indonesian Javanese theatre is popular in parts of Malaysia, especially in Kelantan.

4. I have discussed elsewhere (Bartholomew 1994c, 1995a, 1995b) the incongruence between the words and actions of latah subjects. Although most "mild" cases involving profanity or nonsense words are viewed humorously, this disparity is especially conspicuous with "severe" subjects who would ordinarily receive serious social sanctions. "Severes" do not typically avoid large social gatherings where they are likely to be teased, heartily enjoy their performances, and are met with crowds of friends and relatives who cheer and applaud their antics. I find it incredulous that teasers (usually

relatives or friends) would intentionally induce embarrassing, degrading, potentially harmful reactions, as elders are treated with utmost respect and dignity in Malayo-Indonesian culture. Latahs must make such claims of having no control over their paroxysms to deflect the attribution of blame. During paroxysms, Malays can engage in various proscribed behaviors with impunity.

5. These publications and dates were searched, as they were all of the Malaysian law journals available to me.

6. These topic headings were selected after consulting with Malaysian attorney Matthew Thomas Philip, to whom I am grateful.

7. Based on my examination of amok-related articles at the archives of the *New Straits Times* and the *Star*, two of Malaysia's largest circulating daily newspapers.

8. For prominent representative examples refer to Norris (1849); Mohamed Isa bin Leman Versus the Public Prosecutor (*Malaysian Law Journal* 1939, 8, pp. 161–162); and Jusoh Versus the Public Prosecutor (*Malaysian Law Journal* 1963, 29, pp. 84–87).

9. The term *urban legend* was popularized by University of Utah folklorist Jan Harold Brunvand in his classic best-selling study, *The Vanishing Hitchhiker: Urban Legends and Their Meanings* (1981). Urban legends are sometimes referred to by folklorists, sociologists, and social psychologists as contemporary legends, urban myths, or urban folklore. These are narratives the teller believes to be of recent origin, that pass orally by word of mouth, and are commonly purported to have transpired in a metropolitan environment. Brunvand states that urban legends involve improbable events that are repeated as truth and embellished with local details. Typically attributed to a media source or what folklorists sometimes call "FOAFS" (friend of a friend stories), they are usually impossible to verify. The basic themes of many contemporary urban legends can be traced back centuries and in some cases even millennia. For recent examples refer to Bartholomew and Cole (1997) and Bartholomew (1998c). Although the article by myself and Philip Cole (1997) is titled "The Myth of Aboriginal Cannibalism," we do not claim that Aboriginal cannibalism is a myth but are referring to recent Australian urban myths about its purported relatively recent widespread practice among Aborigines as claimed by the Pauline Hanson political movement in Queensland.

10. This was made possible in my capacity as a senior teacher training instructor for the Malaysian government's Ministry of Human Resources at the Centre for Instructor and Advanced Skill Training in Shah Alam, Malaysia, between 1993 and 1994, which allowed me to discuss latah with teachers from every state in Malaysia.

11. Here Forbes uses the Indonesian spelling of latah.

12. Also spelled *kebaya*, this word refers to a tight-fitting sleeved garment worn by female Malays that typically extends downward to encompass the full or three-quarters length of the body. It is usually worn with a sarong, a tight-fitting tube-shaped Malay skirt donned by both males and females.

13. Malay Muslims are forbidden by Islam to consume any foods derived from pigs. Muslims believe the Koran is the word of God as revealed to the Prophet Mohammed (circa 570–632) by the Angel Gabriel. *Surah* (Arabic for a Koranic verse or chapter division) 5:3 of the Koran states: "You are forbidden carrion, blood, and the flesh of swine" (Dawood 1977, p. 387).

14. Beard was famous during this period for developing the concept of neurasthenia, which is no longer considered a valid disorder entity in Western medicine. Neurasthenia was thought to be a condition involving chronic cerebral cortex malfunction resulting in such ambiguous symptoms as weakness, dizziness, and headache. In an interesting example of the interpretive nature of psychiatric diagnoses and nosology construction, neurasthenia remains part of conventional psychiatric and medical practice in Eastern Europe, China, and parts of Southeast Asia (Porter 1987, p. 9; Kleinman 1988, pp. 12–14).

15. The most influential of these publications was by a student of French neurologist Jean-Martin Charcot, Georges Gilles de la Tourette (1884), who at his mentor's request to classify movement disorders located examples in the scientific literature of what appeared to be similar psychiatric conditions (Lajonchere, Nortz, and Finger 1996).

16. For specific numerical references to the Malay presence in these regions, refer to the *New Encyclopedia Britannica* (1974), "Namib Desert," Vol. 12, p. 820; "South Africa," Vol. 17, p. 67.

17. Also spelled *Ramanenjana,* this term was used to describe zealous dancing, running, leaping, and claims of communication with deceased ancestors reported near the capital of Madagascar (Malagasy) during February 1863, just prior to the political overthrow of unpopular King Radama II. Many historians have described this behavior as a form of psychological disturbance (see McLeod 1865, p. 187; Davidson 1867; Mutibwa 1974, p. 88). For a detailed discussion of this incident, refer to Chapter 5.

18. The Ainu are an indigenous people of Japan who reside on the northern island of Hokkaido, the southern portion of the Kurile Islands, and southern Sakhalin.

19. A notable exception to this pattern is seen in descriptions of "latah" in Afro-Arab countries where "automatic obedience" is not noted, coprolalia is rare, and those affected are reported to be primarily men (Winzeler 1995, p. 50).

20. Also spelled *miryachit, meriachit,* or *meryachit,* the few reports of this behavior pattern involve both verbal and body movement mimicry and occasionally "automatic obedience." Coprolalia per se is absent unless it occurs while imitating the words of others (Czaplicka 1914; Shirokogoroff 1935; Chapel 1970). The literature on myriachit is limited to a handful of historical descriptions involving secondhand accounts.

21. The existence of a universal human startle reflex was first described in detail by Carney Landis and William Hunt (1939), and the literature supporting this condition is considerable (see Simons 1985a). However, a startle mechanism may be irrelevant to understanding latah as a cross-cultural disorder.

22. This is unlike Beard (1880a, 1880b), Stevens (1965), and Kunkle (1967) who have noted fleeting demonstrations of "forced obedience" or "automatic obedience" in some subjects.

23. Beard (1880a, p. 489) noted that a characteristic feature of jumping was "the temporariness and momentariness of the phenomenon: it was all over in a second."

24. This is also distinct from jumpers who exhibit a brief, involuntary response that can be slightly elaborated through cultural conditioning.

25. When they appear to act sleepy or tired, teasers typically cease their teasing.

26. Percy Gerrard (1904), a surgeon in Pahang, Malaya, hypnotized a "severe" latah woman with the specific intent of alleviating symptoms. It was not reported whether her symptoms permanently disappeared, perhaps because Gerrard's brief hypnotic experiment was conducted at his own initiative while visiting friends at the woman's house.

27. The literal translation of *orang latah* is "latah man."

28. Holy Roller typically refers to "a member of one of the religious sects whose meetings are characterized by frenzied excitement—often taken to be offensive" (Gove 1972, p. 397).

29. Noegroho Notosusanto (1961, pp. 87–91) reports that when Indonesian forces were conducting practice exercises for military engagement with the Dutch in an effort to expel them from the Dutch East Indies during the first half of the twentieth century, one soldier was excused from active duty on the basis of his propensity to latah upon hearing weapons discharge. He recounts the story of Taslim who, although noted for his bravery, would latah in the form of swearing and screaming. As a result, his commanding officer transferred him to a less dangerous administrative desk position despite Taslim's protestations to remain. In this instance, latah became an idiom through which Taslim was able to avoid dangerous combat while simultaneously "saving face."

4

Medicalizing Deviant Perceptual Sets and Sexual Worldviews: A Sociological Perspective on Epidemic *Koro* and Similar Collective Behaviors

> We cannot think about sexuality, it seems, without evoking imagery of . . . powerful drives, dysfunctioning organs and clinical nomenclature. The field of inquiry has been thoroughly medicalized. . . . Much discussion of sexuality for the past century or so has been either with an explicit condemnation of diversity (through law and morality) or with an implicit attack (through the conversion of diversity into sickness and clinical problems by medicine and psychiatry). It has been impossible to think about patterns of non-procreative sexuality without evoking some sense of stigma. . . .
>
> It seems hard to grasp that the stigma which is assumed in so much writing may actually be the problem to be analyzed (Kenneth Plummer 1984, pp. 221, 228).

THE PSYCHIATRIC STATUS OF KORO

This chapter challenges the common contemporary psychiatric designation of "epidemic" koro as a mental disorder, arguing that individual and collective episodes are separate entities, with the former appropriately typified as a psychological disturbance and the latter a non-Western example of a collective social delusion. I begin by briefly reviewing the history of both individual and "epidemic" koro and their present psychiatric status. Then I shall argue that this state of affairs is the result of scientists trained in the Western medical tradition superimposing their narrow conceptions of normality, rationality, and reality in pathologizing deviant perceptual sets and sexual worldviews, whereby the consequences of beliefs have been mischaracterized as a medical syndrome. The appearance of what are typically assumed to be somatoform symptoms are explainable as the transient consequences of anxiety. Finally, parallels will be drawn between the common features of "epidemic" koro and a category of mass social delusion involving the overscrutinization and subsequent redefinition of ambiguous objects precipitated by the adherence to deviant perceptual outlooks.

Koro is a Malay word that has gained acceptance as standard psychiatric nomenclature to describe cases of perceived genitalia shrinkage or retraction and the accompanying panic. Of uncertain derivation, it may have arisen from the Malay word *keruk*, "to shrink" (Gwee 1968, p. 3) or Malayo-Indonesian words for tortoise—*kura*, *kura-kura*, and *kuro*. In Malaysia and Indonesia the penis, especially the glans, is commonly referred to as a tortoise head: "The fact that a tortoise can withdraw its head with its wrinkled neck under its shell literally into its body, suggested . . . the mechanism . . . in 'Koro' ('kura') and gave it its name" (Van Wulfften-Palthe 1936, p. 536). Although the condition of genital retraction is described in ancient Chinese medical texts,[1] koro first entered the Western scientific literature with a report by Dutch physician J. C. Blonk (1895) involving a native healer among the non-Chinese Macassaran peoples of southern Celebes in the Netherlands Indies (now Sulawesi, Indonesia).

Although the origin and nature of koro continue to be debated within transcultural psychiatry, there is virtual unanimity that both individual and "epidemic" forms of this condition represent a mental disorder.[2] Koro is typically defined as a culture-bound syndrome involving delusions of genitalia shrinkage, acute anxiety, psychosomatic complaints, and a conviction in some subjects that death will occur once the external genitalia fully retract.[3] The condition is primarily confined to parts of Asia where it has extensive cultural traditions and related beliefs (southern China, Malaysia, Indonesia, Thailand, and India) and is most commonly reported among Chinese descendants in Southeast Asia and southern China.[4] Since the early 1960s, sporadic individual cases have been reported in the psychiatric literature with increasing frequency across a disperse cultural and geographical spectrum among subjects of diverse ethnic backgrounds: an Israeli Jew (Modai, Munitz, and Aizenberg 1986) and Israeli Jewish immigrants from Yemen and Soviet Georgia (Hes and Nassi 1977); Americans (Malinick, Flaherty, and Jobe 1985; Kendall and Jenkins 1987; Scher 1987) and an American of Greek heritage (Edwards 1970); Canadians of Anglo-Saxon background (Arbitman 1975; Ede 1976; Waldenberg 1981) and French descent (Lapierre 1972); subjects from the Sudan (Baasher 1963) and South Africa (Menezes 1992), France (Bourgeois 1968; Turnier and Chouinard 1990), Nigeria (Ifabumuyi and Rwegellera 1979), Italy (de Leo, Mauro, and Pellegrini 1989), Great Britain (Barrett 1978; Constable 1979; Cremona 1981; Hawley and Owen 1988; Adeniran and Jones 1994); a British-born citizen of West Indian parentage (Smyth and Dean 1992), and a Greek Cypriot British immigrant (Ang and Weller 1984).

The earliest known reference to a condition involving the shrinking or retraction of human genitalia appeared in a Chinese medical textbook variously translated as *Huangdi Neiching* or *Huang-Di Nei-jing,* meaning *Yellow Emperor's Classic of Internal Medicine* (circa 200 to 476 B.P.).[5] Containing a series of dialogues between the Yellow Emperor and his physician, Ch'i Po, this document describes *suo-yang,* a fatal condition of male genital retraction into the abdomen (Tseng et al. 1988, p. 1538; Ng and Kua 1996).[6] Many subsequent Chinese medical books referred to this condition as *shook yin,* a disease affecting male and female genitalia. Some writers use the word *sou-yang* to refer to males with this condition and *suo-yin* for females. Descriptions of *suo-yang* or *shook yin* appear in classical Chinese medical texts from the Han dynasty (206 B.P.–A.D. 200), Jin dynasty (A.D. 265–420), Sui dynasty (A.D. 589–618), Tang dynasty (A.D. 618–907), Sung dynasty (A.D. 960–1280), Ming dynasty (A.D. 1368–1644), and Qing dynasty (A.D. 1644–1911) (Ng and Kua 1996). Numerous nineteenth-century Chinese medical practitioners continued to view koro as a disease capable of reducing genitalia size (Gwee 1968, p. 4). As the *Yellow Emperor's Classic of Internal Medicine* was highly influential and dominated subsequent descriptions of koro throughout the various dynasties, it is worthy of citation:

> When the pulse corresponding to the liver is slightly big there is numbness of the liver. The penis will shrink and there is persistent cough which causes abdominal pain. Illness due to internal pathogenic factors causes impotence ... illness due to cold causes retraction of the penis. In the case of the liver, grief moves the innermost self and causes harm to the mind resulting in madness, amnesia and lack of sperm. Without sperm, a person will not be well, and the manifestation is one of retraction of the genitals with spasm of muscles, the bones of the chest are depressed, and the hair colour poor. Death usually occurs in Autumn. (Ng and Kua 1996, p. 565)

The contemporary psychiatric consensus typifies koro as a hysterical variant of universal categories of human sexual dysfunction, precipitated by culture-specific koro-related folk beliefs or Freudian concepts of castration anxiety. It has been variously classified as an obsessive-compulsive disorder (Van Brero

1897), pathological castration fear (Kobler 1948), sexual conflict neuroses (Manson-Bahr 1983, p. 16), psychosexual disorder (Rack 1982, p. 148), and acute hysterical panic syndrome (Gwee 1963, p. 120). Yap (1965, p. 49) typified his patients as young, poorly educated males with immature dependent personalities lacking in sexual confidence, a position supported by Kiev (1972, p. 66). Berrois and Morley (1984) suggested the presence of a unitary psychiatric disorder that varies according to social and cultural context, basing their argument on the presence of korolike symptoms in fifteen non-Chinese subjects who hailed from disperse geographical locations and claimed no prior knowledge of koro-related folk beliefs. They concluded that "koro-like symptoms in non-Chinese subjects may constitute behavioural phenotypes without any underlying cultural genesis" (p. 333). Simons (1985b) also argues for a universal biological etiology ("genital retraction taxon"). Raymond Prince (1992a, 1992b) contends that a panhuman fear of castration and impotence in males is the root stimulus for both individual and "epidemic" koro, citing as supporting evidence numerous examples of transcultural and transhistorical castration themes, especially involving female castrators.[7,8]

By considering the social and cultural context of epidemic koro participants and those diagnosing the "disorder," it is argued that the psychiatric designation of participants as psychologically aberrant is pejorative and Eurocentric, imposing Western standards of normality, reality, and rationality. Such pathological interpretations reflect the medicalization of sexual variance,[9] and unlike rare, sporadic individual koro cases without related social or cultural beliefs, no consistent pattern of psychological disturbance has been identified in the literature.

Ironically, the most prolific advocate of epidemic koro as a mental disorder is Indian psychiatrist Arabinda N. Chowdhury, who typically utilizes Western-based personality inventories and profiles to demonstrate that subjects are sexually maladjusted. The results of his findings are ambiguous. For instance, in examining the behavioral profiles of 162 koro subjects with 160 controls (all Indian males), Chowdhury (1992) found that those experiencing epidemic koro had a greater incidence of aberrant sexual behavior, conflicts, and guilt than the control group. However, "aberrant" can also be viewed as creative, inventive, expressive, intense, or different. These subjects may have been more sexually cognizant. Indeed, as discussed in Chapter 1, the history of the social sciences is replete with examples whereby unfamiliar, "immoral," or unpopular non-Western behavioral idioms have received inappropriate disease or disorder labels. Further, sexual "difficulties" per se do not necessarily validate the existence of a psychosexual disturbance, as historically such arbitrary labels have been couched in "neutral" medical terminology when in fact they were unsubstantiated assumptions reflecting prevailing social and cultural mores (e.g., masturbation, homosexuality, and premarital intercourse). As Szasz (1990, p. 4) remarks, the acceptance of terms such as *sexual disorder, pathology,* or *dysfunction* assists in their mythological conceptualization, as such language informs and defines our constructs of reality: "When we talk about sexual dysfunctions the [erroneous] implication is that the labels for such alleged disorders name abnormal sexual conditions that exist—in the same sense in which, say, [colon cancer] . . . exists."

The characteristic features of epidemic koro unambiguously meet the standard social science criteria for the constitution of a collective delusion, with participants experiencing the cognitive consequences of deviant perceptual sets and the psychosomatic consequences of sexual social realities that become self-fulfilling and real in their consequences. Although some contemporary behavior models of social delusions attribute episodes to irrationality or societal "strains" (social disorganizational theories), such social pathological explanations of collective behavior, which view the participants or their society as "sick," are thoroughly discredited (Turner and Killian 1987; Goode 1992; Goode and Ben-Yehuda 1994).[10] Yet because koro-related folk beliefs are not plausible social realities among mainstream Western-biased psychiatric evaluators, images of psychological disturbance continue to be the predominant explanatory models.

It is important to make a clear distinction between the medical/psychiatric use of the word *delusion* as a persistent pathological belief associated with a psychotic condition as opposed to its loose usage to denote the collective sharing of a temporary false belief. Throughout this chapter the terms *social delusion* and *collective delusion* are used interchangeably in referring to the nonpathological mass adherence to a false belief. This terminology is consistent with common sociological employment. The issue is often confusing and requires clarification, as many social scientists continue to loosely use such terms as *epidemic hysteria, moral panic, mass psychopathology,* and *collective mental disorder* interchangeably with collective or social delusions. Some writers cloud the issue by using such terms as *collective paranoia* to describe a national character (e.g., Calhoun 1976, p. 214), *mass psychosis* in depicting participants in Melanesian cargo "cults" (e.g., Vittorio 1963, p. 315), and *collective mental disorder* to describe adherents of unpopular social movements such as Nazism (e.g., Cartwright and Biddiss 1972), group suicide among People's Temple members (e.g., Kruse 1986), and various flagellant adherents in expectation of divine rewards (e.g., Cohn 1957, p. 127; Faguet and Faguet 1982, p. 11).

COLLECTIVE KORO

Collective koro episodes have been recorded in India, Thailand, China, and Singapore. Because of the large number of affected subjects and abrupt onset, biological explanations have been excluded by medical and social scientists in favor of psychoanalytical models that seek to identify unresolved conflicts in the unconscious mind, panhuman castration fears, and psychological explanations that attribute episodes to abnormal personality traits. Gwee and colleagues (1969, p. 240) consider epidemic koro to be a culture-bound panic syndrome. J. A. Harrington (1982) interprets mass koro as a form of "epidemic psychosis" paralleling the European dancing manias, tarantism, and contemporary episodes of mass psychogenic illness. Simons (1985b, p. 152) argues that as in individual cases, mass episodes also reflect the existence of a universal genital retraction syndrome.

Chowdhury (1989a, 1989b) studied the penile length perceptions of forty single male koro subjects who were affected during an episode involving thousands in North Bengal, India. Two years after the episode most "victims" perceived themselves to possess shorter penises than control subjects, so it was concluded that they were vulnerable to "outbreaks," as they suffered from "dysmorphic penis image perception." Chowdhury (1989a, p. 183) views this as an abnormal psychiatric condition akin to other body image disorders such as anorexia and bulimia, where victims who are undernourished perceive themselves as obese.[11] However, "body dysmorphic disorder" typically begins in adolescence, does not occur abruptly in epidemic form, and persists for years with diagnoses marked by denial and resistance. Collective koro involves different accompanying features (such as extreme anxiety and fear of dying), desire for immediate treatment, and complete recovery within a few minutes, hours, or days following reassurance (American Psychiatric Association 1994, pp. 467–468).[12]

Individual koro reports are rare, even in countries with koro-related folk beliefs, with Yap (1965) locating nineteen cases in Hong Kong over 15 years, Gwee (1963) encountering three Singaporian subjects, Hsien Rin (1965) treating two Taiwanese patients, and sporadic cases from Guangdong province, China (Cai 1982; Mo 1991). Individual cases are associated with physiological and psychiatric origins that, in rare instances, may be exacerbated by folk beliefs. Of the approximately forty individual case reports in the scientific literature, most unambiguously exhibited major psychiatric pathologies (e.g., schizophrenia and affective disorder) associated with sexual inadequacies or conflicts, occasionally coinciding with organic disease[13] or drug ingestion.[14,15] However, all subjects experiencing collective episodes involve populations with extensive koro-related traditions or beliefs and are explainable using main-stream theories of social psychology. This chapter reviews the known documented incidents of mass koro to demonstrate that such episodes are most accurately explained as collective delusions precipitated by social, cultural, physiological, and cognitive influences.

HISTORICAL OVERVIEW OF "EPIDEMIC" KORO

In reviewing historical episodes of mass koro, it is crucial to emphasize that during each incident unambiguous evidence revealed koro-related cultural traditions exacerbated by folk beliefs associated with sexual potency or semen loss, which in turn facilitated the episode, rendering the rumors of genitalia shrinkage (or other yang organs in the case of some Chinese reports) plausible. During October and November 1967, hospitals on the tiny Southeast Asian island Republic of Singapore were inundated by anxious citizens convinced that their penises were shrinking and would eventually disappear, at which time, many believed, death would result. Panicked "victims" often used clamps, string, rubber bands, and even clothespins in an effort to prevent further perceived retraction. These methods occasionally resulted in severe damage to the organ. In some cases friends and relatives would hold the penis in relays until assistance was obtained from medical doctors or local healers. At the height of the "epidemic," the outdoor clinic of the Singapore Hospital treated about seventy-five cases per day. The episode occurred amid widespread rumors circulated in the Singaporean press that the consumption of pork, vaccinated for swine fever prior to slaughter, could precipitate genitalia shrinkage. One report even claimed a pig had died after being inoculated and experiencing penile retraction (Ng 1997, p. 356). Several weeks following the first reports, the panic ended abruptly after authority figures from the Singapore Medical Association and Health Ministry held public news conferences to dispel fears. C. I. Mun (1968, p. 641) provides examples of two characteristic cases:

> A typical case was that of a 16-year-old schoolboy who dashed into the clinic with his parents shouting for the doctor to attend to him quickly because he had "Shook Yong." The boy looked frightened and pale and he was pulling hard on his penis to prevent the organ from disappearing into his abdomen. The doctor explained and reassured both parents and patient. A tablet of 10 mg. of chlordiazepoxide was given at once and he was sent home with two days' supply of chlordiazepoxide. There was no recurrence. The boy had heard about Koro in school. That morning he took "Pow," which contained pork, for breakfast. Then he went to pass

urine and noticed his penis shrunk at the end of micturition. Frightened, he quickly grasped the organ and rushed to his parents shouting for help.

A young mother rushed into the clinic holding on to her 4-month-old baby's penis and asking the doctor to treat her child quickly because he had Koro. The child had not been well for two days with cold and a little diarrhoea. The mother was changing his napkin and washing his perineum when the child had colic and screamed. The mother saw the penis getting smaller and the child screamed and [she] thought he had Koro. She had previously heard the rumours. The mother was first reassured, and the baby's cold and diarrhoea treated. The child was all right after that.

From a cultural perspective, it is noteworthy that Singapore and surrounding countries have extensive traditions promoting koro folk realities (Gwee 1968). Several textbooks on tropical diseases mention previous episodes in nearby West Borneo and Celebes. Chinese medical texts from the nineteenth century describe koro as an identifiable "disease." Pao Sian-Ow's treatise, *New Collection of Remedies of Value* (1834), states authoritatively that koro occurs when "the penis retracts into the abdomen. If treatment is not instituted at once and effective, the case [patient] will die. The disease is due to the invasion of cold vapors and the treatment is to employ the 'heaty' drugs" (cited in Gwee 1963, p. 120). At the time of the initial circulation of rumors and inaccurate press reports that contaminated pork was causing koro, its existence was institutionalized and legitimated within the Singaporean society to the extent that some Chinese Singaporean physicians believed a physical disease called koro actually existed and could cause genital shrinkage (Gwee 1968, p. 4).

In arguing for the existence of a panhuman castration anxiety among males, Prince (1992a, p. 121) notes that only 25 percent of the Singaporean victims (95 percent male) had knowledge of korolike conditions prior to their "attacks."[16] However, as the literature on social delusions demonstrates, rumors need only be plausible to be cogent and initiate reality testing to confirm or deny their existence. Many collective delusions begin with false social beliefs held by a relatively small portion of the population and an absence of any cultural traditions related to these convictions. Examples include social delusions in which the threatening agent involved imaginary gassers (Johnson 1945), slashers (Jacobs 1965), stabbers (Burnham 1924), Martians (Cantril 1947 [1940]), atomic fallout (Medalia and Larsen 1958), monsters (McCloy and Miller 1976), and rockets (Bartholomew 1993a). On the other hand, episodes begin with cultural traditions held by a few individuals that become increasingly plausible to the remaining population in the wake of rumors, misperceptions, and media reports. Examples include waves of claims and public discourse surrounding widespread sightings of legendary creatures such as Sasquatch (Stewart 1989; Bartholomew and Bartholomew 1991; Bartholomew et al. 1992), extinct animals like the Tasmanian "tiger" (Park 1986), or supernatural beings such as fairies (Kirk 1815; Evans-Wentz 1909; Evans 1984).

At least 5,000 inhabitants in a remote area of southern Guangdong province, China, were affected by koro between August 1984 and the summer of 1985 (Jilek 1986, p. 273). Wen-Shing Tseng and colleagues (1988, p. 1538) note the prevalence of a popular folk belief within the region that was related to "evil-induced genital retraction." Male residents of the region are socialized to practice restraint in matters of sexual desire and activity, as excessive semen discharge is believed to weaken physical and mental health, even inducing death. Further, many residents believe certain spirits of the dead, especially female fox maidens, wander in search of penises that will give them powers. Each of the 232 "victims" surveyed by Tseng and colleagues (1988, p. 1539) were convinced that an evil female fox spirit could cause suoyang, and 76 percent had witnessed "victims" being "rescued." Most of these cases occurred at night following a chilly sensation that would precipitate a feeling of penile shrinkage: "Thinking this [chill] to be a fatal sign and believing that they were affected by an evil ghost, they [koro 'victims'] became panic stricken and tried to pull at their penises, while, at the same time, shouting for help" (Tseng et al. 1988, p. 1540).[17] It is noteworthy that during this episode, several children reported shrinkage of their tongue, nose, and ears, reflecting the prevalent ancient Chinese belief that any male (yang) organs can shrink or retract (Tseng et al. 1987, 1988). A separate epidemic in 1987 affected at least 300 residents in the vicinity of Haikang Town on the Leizhou Peninsula of Guangdong province (Tseng et al. 1992).

Koro is endemic in parts of southern China, with sporadic annual reports, occasional case clusters, and confirmed epidemics in 1865, 1948, 1955, 1966, and 1974—all involving at least several hundred residents (Murphy 1986; Jilek 1986, p. 274; Tseng et al. 1992, p. 117). J. Legendre (1936) reports on a koro episode affecting about twenty males in a school in Szechwan, China, during "the 10th moon of the 32nd year of Quang-Sou" (circa 1908), when he heard rumors that numerous pupils attending the schools of *la Ville Jaune* (the Yellow City) were reported to have been simultaneously afflicted with *so in tchen*. This "illness" involved perceptions that the penis was shriveling, followed by a sudden shrinkage and disappearance into the abdominal cavity. It was believed death would ensue if immediate treatment could not induce a reemergence of the organ. Intrigued by these stories, Legendre visited the affected schools, talked with several administrators, and ascertained that the episode began one evening and affected a single pupil who noticed "that his penis was no longer as developed as he had known it to be." Legendre (1936) states that the student "immediately diagnosed 'so in tchen,' so well-known and dreaded in his country, and without hesitation" he applied "methodical tractions" to his penis. That same evening and the following day, approximately twenty more cases appeared in male students attending the schools. They were all treated with tractions placed on the penis, and all re-covered within a few days.

Legendre (1936) was able to locate and interview the final student stricken, "at that time out of danger but not completely restored and still staying in-doors." The "affliction" began 4 days earlier when he apparently felt "light pains" in his genital area, persisting for several hours. The pupil stated that his penis had shrunk to between 3 and 4 centimeters in length. Legendre exam-ined the subject, noting that his physical condition was unremarkable, having a healthy tongue, normal temperature, and a soft and painless stomach. His genitals appeared entirely normal in terms of size and health. Legendre specu-lated that his subject most likely experienced "light alimentary intoxication expressed in insignificant abdominal symptoms," and it was possible that "fairly notable shrinkage" may have occurred. Legendre (1936, p. 1534) attributes the cause of the "imaginary illness" to Chinese superstition: "The scared imagination of Celestial youths, inheritors of twenty centuries of superstition, and legatees from long ancestry to an exclusively literary culture, had not hesitated to attribute this syndrome to the rank of a feared, morbid entity."

Legendre states his conviction that so in tchen and koro are the same "imaginary illness." He also describes it as an "exotic pathology" and "Asian psychosis" that occurs both individually and in collectives. As for its cause, he speculates that it is related to the Chinese fear of impotence and not being able to produce a male descendant to continue the family heritage and to be able to conduct family religious rituals believed to ensure the happiness of deceased ancestors' souls in the afterlife. Legendre observed that "if I did not see before my very eyes the notes that I took then, I would think I had dreamt it, the adventure of these young people was so entertaining and improbable."[18]

Tseng and colleagues (1992) sought to determine why episodes repeatedly occur in the vicinity of Leizhou Peninsula and Hainan Island but never spread to the principal section of Guangdong province or other parts of China, and why only certain residents in a region report koro while others do not. It was found that those affected held the more intense koro-related folk beliefs rela-tive to a control group from the adjacent nonaffected area (Tseng et al. 1992,

p. 122), partially explaining "why each time the koro epidemic spread from the Peninsula, it would cease when it reached the urban area of Guangzhou, where the people are more educated and hold less belief in koro." Although recognizing the importance of rumors and traditional beliefs in precipitating episodes, Tseng and colleagues (1988, p. 1542; 1992, p. 117) consider epidemics in southern China to be a psychiatric disorder ("genital retraction panic disorder") that primarily affects susceptible individuals, such as the poorly educated and those possessing below-normal intellectual endowment who are experiencing social crisis or tension.[19]

Another koro episode transpired in northeast Thailand between approximately November and December 1976, affecting an estimated 2,000 people, primarily rural Thai residents in the border provinces of Maha Sarakham, Nakhon Phanom, Nong Khai, and Udon Thani.[20] Symptoms included the perception of genitalia shrinkage and impotence among males, whereas females typically reported sexual frigidity, with breast and vulva shrinkage. Other symptoms were panic, anxiety, dizziness, diarrhea, discomfort during urination, nausea, headaches, facial numbness, and abdominal pain. Some patients temporarily lost consciousness, and many feared imminent death (Jilek and Jilek-Aall 1977a, p. 58). Of 350 subjects studied in detail, irrespective of whether they sought treatment from native healers or physicians, "most patients had recovered within one day and all within one week" (Suwanlert and Coates 1979, p. 65).

The episode apparently began at a technical college in Udon Thani province, with the circulation of rumors that Vietnamese immigrants had deliberately contaminated food and cigarettes with a koro-inducing powder. It is significant that during this period a strong anti-Vietnamese sentiment existed throughout Thailand. At the time, Australian sociologist James Coughlan (1997, personal communication) notes that legal restrictions had been placed on the movement of Vietnamese in Thailand, and they were ineligible for Thai citizenship. Other factors contributing to Vietnamese xenophobia among the Thai included the October 1976 student revolution in Bangkok, precipitating the overthrow of the fascist government. Additional factors included communist "victories" within Southeast Asia in 1975, the growing influence of the Communist Party of Thailand, and the perceived control of Cambodia and Laos by the Vietnamese. Anti-Vietnamese sentiments in the region were especially strong in the month before the episode (Andelman 1976a, 1976b), with allegations by Thailand's interior minister that "solid evidence" indicated a plot whereby "Vietnamese refugees would incite rioting in northeast Thailand, providing Vietnam with an excuse to invade" on February 15 (Andelman 1976c). As the episode continued, the poisoning rumors became self-fulfilling, as numerous Thai citizens recalled that previously consumed food and cigarettes recently purchased from Vietnamese establishments had an unusual smell and taste. However, an analysis of suspected sources by the Government Medical Science Department "detected no foreign substance that could possibly cause sexual impotence or contraction of the male sex organ" (Jilek and Jilek-Aall 1977a, p. 58).

The episode appears clearly related to the worldview of the Thai population that was almost exclusively affected. Thailand is situated in the vicinity of several Southeast Asian countries with koro traditions. It appears that koro rumors, combined with preexisting awareness of the "disease," served to foster and legitimate its plausible existence. For instance, Sangun Suwanlert and D. Coats (1979, p. 65) found that 94 percent of "victims" studied "were convinced that they had been poisoned." Further, the negative government analysis of alleged tainted substances was undermined by contradictory statements issued by authority figures in the press. Wolfgang Jilek and his wife, Louise Jilek-Aall (1977a, p. 58), note that Thai newspapers cited security officials as attributing the tainting substances believed responsible for precipitating the koro in food to a mixture of vegetable sources undetectable by medical devices.

Another epidemic of koro occurred in the Assam, Meghalya, and Bengal regions of India during July and September 1982. Cases numbered in the thousands, as males claimed penile shrinkage and females perceived their breasts were getting smaller. The panic reached such proportions that medical personnel toured the region, reassuring those affected with loudspeakers (Chakraborty, Das, and Mukherji 1983). Parents typically tied string to their sons' penises to reduce or stop retraction, a practice that occasionally produced penile ulcers. Although evidence indicated preexisting koro-related beliefs among some residents, the episode spread across various religious and ethnic groups, social castes, and geographical areas by way of rumors.[21] In addition to using various means to physically prevent further perceived retraction, other local remedies consisted of dowsing the patient's head with buckets of cold water and consuming lemon juice. Based on psychiatric interviews with thirty "victims" (seventeen male, thirteen female), although Sachdev and Shukla (1982) were unable to identify obvious signs of psychological disturbance, they supported Rin's (1965) psychoanalytical interpretation involving castration anxiety, oral deprivation, and cultural conditioning.[22] Here Sachdev and Shukla appear to support the existing pathological paradigm despite their own evidence to the contrary, highlighting the influence of the zeitgeist in making diagnostic assessments.

MAGICAL GENITALIA LOSS IN NIGERIA

Collective episodes of a korolike condition called magical genitalia loss in Nigeria have also been interpreted as an exotic, unambiguous example of isolated individual mental disturbance.[23] The influence of sociocultural context is evident in these episodes, which have been reported for at least 20 years. While working at a teaching hospital in Kaduna, northern Nigeria, in 1975, psychiatrist Sunny Ilechukwu (1988) reports that he was approached by a police officer who was accompanied by two men. One of the men made the startling claim that the other had caused his penis to vanish; the officer, acting on orders from his superior, was to obtain a medical report to settle the dispute. The patient explained that he was walking along a street and "felt his penis go" after the robes the other man wore had touched him. Incredulous, Ilechukwu initially refused to handle the case but later agreed to conduct a physical exam, which transpired in full view of the concerned parties. The patient stared straight ahead until it was announced that his genitals were normal. Reacting in disbelief, the patient glanced down at his genitals and suggested that they had just reappeared! The policeman then indicated that charges would be filed against the man for falsely reporting an incident.

This case may appear to be an exotic, unambiguous example of isolated individual mental disturbance, as it is beyond Western credulity that people could believe entire body parts were missing when clearly they were not. Yet Ilechukwu reports on epidemics of temporary magical penis loss in Nigeria during the mid-1970s[24] and again in 1990. A major Nigerian episode of "vanishing" genitalia in 1990 mainly affected men but also sometimes women while walking in public places. Accusations were typically triggered by incidental body contact with a stranger interpreted as intentionally contrived, followed by unusual sensations within the scrotum. The affected person would then physically grab the external genitals to confirm that all or parts were missing, after which he would shout a phrase such as "Thief! My genitals are gone" (Ilechukwu 1992, p. 95). The "victim" would completely disrobe to convince quickly gathering crowds of bystanders that his penis was actually missing. The accused was threatened and usually beaten (sometimes fatally) until the genitals were "returned." Although some "victims" soon realized that their genitalia were intact, "many then claimed that they were 'returned' at the time they raised the alarm or that, although the penis had been 'returned,' it was shrunken and so probably a 'wrong' one or just the ghost of a penis" (p. 95). In such instances the assault or lynching would usually continue until the "original, real" penis reappeared.

Incidents quickly spread throughout the country. . . . Men could be seen in
the streets of Lagos holding on to their genitalia either openly or discretely
with their hands in their pockets. Women were also seen holding on to their
breasts directly or discretely by crossing the hands across the chest. It was
thought that inattention and a weak will facilitated the "taking" of the
penis or breasts. Vigilance and anticipatory aggression were thought to be
good prophylaxis. (Ilechukwu 1992, p. 96)

The role of sociocultural traditions in triggering episodes is evident, as
many Nigerian ethnic groups "ascribe high potency to the external genitalia as
ritual and magical objects to promote fecundity or material prosperity to the
unscrupulous. Ritually murdered persons are often said to have these parts
missing" (Ilechukwu 1988, p. 313). The reality of vanishing genitalia is institutionalized to such an extent that during the 1990 episode several influential
Nigerians, including a court judge, protested vehemently when police released
suspected genital thieves, and many knowledgeable citizens "claimed that there
was a real—even if magical—basis for the incidents" (Ilechukwu 1992, pp.
96–97). One Christian priest supported cultural beliefs in genital theft by
citing a biblical passage where Christ asked, "Who touched me?" because the
"power had gone out of him," claiming it was a reference to genital stealing
(pp. 101–102). Ilechukwu concludes that sociocultural beliefs related to magical genitalia loss in Nigeria render sexually maladjusted individuals susceptible to "attacks." He bases this view on his clinical assessment of just two
cases. This generalization is not warranted, especially as the widespread
reports of magical genitalia loss in Nigeria can be explained in social psychological terms and without reference to individual or group pathology.

SOCIAL PATHOLOGY OR SOCIAL PSYCHOLOGY?

Virtually all known "victims" of collective koro or korolike phenomena
return to a normal state of health within hours or days after being convinced
the "illness" is over or never existed.[25] Cases share a similar range of symptoms, including anxiety, sweating, nausea, headache, transient pain, pale skin,
palpitations, blurred vision, faintness, paraesthesia, insomnia, and the koro-
related "delusionary" conviction. The appearance of these symptoms per se is
not necessarily indicative of psychopathology, as they reflect the spectrum of
"normal" physiological responses to extreme anxiety in all cultures. For
instance, because of the similarity of signs and symptoms associated with
koro as described in various Chinese texts over the past two centuries, Beng
Yeong Ng and Ee Heok Kua (1996, p. 569) assume that koro is a culturally
masked manifestation of panic disorder: "The description of the presentation

has features of an acute anxiety attack, including a sense of fear, sweating, pallor, rapid pulse, tinnitus, diarrhoea, urinary frequency, giddiness and blurred vision" (pp. 568–569). Yet these characteristic features of koro are consistent with extreme anxiety precipitated by koro folk beliefs, including the conviction in many subjects that koro may result in death.

The inclusion of the "delusionary" conviction and perception within the collective koro symptom pattern is consistent with perceptual psychology research, which supports the predisposition of an observer to interpret information patterns in a particular manner that is significantly influenced by his or her mental state and broad sociocultural reference system at the time. Studies on the fallibility of human perception and conformity dynamics are apposite (see Asch 1955; Zimbardo 1972). The accuracy of eyewitness testimony is notoriously unreliable, remarkably subject to error, and preconditioned by mental outlook and sociocultural reference system (Buckhout 1974, 1980; Ross, Read, and Toglia 1994). The selective and organizational nature of perception is based more on inference than reality, allowing for interpretations that often differ substantially from reality. Hence, "inference can perform the work of perception by filling in missing information in instances where perception is either inefficient or inadequate" (Massad, Hubbard, and Newtson 1979, p. 531). The variance of interpretations from objective reality is especially pronounced involving the perception of ambiguous stimuli or conflicting information patterns within a group setting, which may result in members developing an increased need to define the situation, depending less on their own judgment for reality validation and more on the judgment of others. As individuals are more dependent on others and less on themselves in their construction of social reality, an opinion, attitude, or conviction "is 'correct,' 'valid,' and 'proper' to the extent that it is anchored in a group of people with similar beliefs, opinions and attitudes" (Festinger 1950, p. 272). Individuals continually engage in reality testing by comparing their perceptions with those of others around them. Hence, it should not be surprising that the process of human perception can and often does result in an array of perceptual observations that do not reflect what exists in the real world but in the socially constructed world of the observers.

What constitutes reality for any particular individual, group, or culture is socially constructed (Berger and Luckmann 1971 [1966]), a process that assists in maintaining social continuity and meaning. Humans arbitrarily create their own social order and meanings based primarily on faith, and an integral part of ordering social reality is the formation of perceptual frames of meaning, which are orientations toward viewing the world. Hence culture, in a strict cognitive sense, is a collection of similar perceptual sets through which a particular people impose order by defining "reality" (Conner 1975, p. 367). In defending the fruitfulness of utilizing interpretive approaches in cognitive anthropology to explicate the meaning of "foreign" conduct codes, Shweder (1984, p. 29) suggests that many "exotic" social realities are not amenable to evaluation through the traditional rational/irrational dichotomy but are nonrational, as perceptual outlooks may support beliefs that foster social realities at extreme variance with Western constructions of reality, rationality, and normality. Similarly, the possibility that certain peoples could erroneously believe their genitalia to be shrinking or disappearing altogether has typically received deviant, abnormal, or psychopathological evaluations by Western-trained scientists, who through cultural conditioning find such realities implausible. In fact, "rationality" appears to be a social construct that varies transculturally.

PHYSIOLOGICAL FACTORS

Exacerbating social and cultural influences is the role of physiological factors in the genesis of collective koro. For instance, James Edwards (1984, pp. 15–16) cites physician-investigated cases of genital retraction resulting from both physical trauma and unknown reasons, in addition to the common experience of genital shrinkage in response to cold, excessive physical exertion, and aging.[26] The penis, scrotum, breasts, and nipples are the most physiologically plastic external body parts, regularly changing size and shape in response to various stimuli.[27] Mun (1968, p. 641) states that diminution of penis size typically occurs in conjunction with illness and following micturition. Patrick (1971, p. 85) suggests that the appearance of penile retraction may result from abdominal gas or a vigorous cremasteric reflex. Femi Oyebode and colleagues (1986) found that anxiety can also precipitate discernible penile circumference reduction,[28] and another study noted a significant relationship between diminished penis tumescence and depression (Thase, Reynolds, and Jennings 1988). This may explain the appearance of penile reduction or retraction as a secondary condition to affective disorders, as in virtually all cases the "delusion" of penis diminution ceased once the primary psychiatric condition was effectively treated with drugs, psychotherapy, or a combination (e.g., Ang and Weller 1984; Kendall and Jenkins 1987; Holden 1987; Turnier and Chouinard 1990).[29,30]

As a reduction in penile size can occur in response to anxiety and mood disorders, the appearance of individual koro in persons with no knowledge of related folk beliefs cannot automatically be classified as delusional. However, epidemic koro occurring in societies with koro-related traditions cannot by definition be classified as a psychiatric delusion because, as noted earlier, the common psychiatric definition of "delusion" involves an erroneous belief not ordinarily held by other members within the subject's culture or subculture, whereas a "bizarre delusion" is one the individual's culture would consider entirely implausible (American Psychiatric Association 1994, p. 765). As noted previously, in societies experiencing epidemic koro, it is normal practice for relatives to support the belief in koro (Vorstman 1897; Arieti and Meth 1959, p. 558; Gwee 1963; Mun 1968; Edwards 1984, p. 4). Also, P. M. Van Wulfften-Palthe (1935) notes that folk beliefs associating koro and death may stem from the observation that in some corpses the penis appears to shrink and retract into the body.

"EPIDEMIC" KORO AS A SOCIAL DELUSION

The label *mass hysteria* has been inappropriately applied to a variety of heterogeneous transcultural behaviors in an attempt to categorize what is typically viewed as abnormal, deviant, or bizarre by Western-trained scientists within a familiar, convenient, unitary psychiatric rubric that is both pejorative and ethnocentric (Bartholomew 1990b). Such evaluations typically ignore or underemphasize the complexities of evaluating cultures and subcultures with social realities that differ significantly from those of the Eurocentric Western-trained researcher.[31] Incidents of collective koro, which have also been viewed as a culture-specific variant of epidemic conversion hysteria (see Gwee 1968, p. 5; Gwee and Ransome 1973, p. 289; Sirois 1974, p. 26; Jilek and Jilek-Aall 1977a; Tan 1980, p. 381; Massey, Brannon, and Riley 1981, p. 607; Harrington 1982, p. 98), share similar characteristics with a variety of diverse social phenomena that have been similarly misclassified. Classic examples include the reinterpretation of prosaic phenomena in the wake of a perceived Martian invasion (Cantril 1947 [1940]), ever-present windshield damage (Medalia and Larsen 1958), and mundane odors and body sensations in the case of a phantom gasser (Johnson 1945). It is important to emphasize that physical symptoms are occasionally associated with collective misperceptions, but these symptoms reflect the consequences of anxiety or excitement, and like epidemic koro they have been medicalized under the assumption that the symptoms are hysterical in nature.

Several examples in the collective behavior literature involving mass misperceptions of a rumor-related object appear in Table 4.1. This subcategory of social delusion involves the rapid spread of false beliefs that are reified within a particular demographic and sociocultural context. As participants attempt to confirm or deny the accuracy of plausible, unsubstantiated stories, they focus extraordinary attention on objects, events, or circumstances related to the rumors. In doing so, they reinterpret ever-present prosaic phenomena in accordance with this newly emerging definition of the situation. The resulting self-fulfilling prophecies can create remarkable distortions of objective reality consistent with the collective delusion scenarios. During the famous Orson Welles live radio drama on October 30, 1938, some U.S. residents panicked after listening to a realistic reenactment of a novel by H. G. Wells, *War of the Worlds*, depicting a fictitious Martian landing in New Jersey and subsequent attack on New York City. Concordant with this new definition of reality and perceptual orientation, several residents in the region of the bogus invasion reported observations consistent with what was being described on the radio. Several persons telephoned police and said they could see "Martians on their giant machines poised on the Jersey Palisades" (Markush 1973, p. 379).[32] One person became convinced he could smell the poison gas and feel the heat rays as described on the radio, and another became emotionally distraught and felt a choking sensation from the imaginary gas (Cantril 1947 [1940], pp. 94–95). After checking various descriptions of the panic, Joseph Bulgatz (1992, p. 129) reported that a Boston woman said she could actually see the fire as described on the radio; other persons told of hearing machine gun fire or the "swish" sound of the Martians. A man even climbed atop a Manhattan building with binoculars and described seeing "the flames of battle."

Another example of collective misperception involves a flurry of press reports about the appearance of strange pit marks on automobile windshields in the vicinity of Seattle, Washington, during 1954. The event began in late March with accounts in Seattle newspapers detailing windshield damage in a city 80 miles to the north. As time passed, reports of damaged windshields moved closer to Seattle. Between nightfall on April 14, when the mysterious agent had first reached the city, and April 18, police had logged 242 telephone calls from concerned residents telling of tiny windshield pit marks across Seattle. The reports then rapidly declined and ceased altogether. The sudden presence of the "pits" created widespread anxiety, as they were typically attributed to atomic fallout from hydrogen bomb tests that had been recently conducted in the Pacific and received saturation media coverage. The Seattle mayor even sought help from U.S. President Dwight Eisenhower. However, an investigation by Nahum Z. Medalia and Otto N. Larsen (1958) determined that the pits had always existed and resulted from mundane events such as ordinary road wear but had gone unnoticed. In the wake of rumors such as the presence of harmful fallout, and spurred by a few initial cases amplified by the news media, residents began looking *at* instead of *through* their windshields.

Although some episodes, such as mass fears of perceived genital shrinkage or of a mad gasser poisoning women, may seem fantastic and naive to

Table 4.1—Social Delusions Involving the Misperception of Rumor-Related Objects

Investigator	Location and Year	Form	Precipitating Events	Mechanism	Min. # Affected
Legendre (1936)	Szechwan, China, circa 1908	shrinking genitalia	rumors; folk belief	scrutinization and plasticity of genitalia	12
Bartholomew (1998d)	New Zealand, 1909	Zeppelins	German military buildup; press	autokinetic movement; misperceptions	1,000s
Bartholomew (1989a)	South Africa, 1914	monoplanes	World War I; rumors; press	autokinetic movement; misperceptions	1,000s
Bartholomew (1997g)	Canada, 1896–1897	ghost balloons	Andree's polar expedition; rumors; press	autokinetic movement; misperceptions	1,000s
Bartholomew (1997c, 1997f, 1998b, 1998f)	USA, 1896–1897	phantom airships	sensational initial rumors; press	autokinetic movement; misperceptions	100,000
McCloy & Miller (1976)	New Jersey, 1909	Jersey Devil	sensational initial case; rumors; press	misperceptions; misidentification of footprints	1,000s
Burnham (1924)	Paris, France, circa 1920	hat pin stabber	rumors; press	scrutinization of mundane lacerations	multiple
Park (1986); Bartholomew (1992a)	Australia, since 1936	Tasmanian "tiger"	mass media; wilderness	misperceptions of ambiguous objects	600
Cantril (1947[1941])	USA, 1938	Martian space-ships	hoax radio play; rumors; nighttime	misperception of prosaic nocturnal aerial stimuli	several
Sieveking (1993)	Yorkshire, UK, 1938–1939	razor maniac	rumors; hoaxes; media	scrutinization of media, mundane lacerations	multiple

Continued on next page

Table 4.1—continued

Investigator	Location and Year	Form	Precipitating Events	Mechanism	Min. # Affected
Johnson (1945)	Illinois, 1944	phantom gasser	sensational initial case	focus on mundane body paralysis; odors	25
Bartholomew (1993a)	Sweden, 1946	ghost rockets	cometary debris; fear of Russia; rumors; media	misperceptions of ambiguous objects	1,000s
Bartholomew (1989b, 1991b)	worldwide, since 1947	flying saucers	sensational initial case; rumors; media & films	autokinetic movement; misperceptions	millions
Tumin & Feldman (1955)	Puerto Rico, 1953	Virgin Mary sightings	visions & subsequent predicted appearance	autokinetic effect; misidentification of mundane phenomena	1,000s
Medalia & Larsen (1958)	Seattle, Washington, 1954	windshield pitting	atomic tests; rumors; media	reinterpretation of mundane damage	300
Jacobs (1965)	Taipei, Taiwan 1956	knife attacks	rumors; media	scrutinization of mundane lacerations	21
Mun (1968); Ngui (1969)	Singapore, 1967	shrinking genitalia	contaminated pork rumors; folk beliefs	scrutinization and plasticity of genitalia	536
Yassa (1980); Persinger & Derr (1989)	Zeitoun, Egypt 1968	Virgin Mary sightings	sensational initial case; seismic fault luminosity; religious beliefs; media; rumors	misperception of ambiguous stimulus	crowds
Miller, Mieus, & Mathers (1978)	Illinois, 1973	monster	sensational initial case; rumors; media	misperceptions	several
Stewart (1977); Bartholomew (1992b)	Midwest USA, 1974	cattle mutilations	UFO reports; rumors; predatory animal habits	scrutinization of decaying cattle carcasses	dozens
Ilechukwu (1988)	Nigeria, 1975–1976	vanishing genitalia	rumors; media; folk beliefs	self-fulfilling belief in magic; reinterpretation of genital tingling after incidental body contact (possible sexual arousal)	multiple

Source	Location, Year	Perception	Causes	Explanation	Number
Jilek & Jilek-Aall (1977a, 1977b)	Thailand, 1976	shrinking genitalia	rumors of tobacco & food poisoning; fear of Vietnamese; media; folk beliefs	scrutinization & pasticity of genitalia	2,000
Toibin (1985)	Eire, Ireland, early 1980s	moving statues	sensational initial case; religious beliefs; rumors: media	visual illusion precipitated by overscrutinization (autokinetic effect)	1,000s
Harrington (1982)	Thailand circa 1981	shrinking genitalia	rumors of food & tobacco contamination; fear of Vietnamese; media; folk beliefs	scrutinization & plasticity of genitalia	100s
Dutta, Phookan, & Das (1982); Sachev (1985)	India, 1982	shrinking genitalia	rumors; folk beliefs	scrutinization & plasticity of genitalia	1,000s
Tseng et al. (1988)	China, 1984–1985	shrinking genitalia, ears, tongue, nose	rumors; folk beliefs	scrutinization of affected body parts	2,000
Tseng et al. (1992)	China, 1987	shrinking genitalia	rumors; folk beliefs	scrutinization & plasticity of genitalia	300
Bartholomew et al. (1992)	New York & Vermont, since indigenous settlement	Bigfoot	rumors; folk beliefs; media	misidentification of prosaic events & objects	100s
Ilechukwu (1992)	Nigeria, 1990	vanishing genitalia	rumors; folk beliefs; media	self-fulfilling belief in magic; reinterpretation of genital tingling after incidental body contact	numerous
Bartholomew (1993b)	Klang, Malaysia, 1992	Islamic pictographs in clouds	sensational initial report; religious setting	misidentification of mundane clouds	201

Western observers, each of the cases of collective misperception in Table 4.1 occurred among cultures or subcultures exposed to plausible information suggesting that the particular rumors were real. For instance, in the case of the "phantom anesthetist" of Mattoon (Johnson 1945), local newspapers, citing authorities such as police and chemical experts, initially reported the existence of a crazed gasser as an established fact, the target of whom was apparently women. This prevailing definition of the situation encouraged Mattoon females to alter their perceptual sets and reinterpret mundane events. The formation of vigilante groups patrolling the streets at night further reinforced the legitimacy of media and authority pronouncements.

OTHER EXAMPLES OF COLLECTIVE MISPERCEPTION

This section will consider several examples of collective misperception. In Mattoon, Illinois, between September 1 and 12, 1944, police received twenty-five separate reports involving twenty-seven females and two males claiming to have been sprayed with a mysterious incapacitating gas by someone dubbed the "phantom anesthetist." The initial ambiguous incident received sensational hometown newspaper coverage after a woman reported that someone had opened her bedroom window as she was retiring for the night. Simultaneously, she noticed a shadowy figure near the window, experienced temporary difficulty walking, and perceived a sickish odor. Psychologist Donald M. Johnson (1945) described the following series of reports as an episode of mass hysteria, noting that 93 percent of the "victims" were females of low socioeconomic status who were uncritical in evaluating the situation and concluding that they were exhibiting hysterical conversion reactions. The transient symptoms reported by those "gassed" were limited to nausea, vomiting, dry mouth, palpitations, difficulty walking, and in one instance, a burning sensation in the mouth. These symptoms may be accounted for by anxiety generated by "gasser" publicity, whereas a series of early cases involved the redefinition of mundane physical reactions that would have ordinarily gone unnoticed but were subsequently attributed to the "phantom anesthetist."

Johnson (1945, p. 176) provides two examples of this latter process. The day after the initial press report ("Anesthetic Prowler on Loose"), a resident identified as Mr. B contacted police to report that on the night prior to the "attack" described in the Mattoon *Daily Journal-Gazette* "he woke up sick, and retched, and asked his wife if the gas had been left on. When she woke up she was unable to walk. At first they had attributed these symptoms to hot dogs eaten the evening before. About the same time, Mr. C, who works nights, told the press that his wife and daughter had likewise been attacked. The daughter woke up coughing and, when Mrs. C got up to take care of her, she could hardly walk. They did not suspect gas until they read the newspaper [the] next day."

In reexamining the case, sociologist David Miller (1985, p. 100) found that several newsmen documenting the event reported headaches attributed to the phantom's gas yet were excluded as victims because they were not female. In at least four instances husbands were accompanying their wives when "attacked," and although both were described as experiencing gassing symptoms, only wives were counted as victims (Miller 1985, p. 110). This is significant, as Johnson used the predominance of female victims to confirm the diagnosis of mass hysteria, and the news media initially defined women as perceived targets. Consequently, the perceptual outlook of Mattoon females became orientated to redefine ordinarily prosaic events and circumstances as gasser related. Further, local media initially reported the gasser's existence as an absolute fact, citing police and other authorities. A police chemist even made a tentative, erroneous identification of chloropicrin as the agent involved. Following the initial sensational case and subsequent police search for the gasser, which received spectacular newspaper coverage, several residents reinterpreted as gasser related mundane occurrences such as nocturnal shadows, chemical odors from numerous local factories, and anxiety states.

During a two-week period in 1956, newspapers in the vicinity of Taipei, Taiwan, reported that a maniacal figure was randomly slashing victims in public with a razor or similar-type weapon (Jacobs 1965). At least twenty-one persons reported attacks. University of Kansas behavioral scientist Norman Jacobs was teaching in Taipei at the time and concluded that affected persons, mainly women and children of low income and education, attributed mundane slash marks to a crazed slasher. The social delusion occurred in conjunction with rumors amplified by widespread sensational press coverage treating the existence of the enigmatic figure as a reality. In the wake of plausible newspaper accounts, which altered the perceptual outlook of residents to include the existence of a daring slasher, police eventually determined that various prosaic lacerations from inadvertent contact in public places were erroneously attributed to the phantom. In one case a middle-aged man described to police in detail how he was slashed by a cavorting figure carrying a mysterious black bag. After a physician determined that the wound could not have resulted from a razor but had been caused by a blunt object, the "victim" admitted to being unable to recall the circumstances surrounding its appearance, assuming he was slashed "because of all the talk going around." Another typical incident involved an elderly man who sought medical treatment for a wrist laceration. The incident was reported to police after the attending physician became suspicious when the man casually described being touched by a stranger, coinciding with the time he first realized he was bleeding. It was subsequently determined that the "slash" was actually an old wound that had been reopened by inadvertent scratching.

There are other historical examples of imaginary attackers. In Paris, France, near the turn of the twentieth century, numerous residents mistakenly reported being "pricked with a long hat pin or the like" (Burnham 1924, pp. 337–338), and several communities in the vicinity of Yorkshire, England, between 1938 and 1939 recounted attacks by "a razor-welding maniac" until police determined that the episode was entirely imaginary (Sieveking 1993).

A variant of slasher-related social delusions involves rumors of sporadic episodes of cattle "mutilations" reported across the midwestern United States between 1969 and 1980 (Stewart 1977; Hines 1988, pp. 278–280). During this period hundreds of dead cattle were found with one or more parts missing, most commonly the sex organs, ears, or mouth. The episodes occurred amid rumors that Satan worshippers or extraterrestrials were responsible. The widespread belief in the existence of extraterrestrial visitants was common in the United States during this period (Bartholomew 1991b, p. 6), with several popular books (Smith 1976; Dalton 1980) and television programs (e.g., Howe 1980) suggesting an association between perceived mutilations and either cultists or extraterrestrials. Hundreds of circumstantial UFO and cult-related press speculations appeared during this period in ordinarily credible media,[33] lending further plausibility to the rumors. As mutilation stories gained widespread media attention within the affected areas, the number of cases rose dramatically. Although the organs of dead cattle are often consumed by various natural predators, many ranchers—who would not ordinarily pay close attention to their animal carcasses—in the presence of the mutilation publicity began scrutinizing the cadavers for evidence of alleged alien or cultic surgical removal of body parts. According to sociologist James R. Stewart (1977, pp. 64–65), the "mutilations" were caused by small nocturnal predators that are unable to easily penetrate cattle hides, gravitating to the most exposed and softest parts, with sharp side teeth giving the impression of surgical incisions. The lack of blood in many of the animals provided credence to the blood-cult rumors, despite veterinarians' cautioning that the blood in dead animals coagulates after several days, giving the impression that the carcasses were drained.[34]

Widespread observations of phantom airships across the United States during 1896–1897 coincided with the U.S. national obsession with science, invention, and rationalism at the time. Voluminous plausible newspaper speculation, in conjunction with numerous highly publicized attempts at powered flight, resulted in tens of thousands of citizens misperceiving mundane astronomical and meteorological phenomena as airships with a technological capability far exceeding that of the period (Sanarov 1981; Bartholomew 1990a, 1991b). The sightings served as a projected Rorschach inkblot test of the collective psyche, underscoring the promise of rapid technological advancement during a period of spiritual decline (Bartholomew 1991b). The Rorschach inkblot test was designed by Swiss psychiatrist Hermann Rorschach and involves a subject interpreting inkblot designs that reflect his or her inner feelings. It is interesting to note that since mass sightings of flying saucers were first reported globally after Idaho businessman Kenneth Arnold's highly publicized 1947 report, many persons involved in small-group "UFO" sightings and who believe they may have been abducted, scanned, or exposed to alien power sources report transient breathing difficulties, dizziness, blurred vision, rashes, headache, and itchy or watery eyes (common anxiety-related features), consistent with the "encounter" scenarios (see Bartholomew, Basterfield, and Howard 1991).

In another example, on May 25, 1953, upwards of 150,000 people converged on a 10-acre site surrounding a well at Rincorn, Puerto Rico, to observe the predicted appearance of the Virgin Mary by seven local children at 11 A.M. As the hour approached, many miracles were reported: colored rings appeared around the sun, an image of the Virgin was silhouetted among the clouds, the infirm were healed, and a general sense of well-being prevailed (Tumin and Feldman 1955). By 5 P.M., when most of the crowd had dispersed, others who had been in attendance reported that they saw or experienced nothing extraordinary. Significantly, intense media publicity preceded the event, and a local politician enthusiastically endorsed the prediction, organizing the children to lead throngs of pilgrims in mass prayers and processions prior to the event (Goode 1992, p. 166). During the "miracle" a team of sociologists who mingled with the crowd and conducted interviews found that the majority of pilgrims believed in the authenticity of the children's claim and were seeking cures for either themselves or friends and relatives (Tumin and Feldman 1955). A variety of ambiguous objects in the immediate surroundings mirrored the hopeful and expectant religious state of mind of many participants at the time.[35]

On the night of July 29, 1992, beginning at about 11 P.M., about 200 students and a female instructor at the Hishamuddin Secondary Islamic School in Klang, Malaysia, observed a variety of seemingly miraculous sights in the sky during a five-hour period. These included the word *Allah* (God) in Arabic script (the language of the Islamic Holy Koran)—a total of twenty-six images were reported. The following evening at about 6:50 P.M., the words *Allah* and *Muhammad* reportedly appeared while students were praying in a school field.

The script was said to be much larger than that in the first episode. During both episodes the images were reportedly formed in, on, or by clouds. In all, students made twenty-six drawings of the perceived images (Abdullah, no date). Bartholomew (1993b) concludes that the pupils misperceived ambiguous nocturnal stimuli (clouds) reflective of their strict religious regimen at the school.[36]

Each of the episodes listed in Table 4.1 is characterized by the existence of plausible rumors of perceived importance that gave widespread credibility to the likely presence of a particular fantastic belief. In attempting to confirm or deny the rumors, individuals focused extraordinary attention on rumor-related objects—be it mundane lacerations (Jacobs 1965), ever-present windscreen pits (Medalia and Larsen 1958), or genitalia (Mun 1968). Ambiguity, anxiety, and extreme positive (e.g., Yassa 1980) or negative (e.g., Johnson 1945) emotions were present, as was the redefinition of a situation from general and ambiguous to specific and absolute. In other words, each of the episodes of epidemic koro in Table 4.1 shares a constellation of elements which suggest that mass koro "outbreaks" are a social delusion and not collective psychopathology.

PSYCHIATRIC ENTITY OR THE CONSEQUENCES OF BELIEFS?

The use of universalist approaches to evaluate unusual or unfamiliar behavior patterns such as koro, or seemingly bizarre Western beliefs such as the existence of phantom mutilators, heavenly saviors, extinct or legendary creatures, fails to adequately assess the significance of transcultural realities. Social realities need only be plausible to the affected groups, no matter how seemingly implausible they appear to those outside of the particular affected social dynamic. Koro-related beliefs alter perceptual sets and are formed within a complex mosaic of social, cultural, physiological, and cognitive influences. By focusing on the "exotic" nature of koro-folk realities per se and underemphasizing their specific social and cultural context in engendering extreme anxiety, Western-trained scientists place their own social realities (including the speculative art of psychoanalysis) as superior, with their implicit assumption that no rational or psychologically healthy individual in his or her "right mind" could possibly believe their genitalia, nose, ears, or tongue were shrinking and that death may ensue. As a result, unfamiliar social reality is viewed as an "exotic" syndrome; fear appropriate to the perceived circumstance becomes "sexual neurosis" and "panic reaction"; the consequences of anxiety are viewed as "hysterical conversion"; concern over sexual potency is interpreted as "obsession," "phobia," and "castration anxiety"; and cultural tradition is mistranslated as "delusionary belief."

Participants in charismatic religious movements commonly experience a variety of transient signs, symptoms, conditions, and states that are the consequences of beliefs and emotional zeal, such as psychomotor agitation, ecstatic states, fainting, tingling, uncontrollable crying, laughing, and visions. Western psychiatry no longer typifies these meaning-oriented expressions of emotions and beliefs as disorders or syndromes, as in recent years various minority religious movements have gained popularity and familiarity in Western countries.

The continuing hypocritical designation of epidemic koro as a convenient, singular psychiatric rubric is a classic example of the medicalization of "exotic" deviance (Bartholomew 1994a, 1994b, 1994d, 1995a, 1995b). To devalue foreign social realities—that is to say, those beliefs defined as such by Western-trained scientists—because of the fantastic nature of the beliefs or to classify them as exemplifying irrationality or psychopathology is to obscure their symbolic meaning whereby diversity is transformed into eccentricity and variance becomes abnormality. To medicalize the perceptual consequences of deviant worldviews and resultant psychosomatic reactions is to deprive the non-Western world of its own cultural heritage and to ignore and censor the enormously rich and diverse ethnographic record.

SUMMARY

In this chapter I have examined the characteristic features of individual koro cases, whereby victims believe their genitalia are shrinking. Recorded cases of individual koro are rare, comprising approximately forty incidents in the scientific literature. Perceptions of genitalia shrinkage have been correlated with major physiological precipitants such as schizophrenia, tumors, urogenital operations, and drug ingestion. A second category involves subjects unambiguously suffering from psychosexual disturbances and body image disorders. Episodes involving collective perceptions of genitalia shrinkage are also typified by scientists as examples of psychosexual and body image disturbances on a mass scale.

However, superimposing medical and psychiatric models of individual koro causation to collective episodes is unsubstantiated. The characteristic features of individual koro are different from epidemic forms, with the latter corresponding to the major features of a collective social delusion. Koro epidemics (1) occur in cultures with social or cultural traditions and beliefs of its existence as a genuine disease entity, (2) persist for a very brief period (virtually all "victims" recover fully within a few hours to a week and always within one month), and (3) involve symptoms reflecting the consequences of anxiety following exposure to koro-related rumors deemed plausible by participants. In accounting for the reason epidemic koro continues to be labeled a form of mass psychopathology, I have suggested that it is principally a result of the "bizarre" nature of the behavior per se, relative to medical and psychiatric theories of koro dominated by narrow Western-biased conceptions of normality. In other words, Western scientists find it incredible that any psychologically normal person could believe his or her genitalia were shrinking and will eventually disappear and they will die as a result. Further, these universalist theorists have failed to adequately assess the impact of the social and cultural koro-related beliefs of those affected and the context of "victims." The medicalization of collective koro is yet one more example where "exotic" culture-specific behaviors that appear strange or unfamiliar to Western scientists have been evaluated without adequately assessing their local meaning and cultural context.

Chapter 5 examines "dancing mania," or Saint Vitus' dance, which occurred in medieval Europe. These behaviors included zealous public dancing, singing, screaming, shouting, alcohol consumption, and orgies that often persisted for days or weeks and coincided with stressful events such as plagues and famines. They are typified within the psychiatric and medical literature as culture-specific examples of stress-induced mass psychopathology. However, by scrutinizing the history, context, and meaning of the "dancing mania," I shall argue that an alternative nonpsychopathological explanation can best explain these episodes—that they were history- and culture-specific forms of religious worship in expectation of divine assistance with earthly problems.

NOTES

1. The most comprehensive description of these texts is provided by Gwee (1963).

2. For exceptions, refer to Bartholomew (1994b, 1998e). Hotopf and Mullen (1992), in a brief letter to the *British Journal of Psychiatry*, note that in societies with koro-related beliefs, individual and epidemic cases may manifest "in otherwise healthy people." Both Wolfgang Jilek (1986, p. 280) and Ng (1997, p. 357) attribute collective episodes to "mass hysteria," although it is not explicitly clear what they mean by this.

3. A delusion is commonly defined by psychiatrists as a false conviction or belief that exists despite evidence to the contrary and that is not supported by members of the deluded person's sociocultural milieu. Delusions are characteristic of certain types of mental disorders.

4. References to koro are found in Mandarin (*suoyang, suo-yang*), Cantonese (*suk-yang, sookyong*), parts of mainland China (*shook yang, shook yong, suk-yong,* and *so in tchen*), and among the Buginese (*lasa koro*) in southern Sulawesi. All of these words translate into "shrinking penis" (see, respectively, Rubin 1982, p. 155; Jilek 1986, p. 269; Tseng et al. 1988, p. 1538; Prins 1990, p. 52; Van Wulfften-Palthe 1936, p. 536; Edwards 1984, p. 2; Legendre 1936). Among the Tagabawa Bagobo peoples of south-central Mindanao, the Philippines, it is termed *lannuk e laso* (approximate translation "retracting penis") (Payne in Edwards 1984, p. 7). In sections of northeast India it is

referred to as *jinjinia* ("tingling") or *jhinjhini* ("tingling disease"), *disco* near Calcutta (a generic word for any type of novelty), and *kattao* ("cut off") among the Northern Bengalese (see, respectively, Dutta, Phookan, and Das 1982; Sachdev and Shukla 1982; Chakraborty, Das, and Mukherji 1983). In Thailand the term is *Rok Joo* (Edwards 1984, p. 17).

5. I am employing the more neutral term B.P. ("before present") as opposed to the Christian reference of human historical chronological measurement, B.C. ("before Christ").

6. Based on traditional Chinese humoral medical theories, it is widely believed that koro-related conditions result from an imbalance of the yin (female) and yang (male) forces. Koro occurs when the yin dominates the yang, whereby any protruding male or female body parts are considered to be yang (i.e., penis, breasts, nipples, tongue, nose, hands, feet, and ears) and can potentially shrink or retract (Gwee 1963; Prince 1992a). Hence, curative or prophylactic measures include the application or consumption of yang elements, such as ginger, powdered black pepper, liquor, or red pepper jam, or tying the penis with a yam stem (Tseng et al. 1988). A second, separate belief system engenders koro epidemics on Hainan Island, China, involving ghosts and fox spirits who steal penises (Prince 1992a, p. 128).

7. Although this does not explain why females also experience koro, Raymond Prince (1992a, p. 119) notes that male episodes are more serious and common, and he is unable to locate a single female case description. However, the neglect of female cases may be an artifact of the historically male-dominated medical profession. For instance, of the cases investigated by Sachdev and Shukla (1982), nearly as many females as males were affected. A supporting factor may involve prohibitions in some societies with koro traditions, such as parts of Indonesia where males are not allowed to assist "victims" by holding the vulva or nipples (Slot 1935). Further, the male genitals appear to be more physiologically plastic than female breasts, nipples, or vulva. The male testicles and penis are vital for reproduction (although the penis may not be essential in the case of in vitro fertilization), whereas the female breast and nipples are not. Of the female breasts, nipples, or vulva, the latter, more vital organ shows the least physiological plasticity.

8. Many contemporary investigators support the theme of castration anxiety in precipitating individual (Fishbain, Barsky, and Goldberg 1989, p. 90) and epidemic koro (e.g., Nandi and Banerjee 1986; Kirmayer 1992; Gerlach 1995). However, Jilek (1985, p. 207) observes that acceptance of the influence of Freudian Oedipal castration anxiety in triggering mass koro would require its exclusive confinement to males, onset precipitated by circumstances "interpreted as somehow analogous to the Oedipal constellation of male childhood," and the link between onset and "sexual relationships that have some metaphoric or symbolic incestual connotation." Yet based on data gathered during koro epidemics, the Oedipal castration anxiety perspective cannot account for epidemics involving a significant portion of females, the rare association between sexual activity and onset among collectivities, and finally the supposed projection of paranoia toward an "outgroup which is widely perceived as posing a threat to the survival of the patient's ethnic-cultural group. Such a clearly defined social situation would not lend itself easily to identification with an Oedipal constellation" (Jilek 1985, p. 208).

9. Although human sexual experiences are governed by biological processes like the acquisition of language or mores, their expressions are primarily a symbolic, scripted

process. The range of expressions particular cultures or subcultures consider to be "normal" sexual practice or experience is historically diverse and variable, both transculturally (Ford and Beach 1951; Bullough 1976) and intraculturally (Kinsey, Pomeroy, and Martin 1948; Kinsey et al. 1953; Plummer 1984). Kevin Howells (1984, p. 2) notes that when it comes to evaluating sexual diversity, "psychologists, doctors and other scientists are often poor cultural and temporal relativists."

Sexual norms and experiences within whole societies have included homosexual relations between an older male and a boy in both fifth-century Athens, Greece (Simon 1978, p. 193) and among certain peoples in contemporary Paupa New Guinea (Shweder 1984, p. 29), public bestiality in Brazil, and open masturbation of children in Bali (Doug Miles, personal communication, May 1, 1996).

10. As discussed in Chapter 1, a classic example is the claim that Nazi adherents and German society during World War II were psychologically disturbed.

11. These drawings were made retrospective to the epidemics and may have reflected greater genital anxiety and concern (vis-à-vis controls) as a result of previous traumatic koro experiences.

12. For example, in an Indian epidemic the majority of cases lasted between 15 and 60 minutes (Sachdev and Shukla 1982), whereas in China 60 percent of the subjects surveyed experienced symptoms from 20 to 60 minutes in duration (Tseng et al. 1988, p. 1540). In all collective episodes, subjects may experience occasional relapses, but symptoms always dissipate within a few days, although genital-related anxiety may endure. Ilechukwu (1992, p. 95), reports that korolike symptoms (sensations of vanishing genitalia) in Nigeria typically last only a few minutes.

13. Although koro has been associated with phimosis (de Leo, Mauro, and Pellegrini 1989), urogenital system pathology (Cohen et al. 1995), prostate removal (Puranik and Dunn 1995), brain tumors (Lapierre 1972; Durst and Rosca-Rebaudengo 1988), and stroke (Anderson 1990), these patients typically have identifiable affective disorders accompanying their organic disturbances.

14. For example, intake of anti-Parkinsonian medication (Chen 1991), abuse of various drugs (Dow and Silver 1973), and cannabis smoking (Chowdhury and Bera 1994), as well as during heroin withdrawal. These cases typically have a sexual component. In the episode of koro in a twenty-six-year-old Hindu, the man not only exhibited affective disorder, but increased masturbation as a coping response to withdrawal, induced discernible reduction in penis size from diminished vascular congestion (Chowdhury and Bagchi 1993).

15. Tseng and colleagues (1988, p. 1538) note that most of Berrois and Morley's subjects "manifested incomplete symptoms (as a koro case is defined). Such korolike states, as secondary symptoms, are usually observed as a part of the primary psychiatric condition, such as affective disorder or psychosis." For instance, in most individual cases in settings with no prior knowledge of the phenomenon, a belief that the penis will fully retract—with fatal consequences—is not reported.

16. Mun (1968, p. 641) states that sporadic cases of individual koro were treated by Singaporean physicians annually for at least a decade prior to the 1967 episode, adding that of the cases examined by twelve doctors in Singapore during 1967, all patients had previous koro knowledge.

17. The following firsthand case description is typical and was reported on May 20, 1985, by an eighteen-year-old agricultural student with no family history of mental illness, on Hainan Island near the end of a major epidemic:

> I woke up at midnight and felt sore and numb in my genitals. I felt with my hands . . . [and my penis was] the size of a fingertip; it was shrinking, disappearing. I yelled for help, my family and neighbours came and held my penis. They covered me with a fish net and beat me with branches of a peach tree. . . . The peach tree branches are the best to drive out ghosts or devils. They said they'd catch the ghost in the net. They were also beating drums and setting off firecrackers. They said it was a fox ghost that got into my body, a female fox spirit, she wants to catch the male genitals. They yelled, 'Get out of him, fox ghost!' They pulled my genitals at the same time as they beat me under the net. . . . I felt better after about one hour but at 2 A.M. I felt my genitals shrinking again. They had to repeat the procedure until I was well again, until the ghost was killed by the beating. The fox ghost is dead when the genitals are coming out again. Now I have no complaints, sleep well, no worries. (Jilek 1986, p. 276)

18. For a translation and discussion of the article by Legendre, the first known detailed documented case of collective koro, refer to Robert Bartholomew and Jane Gregory (1996).

19. Tseng and colleagues (1992) conducted detailed psychometric testing of 214 epidemic koro victims (41 female) in southern China, with a control group of 153 subjects and a third group of 56 patients presenting with minor psychiatric conditions. Surprisingly, the controls tested highest for levels of problems associated with work, school, and their interpersonal lives. The only aberrant findings among the koro subjects were elevated phobic and anxiety levels, but no differences with controls were found on subscales related to neurasthenia, hypochondriasis, and dissociation—suggesting that koro should not be classified as a depersonalization condition or dissociative disorder, whereas the similarity with controls for symptoms of neurasthenia or hypochondriasis argues against its placement as a somatoform disorder (see Kirmayer 1992, pp. 137–139). Although on the basis of these findings Laurence Kirmayer (1992, p. 139) concludes that koro appears to be a condition evoked by severe anxiety exacerbated by folk beliefs and social stresses, he also describes koro as a pathogenic syndrome related to castration anxiety.

20. Surprisingly, no cases were reported among the Chinese who comprise the country's largest ethnic minority. This may be because not many Chinese in Thailand are from Guangzhou or Hainan Island, and most Chinese in Thailand are urbanized.

21. The first known recorded Indian case of koro was reported during 1981 in a psychotic patient but was not associated with the mass episode (see Shukla and Mishra 1981).

22. This conclusion by Sachdev and Shukla (1982, p. 1161) is made despite noting that the typical maladjusted, sexually immature personality characteristics found among koro subjects (see Yap 1965) "were lacking, sexual histories did not usually suggest conflicts or maladjustment in most cases, [and] patients had generally been well-

adjusted previously (though about one-third had significant anxiety traits and depen-
dence-passivity)."

23. This condition is called "magical" in Nigeria as it is widely believed to be caused
by persons with magical powers.

24. The *Transcultural Psychiatric Research Review* 25, p. 314, 1988, also makes
reference to a "minor outbreak" of korolike symptoms in Lagos, Nigeria, during 1979.

25. This pattern contrasts with isolated individual koro cases in association with
mental disorder or organ disease, which typically endure for weeks or months and, if the
underlying pathology is untreated, can persist indefinitely.

26. T. Raven (1886, p. 250) describes a physician-investigated case of penile
hyperinvolution:

> A. B-. a healthy, steady, single man, aged twenty-seven years, shortly after
> he had gone to bed one night, felt a sensation of cold in the region of the
> penis. He was agitated to find that the organ, a fairly developed one, was
> rapidly shrinking, and was, he thought, finally retiring. He at once gave the
> alarm, and I was hastily summoned from my bed to attend him. I found
> him highly nervous and alarmed. The penis had almost disappeared, the
> glans being just perceptible under the pubic arch. The skin of the penis
> alone was visible, and looking as it does when the organ is buried in a
> hydrocele, or, in an extreme degree, as it does after death by drowning. I
> reassured him, and gave him some ammonia, and found [the] next day that
> the natural state of things had returned. But he remained weak and
> nervous for some days. He could give no explanation of the occurrence, and
> the un-natural condition has never returned.

27. As an example of penile plasticity, it is routine practice for all boys among the
Tupari and Tapirape peoples of South America to luxate this organ, whereby except
during urination or copulation "it is completely tucked inside his body" (Devereux
1980, p. 316).

28. In the single case examined, the investigators remarked that reduction in penis
size may be normal, but the subject's awareness is increased "by personal factors, such as
obsessional self-scrutiny or sexual conflicts" (Oyebode, Jamieson, and Davison 1986, p.
214).

29. In one report (Emsley 1985) a primary psychiatric condition was effectively
treated, yet koro persisted. However, the case description, in the form of a brief ten-
sentence letter, suggested the likelihood of significant sexual conflicts, as the subject had
experienced fear of impotence over 8 months after being unwillingly circumcised in a
tribal ritual, with the koro occurring immediately following erectile failure while attempting coitus. David Fishbain and colleagues (1989, p. 90) speculate that "perhaps
if these conflicts were [unambiguously] present, and would have been addressed the
Koro would have resolved." Berrios and Morley (1984) successfully treated a patient
with phenelzine and behavior therapy after a 20-year history of koro episodes associated
with agoraphobia.

30. Overvalued notions or delusions regarding damaged or impaired sexual organs
can be found in schizophrenics (see Gittelson and Levine 1966). Many examples
involve koro and schizophrenia (see Edwards 1970; Cremona 1981; Devan and Hong

1987). A description by Kendall and Jenkins (1987) involves a koro patient who had delusions of having "the largest penis in the world" and shortly thereafter that he was changing into a woman.

31. Sociologist Neil J. Smelser's (1962) widely used paradigm typifies this position. Most mass hysteria studies implicitly or explicitly utilize his value-added theory of collective behavior, which emphasizes the role of grandiose structural elements in facilitating irrational, abnormal "hysterical" episodes. However, although Smelser's perspective is used to argue that such elements as extraordinary ambiguity, anxiety, and structural strains are present in all episodes, these categories are only identified retrospective to "outbreaks" and are so vaguely defined as to be present in all societies during all periods (Bartholomew 1989a). Many investigators relate epidemic koro to societal strains. For instance, Ilechukwu (1992) links the epidemic of magical penis "loss" in Nigeria during 1990 to political and economic upheavals, and Kan-Ming Mo (1991) associates a series of koro epidemics in southern China since 1948 with social and political tensions.

32. Mass panics are often typified as exemplifying collective irrationality. Yet such incidents are characterized by plausibility and a degree of realism for the participants. During the *War of the Worlds* broadcast, of an estimated 6 million people who heard the radio drama, about 1.2 million were frightened, believing it to be a real event (Cantril 1947 [1940]). Bainbridge (1987) contends that relatively few people panicked, arguing that Princeton University psychologist Hadley Cantril, who undertook the first major study of the episode, quotes a few colorful stories from a small number of people who claimed to have panicked. Bainbridge contends that on any given night, out of a pool of over 1 million people, at least a thousand would have been driving excessively fast or engaging in rambunctious behavior. In this manner, various ever-present actions were reinterpreted following media reports of the panic as attributed to the fictitious Martian invasion. From this perspective the event was primarily a news media creation. However, a similar broadcast in South America 11 years later erupted indisputably into a full-fledged panic. During 1949, in the vicinity of Quito, Ecuador, a radio play based on the *War of the Worlds* novel resulted in tens of thousands of frantic residents pouring into the streets and fleeing for their lives or preparing to defend themselves. Broadcast in Spanish, the program was highly realistic, including the name of a local community, Cotocallo, as the Martian landing site. The play included impersonations of politicians and vivid eyewitness descriptions and was so convincing that police gallantly rushed to the nearby town to repel the invaders. Quito was left with a skeleton police presence that was unable to prevent an angry mob from burning down the building housing the radio station that broadcast the drama, in which fifteen people—including the mastermind of the event—were killed. For a detailed description of this episode, refer to Anonymous (1949).

Other radio adaptations of *The War of the Worlds* have had less dramatic consequences. A widespread panic was triggered in parts of Chile following a broadcast of the Wells play by a radio station in Santiago on November 12, 1944. In one province the governor briefly placed troops and artillery on alert. The broadcast was highly realistic and included the use of an actor to impersonate the interior minister (Bulgatz 1992, p. 137). Other broadcasts frightened listeners in the vicinity of Providence, Rhode

Island, at 11 P.M. on October 31, 1974, and in northern Portugal in 1988 (Bulgatz 1992, p. 139).

33. See for examples, Cattle Mutilations Remain a Mystery, *Eagle River News Review* (Wisconsin), January 26, 1978; Mystery Still Surrounds Animal Mutilations, *Springdale News* (Arizona), November 26, 1978; Tracking the Cattle Mutilators: Satanic Groups Suspected, *Newsweek* 95, p. 16 (January 21, 1980); Did Horse Mutilator Come From Outer Space, *Gastonia Gazette* (North Carolina), May 24, 1980; Cattle Ripper Returns, the *Sun* (Edmonton, Alberta, Canada), September 17, 1981; Dluce Rancher Loses Another Cow to Mysterious Mutilation, *Albuquerque Journal* (New Mexico), May 31, 1982.

34. In terms of legitimation by institutions of social control and authority figures, during April 1979 the U.S. federal government approved a US$44,170 grant to investigate a series of mutilations in New Mexico. Despite finding only prosaic explanations—predators, scavengers, and decomposition—U.S. Senator and former astronaut Harrison Schmitt continued to focus national attention on the issue by urging the United States Justice Department to initiate a separate probe into the cause of the cattle mutilations (Olson 1980). For an examination of the apparent genesis of the cattle mutilation myth, refer to Bartholomew (1992b).

35. Numerous similar journalistic reports document religious faithful claiming to observe miraculous events or objects. In 1986 a devout Catholic grandmother, Rita Ratchen, residing in a tiny Ohio town, saw what appeared to be a miraculous image on the side of a soybean oil tank. The yellowish-orange tank had rust spots that resembled an image of a man dressed in robes with outstretched arms. A child appeared next to the man. The figure was thought to be that of Jesus Christ. Once the media reported the story, hundreds of people began flocking to the tower, many of whom agreed that it contained a miraculous image. It is noteworthy that the tower "image" was highly ambiguous. The perceived figures were so faint that when a local newspaper published a picture of the tower, the editor solicited an artist to enhance the photos!

In 1988 a somewhat similar incident occurred at a church in Lubbock, Texas. The pastor had recently returned from a pilgrimage to the former Yugoslavia, where visions of the Virgin Mary had been reported for years. Several miraculous occurrences were claimed by Lubbock church members, including smelling an odor resembling roses and receiving messages allegedly delivered by the Virgin Mary to at least three parishioners. In August 1988 about 12,000 people were attending a celebration of the Virgin Mary's alleged ascension into heaven when several extraordinary events were claimed. One man said he could see a flock of doves flying over the church. Sociologist Erich Goode remarks that during a mass conducted near dusk, some crowd members shrieked as the sun began to shine through the clouds. In response, "Some prayed, and some pointed toward the clouds. Others said they saw Jesus in the clouds, some saw Mary, and some saw heaven's gates. Church deacons took testimony from individuals who had seen visions and apparitions." For a discussion of these two cases, refer to Goode (1992, p. 171).

36. A similar incident was reported on June 12, 1990, in Algeria when the Islamic Salvation Front Party won an upset election victory. While the party leader was speaking to a crowd of supporters standing and shouting "*Allah Akhbar*" (God is great!) in the

direction of the Muslim Holy City of Mecca, a cloud reportedly formed the shape of the word *Allah* (refer to the *Daily Telegraph* [London], June 16, 1990). Since 1990 there have been numerous reports of Muslims reporting the appearance of Islamic symbols, most typically Arabic script, in various countries and settings.

5

Medieval Dancing Manias as History-Specific Variants of "Mass Psychogenic Illness": A Critique and Reappraisal

The interpretive study of culture represents an attempt to come to terms with the diversity of the ways human beings construct their lives in the act of leading them. . . .

To see ourselves as others see us can be eye-opening. . . . But it is from the far more difficult achievement of seeing ourselves amongst others, as a local example of the forms human life has locally taken, a case among cases, a world among worlds, that the largeness of mind . . . comes. If interpretive anthropology has any general office in the world it is to keep reteaching this fugitive truth (Clifford Geertz 1983, p. 16).

DANCING MANIA AS "EPIDEMIC HYSTERIA"

Many within the male-dominated contemporary psychiatric community accept that females are innately susceptible to communicable hysteria. Scientists commonly support this position by noting that the preponderance of female participants in episodes of collective hysteria is historically well documented. This chapter examines the earliest known recorded episodes of behavior labeled epidemic hysteria: two types of deviant collective behavior that became prominent in parts of Europe during the late Middle Ages—namely, tarantism and dancing mania—typified within mainstream psychiatric nomenclature as exemplifying culture and history-specific variants of a unitary hysterical psychiatric entity.[1] This widely held assumption is deconstructed as a category fallacy, and the argument is advanced that such diagnoses are based on subjective, ambiguous categories that reflect the unsubstantiated view that females are innately susceptible to collective conversion symptoms, underemphasizing or ignoring the significance of episodes as culturally conditioned roles of social action. "Victims" are typified as psychologically disturbed females possessing abnormal personality characteristics who are exhibiting cathartic reactions to stress (Deutsch 1967, pp. 1–38; Millon 1969, pp. 6–7; Bromberg 1975; Duke and Nowicki 1986, p. 47; Meyer and Salmon 1988, p. 17). However, a more plausible explanation is that episodes involve normal, rational participants who possess unfamiliar conduct codes, worldviews, and political agendas that differ significantly from those of Western-trained investigators who have judged these illness behaviors independent of their local context and meaning (Bartholomew 1998a). The significance of examining these behaviors and exposing this myth is that they continue to be cited as compelling evidence for pejorative contemporary reckless labeling of females as hysterical.[2]

Conversion hysteria is a term devised by Sigmund Freud and refers to the presentation of physical complaints for which there is no organic basis. The term *mass psychogenic illness* (MPI) is frequently used interchangeably with mass or "epidemic" hysteria and hysterical contagion as the most common contemporary designation to describe the collective occurrence of a constellation of similar symptoms and related beliefs that have no plausible pathogenic explanation (see Olkinuora 1984; Hall and Johnson 1989).[3] Mass "sickness" judged to be of psychogenic origin is typically viewed as abnormal behavior (Wessely 1987, p. 118; Appleby and Forshaw 1990, p. 314), paralleling mental disorders (Tseng and McDermott 1981, p. 69), or as an explicit example of socially shared psychopathology (Sirois 1974).[4] Symptoms include one or a combination of complaints, most commonly hyperventilation, headache, abdominal pain with and without nausea and vomiting, tremor, itching and rash, dizziness, fainting, and malaise (see Bartholomew 1990b, p. 466).[5]

Some of the symptoms reported in episodes of mass psychogenic illness are not considered to be illness categories in the conventional Western medical tradition but characteristics of collective actions Western-trained investigators would typically classify as unusual behavior. For instance, laughing, crying, and running are not typically considered to be illness symptoms, yet several episodes of this nature were reported in East Africa during the twentieth century and received the label of "epidemic" hysterical illness. The following report is characteristic of such "outbreaks":

> NAIROBI, Kenya, 8 Aug. Mass hysteria was suggested as the most likely answer today to the epidemic of laughing sickness along the shores of Lake Victoria.

"I am certain that the outbreak does not have an organic basis," said Dr. Alexander Rankin, one of the medical investigators who uncovered the epidemic.

"It must be purely mental," he said. "People in this area are highly superstitious."

More than 1,000 Africans, most of them youngsters, have suffered fits of laughing and crying in the outbreak in the last 18 months.

No deaths were reported, but the sickness has lasted from several hours to 16 days. The average has been seven days.

"Abnormal emotional behavior may be spread from person to person, giving the impressions of an epidemic," Dr. Rankin said.

No teachers, policemen, village headmen or other relatively sophisticated adults in the area have contracted the symptoms.

The epidemic has centered around the village of Bukoba in Tanganyika, on the western shores of Lake Victoria. (Anonymous 1963a, p. 4)[6]

Other primary "symptoms" reported during similar East African incidents include general disobedience to authority, destruction of missionary schools, and violence. These characteristics suggest that episodes in this part of the world may represent culturally conditioned forms of deviant social behavior or political protest. For instance, during an investigation of three "laughing mania" episodes in Tanzania during the early 1960s, G. J. Ebrahim (1968, p. 437) remarked that natives believed the symptoms were a response to the wishes of ancestral spirits: "Patients ran about aimlessly, sleeping out of doors near ancestral graves. They frequently wore white chicken feathers on their heads or a twig from a specific tree." Native healers conducted sacrifices to appease the spirits believed responsible. Although such descriptions suggest the potentially significant role of anthropolitical factors[7] in facilitating and patterning the "mania," investigators have not vigorously pursued these lines of inquiry. Claims that such actions are either disordered or hysterical have been made using ambiguous and arbitrary criteria.

Based on a literature review, most MPI incidents occur within closed, cohesive social settings: schools, factories, convents, and hospitals. Episodes typically begin with a single individual exhibiting various ambiguous somatic complaints that often appear dramatic, such as fainting or hyperventilation, arousing considerable anxiety among others in the group or observers. Other group members, most commonly females, exhibit the rapid spread of similar symptoms. Personal observations of stricken cohorts, rumors, and media publicity exacerbate the spread of symptoms. Incidents may span from a few hours, such as overbreathing among marching band members (e.g., Pfeiffer

1964), to recurrent episodes persisting for several years, such as demonopathy in Christian convents (e.g., Madden 1857), and even centuries, as in the case of tarantism, although most cases last a few days to one month. The incident is usually preceded by an atmosphere of social stress and the presence of an unusual agent, such as an insect or a strange odor. An investigation of the immediate environment reveals no harmful levels of toxic substances, and medical evaluations of those affected are inconclusive. The episode usually declines once authority figures reassure victims that the offending agent either did not exist or was eliminated. Discussion that the incident was a form of mass hysteria is typically met with hostile resistance and can hamper further cooperation between investigators and those affected.

THEORIES OF "MASS PSYCHOGENIC ILLNESS"

No single dominant explanation of MPI exists, and many of the theories utilized are not considered mutually exclusive. Perhaps the earliest explanation is the supernatural agent perspective, which holds that victims are possessed by evil or benevolent spirits. This popular folk theory was prevalent during episodes of collective demon possession that appeared in dozens of European Christian convents between 1494 and 1662. Symptoms included fainting, twitching, shaking, hallucinations, choking, suffocation, globus, vomiting, laryngismus, and paralysis (Calmeil 1845; Madden 1857; Huxley 1952). These temporary episodes usually subsided once the "devils" were exorcised and the offending "witch" was identified and punished. Similar symptoms and beliefs were recorded during the Salem witch trials of 1692, in addition to historical and contemporary accounts of benevolent spirit possession in various ecstatic religious movements such as the Dutch and German Anabaptists between 1521 and 1592, French Calvinists between 1686 and 1706, and Janeist convulsionaries in 1731. Modern episodes within non-Western countries continue to be attributed to the work of supernatural forces, such as ancestral bush entities in Papua New Guinea (Frankel 1976), *jin* spirits in Malaysia (Teoh, Soewondo, and Sidharta 1975), the female fox ghost in regions of China, and spirits of deceased relatives in Tanzania (Ebrahim 1968).

Another prominent explanation considered the likelihood that some or all participants were consciously feigning illness or unusual behavior for social or monetary benefit. This opinion was espoused by Dominico Cirillo, an Italian natural history professor who implied that tarantism episodes were created to generate money for musicians who were required to perform curative tarantellas (Cirillo 1770), whereas others participated for companionship (Sigerist 1943, p. 221). Justus Friedrich Hecker (1970 [1837], pp. 3-4) states that vagabonds imitated the European dancing mania to seek vice, food, and adventure. More recently, this theory has been modified to include political gain. After 900 persons on the Jordan West Bank were reportedly made ill by mysterious "poison gas" attributed to Israeli sources, several physicians considered the condition factitious and a deliberate, conscious conspiracy among participants to foster anti-Israeli sentiment at the prompting of Palestinian sympathizers (Hafez 1985).

The "sick role" perspective holds that participants are involved in an unconscious desire to obtain various benefits. In their investigation of spasmodic twitching at a Louisiana high school, Schuler and Parenton (1943) note that the initial victim gained attention, sympathy, and avoidance of an undesirable situation. In addition to concern from friends and school officials, her illness status renewed the waning affection of a boyfriend and allowed her to avoid compulsory dance classes. The other subsequently afflicted girls were viewed as adopting the sick role for a variety of secondary gains after observing the success of the initial case. Instances may also involve the simultaneous presence of both conscious and unconscious efforts by participants to attain specific objectives, although the possibility of unanimous conspiratory deception cannot be excluded. An episode of collective "hysterical" tremor in a Swiss girls' school at Basel in 1893 and at the same school 11 years later was attributed to unconscious attempts to avoid school work (Aemmer 1893; Truper 1908).

Some episodes are attributed to various combinations of environmental, organic, and psychological causes. For example, Halley Faust and Lawrence Brilliant (1981) suggest that many incidents of "epidemic" psychogenic illness result solely from the interaction of low levels of toxicants, arguing that women and adolescents are vulnerable because of their relatively lower body weight. Although symptoms associated with "sick building syndrome" are commonly implicated as MPI, Bauer and colleagues (1992) conclude that "real environmental contaminants" account for the vast majority of sufferers. Harold Shapiro (1936) considered that an outbreak of apparent "epidemic" mental disorder by suggestion, involving visions and memory loss among the inhabitants of Pitcairn Island between 1880 and 1884, may have actually been caused by the noxious jimsonweed. Alice Hamilton (1943) concluded that an episode of "epidemic insanity" at a U.S. rayon plant during the 1930s was caused by carbon disulfide. Others contend that certain incidents are misdiagnoses of physical disease, such as chorea (Guthrie 1960, p. 100), epidemic malaise, neuromyasthenia, and atypical poliomyelitis (Stricklin, Sewell, and Austas 1990). Some incidents are viewed as being of primarily bacteriological or viral origin with secondary psychological elements, such as the outbreak of "epidemic" collapse at three British secondary schools, which was partially attributed to a virus (Pollock and Clayton 1964). A similarly mixed diagnosis was made by Levine (1977) in implicating heat stroke for the collapse of marching band members. Massey and colleagues (1981) suggest that involuntary convulsions during nocturnal religious revivals may have been triggered by epileptics experiencing seizures induced by flickering torches, which were quickly imitated by emotionally charged, suggestive followers.

Convergence theory suggests that persons with certain characteristics (e.g., needs, beliefs, purposes) are predisposed to MPI. Tseng and colleagues (1992) conclude, for instance, that a variety of somatic complaints associated with episodes of perceived penis shrinking in Guangdong province, China, are related to "low intellectual endowment." Small and Nicholi (1982) associate divorce and death of a family member with vulnerability to psychogenic symptoms among elementary school students near Boston. Other investigators have identified correlations with disciplinary problems (McEvedy, Griffith, and Hall 1966), neuroticism (Moss and McEvedy 1966), and hysterical traits (Knight, Friedman, and Sulianti 1965) with low socioeconomic status (Johnson 1945; Parigi and Biagiotti 1956).

In the absence of physical findings to suggest a specific organic cause, investigators rely on the presence of other criteria commonly believed to be MPI characteristics. Although no universally agreed set of criteria exists to determine an MPI diagnosis, the three most specific categories most often utilized reflect Western culture-biased stereotypes of normality that have yet to be substantiated. These include a preponderance of female victims, the existence of physical or psychological stress, and the increased presence of mental abnormality among those affected. In reevaluating the appropriateness of these characteristics, the earliest documented episodes of MPI will be scrutinized. The diagnostic criteria and theoretical framework for the modern-day designation of MPI as an illness category were established during the Middle Ages under the heading of "psychic epidemics" and were subsequently refined by contemporary social, medical, and psychiatric professionals. The view that tarantism and dancing mania participants were primarily females who were illiterate, mentally disturbed, and reacting to physical and social stress remains in effect today.

Episodes of dancing mania and tarantism are typically regarded as history-specific forms of MPI[8] (see Dhadphale and Shaikh 1983, p. 85; Olkinuora 1984, p. 501; Boxer 1985, p. 868; Gamino, Elkins, and Hackney 1989, p. 446; Selden 1989, p. 893), as is collective demon possession (Rosen 1968, pp. 205–207; Sirois 1982, pp. 218–219; Singer et al. 1982). The determination that these episodes should be placed under the MPI rubric is based on descriptive, retrospective judgments of primarily anecdotal evidence for which it is not possible to determine the presence of a viral, bacteriological, or toxicological agent.[9] Comparisons will be made between descriptions of tarantism, dancing mania, and demonopathy and specific diagnostic characteristics of MPI. This chapter challenges these interpretations, illustrating how scientists have imposed contemporary Eurocentric criteria of normality and rationality in their assessments, overlooking or underemphasizing the potential political, symbolic, and ritualistic aspects of the behavior under scrutiny.

TARANTISM

One of the earliest cited examples of seemingly bizarre behavior to be labeled as exemplifying MPI and group mental disturbance is what Harold Gloyne (1950, p. 29) terms the "mass hysterical reaction" to perceived bites of the tarantula spider during the Middle Ages in southern Italy. The first recorded description of this "contagious" mental "disease" classified by physicians as tarantism,[10] or less commonly tarantulism, appeared during the thirteenth century and persisted on a widespread scale in southern Europe for 400 years, reaching its height in the seventeenth century after which it died out.[11] Tarantism was reported almost exclusively during the height of the hot, dry summer months of July and August:

> People, asleep or awake, would suddenly jump up, feeling an acute pain like the sting of a bee. Some saw the spider, others did not, but they knew that it must be the tarantula. They ran out of the house into the street, to the market place dancing in great excitement. Soon they were joined by others who like them had just been bitten, or by people who had been stung in previous years, for the disease was never quite cured. The poison remained in the body and was reactivated every year by the heat of summer. . . .
>
> Music and dancing were the only effective remedies, and people were known to have died within an hour or in a few days because music was not available. (Sigerist 1943, pp. 218–219)

Symptoms experienced by participants included breathing difficulty, chest pain, headache, giddiness, fainting, trembling, vomiting, twitching, thirst, appetite loss, general soreness, and delusions. "Victims" occasionally claimed that a sore or swelling was precipitated from a tarantula bite, but such assertions were typically ambiguous and difficult to verify, as the bite appeared similar to that caused by other insects. These symptoms resemble typical modern episodes of mass psychogenic illness, in addition to expected reactions from engaging in periods of exhaustive physical activity and excessive alcohol consumption.

Psychiatrists typify tarantism as a form of MPI because of its psychogenic character and claims that the majority of those affected were females (e.g., Sigerist 1943, p. 218; Rosen 1968, p. 204). Although the identical species of tarantula is common throughout southern Europe and is considered relatively harmless, frenzied reactions to perceived bites were almost exclusively reported in the vicinity of the southern Italian state of Apulia.[12] Early medical observers theorized that a single bite from a venomous species of tarantula indigenous only to Apulia was capable of producing sporadic tarantism symptoms each summer, but modern investigators testing spiders of the region have failed to substantiate these suspicions (Gloyne 1950, p. 35).[13] Other psychogenic aspects include the only reliable cure: dancing to certain types of music. "Victims" would typically perform one of numerous versions of the tarantella, a rapid tempo score characterized by brief repetitive phrases that increase in intensity. Such performances also allowed "victims" to exhibit social behavior prohibited any other time. Dancing persisted intermittently for hours and days and sometimes weeks. Participants would eventually proclaim themselves "cured" for the remainder of the summer, only to relapse in subsequent summers. Many "victims" never claimed to have been bitten but were believed to have been infected from those who had or from simply brushing against a spider. All that was needed to reactivate the venom was to hear the strains of certain music being played to cure those who had been bitten. Claims of tarantism and the accompanying symptoms were almost exclusively confined to July and August.

ANTHROPOLOGICAL AND POLITICAL ASPECTS OF "MPI"

In basing judgment primarily on descriptions of the behavior per se, it is unsurprising that contemporary psychiatry typifies tarantism as a form of group psychopathology involving spontaneous chaotic outbursts of bizarre behavior. For instance, during dances many immodestly tore off their clothing and pranced naked through the streets. Some screamed and beckoned to be tossed into the air, and others danced furiously in what some observers described as strange, colorful attire. A few reportedly laughed or wept to the point of death. Women howled and made obscene gestures. Some participants rolled in the dirt, and others relished being struck on the soles of their feet.

Since the recording of tarantism and dancing manias by medical observers, various psychopathological explanations have been advanced. Naples physician Francesco Serao (1750) suggested that tarantism was prevalent among the Apulian lower class because of their tendency toward melancholy and unhealthy living conditions. Wilhelm Katner (1956) credits the scorching

Apulian climate for fostering delusions precipitated by heat exhaustion; a similar view is held by Turnbull (1771). In analyzing tarantism and related medieval "psychic epidemics," Rosen (1962, p. 15) remarks on the importance of not labeling "strange" or unfamiliar behaviors as psychopathological, even though certain groups may act in a bizarre manner by ordinary criteria. In the same article he presents compelling evidence that tarantism and dancing manias originated from traditional religious ceremonies. However, blinded by the scientific milieu of his day, Rosen assumes that these dance frenzies were "bizarre" cathartic reactions to a variety of overwhelming social, cultural, and economic stresses (Rosen 1962, pp. 42–43), the disorder attracting the mentally disturbed and being masked under the guise of such rites.

Another prominent twentieth-century medical historian, Henry Sigerist, in *Civilization and Disease* (1943, p. 225), also mentions striking similarities between ancient Greek rites and tarantism symptoms. Sigerist speculates that tarantism may have provided a means for the expression of traditional regional heathen customs—in this case a ritual composed almost exclusively of the neurotic, insane, and melancholy that was transformed over the years into the conscious or subconscious guise of being instigated by spider bites so as not to conflict with the rising prominence of Christianity. Like Rosen, Sigerist also assumes, based on predominate psychiatric theories of the period, that such activities attracted the mentally deranged. Sigerist (1943, p. 226) concludes that tarantism originated from Apulian inbreeding, as "there can be no doubt that the great majority of all tarantati were neurotics. Tarantism was a neurosis peculiar to that region." Psychiatrists Silvano Arieti and Eugene Brody (1972, p. 719) take a similar position in labeling such behavior "psychoneuroses of hysterical nature . . . induced by the effect the crowd had on the predisposed person." These investigators fail to address adequately the social and cultural patterning of episodes.

By focusing on "bizarre," descriptive aspects of tarantism per se, and blinded by Western culture-biased definitions of normality, researchers have overlooked its symbolic significance and the influence of existing social and cultural norms. Socially, the existence of tarantism in southern Italy was considered a fact. Medieval-period physicians legitimated its reality despite questions about its anomalous confinement to the Apulia region. Most sixteenth-century physicians held views similar to Italian medical authority Giorgio Baglivi (1723), that tarantulas in the vicinity of Apulia, when angry, produced a hallucinatory venom whose only reliable temporary cure was dancing to certain tunes. A clear relationship seems to exist between telesic or ritual madness in ancient Greece and tarantism. These collective rituals were intended to relieve anxiety and assure future happiness (Mora 1963, p. 430).

They were particularly geared toward arousing the interest of new participants to the benefits of uninhibited emotional release. Corybantoc rites, typically associated with telete rituals, are described in part as follows:

> The candidate was seated in a chair and the ministrants danced around him
> and raised a great din. The effect of this was to rouse his excitement and stir
> his emotions, so that he gradually lost consciousness of all but the whirling
> rhythm of the dance. This was followed by what was called telete proper, in
> which, we may suppose, the candidate threw himself into the dance with
> the rest and yielded to the intoxication of the rhythm. In the end, when all
> was over, the participants emerged from the tumult to a state of calm and
> tranquillity, and their minds were at peace. (Mora 1963, p. 430)

Tarantism and dance mania did not suddenly appear as hysterical responses
to stress, but the social and cultural origins of these rituals and behavioral
idioms can be traced at least a millennium before what most researchers
consider their initial appearance in medieval Europe. Over a thousand years
prior to the first documented tarantism accounts, followers of Pythagoras had
spread similar beliefs about music and healing across Italy (Inglis 1965, p.
66), the Apulia region once part of ancient Greece, and, later, Rome. The
Greeks traditionally used music to evoke ecstatic healing, eroticism, and pu-
rification to foster a return to mental equilibrium. Politically, the symbolism
of the tarantula bite and annual arachnoid curing rituals provided a means to
practice and maintain ancient pagan rituals without fear of sanction. Following the conversion of Roman Emperor Constantine in 312, Christianity
became the official state religion, and pagan worship was gradually discouraged. This was as aggressive as Constantine could be, since at the time of his
decree at least 80 percent of the Empire's population lay outside the church
(Bury 1958, p. 366). Although antipagan laws were enacted, enforcement was
lax and spasmodic during the fourth through sixth centuries. More significantly, during this period Christianity became a secure and fashionable means
to official advancement, as pagans dwindled from the ranks of the aristocracy.
Honorius and Theodosius II excluded non-Christians from governmental
positions, Leo prohibited them from joining the legal profession, and Justin-
ian excluded them from holding academic chairs (Jones 1984, p. 323).

Immediately prior to the first recorded appearance of tarantism, southern Italy schismed into a series of politically distinct communes that, although
under papal rule, were more relaxed toward the practice of local customs,
with their own constitutions and regional administrators (Hyde 1973, pp.
94–123). This paved the way for greater religious expression, so long as it did
not blatantly challenge Christianity. Once the Roman Empire had collapsed in

the West in 476, the next 500 years were marked by a conglomeration of "primitive" beliefs with Christian theology (Cockerham 1981, p. 14). Furthermore, pagans of the declining Roman Empire were pragmatic in the sense that "there were few pagan martyrs, and most were content to bribe the authorities to connive at their worship or to carry it on secretly" (Jones 1984, p. 325).

Tarantism and dancing manias also conveniently revived the fledgling careers of many musicians, who were restricted from performing by church leaders who condemned them for their moral license and regarded their activities as evil. Sir Malcolm Sargent and Martin Cooper (1962, p. 453) state that "players were excommunicated, and what could not be brought somehow into the service of the Church was condemned—at least officially." These heathen rites, proscribed following the Christianization of the region, became institutionalized under the new title of tarantism as an annual event, with musicians flocking to Apulia every summer to earn money playing "the appropriate" curative tunes. Some municipalities even hired special musicians for the dancers and provided "corps of substitutes to relieve the regular accompanists as they became exhausted" (Gloyne 1950, p. 33).

Tarantism is typically compared with contemporary reports of MPI, as both are characterized by spontaneous, uncontrolled behaviors and somatic complaints, prompting suggestions that both are manifestations of a unitary disorder entity (Colligan, Pennebaker, and Murphy 1982, p. 2). The physical symptoms associated with tarantism are virtually identical to those of participants in both historical and contemporary ecstatic religious enthusiasms, which are ritualized and institutionalized, known by such aptly descriptive names as the Shakers and Quakers. Although *taranti,* as victims were known, are typically described as participating in uncontrollable behaviors in chaotic, frenzied throngs, like their more contemporary religious counterparts (ecstatic religious sects) adherents worshipped in a discernible pattern. They would typically commence dancing at sunrise, stop during midday to sleep and sweat, then bathe before resuming dancing until evening, when they would again sleep and sweat, consume a light meal, then sleep until sunrise. This ritual was usually repeated over four or five days and sometimes for weeks (Russell 1979, p. 413).

DANCING MANIAS

A variation of tarantism spread throughout much of Europe between the thirteenth and seventeenth centuries, where it was known as the dancing mania,[14] or Saint Vitus' dance,[15] because participants often ended their processions in the vicinity of chapels and shrines dedicated to this saint. Like its

Italian counterpart, "epidemics" seized groups of people who engaged in frenzied dancing, often naked, intermittently for days or weeks. Social scientists
typify "victims" as maladjusted, deviant, irrational, or mentally disturbed,
primarily females.[16] These activities were typically accompanied by symptoms
similar to tarantism, including screaming, hallucinations, convulsive body
movements, chest pains, hyperventilation, sexually suggestive gestures, and
even sexual intercourse. Devoid of arachnoid symbolism prevalent in taranti,
participants usually claimed they were possessed by demons who had induced
a seemingly uncontrollable urge to dance. Like tarantism, however, music was
typically played during these "outbreaks" and was considered a potent rem-
edy. Detailed accounts of many episodes appear in Hecker's classic *Epidemics
of the Middle Ages* (1844). He considered the origin of these "epidemics" to be
"morbid sympathy" coinciding with periods of severe disease that resulted in
high numbers of fatalities, such as the widespread feeling of pessimism and
despair from the effects of the Black Death (Hecker 1844, p. 87). This epic
disease epidemic subsided about 20 years prior to 1374, the year most scholars identify with the onset of the dancing mania. Benjamin Gordon, in *Medieval and Renaissance Medicine* (1959, p. 562), provides this description:

> From Italy it [the dancing mania] spread to Aachen (Aix-la Chapelle),
> Prussia, and one morning, without warning, the streets were filled with
> men and women who joined hands, formed circles and seemingly lost all
> control over their actions. They danced together, ceaselessly, for hours or
> days, and in wild delirium, the dancers collapsed and fell to the ground
> exhausted, groaning and sighing as if in the agonies of death. When
> recuperated, they swathed themselves tightly with cloth around their waists
> and resumed their convulsive movements. They contorted their bodies,
> writhing, screaming and jumping in a mad frenzy. One by one they fell
> from exhaustion, but as they fell, others of the town took their places.
> These wild dancers seemed insensible to external impressions. . . .
>
> Dancing attacks were often followed by epileptiform convulsions. The
> victims fell to the ground, fainting, and laboring for breath. They foamed
> from the mouth and suddenly sprang up to dance once again. Many later
> claimed that they had seen the walls of heaven split open and that Jesus
> and the Virgin Mary had appeared before them.

As with tarantism, dancing mania episodes were considered to have
occurred spontaneously, with participants unable to control their actions, and
to be largely confined to psychologically vulnerable individuals, particularly
females—a typical contention of modern-day MPI reports. Accordingly,
Frederick Redlich and D. Freedman (1966, p. 31) suggest that medieval danc-

ing manias were "mass psychoses," Charles Singer and Edgar Underwood (1962, p. 504) describe them as a "strange neurosis," and psychiatrists Kaplan and Sadock (1985, p. 1227) use the term *collective mental disorder.*

Although medical historians such as Hecker, Sigerist, Mora, Rosen, and Russell acknowledge the integration of ritualistic elements in the dancing manias, each assumes, based on the prominent stress-strain paradigm of his or her contemporary social science milieu, that participants were using these traditions as a socially acceptable means to engage in shared psychopathology that manifested as cathartic reactions to intolerable social conditions. It is a testament to the blinding power of the social and cultural zeitgeist that each of these prominent researchers overlooks the likelihood that the appearance of such ancient rituals was not facilitated by stress per se, which fostered a hypothesized state of MPI or "epidemic" hysteria, but that they were simply rituals in their own right; that instead of representing spontaneous, uncontrollable hysterical reactions to pent-up emotions per se, participants were partaking in the widespread European belief of the period, which held that dancing in the vicinity of religious shrines, particularly Saint Vitus, was a means to obtain divine favor and protection.

Rosen (1968) contends that dance frenzies appeared most often during periods of crop failures, famine, epidemics, and social upheaval. However, these same events were likely to facilitate attempts at divine intervention through ritualized dancing, which often fostered ecstatic trance and possession states. Although Mora (1963, pp. 436–438) writes that tarantism and dance manias offered a socially acceptable means of "expression, through ritual, of deeply rooted emotional conflicts," he categorizes participants as engaging in psychotherapeutic attempts to cope with either individual or societal maladjustments that fostered "psychopathological" manifestations. This position is typified in a recent book on abnormal psychology (Carson, Butcher, and Mineka 1996, p. 37), which cites Sigerist and notes that although Saint Vitus' dance and tarantism were similar to ancient Greek orgiastic rites, which had been outlawed by Christian authorities but were secretly practiced, the authors assume these "secret gatherings . . . probably led to considerable guilt and conflict," which precipitated collective hysterical disorders.

It could be argued that these "manias" were actually culturally masked examples of MPI, since they were often described by observers of the period as possessing elements of deviance. However, based on period chronicles, most participants did not reside in the municipalities where the "manias" occurred but hailed from other regions, traveling through communities as they sought out shrines and churchyards to perform in. For instance, in the largest and most thoroughly documented dance frenzy, that of 1374 involving massive crowds of "dancers" in Germany and Holland, participants were "pil-grims" who traveled, "according to Beka's chronicle, from Bohemia, but also from Hungary, Poland, Carinthia, Austria, and Germany. Great hosts from the Netherlands and France joined them" (Backman 1952, p. 331).[17] As with tarantism, these "spontaneous" episodes were institutionalized. For instance, German magistrates hired musicians to play for participants and serve as dancing companions, the latter of which were designed to reduce their inju-ries and mischief during their procession to the Saint Vitus chapel where divine cures and favors were granted and the mania subsequently subsided—or, perhaps more accurately, the ritual ended (Hecker 1970 [1837], p. 4).[18]

Sirois (1982, p. 218) observes that the dance mania was predominantly confined to "lower social groups." As such, and like its Italian counterpart, the dancing mania offered a means for the disadvantaged to implement hid-den political agendas with impunity. For instance, a dancing frenzy in 1374 allowed for the public chastisement and near overthrow of a group of despised local clergy. Many residents of Liege attributed their possession by demons to unsanctified baptisms, as most of the priests had concubines; "for this reason the populace proposed that they rise against the priests, kill them and take their property" (Hecker, cited in Rosen 1968, p. 197). The mania eventually subsided following exorcisms by the clergy, who became much more respon-sive in attending to their subjects (Hecker 1970 [1837], p. 3), thus retaining their power. Through the idiom of temporary possession, the repressed were afforded the opportunity to participate in otherwise proscribed heathen rites. Further, the existence of the dance itself, with most participants collectively, publicly, and in rather dramatic fashion requesting divine assistance, implied that the existing political system was woefully inadequate.[19]

Hecker (1970 [1837], p. 6) states that the dancing mania was a "half-heathen, half-christian festival" that incorporated into the festival of St. John's day as early as the fourth century "the kindling of the 'Nodfyr,' which was forbidden them by St. Boniface." This ritual involved leaping through smoke or flames, which was believed to protect participants from various diseases during the ensuing year. A central feature of the dance frenzy was the Baccha-nalian leaps, where those affected would jump for periods up to several hours through what they claimed were invisible fires until collapsing in exhaustion.

Working on the assumption that MPI is a stress-induced unitary psychi-atric disorder masked by cultural custom, it is noted that episodes with broadly similar behavioral characteristics have been labeled dancing manias. These include enthusiastic dancing, shouting, jumping, laughing, hallucinations, and involuntary muscular spasms associated with religious revivals in Kentucky and Tennessee between 1803 and 1805 (Robertson 1806; Yandell 1882). Hecker

(1970 [1837], p. 39) remarks that an outbreak of Methodist revivalism at Redruth, England, in 1812 "completely resembled the St. Vitus's dance," and Rosen (1968, p. 205) states that "bizarre forms of group behavior similar to the dance frenzies have occurred widely separated in time and place," appearing "in various contexts and under different names." Harrington (1982) takes a similar position in equating "epidemic" episodes of collective *koro* in Southeast Asia with "epidemic psychoses" affecting dancing mania and tarantism participants, in addition to more contemporary incidents of MPI. Gwee (1968) and Tan (1980) concur with this view. Yap (1952, p. 517) compared reports of *delire 'a Java* in Indonesia, an "epidemic" form of latahlike behavior, "with the hysterical epidemics of medieval Europe." Historian E. H. Norman (1945), in an article entitled "Mass Hysteria in Japan," invites similar comparisons in describing episodes of frenzied dancing, singing, crying, shouting obscenities, and amnesia during widespread civil unrest at the end of the Tokugawa era during the mid-nineteenth century.[20] Each of these "disorders" almost exclusively affected the peasantry preceding periods of political upheaval in their respective countries, and their categorization as a variant of dancing mania reduces and alienates human behavior from its anthropolitical complexity.[21]

Another example of this reductionism is illustrated in the "epidemic choreomania," known to the natives of Madagascar as *Ramanenjana,* which appeared amid the political turmoil that preceded the assassination of King Radama II in 1863. The symptoms of this "ailment" were described as virtually identical to those of the dancing mania, especially as women of the lowest classes were particularly affected (Davidson 1867; Markush 1973, p. 374).

Radama II succeeded to the throne in 1861, quickly reversing European isolationist policies that had been in effect since 1835. A series of charters and treaties appearing to favor the Europeans, the subsequent influx of missionaries, and rumors that Radama II had converted to Christianity caused great consternation among the island's non-Christian majority, who practiced ancestor-cult worship. It is within this context that in February 1863, a "mental epidemic" appeared in the vicinity of the capital, exclusive to Malagasy, in which natives "pretended to be unconscious of their actions, being unable to refrain from leaping, running, dancing" and ancestral visions were perceived (McLeod 1865, p. 187). A commonly reported vision involved a request by the king's ancestors to deliver the message to Radama II that if he did not "stop the praying" in their homeland, a calamity would befall him.

The majority of those participating in the Malagasy revolution suffered from the dancing mania (Mutibwa 1974, p. 88), and although the word of Radama II was sacred and unchallengeable, those protesting the king's rule were able to express their opposition with impunity, as they were afflicted with *Ramanenjana*. The dance participants were viewed as a medium through which their ancestors could voice dissatisfaction. The appearance of the affliction afforded the anti-Christians, xenophobics, and those seeking power an excellent opportunity to succeed.

> King Ramada II . . . was morally and intellectually ill-equipped to deal with a situation such as the one created by the Dancing Mania. As the Malagasy believed in the ancestor-cult, the dancers did not find it difficult to convince the king that they had seen the visions of his ancestors, who had sent a message to him that all Europeans should be expelled from the country and that Christianity should be banned, otherwise some dreadful calamity would soon come upon him and his country. His resistance broke when his own son became affected by the disease. The king had been won over to the movement; and those who supported it, particularly the idol-keepers, had triumphed. (Mutibwa 1974, p. 83)

The anti-European movement eventually failed in its objectives when the king was assassinated shortly thereafter.

In questioning the purported association between "epidemics" of tarantism, dancing mania, and demonopathy as culture and history-specific manifestations of a unitary mental disorder, comparisons will next be made with the three most prominent specific elements typically considered to be MPI features: female susceptibility, abnormal personality correlates, and stress. Researchers typically classify these episodes as historical examples based on the presence of these ambiguous, chameleonlike categories.

FEMALE SUSCEPTIBILITY

Given the subjective, exclusionary nature of the diagnosis of any particular MPI episode, investigators typically become engaged in a self-fulfilling search for supportive characteristics, categorizing collective behavior deviating from their Eurocentric notions of normality. The presence of such elements is ambiguous and entirely descriptive. Innate female susceptibility has long been held to be a MPI characteristic (Lang and Lang 1961, p. 227; Rawnsley and Loudon 1964, p. 839; Tan 1972, p. 8; Trethowan and Sims 1983, p. 208; Hill, Murray, and Thorley 1986, p. 237). To support this contention, it has been stated that tarantism episodes were commonly referred to as "the woman's little carnival" (*Il carnevaletto delle donne*). For instance, medical historian Henry Sigerist (1943, p. 221) makes this suggestion, as does Mora (1963, p. 423). However, this phrase is traceable to Italian physician Giorgio Baglivi's book, *The Practice of Physick* (1723, p. 617), referring to the observation that women most often made arrangements in preparation for the tarantism festival (Hecker 1970 [1837], p. 23). Sigerist (1943, p. 218) also contends that tarantism affected "women more than men." However, historical writings, especially those based on firsthand observations, indicate otherwise. Hecker (1970 [1837], p. 28), a medieval medical authority who has written a comprehensive review of early writings on the subject, states that although in some cities women were most often afflicted, "upon the whole it appears, from concurrent accounts, that women by no means enjoyed the distinction of being attacked by tarantism more frequently than men."[22]

Indeed, a revisiting of the descriptions of dancing manias based on the original chronicles of these events clearly states that both men and women were affected with equal frequency. This is most evident in the work of E. Louis Backman (1952), who provides verbatim accounts from numerous French, Dutch, and German chronicles involving descriptions of dance frenzy participants and their gender. There is no indication of females being over-represented in all but a couple of reported episodes. The same can be said of males, who in some instances were said to have outnumbered females. In fact, one of the earliest accounts of a dance mania at Kolbigk in 1021 was said to have involved fifteen men and either three or four women (Backman 1952, p. 175).

Based on Backman's translations of these chronicles in which the gender of the participants was noted, the following comments were representative: A. Bzovius writing in *Annalium Ecclesiasticorum* states that a dance mania in 1268 involved "many youths and maidens, men and women"; Petrus de Herenthal's chronicle *Vita Gregorii XI* remarks that "persons of both sexes . . . danced"; according to Radulpho de Rivo's *Decani Tongrensis,* "persons of both sexes, possessed by devils and half naked, set wreathes on their heads, and began their dances"; Joannes de Beka's *Canonicus Ultrajectinus et Heda, Wilhelmus, Praepositus Arnhemensis: De Episcopis Ultraiectinis, Recogniti,* states that in 1385 "there spread along the Rhine . . . a strange plague . . . whereby persons of both sexes, in great crowds . . . danced and sang, both inside and outside of churches, till they were so weary that they fell to the ground"; according to *Koelhoff's Chronicle,* published in 1499, "Many people, men and women, old and young, had the disease [of dancing mania]"; Casper Hedion, in *Ein Ausserlessne Chronik von Anfang der Welt bis auff das iar nach Christi unsers Eynigen Heylands Gepurt M.D.,* writes that in 1374 "a terrible disease, called St. John's dance . . . attacked many women and girls, men and boys"; A. Slichtenhorst's *Gelersee Geschiedenissen* states that "men and women were smitten by the fantastic frenzy"; *The Chronicle of Metz,* published by Molinier in 1698, states that "in 1374 certain men and women appeared in Metz, dancing and singing like corybantes"; and an astrological chronicle published by A. Goldmeyer in 1636 (*Strassburgische Chronica Astrologisch Beschrieben*) notes that an episode of dancing mania in 1518 "occurred among men . . . men in their madness began to dance day and night until finally they fell down." Although this latter account probably used the word *men* to mean humankind, it is difficult to envision the term being used if the majority of participants were female.

Within the psychiatric, psychological, and medical professions, such unsubstantiated present-day typifications of tarantism and dancing mania participants as mostly innately susceptible female hysterics and the mentally disturbed parallel the predominant similar view held until the 1990s of those accused of witchcraft. During the Continental European witch persecutions between the fifteenth and seventeenth centuries, the majority of persons accused of witchcraft were "deviant" females (Rosen 1968, p. 13; Szasz 1970, p. 8; Heinsohn and Steiger 1982; Goode and Ben-Yehuda 1994, p. 157), and clearly the paramount single factor was being female per se. As Monter (1976, p. 124) remarks, "Compared to sex [gender], poverty and other factors seem to be secondary." Similar interpretations were held for those accused of engaging in collective demon possession. Indeed, the *Malleus Maleficarum* (Hammer of Witches) of Heinrich Framer and Jakob Sprenger, used as a guideline at so many witch trials, stated that most witches were females, as "all witchcraft comes from carnal lust, which is in women insatiable," whereas males were favored with special immunity because Jesus was male (cited in Szasz 1970, p. 8).

ABNORMAL PERSONALITY CHARACTERISTICS

Some MPI investigators continue to draw on unsubstantiated or antiquated assumptions of crowd behavior (i.e., riots, lynchings, revolutions), especially those that appear to mimic explanations for dancing manias, which do not vary considerably from their original formulations.[23] Just as various psychiatric studies on hypnosis in the early 1880s were used to construct a model of collective hallucination, mass hypnosis, or extreme forms of *folie a deux* psychosis (Harris 1985), contemporary social scientists have acted likewise. Anthropologist Anthony Wallace (1963, p. 989) makes this suggestion, noting that "the victim of mass hysteria may be compared to a person under hypnosis. He has entered a trancelike state in which he will, within certain limits, believe, feel, and do what [he] is told by the group or the leader." Elkins and colleagues (1988) speculate that an "active-alert" form of hypnotic trance, as opposed to the well-known sleep-relaxation type, is a plausible explanation in psychogenic illness. The authors base this hypothesis on a purely descriptive observation by Ernest Hilgard (1977, p. 165), who noted that the production of hypnoticlike states is not only limited to deep relaxation, as "the trance states of the whirling dervishes or the dancing Balinese are just as real as the states of those who achieve trance state by quiet meditation, and all may resemble hypnosis." Although Elkins and colleagues (1988) note a relationship between hypnotically susceptible individuals and the development of individual psychosomatic symptoms, no consistent pattern is found of tendencies toward hypnotic susceptibility, hysterical traits, neuroticism, and paranoia in populations judged to have undergone MPI (Tam et al. 1982; Wessely 1987; Bartholomew 1990b).

Although behavior can be both hysteria and ritual, it seems unlikely that the majority of Europeans affected by the dancing mania and tarantism during the Middle Ages were hysterics, given the descriptions of these episodes as "pandemic" (Lidz 1963, p. 822; Millon and Millon 1974, p. 22). Characterizations of most "contagious" tarantism and dancing mania participants as mentally disturbed ignore the social patterning of episodes. Although some "victims" may have been epileptics, schizophrenics, or hysterics, the large percentage of the populations affected suggests otherwise.

Not only did the dancing manias reflect established religious rituals and offer a means to express pagan and antiestablishment traditions without the fear of sanction, but many participants attended episodes for a variety of deliberate reasons. For example, the ranks of the dancing mania processions were increased by a multitude of spectators (Hecker 1970 [1837], p. 4), which included children searching for their parents who were among the dancers, and vice versa (Haggard 1934, p. 187). Some observers were threatened with violence if they did not dance (Backman 1952, p. 147). Many apparently participated out of loneliness and carnal pleasure, whereas others joined in out of curiosity and for the exhilaration (Rust 1969, p. 22). Hecker (1970 [1837], pp. 3–4) remarks that "numerous beggars, stimulated by vice and misery, availed themselves of this new complaint to gain a temporary livelihood," and gangs of vagabonds imitated the dance, roving "from place to place seeking maintenance and adventures." Similar observations have been noted of tarantism episodes. Additionally, many of the physical symptoms associated with tarantism and dancing mania likely resulted from the effects of sleep deprivation, excessive alcohol consumption, emotional excitement, and vigorous, prolonged physical activity. A German chronicle reports that during a dance mania episode at Strasbourg in 1418, "many of them went without food for days and nights" (Rust 1969, p. 20).[24]

DANCING MANIAS AND STRESS

Almost universally, those investigating episodes of dancing mania, tarantism, and demonopathy have assumed they are a cathartic response to pent-up stress. The analysis in this chapter involves a meaning-oriented approach that emphasizes the importance of ascertaining the context of a particular set of collective beliefs. This approach views stress "as a matter of definition in a specific sociocultural context rather than as an objective given from which predictions can be made" (see Lee and Ackerman 1980, p. 79).

SUMMARY

This chapter has examined the European "dancing mania" and its Italian variant, tarantism. These behaviors are typified as representing the first recorded episodes of "epidemic hysteria." They are also typified within the psychiatric literature as spontaneous, stress-induced outbursts of psychological disturbance that primarily affected females. This depiction is typically founded on secondary sources or the selective use of period quotations by medical historians such as George Rosen and Henry Sigerist, who were reflecting popular stereotypes of female susceptibility to mental disorders. However, based on a series of translations of medieval European chronicles describing these events, typically firsthand, and by scrutinizing various other historical sources that provide a degree of social, cultural, historical, and political perspective to these events, it is evident that contemporary depictions of "dancing manias" have been misrepresented by scholars.[25] Contrary to popular psychiatric portrayals, females were not overrepresented among participants, episodes were not spontaneous but highly structured, and they involved unfamiliar religious sects engaging in strange or unfamiliar customs redefined as a behavioral abnormality. Therefore, based on an examination of the social, cultural, and historical events and circumstances involving the appearance of tarantism and dance mania in medieval Europe, these episodes are best explained as behavioral idioms that have been "mistranslated" by scholars judging these behaviors per se, removed from their regional context and meaning.

In the modern-day field of psychological medicine, the topic of "epidemic hysteria" or "mass psychogenic illness" is highly contentious, and virtually all psychiatrists have assumed that the first known recorded episodes of MPI occurred in the form of medieval dance manias and tarantism. In this chapter I have shown the unfounded basis for this assumption and how it is pejorative to females, arguing that a more appropriate explanation for these actions (which are behavioral idioms) becomes evident upon scrutinizing the worldview of the participants. In Chapter 6 I shall examine various contemporary behaviors that continue to be erroneously labeled by scientists as MPI and claims that females are innately susceptible. However, as will become evident in the next chapter, we should not therefore assume that all actions deemed "strange" by modern Western normality standards are a social construction of Western-biased researchers or that mental disorder does not exist, as is claimed by a few radical feminists and so-called antipsychiatrists. In Chapter 6 I shall highlight the important contributions of the contemporary medical-psychiatric model of mental disorder and the caveats of phenomenological approaches by radical feminists and antipsychiatrists, who contend that the notion of mental illness is almost entirely socially constructed, by examining the concept of individual and collective hysteria. All known reports of communicable conversion symptoms in school settings will be examined. Based on the characteristic features of episodes, it will be argued that whereas the term *epidemic hysteria* has often been used pejoratively to marginalize various groups, especially females, a transcultural, transhistorical psychological disorder rubric exists involving the rapid spread of conversion symptoms. However, although the overwhelming number of sufferers in mass conversion episodes are females, I shall underscore the importance of the context and meaning of episodes and the social structural conditions that precipitate anxiety, which engenders incidents, and criticize claims that such cases are precipitated by innate female susceptibility, individuals with abnormal personality traits, or stress per se.

NOTES

1. In discussing the dancing mania and tarantism, Hecker (1844, p. 85) states that "they are a portion of history, and will never return in the form in which they are there recorded."

2. Typical of the influence of this myth is the following editorial from the *British Medical Journal* (Anonymous 1966a, p. 1280): "Epidemic hysteria has always tended to involve women more than men, particularly those in the younger age groups. Few men, for instance, were affected in the dancing manias which recurred from time to time throughout Europe in the Middle Ages. In the Blackburn [England] epidemic, symptoms first began among 14-year-old girls and rapidly spread to affect most heavily the youngest, and therefore more susceptible, girls." The editors refrained from discussing the differences in transcultural gender roles that may be mistaken for group "hysteria," such as Western females typically acquiring emotionally expressive, sympathetic, and submissive character traits (Parsons 1955; Kagan 1969).

3. Other twentieth-century synonyms used to describe the rapid spread of conversion symptoms within a particular collective include *mass sociogenic illness,* a term preferred by Stahl (1982, p. 196), as most cases "have as much group or peer input as

they have psychological explanations." Other descriptions include collective stress reaction (Yassi et al. 1989), group contagious hysteria (Nandi et al. 1985), group conversion reaction (Boxer 1985), communicable hysteria (Merskey 1979), collective stress syndrome (Mann and Rosenblatt 1979), group hysteria (Olczak et al. 1971), mass psychology (Jaspers 1968), and behavior contagion (Wheeler 1966).

4. This is evident in such descriptive synonyms as epidemic insanity (Despine 1875), psychic disturbance (Anonymous 1888), social insanity (Friedmann 1901), hallucination by suggestion (Anonymous 1913), mass psychosis (Schumacher 1940), mass psychopathology (Simmel 1946), socially shared collective madness (Lefebvre 1954), shared group psychopathology (Gruenberg 1957), shared psychopathology (Lang and Lang 1961), hysterical psychosis (Langness 1965), collective psychosis (Goldenson 1970), group mental disorder (Coleman 1976), transient collective psychosis (Raschka 1976), epidemic psychological disturbance (Tseng and Hsu 1980), and psychotic epidemics (Faguet and Faguet 1982).

5. The range of symptoms reported in mass psychogenic illness investigations is varied and also includes numbness (Reig-y-Casco 1881; Dubnikov 1927), twitching (Schuler and Parenton 1943; Dhadphale and Shaikh 1983), lockjaw (Genik 1898), crying (Davy 1880; Helvie 1968), screaming (Chew 1978; Phoon 1982), paralysis (Watson 1982), depression (Ikeda 1966), burning eyes (Gamino, Elkins, and Hackney 1989; Goldsmith 1989), sore throat (Pollock and Clayton 1964; Sinks, Kerndt, and Wallingford 1989), running (Kagwa 1964), laughing (Rankin and Philip 1963; Muhangi 1973), jumping (Beard 1880a; Thornton 1885), insomnia (Pullela 1986), trance states (Muluka, Dhadphale, and Mwita 1985), possession states (Teoh, Soewondo, and Sidharta 1975; Mohr 1980), hallucinations (Shapiro 1936; Lee and Ackerman 1980), blindness (Mohr and Bond 1982), diarrhea (Colligan et al. 1979), echolalia (Yap 1952), foul mouth taste (Folland 1975; Colligan 1978), choking (Christophersen 1946; Rawnsley and Loudon 1964), globus (Seeligmuller 1876), coughing (Bozzolo 1894; Szego 1896), hiccup (Markush 1973), nose bleeding (Babington 1859), muscle weakness (Shepard and Kroes 1975), sleepiness (Colligan and Urtes 1978), chest discomfort (Araki and Honma 1986), tinnitus (Faust and Brilliant 1981), shivering (Moss and McEvedy 1966), "catalepsy" (Hirsch 1883), memory loss (Sigurdsson et al. 1950), fever (Acheson 1959), digestive disorders (Ikeda 1966), and yawning (Cornish 1814).

6. For reports of similar episodes in East Africa, refer to Rankin and Philip (1963), Anonymous (1963b), Kagwa (1964), Anonymous (1966b), Ebrahim (1968), and Muhangi (1973).

7. That is, the influence of factors anthropologists would typically focus on (e.g., cultural and social developments of humankind) and factors political scientists would consider of importance (i.e., activities related to government or the administering of governmental affairs).

8. Prior to the twentieth century, behavior contemporary writers labeled mass or "epidemic" hysteria was commonly referred to as psychic contagion, psychic epidemic, chorea, or epidemic chorea. The popular usage of the word *chorea* is traceable to the dancing manias of the Middle Ages in which participants were thought to be exhibiting symptoms of chorea, a central nervous system disorder characterized by brief involuntary, irregular jerky movements that can resemble dancing. Chorea is also known as

Sydenham's chorea, named after British physician Thomas Sydenham (1624–1689). Very few modern-day researchers (for example, Dajer 1990) continue to claim that dancing mania participants were literally suffering from chorea. Such speculations are based entirely on descriptive similarities between the two. Further, no evidence suggests that chorea is contagious.

9. For instance, Backman (1952, pp. 306–327) argues that ergot contamination of the food supply triggered dancing manias and tarantism.

10. The word *tarantism* is often used interchangeably with dancing mania. Other words used specifically to describe tarantism include stellio, astaragazza, and tarantulismo.

11. Present-day annual tarantism reports persist in parts of southern Italy. Hans Schadewaldt (1971) investigated an outbreak in the community of Wardo during 1957. An Italian religious history professor, Ernesto de Martino (1966), identified thirty-five cases of tarantism in Galatina, Apulia, during 1959. De Martino conducted his survey between June 28 and 30, as June 29 is the festival day of St. Peter and St. Paul. On that day it is customary for "victims" to travel from regional villages to the chapel of St. Paul to obtain a cure for various ailments. Refer to Anonymous (1967) for a summary of de Martino's investigation.

12. Isolated, apparently individual cases described as tarantism have appeared in other parts of Europe and Italy. Episodes have also been reported in Persia, Albania, America, Ethiopia, and Asia Minor, although none remotely resemble the scale of cases in southern Italy.

13. *Latrodectus tarantula,* a nonaggressive, slow-moving spider indigenous to Apulia, is capable of producing psychoactive effects in people it bites, which in severe cases may temporarily mimic many of the symptoms characteristic of tarantism, including psychomotor agitation, weakness, nausea, and muscular pains (Lewis 1991, p. 514). Ironically, *Lycosa tarantula* was typically blamed for tarantism symptoms, as it is larger, more aggressive, ferocious in appearance, and has a painful bite. However, neither spider can account for the predominantly symbolic and psychogenic character of tarantism attacks. Further, *Latrodectus tarantula* is found in other countries where tarantism does not occur (Russell 1979, p. 416), including the United States (Lewis 1991, p. 517). No evidence suggests that a venomous species of tarantula, native only to Apulia, may have existed during this period and later died out. As Sigerist (1943, p. 221) remarks, "The same tarantula shipped to other parts of the country seemed to lose most of its venom, and what remained acted differently." It is also doubtful that some other insect or agent was responsible for causing "attacks," as the vast majority of participants did not claim to have been bitten and would only participate in tarantism episodes at designated times.

14. The term *dancing mania* is derived from the Greek word *choros,* a dance, and *mania,* madness. The literal translation of *choros mania* is dancing madness. It was known in Germany as *Tanzwut* (dancing frenzy or madness), *tanzplage* (dancing plague), and, later, *chorea Germanorum.* Prior to the twentieth century it was commonly referred to as epidemic chorea, choreomania, the lascivious dance, Saint Vitus's dance, Saint Vitus' dance, Chorea Sancti viti, Viti Saltus, Saint Anthony's dance, Saint Guy's dance, Saint John's dance, and the dance of Saint Modestir. The controversial Swiss physician Paracelsus (1493–1541), one of the first to argue that such behaviors are not the work

of demons but have medical causes, identified three types of dancing mania: chorea imaginativa, chorea lasciva, and chorea naturalis (Markush 1973, p. 406).

15. Hecker (1844, p. 87) states that the name Saint Vitus was used to describe the dance "on account of the Bacchantic leaps by which it was characterized." However, most twentieth-century writers contend that the name was adopted after a group of about 200 people danced so spiritedly on a bridge above the Maas River in Germany during 1278 that it collapsed, killing many participants. Survivors were treated in a nearby chapel dedicated to Saint Vitus, and many were reportedly restored to full health.

16. The early work of Paracelsus (circa 1532) is often cited for his opinion that the majority of those affected were irrational, imaginative females (see Sigerist 1941).

17. The behavior of these dancers was described as strange because although some actions were part of the Christian tradition and paid homage to Jesus, Mary, and various saints at chapels and shrines, other elements were foreign and sectarian, which is clearly evident in the period chronicles translated into English by Backman (1952). Radulphus de Rivo's chronicle *Decani Tongrensis* states: "In their songs they uttered the names of devils never before heard of . . . this strange sect." According to Petrus de Herenthal in *Vita Gregorii XI,* "There came to Aachen . . . a curious sect (*mira secta*)." The *Chronicon Belgicum Magnum* describes the participants as "a sect of dancers." The actions of dancers were often depicted as immoral, as much uninhibited sexual intercourse occurred. The chronicle of C. Browerus (*Abtiquitatum et Annalium Trevirensium*) states, "They indulged in disgraceful immodesty, for many women, during this shameless dance and mock-bridal singing, bared their bosoms, while others of their own accord offered their virtue." *A Chronicle of Early Roman Kings and Emperors* states that a number of participants engaged in "loose living with the women and young girls who shamelessly wandered about in remote places under the cover of night." If the majority of the participants were pilgrims of Bohemian and Czech origin as Backman asserts, during this period Czechs and Bohemians were noted for a high incidence of then perceived immorality, especially sexual, including prostitution and annual festivals involving free sexual intercourse (Backman 1952, p. 290).

18. The widespread assertion in psychiatric and medical texts describing dance manias as spontaneous is erroneous. It is clear from period chronicles that dance mania participants were pilgrims who also gained local adherents, engaging in emotionally laden displays of worship that were often wild, but such outbursts were clearly structured. This social patterning of episodes is evident in a firsthand account on September 11, 1374, by Jean d'Outremeuse in his chronicle *La Geste de Liege,* who states that "there came from the north to Liege . . . a company of persons who all danced continually. They were linked with clothes, and they jumped and leaped. . . . They called loudly on St. John the Baptist and fiercely clapped their hands. . . . All this I saw indeed, and much more also." Slichtenhorst (cited in Backman 1952, p. 210), in describing the dance frenzy of 1375 and 1376 in Gelderland, France, and Germany, noted that participants "went in couples, and with every couple was another single person . . . they danced, leaped and sang, and embraced each other in friendly fashion."

19. Of course, it could be argued that my observation here is a value judgment made at the dawn of the twenty-first century.

20. Norman (1945) records how the timing of this "hysterical dance frenzy" and its particular severity in the vicinity of the political center of Kyoto paralyzed the ruling Tokugawa government during a critical period in late 1867. The ensuing confusion and chaos brought about large crowds singing, dancing, weeping, shouting obscenities, and claiming amnesia and allowed representatives of the Satsuma and Choshu clans to journey undetected past rival clan agents and government secret police to negotiate an agreement that gained the emperor's support against the Tokugawa. This "spontaneous" and "uncontrollable" dance frenzy affected peasants during their irregular *okage-mairi* pilgrimage to the Ise Shrine, the timing of which was almost miraculously convenient considering that such treks are organized approximately once per generation. Norman (1945) concluded that the stoic Japanese temperament, combined with unbearable economic hardships and repressive policies under feudal authority, induced a state of collective neuroses that unwittingly facilitated the government's fall.

21. Consult Norman (1945) for a detailed discussion of this political upheaval that includes period sources.

22. A more contemporary study of tarantism episodes in the vicinity of Sardinia, Italy, by Gallini (1988) found that the vast majority of "victims" were male, whereas de Martino (1966) reported that most participants near Apulia were female.

23. This is also true in explaining medieval demonopathy. During the late nineteenth century the Italian Scipio Sighele (1892) viewed crowd behavior as unleashing "primitive" impulses within susceptible individuals, a conclusion formulated from Charcot's psychopathological notion of hypnotic suggestibility. In addition to Gustave LeBon's influential work, *La Psychologie des Foules* (1896), which originally appeared in 1895, many social theorists of the period utilized and modified these earlier concepts of suggestibility and mass behavior, including H. Fournial (1892) and Gabriel Tarde (1901). Recent works, particularly by psychologists and psychiatrists, draw on similar intellectual roots relative to collective hypnosis in explaining the fear of witches and mass demon possession. For instance, Eugene Bliss (1986, p. 224) takes a noncontextual universalist approach that blames much of "the insane idea" surrounding demonophobia on spontaneous "self-hypnosis," disregarding more prosaic and plausible explanations such as deviance, labeling, conformity dynamics, and symbol system analysis. Casper Schmidt (1984) holds a similar "group trance" interpretation, whereas Freud (1975 [1923]) views demon possession states psychopathologically. Other more contemporary authors (e.g., U.S. sociologist Neil Smelser) apply the notion of a dysfunctioning "proper" social order and the resultant psychosocial stress as precipitating such behaviors.

24. Repressed medieval females exhibiting demon possession and labeled witches have been typified by scientists as mentally disturbed and suffering from hysteria (Bartholomew 1990b, p. 463; Szasz 1970, 1974b), a view held by Charcot and Freud. However, despite a series of critiques of this paradigm since the late 1970s that discredit pathological evaluations (e.g., Neugebauer 1978; Spanos 1978), historical, sociological, and anthropological interpretations have been slow to be adopted into textbooks on abnormal psychology. T. J. Schoeneman (1984) documents the reluctance of some scientists to incorporate the contemporary paradigm shift, which takes into account the social, cultural, historical, and political context in which females and various deviants were likely to be erroneously labeled witches or hysterics or as engaging in collective

possession. Based on a survey by Schoeneman of recently published abnormal psychology textbooks, most writers supported some form of the psychopathological perspective, with just three texts offering alternative views. Conspicuously, the writers "generally ignored prominent historical and anthropological research on witchcraft and possession . . . [devoting] minimal attention to more recent, socio-culturally oriented histories of psychiatry and to critiques of the older psychiatric paradigm" (Schoeneman
1984, p. 299).

The standard present-day interpretation of this demonophobia among deviance
specialists holds that the fear of witches was a moral panic. Such episodes typically
endure unabated for years, encompassing entire countries and geographical regions,
and are characterized by a general long-term threat. They are primarily symbolic and
rumor driven, consisting of fear over the exaggerated erosion of traditional values characterized by self-fulfilling stereotypes of ethnic minorities and deviants wrongfully
indicted for evil deeds. Goode (1992) aptly summarizes the infamous continental
European witch persecutions as a social panic, noting that they originated from the
disintegration of the Roman Catholic Church during the late Middle Ages and early
Renaissance when the feudal hierarchy was unraveling and peasants were migrating to
cities. Scientific rationalism, with its secular philosophy, conflicted with church doctrine, and new religious denominations were being formed beyond the church's control.
In an unconscious attempt to counteract secularism and reestablish traditional authority, the church-sponsored persecution of witches attempted to redefine moral boundaries, and church inquisitors focused on eradicating various deviants who were viewed
as a threat.

25. These scholars reflect a male bias indicative of the day reflecting (1) the states of
women in society, (2) the power of women in society, and (3) the education/literacy of
women in society.

6

Deconstructing "Epidemic" Conversion "Hysteria" in School Settings: A Cautionary Tale

If men define situations as real, they are real in their consequences (William Thomas 1932, p. 572).

Changes in cultural fashion, psychiatric theory, and public policy have not transformed the imbalance of gender and power that has kept madness a female malady. . . . The cultural connections between "women" and "madness" must be dismantled . . . femininity must not be defined in terms of a male norm, and . . . we can expect no progress when a male-dominated profession determines the concepts of normality and deviance that women perforce must accept (Elaine Showalter 1991, pp. 19–20).

Chapter 5 assessed the validity of scientific interpretations of certain collective illness behaviors during the Middle Ages; the present chapter will concentrate on group "hysterical" episodes in school settings since the seventeenth century.[1] Many health care professionals accept that MPI exists as a unitary disease or disorder entity and that those most vulnerable are innately susceptible females with abnormal personality characteristics who exhibit cathartic reactions to accumulated stress. In this chapter I shall assess this contention and the validity of attempts to apply the MPI rubric to various illness behaviors in transcultural, transhistorical settings under the assumption that participants are exhibiting culture and history-bound manifestations of a unitary syndrome. In examining the literature I shall first discuss the concepts of individual and collective "hysterical" conversion reactions, questions surrounding their very existence, and problematics in diagnosing possible manifestations. Second, I shall demonstrate that ambiguous MPI diagnostic criteria have been generally misused to stigmatize strange, unfamiliar, unpopular, or immoral behaviors, especially those deviating from Western standards of normality. Third, I shall review the MPI literature in school settings since the seventeenth century (the overwhelming majority of reports), describing their characteristic features and assessing evidence for the existence of MPI as a psychiatric category that, although problematic, I conclude does exist, not as an illness per se but as an abnormal state of health. However, I shall argue that social and cultural factors can best account for the enigmatic clustering of cases in certain times and places among almost exclusively those of female gender and demonstrate that it is pejorative for misogynist researchers to contend that the preponderance of female participants is explainable by as yet unspecified gender-specific biological forces purportedly exacerbated by abnormal personality traits and cathartic reactions to stress.[2]

INDIVIDUAL AND COLLECTIVE "HYSTERIA"

Hysteria is arguably the most ambiguous, confusing, misunderstood, and controversial term in the history of science. In psychiatry alone it has been used to describe no fewer than ten distinct individual behavioral manifestations, including the histrionic personality, forms of psychosis, and psychogenic pain disorder (Weintraub 1983; Kendell and Zealley 1993). It is generally used in the medical and psychiatric professions to describe a nervous system disturbance involving a loss or alteration of function, predominantly affecting females, whereby physical symptoms unconsciously exhibited have no corresponding organic etiology. In the standard psychiatric nomenclature this form is subsumed under the general heading of "somatoform disorder," subcategorized as "conversion disorder" or "hysterical neurosis, conversion type" (American Psychiatric Association [APA] 1994). Classic examples include the soldier opposed to killing, whose arm becomes temporarily paralyzed when attempting to fire a weapon (primary gain), or the onset of blindness after witnessing a traumatic event (secondary gain) (APA 1987, p. 257). Primary and secondary gains are the two mechanisms hypothesized for the appearance of conversion disorder. In the former, a psychological need or conflict is internalized, thereby offering a partial solution to an internal conflict. Such cases are typified by "a temporal relationship between an environmental stimulus that is apparently related to a psychological conflict or need and initiation or exacerbation of the symptom," which often manifests as a symbolic projection "and partial solution of the underlying psychological conflict" (APA 1987, p. 257). The achievement of secondary gain is attained through the avoidance of undesirable situations or outcomes, such as leg paralysis to prevent spousal desertion.

A fundamental problem with the concept of "hysterical" conversion is that like so many other psychiatric disorders, the diagnostic criteria are ambiguous and subject to interpretation and misdiagnosis—perhaps hysteria more than any other.[3] Szasz (1974b) does not view hysteria as an illness or disorder but a form of communication precipitated by problems in living. In this sense it can be interpreted as an idiom of distress. Others have also questioned its existence as a clinical entity, most notably the former editor of the *British Journal of Psychiatry*, Eliot Slater (1965).[4] Certainly, the term has been misused to stigmatize a variety of undesirable behaviors and can be analyzed on multiple levels. Indeed, what has been described as hysteria has been interpreted and conceptualized within various academic traditions.[5]

Since the mid-1970s, feminist critiques of hysteria have become fashionable, deconstructing the term and generally interpreting this predominantly female malady as an iatrogenic rubric created and maintained by the male-dominated medical profession (Smith-Rosenberg 1972; Ehrenreich and English 1978; Showalter 1991; Ussher 1991; Russell 1995; Micale 1995, pp. 66–88). These feminist writers document the clear misuse of the term *hysteria* by male-biased researchers who were/are able to consciously assert social, political, and legal dominance over females and their bodies. This has been achieved by medicalizing femininity and characterizing women's psychological constitution as innately unstable and prone to disturbance, relegating these females to the status of the "Other." The ambiguous diagnostic criteria for determining the presence of hysteria were ideal for this purpose, as it is said to mimic any organic disease (Rack 1982, p. 141; Weintraub 1983, p. 5).

The study of conversion symptoms has a checkered history of abuse and misuse, largely because of ambiguous diagnostic criteria and uncertainty surrounding their psychophysiological mechanism. However, although Kleinman (1988, p. 41) considers conversion symptoms "a great mystery at the heart of psychosomatic medicine," he believes "enough is known about conversion symptoms to describe them as the literal embodiment of conflicted meanings, somatic symbols that have psychological and social uses." Virtually all authors of textbooks on psychiatry and abnormal psychology concur with this position, describing conversion reactions as a clinical entity. In defending the concept, although Miller (1987, p. 163; 1988, p. 265) notes that all explanatory models of hysteria have significant weaknesses, health care professionals note a consistent pattern involving subjects presenting with symptoms with no discernible pathology. "If 'hysteria" refers to this and nothing more, then the term does carry useful meaning" (Miller 1987, p. 171).

In this chapter I am concerned solely with the concept of communicable conversion hysteria, which I shall describe with the more neutral term *conversion reaction,* eliminating the pejorative use of the word *hysteria* and its unsubstantiated designation as an illness per se. Although individual conversion reactions have received voluminous treatment and analysis and have been greatly misused and misunderstood, the concept of collective conversion reactions has been virtually neglected, with most discussions limited to brief descriptions of apparent episodes. Although the specific mechanism(s) of conversion reactions are unclear, transculturally and transhistorically physicians have observed a constellation of signs and symptoms signifying psychological distress or disorder for which there is no identifiable viral, toxicological, or bacteriological cause. As in individual conversion disorder, episodes are typified by an anxiety-generating precipitant within the victims' environment, and symptoms occur within close temporal proximity of exposure to the stimulus.

MISUSE OF THE TERM *COLLECTIVE "HYSTERIA"*

Usage of such terms as *mass* or *epidemic hysteria* has been made to marginalize ethnic and ideological minorities holding deviant, unpopular, or unfamiliar beliefs that differ from mainstream Western notions of normality, rationality, and reality. For instance, Bartholomew (1991b, 1993a, 1993b) demonstrates that large diffuse outbreaks of seemingly strange beliefs or actions/reactions typified as exemplifying communicable "hysteria" actually make better sense when understood from the sociocultural circumstances of the participants.[6] He notes, for instance, that such "hysterical" episodes as mutilation scares (Stewart 1977), phantom atomic fallout marks on windscreens (Medalia and Larsen 1958), Virgin Mary sightings (Tumin and Feldman 1955; Yassa 1980), and mysterious aerial objects (Bartholomew 1989a, 1989b) all involve plausible social realities among the participants who overscrutinized and reified the ambiguous rumor-related object, resulting in widespread misperceptions of tangible, not imaginary, environmental stimuli.

In his case study of mass sightings of imaginary rockets over Sweden in 1946, Bartholomew (1993a) notes that they occurred in conjunction with rare cometary debris entering the atmosphere and rumors that remote-controlled German V rockets, confiscated by the Soviets at the close of World War II, were being test fired as a form of political intimidation or a prelude to an invasion. The historical and political contexts were key factors in rendering the rumors plausible, as the episode occurred amid a long history of Soviet mistrust, including invasion fears, border disputes, and spy scandals, that has preoccupied Swedes for centuries. Public statements reinforcing the existence of the rockets were made by top Swedish military officials, politicians, scientists, police, and journalists—many of whom, when it was subsequently determined that the rockets were of psychological origin, stigmatized citizens as "hysterical" when, in fact, they were simply redefining cometary spray sporadically streaking across the sky as enemy rockets.

Bartholomew (1997d) identifies four subtypes of diffuse behaviors commonly erroneously associated with communicable "hysteria." The abovementioned category is of "immediate community threats." Three other categories are described. Community flight panics involve rational attempts to flee a plausible but imaginary threat. Most episodes last a few hours to several days or weeks, subsiding when it is realized that the harmful agent did not materialize.[7] Symbolic community threats typically endure unabated for years, encompassing entire countries and geographical regions. There is less of an immediate concern for safety and welfare (as in the case of immediate community threats) and more of a general long-term threat.[8] Finally, mass wish fulfillments involve similar or identical processes that facilitate community threats and moral panics, except the object of extraordinary interest is esteemed and satisfies psychological needs. Cases typically persist from a few weeks to several months and recur periodically in clusters.[9]

The influx of reports of occupational overuse injuries among Australian keyboard users during the mid-1980s has been attributed to "hysterical" contagion (Lucire 1986; Ferguson 1987; Hopkins 1990, p. 365). Australian psychiatrist Yolande Lucire (1986) explained the reason for the rise in Repetition Strain Injuries (RSI) as a workplace neurosis that manifested as a form of collective conversion "hysteria." A major factor in implicating MPI was a series of reports that the majority of patients were female, which Wayne Hall and Louise Morrow (1988, p. 646) noted "is a characteristic of epidemic hysteria." Such analyses seek to understand the origins of the RSI "epidemic" independent of its local context and meaning. Most Australian keyboard operators are female. Further, although RSI experiences were not unique to Australia, the scale of the "ailment" was (Bell 1989a). Work-related compensation injuries in Australia are regarded as a right, and a consensus emerged prior to the "epidemic" that the Workers' Compensation system could be easily exploited by simply obtaining a doctor's certificate (Hunter 1989).

The epidemiology or spread of RSI followed social networks, decisively establishing that it was neither illness nor injury but was spread by the conscious or unconscious desire for compensation (Bell 1989a, 1989b).[10] The situation was exacerbated by the intervention and support of the then strong Australian trade unions and the ambiguity of the diagnostic criteria (Forsyth 1989). The RSI diagnosis became a vague catchall category for a variety of endemic aches and pains, with its anomalous pervasiveness and persistence in Australia earning it the label *kangaroo paw* (Awerbuch 1985; Sharrod 1985).

A consensus among investigators has now emerged that the RSI label was an overinclusive, ill-defined diagnostic rubric embodying "the causal theory that the symptoms were an injury caused by repetitive movement and over-use. Its creation gave legitimacy to complaints of arm pain as a reason for absence from work and a basis for claims under workers' compensation" (Hall and Morrow 1988, p. 646). In underscoring the social nature of the RSI diagnosis, the incidence of writer's cramp (thought to be an earlier manifesta-tion of RSI under a different label) among Australian keyboard telegraphists in 1971 was 14 percent (Ferguson 1971). However, symptoms were virtually nonexistent "in countries where [workers'] compensation was not paid for it" (Lucire 1986, p. 324).[11] The common attribution of "RSI" symptoms as epi-demic hysteria by many Australian medical practitioners during the 1980s fostered an epidemic of symptoms among predominantly female Australian keyboard operators.[12] This incident underscores the dangers of superimpos-ing popular stereotypes of innate female vulnerability to both individual and collective hysteria.

Western-trained scientists have a long history of marginalizing deviant or unfamiliar collective behaviors and beliefs under the stigmatizing rubric "epi-demic hysteria" (Bartholomew 1990b, 1993a, 1994a, 1994b, 1994d, 1997b). This includes such seemingly heterogeneous collective behaviors as group lycanthropy (Goshen 1967), mass suicide (Faguet and Faguet 1982), the Salem witch hunts (Bonfanti 1977), riots (Smelser 1962), and masturbatory "insanity" (Gilbert 1975). Political movements during World War II, such as Japanese imperialism, have been interpreted as exemplifying mass psychopa-thology (Norman 1945, p. 65), as was Nazism (Baynes 1941; Brown 1944, p. 59), with Cartwright and Biddiss (1972, p. 210) typifying those pledging alle-giance to Hitler as "mentally sick." Clusters of pyromania have been labeled epidemic "hysteria" by L. Boling and C. Brotman (1975), as have mass behav-iors labeled fads, fashions, crazes, and booms (Brown 1954).[13,14]

Other behaviors stigmatized as "mass hysteria" by social scientists can be traced back centuries. Journalist Charles Mackay (1852) chronicled the "tulipomania" in Holland between 1634 and 1637, whereby exorbitant prices were paid for tulip bulbs, describing the event in terms of irrationality. Contem-porary textbooks on collective behavior and sociology continue to describe these behaviors with such terms as *craze, irrationality,* and *mass hysteria.* However, in examining the episode within its social, historical, and economic contexts, P. M. Garber (1989) argues that the seemingly irrational aspects of the "tulip mania" were exaggerated. He disputes as sensational Mackay's claims that many citizens neglected their jobs, becoming overwhelmed by crowd psychology, with the obsessive desire to obtain tulip bulbs. Although some bulb varieties did reach astronomical prices and the tulip market suddenly "crashed," the economic consequences were not nearly as devastating as typically portrayed by Mackay. Nevertheless, under the basic laws of economics and marketplace practice, as bulbs can be propagated and sold at considerable profit, the eventual drop in prices is virtually inevitable because the greater the number of bulbs produced and sold, the less scarce and valuable they become. Goode (1992, p. 382) remarks that "at the height of speculation, a single tulip bulb sold for a weight of gold equivalent, in today's market, to US$50,000; this might in itself seem to represent evidence of frenzied and irrational trading. . . . But even nowadays, in more sober economic times, such prices are not unusual." Clearly, the often loose and inappropriate usage of such words as *mass* or *epidemic hysteria* to describe various social phenomena that are separate from the condition of conversion reactions within individuals or groups has created, and continues to create, considerable confusion among scientists and the lay public. It is therefore necessary in the next section to be explicit in defining what constitutes a collective conversion reaction.

CHARACTERISTIC FEATURES OF MASS CONVERSION REPORTS IN SCHOOLS

This section reviews all known, obtainable reports labeled collective conversion reactions in school settings (the overwhelming majority of reports) under various alternative labels (e.g., "mass hysteria," "epidemic hysteria," "hysterical contagion," and "mass psychogenic illness") (N=115) based on a search of MEDLINE,[15] Sociological Abstracts, Psychological Abstracts, cross-referencing, and reliable, detailed press accounts. The standard definition of a syndrome is the appearance of a constellation of signs and symptoms that when occurring together indicate the appearance of an illness or abnormal condition. As mass conversion symptoms are affected by social, cultural, and precipitating factors, feature distinct presentation patterns, and do not appear to be a normal state of health, Collective Conversion Syndrome (CCS) most appropriately describes the process. The definition of school encompasses not only the formal classroom (educational) setting but also groups of students outside school premises who are participating in school-related activities, such as a field trip, dance, concert, play, chorus, marching band, or sports event. Fifty-seven additional cases fitting this definition were reported in occupational settings (see Bartholomew and Sirois 1997), and singular episodes were located in a prison, an orphanage, and a hospital. For the sake of convenience and manageability, these nonschool cases will be excluded from this discussion, and I shall focus solely on schools.[16]

An episode of collective conversion syndrome comprises two or more subjects in a closed social setting exhibiting perceptions, sensations, and beliefs for which there is no identifiable pathogenic agent or source and which did not originate in an organized, ritualized, or institutionalized manner. Excluded from this definition are fainting, twitching, shaking, glossolalia, altered states of consciousness, and related phenomena originating in an organized, ritualized, or institutionalized manner, such as deliberately induced ecstatic states in school-related charismatic religious organizations. With the exception of a series of Malaysian press reports, primary sources considered in this study are restricted to scientific journal accounts.[17]

What may have been the first recorded episode of "epidemic hysteria" in an educational setting occurred in 1639 at a girls' school in Lille, France, during a period of widespread belief in witchcraft. With great consternation, school founder Antoinette Bourgignon told her pupils she had observed "little black angels" flying about their heads warning them "to beware of the devil, whose imps were hovering about them" (Mackay 1852, pp. 539–540). Each of the fifty students eventually confessed to being a witch, eating the flesh of babies, and flying through the air on broomsticks. The students narrowly avoided burning at the stake when the activities of the headmistress, who escaped, became the focus of public scrutiny. Since Charles Mackay (1852), an accomplished journalist of the period, does not provide further details, this report is given only as a historical illustration and is not included in the list of cases.

THEORETICAL OVERVIEW OF MASS CONVERSION REACTIONS IN SCHOOLS

Contemporary explanations for the appearance of MPI in schools fall within five broad theoretical traditions: (1) psychoanalytic, (2) sociological, (3) social psychological, (4) biological, and (5) anthropological. These theoretical perspectives are not mutually exclusive and often share overlapping features. Although each perspective emphasizes the influence of different mechanisms and processes in precipitating outbreaks, all converge on the pivotal role of extreme psychosocial stress.

First, psychoanalytic theories are formulated based on observations of not collective but individual conversion reactions. It is assumed that the victim is reacting to a state of extreme psychic conflict by subconsciously converting the conflict into physical symptoms. Often the affected body parts are related to the specific conflict. A classic example is the witness to a traumatic event, who subsequently experiences partial or complete blindness (Mohr and Bond 1982).

Psychoanalytical perspectives have been used to explain the prominence of histrionics and playacting among mass conversion victims, which exacerbate outbreaks, especially in enduring episodes involving strict academic discipline. This includes the conscious, subconscious, or partially conscious utilization of the "sick role" to obtain sympathy, attention, and manipulation of cherished or undesirable activities and situations. For example, an outbreak of spasmodic twitching at a Louisiana high school spread after symptoms in the first pupil enabled her to avoid dance classes and rekindle a boyfriend's waning affection. After observing the success of the initial case, over the ensuing weeks six other female students obtained "secondary gains" as a result of their newly acquired illness status (Schuler and Parenton 1943). Silvio Benaim and colleagues (1973) report that Louise, the index case in an episode of falling among sixteen- and seventeen-year-old schoolgirls near London, admitted to faking "drop attacks" after becoming accustomed to the growing attention she received from her initial genuine fainting spells. Psychiatrists typically use the term *secondary gains* to refer to symptoms that are only unintentionally produced, whereas the feigning of symptoms is classified as malingering (APA 1994, p. 457). Histrionics produced during school episodes of collective conversion often do not appear to be intentionally produced with the conscious intent of obtaining secondary benefits, but it appears considerable feigning may occur to convince authority figures to take some immediate action to nullify the perceived threat or anxiety-generating stimulus. This is especially evident in persistent outbreaks where authorities are not perceived as having thoroughly investigated the potential triggering agent. One must remember that even if medical investigators are unable to detect the presence of a toxic gas or biological agent, those experiencing "epidemic" conversion symptoms and their parents are often convinced that the external agent exists but has not been identified.

Second, a major sociological explanation within the positivist-functionalist tradition is outlined by Smelser (1962), who contends that episodes occur within dysfunctional social orders. Rapid social and cultural changes are believed to produce a disequilibrium within the normal state of society. Smelser believes five factors must be present to trigger episodes. First, there must be "structural conduciveness" whereby the structure of society permits the emergence of mass behavior. Hence, a school episode of "epidemic" conversion cannot transpire in a "primitive" society that does not have enclosed classrooms and an organized school system. Similarly, a stock market crash cannot occur in societies that prohibit private entrepreneurship and successfully outlaw the ownership of shares. The second determinant is "structural strain," the existence of stress or conflict, such as an unfamiliar odor or poor student-teacher relations. Third is "growth and spread of a generalized belief" whereby individual group members interpret the "strain"—a false, irrational "hysterical belief"—in a like manner. The strain must (1) be ambiguous, (2) generate extraordinary anxiety, and (3) result in a redefinition of the situation attributed to the stressful agent and is often exacerbated by (4) "precipitating factors," which are usually specific events that exaggerate the effects of the imaginary threat by "providing 'evidence' that something terrible is at work" (Smelser 1962, p. 92). For instance, in Seremban, Malaysia, a sudden electricity disruption was believed to confirm the presence of supernatural forces in a school.[18] Prior to the appearance of a mystery "gas" at a Hong Kong school, which affected over 300 students, rumors of a recent toxic gas scare at a nearby school were in circulation, and several teachers had discussed the incident with their pupils—some to the point of advising them as to what action to take if a similar event should occur there (Wong et al. 1982, p. 430).

"Mobilization for action" and "inadequate social control" are Smelser's final two determinants of collective behavior. The former category considers how communication and leadership contribute to fostering a mass reaction. This is clearly evident in many episodes where symptoms begin in the older, higher-status students and spread to the younger ones. Often the first affected pupil is an influential group member. Finally, "social control" is a counter determinant that is unable to impede or prevent outbreaks. An anxious look, indecision, or confusion or panic by teachers, administrators, medical personnel, or law enforcement officials is counterproductive and fails to contain episodes. Smelser contends that his theory can explain the appearance of such diverse mass behaviors as panics, riots, "crazes," and both norm and value-oriented social movements.[19]

Third, two prominent social psychological perspectives exist—convergence and emergent-norm theories. The former position holds that students sharing similar predispositions, such as atypical personality traits, have the highest risk of exhibiting psychogenic symptoms following exposure to a stressful stimulus—a view that is unsubstantiated, as no consistent pattern has been uncovered by researchers. The emergent-norm perspective rejects the notion that students become "hysterical" per se as a cathartic response to accumulating stress but rather focuses on the influence of sociocultural norms and unique contextual circumstances in structuring episodes (Kerckhoff 1982). Instead of emphasizing the role of stress per se or pathological group processes, focus is on the newly emerging definition of the situation from the viewpoint of those affected, creating what Thomas (1923) first described as a self-fulfilling prophecy.

In investigating an episode of "epidemic" conversion in a Malaysian school, Lee and Ackerman (1980, p. 79) emphasize the importance of examining stress "as a matter of definition in a specific sociocultural context rather than as an objective given from which predictions can be made," focusing attention on how victims and those unaffected retrospectively interpret events. This sociocultural approach examines how victims, observers, and the community at large explain the episode, thereby leading to a situation of "analyzing the consequences of these interpretations" (p. 79). Whether a particular student becomes affected is determined by such factors as physical and visual proximity, social and cultural beliefs, education level, personality traits (not necessarily abnormal), social and spatial distance from the threatening situation, and precipitating events. For instance, based on this theoretical approach and previous observations, students with the strongest social ties with those already affected or in close physical proximity to the perceived threat should experience the highest stress levels, as they are most likely to observe the initial index case. The actions of authority figures such as teachers or administrators, either through calm reassurance or expressions of outward anxiety, can validate or defuse situations.

Kerckhoff (1982) observes that outbreaks are most likely to occur in settings where one or more dramatic illness cases (e.g., fainting, vomiting) or abnormal behavior (e.g., epileptic seizures, drug ingestion) appears. The cause of the illness or illnesses is unknown at the time. These initial dramatic events must be viewed as a direct threat to the remaining students, thus increasing group stress and associated physiological symptoms such as heart palpitations and hyperventilation. The potential threat must be credible to the affected students and teachers. For instance, if a student were to faint during any given school day, it would not ordinarily precipitate CCS. Yet if this incident were to have occurred during the 1991 Middle East War and coincided with the presence of a strange odor, many young, inexperienced schoolchildren might assume they were the subject of an Iraqi poison gas raid. In fact, just such a scenario was reported at a Rhode Island school during the Gulf War (Rockney and Lemke 1992).

Similar episodes of mass psychogenic illness have been reported in school settings following imaginary threats of poison gas attacks in the Israeli-occupied West Bank (Modan et al. 1983; Hafez 1985) and in Soviet Georgia (Goldsmith 1989). In the last two instances political unrest, rumors, recent historical events, and speculative media reports engendered widespread, plausible beliefs that such attacks were a credible possibility. The episode in Soviet Georgia affected about 400 adolescent females in several nearby schools in the wake of a recent highly publicized political rally dissipated by Russian

troops dispensing toxic gas, including chloropicrin. As is typical in MPI episodes, the transient, benign symptoms of the students reflected the complaints
of gas victims: burning eyes, abdominal pain, skin irritation, and dry throat.
Instead of representing abnormal responses to stress, it is arguable that pupils
are conforming to group norms. Thus, upon seeing a classmate fall ill and
soon noting a strange odor, some pupils might assume a connection, triggering immediate and acute conversion reactions.

Although social factors are undeniable in precipitating school outbreaks,
the historical and cross-cultural overrepresentation of females in such episodes suggests the possibility that a fourth theoretical perspective, that of
biological factors, may exacerbate existing social and cultural forces. For
instance, classroom social conditions are fairly uniform for both male and
female students in many Western countries, yet CCS continues to be reported
almost exclusively among females. Also, why does the army not produce similarly high levels of conversion reaction in male recruits? A plausible physiological mechanism for this occurrence is the innate susceptibility of men-
struating females to panic disorder and hyperventilation syndrome (Klein 1993).
Further, the reporting of individual somatic complaints has been associated
with the onset of puberty and menstruation (Aro and Taipale 1987). "Hysterical" disorders in general may have a biological basis, as they are more
frequently diagnosed in females, such as somatization disorder, globus hystericus, and psychogenic pain disorder (APA 1994). Further, the incidence of
individual conversion disorders appears to be more common in females than
males, with reported female to male ratios varying from 2:1 to as high as
10:1. This parallels the range in prevalence ratios of "epidemic" conversion
episodes in schools (APA 1994, p. 455).

Biological theories suggesting innate female susceptibility to CCS were
popular until the late 1960s. Previously, it was commonly believed females
possessed weaker mental constitutions than men and were prone to emotional
lability, making them prime candidates for episodes. Generally, this view has
been labeled sexist, with critics arguing that proponents of a biological basis
for cases have not taken into account the influence of gender socialization, as
females are generally enculturated to possess emotionally expressive, submissive character traits (Parsons 1955). Further, females exhibit a transcultural
tendency to be low in the power hierarchy, increasing their susceptibility to
experience long-term emotional frustration.

Fifth and finally, an anthropological perspective involves a focus on the
context, social status, and local worldview of pupils, utilizing research by British anthropologist Ioan Myrddin Lewis (1971). This model is applied to CCS
episodes in non-Western schools by Lee and Ackerman (1980). In observing

a preponderance of females in spirit possession cults and charismatic religious movements within various cross-cultural settings, Lewis attributes this
situation to their low social status and oppression in male-dominated societies where they are low on the power hierarchy. Women in many of these
societies often experience—sometimes collectively—trance and possession
states, psychomotor agitation, and anxiety-related transient somatic complaints.
Concordantly, females in repressive, intolerable social situations are characteristic features of school life in Malaysia and Central Africa where CCS is
endemic. Although female redress is generally culturally unacceptable in these
societies, males typically believe those affected are possessed by spirits. Outbreaks of dissociation, histrionics, and psychomotor dysfunction among predominantly female pupils in these countries often include insulting authorities
and frank criticism of administration policies. Yet these outbursts are accepted
with impunity, as the temporary possession status deflects the attribution of
blame. As a result, they have developed into idioms of distress and negotiation, whereby outbreaks signal to the wider community that something is
amiss. The anthropological perspective assumes that females are not susceptible per se but are rendered vulnerable through gender socialization.

PATTERNS

Based on the descriptive features of episodes, two distinct presentation
patterns are identifiable—patterns that correspond closely to what Simon
Wessely (1987) terms *mass anxiety hysteria* and *mass motor hysteria.* The former
is of shorter duration, typically one day, and involves sudden, extreme anxiety
following the perception of a false threat. The second type is confined to a
intolerable social setting and is characterized by dissociative states, histrionics, and alterations in psychomotor activity, usually persisting for weeks or
months. I shall also discuss a single third episode type of what I shall term
mass pseudo hysteria, involving the relabeling of mundane symptoms by
hypervigilant authority figures. To avoid the pejorative use of the word *hysteria,* I shall substitute the more neutral term *conversion reactions.* Hence, "mass
anxiety hysteria" becomes "mass anxiety conversion reaction," "mass motor
hysteria" becomes "mass motor conversion reaction," and "mass pseudo hysteria" is relabeled "mass pseudo conversion reaction."

TYPE ONE: MASS ANXIETY CONVERSION REACTIONS

Mass anxiety conversion reaction is prevalent in Western or developed
countries amid a social context conspicuously devoid of preexisting stress.
Outbreaks are characterized by the appearance of illness signs and symptoms
in a single student, which spread rapidly to schoolmates and occasionally

teachers, who experience various ambiguous, anxiety-related somatic complaints. Occasionally, the index case is a sick teacher. The behavior of the index subject is often dramatic, engendering consternation among classmates. Often the first affected student, the index case, exhibits a medical condition such as an epileptic fit, schizophrenia, tonsillitis, or heat stroke. At the time, information as to the specific cause is typically unknown to the remaining students and is usually learned retrospectively. Soon after the appearance of the index case, pupils begin to attribute the cause to an unusual odor assumed to represent a toxic gas, or an agent such as a communicable illness, all of which are believed to pose an immediate personal threat. Food poisoning from the school cafeteria or a toxic chemical spill are common initial suspicions. Such determinations are made either nonverbally or orally through rumors and discussion about the incident among classmates. Sometimes rumors play the same role as a precipitating event. The possible presence of the news media, recent events, local traditions, and folk beliefs exacerbate the situation.[20]

In non-Western countries such as Malaysia, odors or food poisoning are rarely suspected in mass anxiety conversion reactions. Instead, suspicion is placed on an array of diminutive supernatural entities. In such settings the index case typically exhibits screaming, crying, and hyperventilation after seeing what are believed to be such beings. Fellow pupils typically assume the index subject is hexed or charmed or that a ghost is roaming the school, triggering sudden, extreme anxiety as they assume they may be the next victims. The search for potential explanations among pupils is limited only by plausibility, as the lack of educational and life experiences can foster hypotheses potentially fantastic to adults or individuals living outside the culture or subcultural milieu. Students in the closest spatial, visual, or social contact with the index case, and subsequent fallen cohorts, are most susceptible to develop symptoms. In the majority of cases investigators identify a downward spread of symptoms along the age scale, with the oldest student(s) affected first, followed by younger schoolmates. Typical are reports by Schuler and Parenton (1943), Benaim, Horder, and Anderson (1973), and Teoh, Soewondo, and Sidharta (1975) where the index case was a prominent group member of the school class.

Most episodes last a single day and rarely more than a week. Lengthier cases or episodes involving relapses appear related to the inability of medical, school, and community leaders to convince the affected students and their parents of the psychogenic nature of the symptoms. In rare instances where the imaginary agent is believed to persist or authorities are not perceived to have thoroughly examined the premises, cases can endure sporadically for several weeks or months. Episodes of mass anxiety conversion reaction cease rapidly once students are convincingly reassured that the phantom threat, most typically a harmless odor, has been eliminated or never existed.

A classic episode of mass anxiety conversion reaction occurred at a girls' secondary school in Blackburn, England, in 1965. The episode was thoroughly investigated by Moss and McEvedy (1966) and reported in the *British Medical Journal*. On October 6 most of the schoolgirls attended a church ceremony under royal patronage. The service was delayed, and the group had to endure a 3-hour wait, during which 20 people fainted. The next day the fainting incident was the major topic of discussion. At the morning assembly that day one girl fainted, which was not uncommon, as the assembly averaged 2 to 3 faints per week. After the assembly 4 additional girls felt faint and were placed on chairs in a corridor near the center of the building; during the first two periods 6 more girls were added to the distressed group. Because of concerns that they might injure themselves if they were to faint and fall from the chairs, they were asked to lie on the floor.

With the first group of symptomatic girls positioned in the highly visible corridors, the situation appeared more dramatic, and the "epidemic" spread by line of sight soon after the midmorning break. By midday 141 pupils were complaining of various symptoms: dizziness, fainting, headache, shivering, back and stomach pain, nausea, shortness of breath, facial numbness, and tetanic spasms. Ambulances rushed to the scene and transported 85 of the most severely affected to the hospital. The mass media speculated as to the source of the "mysterious illness," adding further anxiety in the following days. Medical tests yielded unremarkable results, and over the next 15 days several clusters of cases occurred at the school in a declining fashion, with fewer numbers of students affected each time. In all, about one-third of the 550 girls were affected. "What became epidemic was a piece of behaviour consequent on an emotional state: excitement or, in the latter stages, frank fear led to overbreathing, with its characteristic sequelae—faintness, dizziness, paraesthesiae, and tetany. Once learned, this self-reinforcing piece of behaviour restarted spontaneously when the school was assembled. By day 12, however, the hysterical nature of the epidemic was generally accepted, and a firm line prevented the behaviour propagating as extensively as it had on the previous occasions" (Moss and McEvedy 1966, p. 1299).

TYPE TWO: MASS MOTOR CONVERSION REACTIONS

The second discernible episode type is typified by an atmosphere of long-term preexisting tension. Twentieth-century cases are primarily confined to schools in non-Western, technologically underdeveloped, traditional societies.

Within such settings both male and adult-dominated power structures often foster strict disciplinary routines among pupils, especially females. Students have little means of redress, as negotiation or protest channels with authorities are inhibited or nonexistent. They are unable to escape the anxiety-generating situation, as school is mandatory. Even if they stay at home and feign illness, homework is still required. Besides, such avoidance strategies will remove them from social contact with many schoolmates. The inescapable, intolerable situation engenders intense frustration internalized as conversion symptoms during the ensuing weeks or months.

This pattern was most prominent in Europe during the second half of the nineteenth and the early twentieth centuries in response to rigid rationalist educational discipline in many schools in such countries as France, Switzerland, and especially Germany. Although the severity of school rules could vary between districts, the school systems in which episodes occurred were typified by performance pressures, monotonous tasks, rote memorization, repetitive writing and arithmetic drills, and a lack of imagination and individuality. During this period curricula in French "primary elementary" schools were characterized as "too intense" and "far too much composed of memory work" (Johnson 1908, p. 26). Article 1384 of the French educational code discouraged physical activities and games during school hours, as teachers were held responsible for accidents occurring under their supervision (p. 26). Scholastic/academic competition was extreme, with excessive pressure on students to perform coming from both teachers and parents and a list of pupils waiting to take their place if a pupil was to "drop out," withdraw, or be expelled. "With such dismissal constantly hanging over their heads, pupils appear to be always at high pressure" (Johnson 1908, p. 27). As early as age eleven, students could enter the secondary schools (*lycees*), "a veritable prison-house for all pupils from the youngest equally to the oldest, with a system of continual espionage known as *surbeillance* (every minute of the day being duly apportioned, even recreation policed), relieved . . . by scarcely a human feature" (p. 27). B. Dumville (1908, pp. 116–117) described the French teaching method as little more than "monotonous and reiterated preaching" whereby at the close of each lesson "a tireless *resume*" must be committed to memory. Concurrently, in some German districts discipline was so rigid that according to Gustav Spiller (1908a, p. 215), even "corporal punishment in the elementary schools is harsh and severe." Jessie Douglas Montgomery (1908, pp. 237–238) observed that the German military training habits of obedience, order, and self-control were also incorporated into the education of women and children. In addition, the Swiss education system during this period was virtually identical to the German system (Spiller 1908b, p. 196), with Spiller noting that discipline was high, games were rare, and free thought and imagination were suppressed (pp. 199, 203).

At a girls' school in Basel, Switzerland, during 1893, contagious trembling and convulsions affected 20 students who were prevented from completing in-school written assignments. Symptoms virtually disappeared after school hours, relapsing only upon reentering school grounds (Aemmer 1893). The previous year a remarkably similar episode was reported at Gross-tinz, Germany. Convulsions and tremors prevented the girls from doing writing class work but ceased when school was closed prematurely for vacation, only to return in the form of severe headaches when classes reopened (Hirt 1892, 1893). At an elementary school in Chemnitz, Germany, during the first decade of the twentieth century, Schoedel (1906), the school physician, documented arm and hand tremors in 21 female students over four weeks. The pupils performed all other manual tasks normally, including gym class, and were affected only during written schoolwork. Symptoms ceased soon after it was announced, "Since you are not able to write, you must unfortunately have mental arithmetic again" (Burnham 1924, p. 327).

During the twentieth century, mass motor conversion reactions were most evident in schools within Malaysia and Central and eastern Africa. The African outbreaks usually affected missionary schools (Rankin and Philip 1963; Kagwa 1964; Ebrahim 1968; Muhangi 1973). A typical African case was investigated by Dhadphale and Shaikh (1983) involving an outbreak of twitching, mental confusion, uncontrollable laughing, running, and anxiety and affecting 126 students at a secondary school in Zambia during May 1976. The researchers noted that "the recent strict disciplinary measures taken by the new administration, such as rigid separation of boys and girls, may have prepared the emotionally charged background" (p. 87). Ebrahim notes that African children are dominated by their "all-powerful elders." Conflict appears to arise from exposure to foreign ideas that challenge traditional beliefs, with escape sought through conversion reactions. According to Ebrahim (1968, p. 438) these episodes are precipitated by "emotional conflict aroused in children who are being brought up at home amidst traditional tribal conservatism, while being exposed in school to thoughts and ideas which challenge accepted beliefs."

In Malaysia the widespread appearance of mass motor conversion reactions in schools coincides with rapid social and cultural changes (Teoh and Yeoh 1973; Teoh and Tan 1976), especially Islamic revivalism, which has rapidly gained influence since the early 1960s. Islamic by birth, ethnic Malays comprise just over half of the Malaysian population. Yet mass motor conversion reaction is almost exclusively confined to female Malays attending religious boarding schools. Episodes have become prevalent primarily in Malaysian Islamic schools since 1962. These schools are notorious for their rigid discipline and lack of privacy, where even basic choices such as which school to attend, courses to take, careers to pursue, and friendships to develop are decided by others (Selvadurai 1985, pp. 7–8). In coeducational Islamic schools boys and girls are strictly segregated, even within the same classroom. Students must account for their whereabouts at all times. Interaction with boys is strictly prohibited by school authorities, courting is also forbidden, and even visits by relatives are closely monitored in special public rooms. Mass motor conversion reaction in Malay boarding schools typically occurs amid "a general feeling of unhappiness about some new condition of study or rule among the girls" (Deva 1990, p. 94). In conjunction with such oppressive practices, social, cultural, and religious protocols prohibit female Malays from direct confrontation with their superiors (Ackerman 1980).

With the continued presence of strict religious discipline, eventually a small number of students begin exhibiting conversion symptoms. Such events foster widespread anxiety in the existence of demonic agents within the school that posses an immediate personal threat. Teoh and colleagues (1975, p. 260) report a "monotonously similar" pattern in Malaysian schools whereby "girls would scream, shout, and run aimlessly all over in terror, with severe hyperventilation followed by muscular twitchings and tetanic spasms of the limbs."

> Some would fall on the floor in a trancelike state, as though in a stupor. Occasionally one or two of the subjects would speak up on behalf of the group, voicing their misdemeanors and frustrations. Very often they became abusive. They characteristically took hints and cues from one another. Most of the subjects . . . would swear amnesia. On questioning, the girls would complain of seeing fearsome objects. . . . Some would see dark flying objects or an ugly woman eight feet tall. The occupants of one hostel complained that a hungry spirit was always stealing their food and raiding the refrigerator. Others complained of ghosts stealing their underwear and jamming their doors. (Teoh, Soewondo, and Sidharta 1975, p. 260)

It is vital to realize that although the interpretations of these events by the pupils may seem bizarre by Western standards, they are entirely consistent with popular Malay folk beliefs (see Skeat 1900; Gimlette 1915; Chen 1970; Endicott 1970). Animistic customs and folk beliefs are prevalent in Malay society, as there is a widespread belief in the existence of various supernatural forces—such as the efficacy of magic potions, spells, amulets, charms, and curses—that are easily obtained by consulting a witchdoctor (*bomoh*), whose

services remain popular. There is also a prevalent Islamic belief in the existence of supernatural beings known as the *Jinn,* which are described in the
Koran, in addition to diminutive fairylike *toyl* creatures and ghosts (*hantus*)
from Malay culture. Extreme anxiety, conversion reactions, and hyperventilation syndrome spread rapidly among pupils in closest proximity or visual
contact or having the strongest social ties with the initial cohort exhibiting
dissociative states. These trancelike states sometimes take the form of spirit
possession, which can be dramatic and convincing to observers. In virtually
every non-Western episode of this type, the services of one or more native
healers were solicited to exorcise the evil spirit(s). Repression-induced conversion symptoms typically persist from one month to several years, depending on the changes implemented by authorities in response to the outbreak. If
discipline is eased and anxiety levels decline, episodes usually subside. However, if the intolerable situation persists, outbreaks can endure indefinitely.

Contemporary Western episodes are uncommon but occasionally occur.
One outbreak of mass motor conversion reaction took the form of epidemic
fainting, dissociation, and histrionics among several pupils at a girls' school
near London amid serious interpersonal and sexual conflicts following the
death of a former schoolmate and lesbian advances by a school mistress
(Benaim, Horder, and Anderson 1973). In this instance, instead of the "drop
attacks" being instigated by academic discipline, the school premises served
as a stage where the girls' personal problems appeared in the form of conversion dramas over a 7-month period.

Another Western example of mass motor conversion reaction occurred at
a Negro school in Louisiana in the southern United States over a 6-month
period in 1962 and was investigated by Schuler and Parenton (1943). All but
one of the 23 affected pupils were female. The students exhibited dizziness,
headaches, and epileptic-type seizures. Most of the "blackout spells" lasted a
few minutes and occasionally up to an hour. A considerable number of the
students, ranging in age from ten to seventeen, were sexually active. The outbreak coincided with rumors that all of the girls were going to be adminis-
tered pregnancy tests and, if determined to be pregnant, they would be sent
away to a correctional school. Treatment with tranquilizers and sedatives was
ineffective, and visits by outside authorities exacerbated the symptoms. Only
with the gradual reduction of stress did the outbreak subside 7 months later.

TYPE THREE: MASS PSEUDO CONVERSION REACTION

One case surveyed involved relabeling mundane symptoms in closed,
cohesive social units instigated and maintained by the erroneous beliefs of
hypervigilant authority figures. During a routine social gathering of parents

Symbols for Tables 6.1 and 6.2 are as follows. The symbol "<" is used in the following manner: < 20 = less than 20, 20< = 20 or less; the symbol "/" (e.g. "M/F") means both males and females were involved in unspecified proportions; the symbol ":" means both sexes were involved but the first letter to appear means that gender was in greater proportion (e.g., F:M means females predominated but the exact number was not specified).

Table 6.1—Chronological List of Mass Anxiety Conversion Reactions in School Settings

Source/Circa	Location	Primary Symptoms	Duration	Sex	No./Age Span	Index Noted
Bokai 1892	Hungary	Hyperventilation	—	female	12	– (9–15)
Legendre 1908	Szechwan, China	Genital sensations	few days	male	20	– (<20)
Olson 1928	USA	Fainting	1 month	female	9	+ (14–17)
Pfeiffer 1964	USA	Hyperventilation	1 day	female	8	+ (16–20)
Moss & McEvedy 1966	Blackburn, England	Hyperventilation	2 weeks	female	140	– (10–16)
McEvedy, Griffith, & Hall, 1966	England	Vomiting	9 days	female	105	– (10–15)
(1–2) 1966	Kajang, Malaysia	Crying, screaming, fainting	1 week	—	18	+ (<20)
Mausner & Gezon 1967	USA	Gonorrhea-like symptoms	15 days	female (80%)	50–100	+ (6–12)
Lyons & Potter 1970	Northern Ireland	Fainting	1 day	female	28	+ (11–14)

Source / Year	Location	Symptoms	Duration	Sex	N	Age
(3–4) 1971	Pahang, Malaysia	Howling, screaming	~2 days	female	5	− (13–17)
(5) 1971	Ipoh, Malaysia	Screaming, crying	1 day	—	16	− (<20)
(6–7) 1972	Junjong, Malaysia	Crying, screaming	1 day	22 F 2 M	24	+ (6–17)
Goldberg 1973	Maryland	Screaming	1 day	47 F 6 M	53	+ (12–18)
Smith & Eastham* 1973	Newcastle Upon Tyne, England	Abdominal pain	1 day	76 F 4 M	130	+ (8–15)
Levine/Polk 1973	Alabama	Pruritus, rash	2 weeks	2F:1M	98	+ (7–12)
Sirois 1974	Quebec, Canada	Fainting	1 day	female	11	− (9–11)
Sirois 1975	Quebec, Canada	Fainting	6 weeks	—	100	+ (12–14)
Nitzkin 1975	Florida	Headache	1 day	2F:1M	34	+ (11–12)
Levine 1977	Alabama	Fainting	1 day	female and male	57	+ (14–17)

Continued on next page

---

*In the case of Smith and Eastham (1973) in Table 6.1, the total number of persons affected does not equal 100 percent. Smith (1973, p. 956) stated that "approximately 130 . . . developed an illness," but only 76 were specifically identified as female and 4 as males.

Table 6.1—continued

Source/Circa	Location	Primary Symptoms	Duration	Sex	No./Age Span	Index Noted
Figueroa 1977	Kingston, Jamaica	Abdominal pain	1 week	3F:1M	196	– (10–11)
(8) 1978	Kuah, Malaysia	Fainting, screaming, seeing ghosts	1 day	female	7	+ (–13–17)
Forrester 1979	England	Fainting	1 day	female	40	– (20<)
Bebbington et al. 1989	Nottinghamshire, England	Fainting	1 day	female	414	+ (7–17)
O'Donnell 1980	Ireland	Abdominal pain	1 day	female and male	47	+ (9–12)
Lee & Ackerman 1980	West Malaysia	Screaming	2 days	16 female 1 male	17	+ (~16–17)
Moffat 1980	Montreal, Canada	Dizziness	1 day	23 female 7 male	30	+ (12–14)
Small & Nicholi 1982	Maine	Dizziness	1 day	male-female	34	+ (9–13)
Wong/Tam 1982	Hong Kong	Abdominal	3 days	2F:1M	355	– (6–14)
(9) 1982	Kuching, Sarawak, Malaysia	Screaming, strange figures seen	3 days	female	30	+ (~6–17)
(10–12) 1982	Kuala Trengganu, Malaysia	Swearing, screaming, crying	3 days	female	~30	– (13, 15–16)

(13) 1982	Labis, Malaysia	Crying, moaning	8 days	female	20	– (12–16)
Modan et al. 1983	Jordan West Bank, Israel	Headache, fainting	14 days	3F:1M	949	– (6–18)
Small & Borus 1983	Massachusetts	Dizziness	1 day	3F:1M	41	+ (9–13)
Wason & Bausher 1983	Ohio	Headache	1 day	3F:1M	41	+ (9–14)
Roback et al. 1983	Tennessee	Screaming	1 day	female	8	+ (8–9)
(14) 1983	Malacca, Malaysia	Screaming, crying	1 day	female	~30	+ (12–16)
(15) 1983	Seremban, Malaysia	Jumping, screaming, fleeing	6.5 hours	female	15	– (20<)
(16–18) 1983	Keningau, Malaysia	Fainting, crying, swearing	1 week	female	13	– (14–16)
Robinson et al. 1984	West Virginia	Pruritus	2 days	3F:1M	57	– (9–12)
Araki & Honma 1984	Tokyo, Japan	Headache	1 day	3F:1M	16	+ (12–15)
(19) 1984	Kuala Terengganu, Malaysia	Itching	½ hour	female	15	– (8)

Continued on next page

Table 6.1—continued

Source/Circa	Location	Primary Symptoms	Duration	Sex	No./Age Span	Index Noted
(20) 1984	Taiping, Malaysia	Fainting, headache	1 day	male	2	– (~6–17)
Goh 1986	Singapore	Dizziness	1 day	5:F to 1:M	65	– (12–15)
(21–23) 1986	Klang, Malaysia	Screaming, fainting, foaming at the mouth	~1 day	female	9	– (~13–17)
Elkins et al. 1987	Texas	Abdominal pain	1 day	female	30	+ (14–16)
(24) 1987	Johore Baru, Malaysia	Crying	—	female	7	– (13–16)
(25) 1987	Seremban, Malaysia	Screaming	—	female	11	– (20<)
(26) 1987	Pasir Mas, Malaysia	Screaming	1 week	most female	43	– (13–17)
Ruiz & Lopez 1988	Spain	Fainting	10 days	female	8	– (11–15)
Cartter et al. 1988	Connecticut	Abdominal pain	1 day	—	39	– (12)
(27) 1988	Seremban, Malaysia	Screaming	1 day	female	10	+ (?)

Study	Location	Symptom	Duration	Sex ratio	Number	Age
Gamino et al. 1989	Texas	Hyperventilation, abdominal pain	1 day	—	119	+ (11–14)
Goldsmith 1989	Soviet Georgia	Abdominal pain	1 day	most female	40	− (<20)
Philen et al. 1989	Georgia (USA)	Headache	2 months	4F:1M	339	− (5–14)
Selden 1989	Alabama	Nausea	1 day	most female	15	− (?)
Cole 1989	North Carolina	Headache	few days	female	103	+ (10–14)
Small et al. 1990	California	Headache	1 day	2.5F:1M	247	− (12–18)
Baker & Selvey 1991	Arizona	Headache	1 day	2F:1M	296	− (17<)
Desenclos, Gardner, & Horan, 1992	Florida	Abdominal pain	1 day	3:F to 1:M	3	− (4–14)
Krug 1992	Ohio	Nausea	—	—	116	+ (10–13)
Rockney & Lemke 1992	Rhode Island	Dizziness, headache, nausea	1 day	18 female 3 male	21	− (12–14)
Taylor & Werbicki 1992	Canada	Nausea	1 day	2 female 7 male	19	+ (9–12)

Table 6.2—Chronological List of Mass Motor Conversion Reaction in School Settings

Source/Circa	Location	Primary Symptoms	Duration	Sex	No./Age Span	Index Noted
Hirsch 1808	Hanover, Germany	Convulsions	—	female	—	– (9–14)
Regnard & Simon 1876	France	Contractures, paresthesia	2 weeks	female	28	+ (8–13)
Armainguad 1879	France	Convulsions, laughing globus	18 days	female	6	+ (11–14)
Laquer 1888	Germany	Shaking	3 months	female	10	– (8–12)
Wichmann 1890	Germany	Shaking	7 months	female 70%	26	+ (12–14)
Schatalow 1891	Germany	Laughing	14 days	female	13	– (10–13)
Palmer 1892	Gross-tinz, Germany	Convulsions, tremor	3 weeks	female	20	+ (10–13)
Rembold 1893	Germany	Fainting, laughing	1 day	female	25	– (9–10)
Hagenbach 1893	Basel, Switzerland	Convulsions	few days	female	62	+ (10–20)
Sirois 1893	Austria	Abnormal movements	1 month	female	7	+ (10–20)
Leuch 1896	Germany	Coughing, headache, abnormal movements	few months	female 96%	25	+ (9–11)

Author, year	Country	Symptoms	Duration	Sex	Number	
Von Holwede 1898	Germany	Abnormal movements	10 days	female	42	− (8–14)
Schutte 1906	Meissen, Germany	Abnormal movements	1 month	female	20	− (9–13)
Schoedel 1906	Chemnitz, Germany	Abnormal movements	4 weeks	female	21	+ (9–10)
Sterling 1936	Poland	Abnormal movements, paresthesia	5 days	female	5	+ (10–12)
Schuler & Parenton 1939	Louisiana	Abnormal movements	~1 month	female	7	+ (16–18)
Michaux et al. 1952	France	Convulsions	15 days	female	4	+ (14–16)
Theopold 1955	Germany	Neuralgia	few days	female	30	− (10–20)
(26) Rankin & Philip, 1962	Tanganyika (Tanzania)	Laughing	18 months	male and female	1,000	+ (12–18)
Tan 1962	Johore Baru, Malaya (Malaysia)	Screaming, crying, fainting, trance	<1 month	female	29	+ (~6–17)
Kagwa 1964	Uganda	Running, agitation	1 month	male and female	300	− (11–40)
Knight et al. 1965	Louisiana	Fainting, epileptic-like fits, tremor, catatonic posturing	6 months	21 female 1 male	22	+ (10–17)

Continued on next page

Table 6.2—continued

Source/Circa	Location	Primary Symptoms	Duration	Sex	No./Age Span	Index Noted
Helvie 1968	USA	Laughing, crying	1 day	female	16	– (14–18)
Olczak et al. 1971	USA	Convulsions, tremor, stomach cramps	1 week	female 66%	55	+ (15–19)
(28–29) 1971	Malaysia	Crying, screaming, fainting, violence	2 days	female	78	+ (-13–17)
Muhangi 1971	Kajara County, Uganda	Grimacing, laughing, foul language, disobedience	—	—	50	+ (12–20)
Teoh 1972	Near Kuala Lumpur, Malaysia	Crying, screaming, spirit possession, hyperventilation	1 month	female	5	+ (<20)
(30–31) 1973	Ipoh, Malaysia	Running, screaming, disobedience	6 days	male	8	– (<18)
Adomakoh 1973	Africa	Laughing	10 days	female	62	– (11–16)
Benaim et al. 1973	London, England	Fainting	7 months	female	8	+ (16–17)
Teoh et al. 1975	Kelang, Malaysia	Tetanic spasms, trance, hyperventilation, screaming	10 weeks	female	8	+ (12–15)
Ackerman & Lee 1978	West Malaysia	Trance, screaming	6 days	8 female 4 male	12	+ (?)
(32) 1981	West Malaysia	"Hysterical" fits, "dreamy"	1 month	female	several	– (20)

Study	Location	Symptoms	Duration	Sex	Number	
Mohr & Bond 1982	England	Loss of consciousness	21 months	60 female 3 male	63	+ (12–15)
Dhadphale & Shaikh, 1982	Mwinilunga, Zambia	Twitching, laughing	3 days	120 female 5 male	126	+ (16–17)
(33–34) 1982	Taiping, Malaysia	Fainting, violent fits	2 months	female	6	– (9–11)
(35–37) 1986	Bahu, Malaysia	"Hysterical" fits	1 month	—	29	– (~6–17)
(38) 1986	Johore Baru, Malaysia	"Hysterical" fits	2 months	—	several	– (~6–17)
(39) 1986	Johore Baru, Malaysia	"Hysterical" fits	2 months	—	several	– (6–17)
(40–41) 1986	Bahu, Malaysia	"Hysterical" fits	1.5 month	—	29	– (6–17)
(42) 1987	Setiu, Malaysia	Screaming, running	4 weeks	female	10	– (~13–17)
(43) 1987	Bahu, Malaysia	Screaming, running away	—	—	16	– (13–17)
(44–47) 1987	Kuala Terengganu, Malaysia	Screaming, running, trance	3 weeks	female	100	+ (12–16)
(48–59) 1987	Alor Star, Malaysia	Shouting, running, violence, spirit possession	5 years	female	36	+ (13–17)

Continued on next page

Table 6.2—continued

Source/Circa	Location	Primary Symptoms	Duration	Sex	No./Age Span	Index Noted
(60) 1989	Gurun, Malaysia	Ghosts waving at them, screaming, fainting	~9 months	female	several	– (12–16)
(61) 1989	West Malaysia	Screaming, ghosts waving at them, fainting	—	female	18	+ (13–17)
(62) 1989	Klang, Malaysia	"Hysteria," ghosts waving, screaming, fainting	38 days	4 female 1 male	5	– (16)
Wittstock et al. 1991	South Africa	Fainting, trance	18 months	male and female	60	– (6–13)
(63) 1991	Johore Baru, Malaysia	"Hysterical" fits	9 days	female	30	–
(64) 1991	Kluang, Malaysia	"Hysterical" fits	1.5 months	—	46	– (?)
(65–68) 1991	Johore Baru, Malaysia	"Hysterical" fits, violence tearing clothes, screaming, trance	2 months	most female	120	–
(69) 1993	Klang, Malaysia	Screaming, running	—	—	10	– (15–16)
(69–70) 1994	Sentul, Malaysia	Screaming, trembling, glossolalia, possession, fainting, verbal abuse	8 days	female	10	– (?)

and students at an elementary school cafeteria in early September 1988, the mother of a student attending the school, located near Atlanta, Georgia, remarked how since the beginning of the term her child had appeared pale and had experienced a variety of minor health problems. Other mothers had noted similar signs and symptoms in their children since the beginning of the term: pallor, dark circles under the eyes, headaches, fatigue, nausea, and occasional vomiting. They were soon convinced that the school building was responsible.

This conviction crystallized further when, on October 11, a small quantity of natural gas leaked during routine maintenance, prompting the school's evacuation. Over the next month a series of minor gas leaks occurred at the school. Despite health assurances from authorities, many parents became distraught, organized pickets, and highlighted the situation to the mass media. Environmental and epidemiological studies reaffirmed the view of the administration that no health threat existed. Rossanne Philen and colleagues (1989, p. 1376) remarked that the children exhibited little public illness and did not seek attention, with concern "expressed almost exclusively by the mothers." Attendance levels remained high throughout the term, and the array of complaints were attributable to ever-present, mundane childhood illnesses. This is the only MPI episode in my sample of affected school students that does not fall into the category of either mass anxiety conversion reactions or mass motor conversion reactions, as no evidence of conversion reactions exists, and can be described as "mass hysteria by proxy."

COMMUNICABLE CONVERSION AS A UNITARY ENTITY

The characteristic features of "epidemic" conversion symptoms in school settings are consistent across disperse geographical and historical periods. The classic school outbreak involves a socially cohesive group of female pupils near the onset of puberty and early adolescence who are exposed to a stressful stimulus. Transient symptoms spread and subside rapidly and occasionally recur. School episodes manifest as variants of a unitary syndrome typified by collective anxiety states and conversion symptoms, with the medical and cultural zeitgeist accounting for the variance in descriptions and nomenclature. Symptoms within each presentation type are interpreted within the prevailing sociocultural milieu. Demonic possession predominates in non-Western traditional societies experiencing mass motor conversion reaction, whereas chemical and food contamination scares typically involve mass anxiety conversion reaction, reflecting contemporary Western preoccupations with environmental and scientific concerns. Although major theories vary in explaining symptom presentation, each acknowledges the pivotal role of extreme psychosocial stress.

By their very nature, CCS outbreaks have the potential to generate public controversy, as most investigators view CCS as a diagnosis of exclusion that can never be confirmed with positive medical test results.[21] A notable exception to this view is Wessely (1987), who does not consider it a diagnosis of exclusion, as the syndrome is characterized by several distinct features, the collective appearance of which almost certainly indicates the presence of CCS. However, prior to the results of medical and environmental tests and detailed interviews with affected students, during the initial phase of the outbreak physicians can only note the transient, ambiguous, benign symptomatology, preponderance of female victims, and lack of a plausible pathogenic agent.

A diagnosis of CCS can be reasonably determined only retrospectively, after eliminating the presence of organic or toxicological pathogens. During the early stages of any outbreak, investigators should be cautious in attributing a psychogenic origin to unidentified illness symptoms prior to receiving laboratory findings. An outbreak of abdominal pain, nausea, and vomiting at a London elementary school in 1990 included such classic CCS features as rapid onset and recovery, overbreathing, line of sight transmission, and a high female attack rate. However, subsequent investigation revealed cucumber pesticide contamination as the cause of the "attack" (Aldous et al. 1994). It may therefore be advisable to close the school until such negative results are returned. Closure should also assist in reducing the stress levels among students and will temporarily break up the group, thus also limiting the potential "spread" of the "illness." This will give investigators time to determine in detail if most or all of the characteristic features (a combination of symptoms and conditions) of CCS are present. These include (1) symptoms with no plausible organic basis, (2) symptoms that are transient and benign, (3) rapid onset and recovery, (4) occurrence in a segregated group, (5) extraordinary anxiety, (6) symptoms spread through sight, sound, or oral communication, (7) spread occurs down the age scale beginning in older or higher-status students, and (8) a preponderance of female participants near puberty and early adolescence.[22]

Although mass anxiety conversion reaction reports dominate the twentieth-century scientific literature and mass motor conversion reaction was more prevalent during the nineteenth century, it does not necessarily follow that mass anxiety conversion reaction was less common in the latter century. During the nineteenth century, psychoanalytic-oriented observers may have taken more notice of prolonged outbreaks affecting small numbers of students while ignoring more short-lived, large-scale episodes by passing them off as the behavior of "immature" schoolgirls.

THE PROBLEMATICS OF MASS CONVERSION REACTIONS

The concept of collective conversion reactions is problematic. As with the appearance of individual conversion symptoms, it is a mysterious disorder, as the psychophysiological mechanism of cause is uncertain. It would be inappropriate to label participants as ill in the disease sense. To describe them as transient reactions would be more neutral and accurate. The personal, social, cultural, political, religious, and historical circumstances of events are different, but the conditions eliciting these behaviors are generally so uniform and specific, transculturally and transhistorically, that despite the inability to account for the specific psychophysiological mechanisms involved, I believe they can be appropriately described as mass psychogenic reactions.

Those writing in the tradition of feminist discourse have argued differently, claiming that collective conversion reactions are a form of social protest, not an illness. Barbara Ehrenreich and Deirdre English (1978, p. 139), referring primarily to the nineteenth-century literature, state that "with hysteria, the cult of invalidism was carried to its logical conclusion. Society had assigned women to a life of confinement and inactivity, and medicine had justified this assignment by describing women as innately sick. In the epidemic of hysteria, women were both accepting their inherent 'sickness' and finding a way to rebel against an intolerable social role." Other researchers refer to more recent twentieth-century examples whereby psychological distress among female collectives has been interpreted as a form of protest (Ong 1987, 1988; Bartholomew 1997b). Although this may be true in the misuse of the concept of individual "hysteria," I do not believe it is applicable in explaining the appearance of transhistorical, transcultural episodes of "epidemic" conversion symptoms. I do acknowledge that mass motor conversion reactions are patterned by, and accurately reflect, the oppression of females in the cases described, whereas the preponderance of females in mass anxiety conversion reaction is an accurate reflection of the internalization of female social roles.[23]

MISOGYNIST DISCOURSE SUPERIMPOSED
ONTO A PSYCHIATRIC SYNDROME

The rest of this chapter challenges the contemporary psychiatric typification of those persons most vulnerable to episodes of "epidemic hysteria" as innately susceptible females with aberrant personality characteristics who are exhibiting cathartic reactions to accumulated stress. I shall demonstrate that such claims are unjustified, pejorative, and sexist and have been inappropriately used to stigmatize females in different cultures and historical settings as psychologically fragile and as a means of male domination. Most researchers fail to provide thorough social and cultural circumstances in which episodes were couched (see Bartholomew 1997e), neglecting to consider that females were more likely to be in repressed situations that elicited conversion responses and how female social roles may have engendered more anxiety and hence precipitated a preponderance of female victims.

INNATE FEMALE SUSCEPTIBILITY

The belief in innate female susceptibility has become accepted as a social fact by many contemporary researchers who continue to use it as a self-fulfilling criterion for determining the presence of mass conversion reactions as these predominantly male researchers perpetuate long-held Western-biased stereotypes of female vulnerability. During the late nineteenth and the early twentieth centuries, the male-dominated Western medical profession even considered femininity to be a disease, which fostered widespread female hypochondria with such processes as menstruation and childbirth being labeled pathological (Ehrenreich and English 1978, pp. 91–126). Women were also ranked lower than men on the evolutionary scale. This representative quotation appeared in a book published in 1878 by French anthropologist Paul Topinard: "The outlines of the adult female cranium are intermediate between those of the child and the adult man: they are softer, more graceful and delicate . . . the superciliary ridges and the gabella are far less developed, often not at all; the crown is higher and more horizontal, the brain weight and cranial capacity are less" (cited in Astbury 1996, p. 47). In describing these and numerous other examples, Jill Astbury draws attention to the use of precise "value-neutral language of scientific discourse" employed to support folk misconceptions "of female otherness and inferiority" (p. 47). Vieda Skultans (1975, pp. 223–240; 1979, pp. 77–97) provides a plethora of nineteenth-century excerpts involving male mental health professionals claiming a taken-for-granted link between innate feminine vulnerability and psychological disturbance. This assumption remained prevalent within twentieth-century medical and psychiatric practice (Tavris 1993; Russell 1995; Astbury 1996, p. 189).

Similar unsubstantiated gender-based associations also abound in the contemporary "mass psychogenic illness" and "epidemic hysteria" literature.[24] For example, Philip Landrigan and Bess Miller (1983, p. 1475) stated that their diagnosis of psychogenic illness was influenced "by the preponderance of female patients, particularly adolescent girls." In their diagnosis of collective psychogenic vomiting and abdominal pain at an English secondary girls' school, McEvedy and colleagues (1966, p. 1302) wrote that "the Portsmouth epidemic satisfied criteria suggested previously for functional outbreaks. It occurred in a girls' school." Goldberg (1973, p. 365) also used this circular logic in his investigation of a phantom gas that reportedly made many students ill; he remarked that "adolescent girls are the group most prone to behaving in an hysterical manner. . . . The persons who were affected in the cafeteria on May 28, 1968, were almost all adolescent girls." In their study of psychogenic sickness among several hundred industrial workers, Hall and Johnson (1989, p. 249) based their diagnosis on its consistency with the purported susceptibility of females in previous "mass psychogenic illness" studies—"the situation that we encountered is consistent with a psychogenic profile, as summarized in the literature review"—noting that "women tend to be more ill and experience greater mental strain than men." Ah Leng Gwee (1968), in evaluating an "epidemic" of perceived genitalia shrinkage in Singapore during 1967, concluded that it represented a form of "mass hysterical delusion." Gwee and colleagues (1969) subsequently recanted this position, citing the overwhelming male bias in the presentation of cases.

In explaining the preponderance of females, researchers refrain from discussing the differences in transcultural gender roles that foster mental states of mind conducive to conversion symptoms. For instance, Western females typically acquire emotionally expressive, sympathetic, and submissive character traits (Parsons 1955; Kagan 1969), whereas Western males are typified by courageous and expressive characteristics. This socialization pattern may render females more vulnerable to MPI and more likely to seek treatment during an episode. Females may also be more susceptible to MPI because of a general global symbolic identity they possess, which encourages states of mind that render them more vulnerable. This issue will be addressed in the next section.

DO FEMALES HAVE A SYMBOLIC IDENTITY?

It is typically assumed that females are innately susceptible to mass conversion reactions, as they represent the overwhelming majority of affected subjects. We may be able to glean important clues about claims of innate female susceptibility to mass conversion reactions from anthropologists who have observed an interesting transcultural, transhistorical phenomena involving females. In numerous cultures there are reports of women exhibiting group trance and possession states with occasional psychomotor agitation and transient somatic symptoms. Such symptoms are rarely recorded among men (but when they do happen, the men are usually clearly oppressed or repressed). At first glance it would appear that something in the female biological makeup renders them susceptible. However, most anthropologists examining this question have concluded that social factors can potentially account for this phenomenon (e.g., Lewis 1971; Kapferer 1983; Ong 1988). I shall apply these anthropological insights to Malaysia, which has by far the highest number of mass conversion reports.

Malaysia is an ideal case study because of its three main ethnic groups and the fact that female Malays in schools and factories are almost exclusively affected, even in settings where other ethnic groups are predominant. Further, from a comprehensive, extensive literature examination and numerous discussions and correspondences prior to 1960, I am unaware of a single episode of "mass hysteria," based on a survey of ethnographic, historical, and journalistic sources. As I examine this anthropological perspective, the question I shall ask is, What has happened since 1960 among Malaysian Malay females under age forty that renders them almost exclusively susceptible to mass spirit possession and psychosomatic symptoms?

Ioan Lewis (1971) attributes the global preponderance of females in spirit possession cults and charismatic religious movements to emotional frustration over their low social status and oppression in male-dominated societies, where females are low on the power hierarchy. Lewis views spirit "attacks" as functional and cathartic, allowing the oppressed to temporarily circumvent their position by inverting the normal social order. Concordantly, beginning in about 1960 a conservative Islamic movement (*dakwah*) spread across Malaysia, resulting in the implementation of strict Muslim rules and regulations, particularly in the educational system. Ethnic Indian and Chinese Malaysian students (of whom only a tiny portion are Islamic) were not required to adhere to these restrictions. In contemporary Malaysia, intolerable social situations are characteristic features of female Malay school and factory settings. Female redress is culturally unacceptable. Malaysian episodes of "mass hysteria" are typified by frank criticisms of authorities and administration policies, with the label *mass hysteria* deflecting the attribution of blame. Because of space limitations, I shall restrict most of this discussion to mass possession "hysteria" in Malaysian educational settings, typified by male headmasters imposing totalitarian rules of academic and religious discipline. Often allegations are made that the headmaster or his administrators were voyeuristic, molested hostelites, or showed favoritism.

Australian-born anthropologist Bruce Kapferer (1983) also assumes that social factors are the most likely explanation for the overrepresentation of females in possession cults in cross-cultural settings but believes it may be related to the global symbolic identity of women. To my knowledge, this perspective has never been discussed in "mass hysteria" studies, except for a passing reference by anthropologist Robert Winzeler (1995, p. 101). Kapferer contends that any explanation must consider "the shared constructions and typifications which men and women have of themselves and of each other" (p. 96). A key element in this position is the widespread transcultural reality among both men and women that women as a category are subordinate to men and are therefore seen to be more susceptible to spirit possession.[25] If this approach is applicable, we should be able to identify cultural constructs that render female Malays vulnerable to collective spirit possession and conversion symptoms in school and factory settings.

Submissiveness to males is an expected cultural trait of female Malays (Ackerman 1980). Malays also hold a racist folk belief that they are inherently suggestible, especially females. This conviction is so ingrained in Malaysian society (probably as a remnant of British colonialism) that in explaining an outbreak of mass possession at an all-female religious school, Malaysia's founding prime minister, Tunku Abdul Rahman (1987), remarked that "as a race the Malays are highly sensitive and are prone to be led to do things which in normal circumstances they would not do. The hysteria that took place in the school . . . was caused by something that may have touched off their mental sensitivity."

Malays believe in an ambiguously defined spiritual life force (*semangat*) that promotes mental fortitude. Those possessing strong semangat can resist and control Otherworldly forces, whereas "weaker semangat is likely to be subsumed and controlled by them," rendering them vulnerable to spirit possession (Nasuruddin 1990, p. 146). Illness, severe mental stress, excessive worry, and improper behavior are the main factors that weaken semangat and precipitate spirit possession (McHugh 1959; Endicott 1970, p. 50; Chen 1970). In Malay society, females and children are believed to possess less of this force than men, rendering them susceptible to possession by a ghost (*dirasok hantu*) (Resner and Hartog 1970, p. 377).[26] Correspondingly, this is precisely the group affected by occasional episodes of mass spirit possession in educational and factory settings—female Malays. In explaining an outbreak of mass spirit possession at a college hostel for female Malays, Lee and Ackerman (1980, p. 85) observed that events surrounding the episode were generally interpreted as spirit possession: "The ideas by which they made this interpretation were based on a world-view which places heavy emphasis on the supernatural and female vulnerability."

The spread of conversion symptoms in Malaysian schools and factories is most commonly attributed to psychosocial stress fostered by rapid social change resulting from educational policies that have prompted the movement of rural Malays, who generally adhere to more traditional folk beliefs, into urban environments. It is typically noted that episodes affect Islamic schools with headmasters who implement the most repressive authoritarian policies on females residing in socially isolated hostels. Although this could be viewed as supporting Lewis's thesis, a closer examination suggests otherwise. Teoh and Yeoh (1973) investigated an outbreak of possession "hysteria" affecting eleven students over 2½ months at a liberal female Muslim college hostel in 1972. Contrary to prevailing opinion, the six girls most severely affected "were highly urbanized individuals in their mode of behavior" (Teoh and Yeoh 1973, p. 287):

> This group of Malay college students do not live in seclusion from the community as it has been normally assumed that the outbreaks of hysteria occur in isolated and closed communities . . . [and they] mingle freely within the township and are in close contact with the outside world. . . . Generally, the rules are more relaxed and the girls can come in and go out at all hours of the day and night. The residential tutor who lives in a house nearby the hostel is called upon only in times of emergency. The principal of the college, a sensible person, administers the college with discretion. (Teoh and Yeoh 1973, p. 286)

Residents must adhere to Islamic tenants such as wearing appropriate attire and disallowing males from entering their dormitories. However, personal, interpersonal, and intergroup conflicts of a social, sexual, and political nature were evident among rival female hostelites (rural conservatives versus urban liberals); thus, according to Teoh and Yeoh (1973), the fostering of status ambiguity was mainly responsible for engendering the episode, which conspicuously lacked elements of male dominance or repression.

Kapferer's perspective may be extended to account for the overrepresentation of females in global reports of general mass conversion reactions in schools and factories. Although such factors as male dominance in repressive settings and status ambiguity can engender episodes, a major overlooked element may involve conceptions about female perceptions of innate vulnerability in countries where "mass hysteria" cases occur. As conversion reactions are engendered by "states of mind" regarding the appearance of an imaginary illness or agent, I would be more inclined to believe a biological component exists if male episodes were absent from the literature, but a few reports contain an equal or majority percentage of males involved (see Bartholomew 1994a, p. 296). Any theory that attempts to explain the appearance of mass conversion symptoms in terms of innate female susceptibility must account for its manifestation in males.

Any discussion of social factors correlated with the preponderance of women in spirit possession religions and behaviors must include the meticulous research of anthropologist Erika Bourguignon who, like Kapferer, is critical of Lewis. Bourguignon believes Lewis's thesis is only a partial explanation for a culturally patterned model of altered states of consciousness that results from a combination of economic and social structural factors. Using ethnographic data collected on 488 societies, she found that trance is predominantly a male phenomenon associated with less complex, low accumulation subsistence economies (i.e., hunting, gathering, fishing) that typically socialize for traits such as self-reliance, assertion, and independence. However, possession trance typically involves women in complex, high accumulation societies (i.e., pastoralism or agriculture), who in their ecological adaptations socialize for obedience, compliance, and dependence (Bourguignon 1978, 1979, pp. 258—261). In this latter instance females entering possession trance deal with the spirits through impersonations and dramatizing the importance of compliance made by these powerful spirits. Yet as "humans play the roles of these impersonated entities, the ASC [altered states of consciousness] allow those in possession trance to act out their own needs for assertion, and they present them with an opportunity to manipulate others and their own real life situations as well" (Bourguignon 1974, p. 24). This finding is entirely consistent with Malay society where females are socialized to be obedient and dependent. It is precisely in such societies that female Malays "will not seek spirit help to augment their own powers to be able to deal with a hostile group. Instead, the[y] call on powerful, authoritative spirits to *act in their place*" (Bourguignon 1979, p. 261).[27] To summarize, Bourguignon's findings indicate that trance is typically male and involves interaction with another to increase individual power in subsistence societies, whereas possession trance is common among females and entails becoming another, which allows subservient women to act out their needs for them.

MASS MOTOR "HYSTERIA"
AND FEMALE POLITICAL SUBORDINATION

The juxtaposition of feminist and medical interpretations on collective conversion reactions is typically polemic. In this section I shall demonstrate that it is possible to take a middle ground by synthesizing the basic tenets of both perspectives, arguing that the social patterning of episodes is what renders females vulnerable to outbreaks of a genuine disorder. I contend that feminist perspectives overemphasize the influence of protest per se in contributing to what they interpret as episodes labeled *mass conversion reaction,* whereas medical observers overemphasize the physiological aspects per se in explaining the preponderance of female participation in "hysterical" episodes. This state of affairs is evident in comparing reports of conversion symptoms among contemporary Malay schoolgirls experiencing rigid Islamic discipline, with reports of virtually identical symptoms among repressed nuns since the late Middle Ages. Elements of conversion disorder and political resistance are evident in both of these examples.[28]

The presentation of mass motor episodes is remarkably similar to scores of hysterical fits, dissociation, and psychomotor agitation among nuns secluded primarily in European Christian convents between the fifteenth and nineteenth centuries (Hecker 1970 [1837]; Calmeil 1845; Madden 1857; Davy 1880; Garnier 1895; Loredan 1912; Huxley 1952; Rosen 1968; de Certeau 1970; Thomas 1971; Bartholomew 1994a). Prominent incidents were reported at Cambrai in 1494, Yvertet (1550), Kintorp (1552), Cologne and Flanders (1560), Aix (1609), Madrid (1628), Loudun (1632), and Louviers (1642). Histrionics and role playing were also a significant part of the syndrome. Like their Malaysian counterparts, young females were typically coerced by elders into joining socially isolating religious orders, practicing rigid discipline in confined, all-female living quarters. Male associations were forbidden. Mass motor conversion reactions conspicuously appeared under the strictest administrations. Instead of witch doctors, priests were summoned to exorcise the "demonic" spirits, and disliked individuals were often accused of casting spells. In both instances the inmates released frustrations by uttering disrespectful, often blasphemous remarks and engaging in aggressive sexual and threatening behavior, their possession status providing them with impunity.

Although Malay schoolgirls often call for the dismissal or transfer of their restrictive headmaster (which under normal circumstances would be viewed as disrespectful), a despised colleague or restrictive convent priest was typically accused by the possessed nuns of causing their condition through witchcraft. Malaysian episodes usually subside when school authorities relax rules or the offending official is removed, whereas in convents symptoms disappeared soon after the accused was transferred, banished, imprisoned, or, more commonly, burned at the stake. Whereas Malaysian episodes typically persist for a few months and occasionally years, convent outbreaks usually endured for several years, as lengthy church inquisitions were required and exorcisms were performed to remove the offending administrator or for punishment to be decided. During this waiting period the nuns remained in their repressive situation, which continued to incubate symptoms.

One episode of mass motor conversion reaction at a female religious school and hostel in Alor Star, in the remote state of Kedah in northern Malaysia, endured for 5 years, affecting thirty-six Islamic females between ages thirteen and seventeen. Episodes were typified by shouting, running, crying, abnormal movements, mental confusion, and spirit possession, with the girls' conduct becoming progressively histrionic and violent. The girls complained of extreme boredom and overly strict religious and academic studies and were confined to their all-female dormitories most of the time with no recreational activities. Scores of witch doctors were used during this period, but they met with only temporary success as the underlying dissatisfaction remained. The struggle between students and administrators continued for years and climaxed during an outbreak in 1987, when several "hysterical" girls took hostages with large chopping knives (*parangs*) and demanded changes. Their "hysterical" status deflected the attribution of blame, and no criminal charges were brought against them. The bouts ceased soon after former Malaysian prime minister Tunku Abdul Rahman intervened, visited the school, "adopted" the pupils, and ensured that they were transferred to a more liberal school.[29]

FROM REPRESSED SCHOOLGIRLS TO REPRESSED NUNS

Most investigators utilize psychiatric, sociological, and medical frameworks to interpret mass conversion reaction episodes (see Bartholomew 1990b). Virtually ignored in the literature is anthropolitical research discussing the likelihood that certain episodes of mass conversion reactions actually represent a culturally conditioned means for the politically weak—that is, primarily females—to consciously or unconsciously critique unsatisfactory social conditions and effect gradual change. For instance, James Scott (1985) documents how everyday forms of peasant resistance in rural West Malaysia involve continuous, creative, prosaic ways of expressing dissatisfaction with government and management policies, including foot dragging, sabotage, slander, desertion, feigned ignorance, and false compliance. As noted earlier, it is a cultural trait of Malay females to be obedient and submissive and to avoid direct confrontation with authority (Ackerman 1980), and expressions of dissatisfaction through "mass hysteria" and spirit possession are culturally acceptable means of indirectly negotiating problematic situations (Lee and Ackerman 1980, p. 85). Anthropologist Aihwa Ong (1987, 1988) has examined the structural and political roots of ideological meanings attached to episodes of mass spirit possession in Malaysian factories, which almost exclusively affect Malay females. She views "hysterical" episodes as forms of ongoing culturally acceptable political resistance to the imposition of dehumanizing capitalist discipline vis-à-vis traditional Malay noncapitalist conduct codes. Collective spirit possession incidents and the common accompanying symptoms (hyperventilation, dizziness, nausea, fainting, headache) can focus public attention to subordinate concerns and amounts to ritualized rebellion.

Collective conversion reactions are traditionally considered to involve relatively spontaneous episodes within familiar social networks. Tactics of political resistance may seem overly contrived and entail detailed collective planning, thus rendering them easily distinguishable from "real" collective "hysterias." However, various forms of Malaysian subversive resistance in factories "were spontaneous, carried out by individual workers independently of each other" (Ong 1987, pp. 210–211), "require[d] little or no coordination or planning," and utilized "implicit understandings and informal networks" (Scott 1985, p. xvi). Some forms of resistance involve feigning illness as a strategy to leave the shop floor (Ong 1987, p. 203). If several workers exit in this manner within a relatively short period, outsiders unfamiliar with this conduct code of resistance could misinterpret the action as "mass psychogenic illness."

The dismissal of native interpretations of mass spirit possession in Malaysian schools and factories by most Western-trained social scientists in favor of a medical worldview represents attempts to describe illness "independent of their local meanings and values" (Ong 1988, pp. 29–30):

> Spirit possession episodes . . . are acts of rebellion, symbolizing what cannot be spoken directly, calling for a renegotiation of obligations between the management and workers. However, technocrats have turned a deaf ear to such protests, to this moral indictment of their woeful cultural judgements about the dispossessed . . . choosing to view possession episodes narrowly as sickness caused by physiological and psychological maladjustment. (Ong 1988, p. 38)

The irony here is that through the act of psychiatric imperialism, native interpretations of these events (e.g., hexing, charming, disturbed spirits, ghosts) are being replaced by local academics who parrot the medical position from Western books and teachers. The legitimation of "scientific" interpretations of possession to the benefit of Western multinational corporations in Malaysia parodies the exploitative use of psychology and anthropology by European colonialists in Melanesia during the early twentieth century. Cargo cult "hysteria" and the accompanying "illness" symptoms not only offered proof that the natives were mentally unstable, irrational, and natural mimics instead of innovators but also justified the need for colonial discipline and surveillance structures (Lattas 1992). The definition of "madness" encompassed only the political use of trance, magic, and "hysterical" reactions that were of potential use against Europeans, becoming a means to police innovation and prescribe which behaviors could be legitimately adopted (Lattas 1992, p. 4).

The political aspects of collective spirit possession in Malaysian factories are comparable to the demonomania that spread throughout European convents during the late Middle Ages and early Renaissance. Most of these episodes involved small groups of socially cohesive women in closed settings who were dissatisfied with the strict Christian discipline imposed by their male superiors, often perceived as hypocritical. The sisters typically claimed to be possessed by demons sent by a person or persons whom they believed was or were responsible for their hardships. In conjunction with various psychosomatic complaints, much of the behavior possessed a histrionic character. In most instances a sorcerer or sorceress was identified, tried, and imprisoned for life, burned at the stake, or, less frequently, excommunicated. In his analysis of twelve episodes of "epidemic" demonopathy at convents between the fifteenth and seventeenth centuries, Madden (1857, p. 405) concludes that the professed presence of demons actually represented a form of collective mental disorder fostered by the "unnatural, unjust" religious discipline imposed on pious subordinates. In response to concerns over the scandalous rigidity of Christian discipline at various European convents during this period, and in an effort to reduce incidents of contagious demonopathy, Pope Paul III subsequently signed a report calling for "the reformation of manners and discipline in religious houses and amongst the subordinate clergy" (Madden 1857, pp. 404–405).

A well-documented example involving the appearance of mass conversion reactions in conjunction with political rebellion is the case of "epidemic" demonic possession at a convent in Loudun, France, beginning in 1632, affecting sixteen religious sisters. In this episode, although clear evidence reveals an involuntary body disorder (abnormal twitching, shaking, and dissociation) and a variety of psychosomatic complaints, there is unambiguous evidence of malingering.[30] A charismatic priest named Urbain Grandier made scores of enemies—including local women, clergy, the police chief, and public prosecutor—for his confrontational nature, hypocritical piety, and sexual liaisons. A scheme was instigated between Canon Mignon, whose cousin Grandier had impregnated, and a scorned prioress, Jeanne des Anges, to capitalize on a series of Halloween pranks instigated by a committee of nuns who had concocted apparitional and poltergeist manifestations. The pair convinced the Ursuline convent members that the events were the sinister conjurations of Grandier, who was already greatly disliked and who had summoned the demons to torment them. Jeanne des Anges began disclosing daily accounts in great detail of Grandier's nightly *incubus* violations and in conjunction with persuasion by the exorcists soon managed to convince eight sisters that they, too, had been deflowered by his nocturnal transgressions (Garnier 1895, pp. 14–15).

The exorcists summoned were all enemies of Grandier. At the direction of Mignon and the prior, the affected nuns became convinced that a variety of ambiguous ailments were induced by Grandier, only to be readily "cured" by the exorcists of such perceived conditions as headache, stomach pain, and colic. The "possessions" took on a definite histrionic character and became a public spectacle when the Ursuline chapel exorcisms were opened to the public. Meanwhile, the Ursulines amassed considerable wealth from gratuities left by the flocks of observers who traveled from all parts of France and even abroad to watch the theatrical confabulations. For the nuns afflicted with what were presumably Grandier's demons, the exorcisms were a means of attracting public attention to his immoral exploits and their pious sufferings. The nuns purportedly vomited various objects during their paroxysms to maintain the deception, including straw, worms, cinders, hair, nail parings, Grandier's blood and semen, and even a piece of heart said to have belonged to a child sacrificed at a witches' Sabbath (Huxley 1952, p. 155).[31] Regarding ulterior motives underlying the theatrics at Loudun, Aldous Huxley (1952, p. 188) remarks:

> For the sake of publicity which was thought to be good for their respective Orders and the Church at large, or with the deliberate intention of using the nuns as instruments for the destruction of Grandier, the exorcists did everything in their power to foster and increase the scandal. The nuns were forced to perform their antics in public, were encouraged to blaspheme for distinguished visitors and to trickle the groundlings with displays of extravagant immodesty. . . . At the beginning of her malady, the Prioress did not believe herself to be possessed. It was only after her confessor and the other exorcists had repeatedly assured her that she was full of devils that Sister Jane came at last to be convinced that she was a demoniac and that her business, henceforth, was to behave as such. And the same was true of some at least of the other nuns.

On numerous occasions the nuns would voice foul blasphemies and sexual indecencies and contort their bodies in lustfully vulgar ways with complete impunity. As in the case of mass spirit possession in Malaysian factories, the affected sisters were never directly sanctioned for these sacrilegious utterances, as it was widely believed they were under the temporary control of the demonic forces or exhibiting fits of "epidemic hysteria." The tradition of collective demonic possession within the Christian church is well documented long before the incidents at Loudun. Although some or all of the affected nuns may have engaged in unconscious spirit possession, a group of physicians ordered by the Parliament of Burgundy to examine the sisters found no evidence of this.[32] Suspiciously, the sisters "were scarcely ever possessed" when the exorcisms were not transpiring (Madden 1857, p. 302). In a similar vein, Malaysian factory workers and boarding school students who exhibit dramatic possession symptoms typically exhibit spontaneous remissions and appear in excellent health once exiting the workplace or school environment, only to be seized again upon reentering the offending premises.[33]

Grandier was subsequently tried, convicted, and burned alive at the stake in 1634. Conveniently, once the king decided to withdraw the pension for the continuance of the exorcists and having achieved the nuns' political motives, shortly thereafter the possessions ceased.

The commonality of "stress" in episodes labeled *mass psychogenic illness* typically involves disputes between workers and management (Ikeda 1966; Stahl and Lebedun 1974; Folland 1975; Shepard and Kroes 1975; Smith, Colligan, and Hurrell 1978, p. 400; Chew 1978; Singer et al. 1982, p. 156). In reviewing twenty-three factory episodes, Colligan and Murphy (1982, p. 43) observed "the tendency of affecteds to have a history of absenteeism from work prior to the contagious outbreak," which is suggestive but not proof of job dissatisfaction. Confrontations between students and teachers are also prevalent (Schuler and Parenton 1943; Tan 1963; Knight, Friedman, and Sulianti 1965; Markush 1973, pp. 405–406; Teoh, Soewondo, and Sidharta 1975, p. 266; Lee and Ackerman 1980; Dhadphale and Shaikh 1983, p. 87). Medical practitioners could typify this as cathartic reactions to suppressed emotions, whereas a feminist perspective could be used to suggest that these "outbreaks" are forms of covert political resistance to oppressive social conditions. Both of these positions would be consistent with the contention of Lewis (1971) that female spirit possession episodes represent veiled protests in efforts to overcome male dominance and oppression. That may also explain why the majority of episodes involve females of low socioeconomic status (Sirois 1974, p. 16; Stahl 1982, p. 189).

ABNORMAL PERSONALITY TRAITS

Several investigators of episodes in school settings have attempted to differentiate the social, psychological, and physical (i.e., gender) characteristics of affected versus unaffected participants within the same group setting by administering standardized personality inventories. However, no consistent pattern of abnormal personality traits appears among "mass hysteria" participants. Some results indicate a tendency for those affected to score higher on scales for paranoia (Goldberg 1973), neuroticism (Moss and McEvedy 1966; McEvedy, Griffith, and Hall 1966), and hysterical traits (Knight, Friedman, and Sulianti 1965). Yet others have found no such correlations (Olson 1928; Olczak et al. 1971; Teoh and Yeoh 1973; Tam et al. 1982; Wong et al. 1982). Goldberg (1973) noted an association between absenteeism and being affected, whereas Cole (1990) did not. Small and colleagues (1991) identified a relationship between academic performance and being stricken, but Goh (1987) found no association. The death of a significant other during early childhood has been correlated (Small and Nicholi 1982; Small et al. 1991), yet this observation was not confirmed in another study by the same investigator (Small and Borus 1983). Although some researchers note that those affected possess below-average IQs (Michaux, Lemperiere, and Juredieu 1952; Knight, Friedman, and Sulianti 1965), others gained the opposite impression (Olson 1928; Schuler and Parenton 1943; Theopold 1955).[34]

STRESS

Contemporary investigators of "mass psychogenic illness" typically attempt to identify a specific source of stress, such as tight band uniforms (Levine 1977), exams (Benaim, Horder, and Anderson 1973), an unusual odor (Stahl and Lebedun 1974), and nuclear fallout fears (Medalia and Larsen 1958). However, the presence of specific "stresses" and predisposing personality correlates is always identified retrospectively, and the investigator typically fails to consider seriously a sociocultural perspective that is sensitive to the taken-for-granted realities of a certain collective of people at a particular time and location.

Social science theorists traditionally view the etiology of episodes of "mass psychogenic illness" and "mass hysteria" as mental disorders or irrational reactions, typically attributable to aspects of the social structure that are in anomie and disequilibrium. Some scientists still use Smelser's *Theory of Collective Behavior* (1962) to explain "mass psychogenic illness," viewing it and all collective behavior as the irrational product of a dysfunctioning social order undergoing "structural strains." For Smelser, "mass hysteria" is an objective given, a taken-for-granted part of contemporary social science reality with its structural elements awaiting transcultural discovery. This position has been the subject of scathing attacks by social constructionists. For instance, although Smelser contends that "ambiguity," "anxiety," and "structural strains" appear in all "hysterical" episodes, these categories are always identified retrospective to "outbreaks" and are so ambiguous as to be present in all societies at all times. Furthermore, how does one measure a "structural strain" or the degree to which ambiguity was present in a particular episode? What is perceived as stressful also varies cross-culturally and transhistorically and within different segments of a society. This approach has the potential to reduce any behaviors differing from Western standards of normality as reactions to structural elements, deemphasizing the motivations underlying such actions, which occur within a unique sociocultural context. Instead of trying to discover universal transcultural elements that comprise episodes labeled *collective psychogenic illness,* meaning-oriented approaches are fruitful, as they seek contextual interpretations of "stresses" and "strains" with "hysterical" episodes.

SUMMARY

In this chapter I have examined problematics surrounding the concepts of individual and collective conversion symptoms, the ambiguity of diagnostic criteria, and the misuse of the term *hysteria* to describe a variety of unrelated phenomena. In reviewing explanations I have concluded that sociological factors can account for the social patterning of the cases described and the overrepresentation of female participation. However, I have rejected recent trends within feminist discourse to view such events purely in terms of female protest and distress. Based on a survey of all known reliable episodes of collective conversion reactions in school settings, a uniformity and consistency of symptom presentation cuts across cultures and time periods, which suggests the existence of a unitary syndrome involving an abnormal state of psychological health.

NOTES

1. No known reports were recorded prior to this period.

2. The numerical references in Tables 6.1 and 6.2 refer to detailed Malaysian press accounts that appear at the end of the reference section under the heading "Malaysian Press Sources."

3. Indeed, it is difficult to differentiate between a conversion subject and a malingerer deliberately producing symptoms, and studies indicate that a majority of those diagnosed with conversion are actually suffering from neurological disorders that are difficult to detect in their early stages (Alloy, Acocella, and Bootzin 1996, p. 197).

4. Slater followed the course of 112 subjects previously diagnosed with hysterical symptoms. After approximately a decade he noted that 60 percent had organic illness, 8 percent had depression or schizophrenia, and the remainder exhibited symptoms of Briquet's Syndrome or ambiguous signs and symptoms that were labeled under the hysteria rubric. According to Slater (1965, p. 1399), "The diagnosis of 'hysteria' is a disguise for ignorance and a fertile source of clinical error." He concludes that "no evidence has yet been offered that patients suffering from 'hysteria' are in medically significant terms anything more than a random selection. . . . The only thing that 'hysterical' patients can be shown to have in common is that they are all patients."

5. Mark S. Micale (1995, pp. 285–286) aptly summarizes these approaches, noting that its disease history has been viewed

> As a scientific, clinical, social, economic, political, sexual, cultural, and aesthetic construction. It has been interpreted as a chapter in the history of medical thought, an episode in the discovery of the unconscious, a study in mind/body relations, and an example of the misdiagnosis of organic disease. It has been written about as a repressed cry for sexual release, an exhibition-

istic erotic performance, and a passive, pathological escape from social oppression; as a caricature of femininity, an exploration of masculinity, and a codification of misogynistic male science; as an exercise in scientific pornography and a program for gender normalization. It has been studied as a social metaphor, a literary typos, a visual icon, and a surrogate form of religious experience; as a morbid manifestation of Victorian civilization, a secret strategy for professional expansion . . . [and] discussed as an actual psychiatric disorder.

6. For example, in a recent review of the published literature on epidemic hysteria between 1973 and 1993, Leslie Boss (1997) of the Centers for Disease Control and Prevention in Atlanta, Georgia, fails to distinguish between epidemic hysteria and collective delusions. These are two separate entities, with the former representing the pathological spread of conversion symptoms and the latter involving the nonpathological manifestation of conformity dynamics and reality testing exacerbated by human perceptual fallibility. As a result of this failure, Boss explicitly and erroneously describes as "epidemic illnesses" the 1938 Martian invasion panic and the 1954 Seattle windshield pitting episode.

7. Perhaps the best-known example is the panic that ensued in the United States on Halloween Eve, 1938, following the realistic radio reenactment of the drama *War of the Worlds* by the CBS Mercury Theatre (Cantril 1947 [1940]). Other examples include mass flights from the city of London in response to prophecies of its destruction by a great flood in 1524, the London Day of Judgment in 1736, and the London earthquake in 1761 (Mackay 1852). One of many contemporary examples involving apocalyptic prophecies and mass panic occurred in Adelaide, Australia, in the month leading up to January 19, 1976. Many people fled the city and some even sold their homes after "psychic" John Nash predicted that an earthquake and tidal wave would strike at midday. In examining the circumstances of the event, many of those who sold their homes or left for the hills for the day were first-generation Greeks and Italians. Both countries have a long history of devastating earthquakes, where the belief in clairvoyants is generally taken very seriously by inhabitants (Bartholomew 1992a).

8. These moral panics are primarily symbolic and rumor driven, consisting of generalized anxiety over the exaggerated erosion of traditional values. One prominent contemporary moral panic has persisted since at least 1984, whereby scores of Western communities possessing predominantly Judeo-Christian traditions have experienced ongoing concern in conjunction with the circulation of rumors about a network of satanic cults kidnapping and sacrificing children. These rumors coincide with the widespread perception of declining Western morality and traditional values. Under similar historical circumstances subversion myths have appeared in which a particular alien group is believed to threaten the moral fabric of society. Common xenophobic scapegoats include minority ethnic groups, Jews, Africans, communists, heretics, deviants, and the poor. Such myths flourish during periods of social tension and economic hardship and are characterized by dramatic, plausible rumors containing meaningful, topical morals or messages reflecting popular fears. During oral transmission local details are supplanted and a credible source is identified. Their function is primarily metaphorical. Sociologist Jeffery S. Victor (1990, p. 290) notes that the contemporary satanic cult

scare coincides with the disintegration of traditional family structures, generally intensifying fears and the desire "to blame someone." Unlike scares involving imminent danger, subversion myths present a more generalized threat not only to people but to a way of life (Hicks 1990, p. 387), as rumors and urban legends of local satanic cults function as cautionary cultural metaphors about the inability of the weakened family to protect children (Victor 1989, 1992).

9. Episodes involve a conscious or subconscious wish related to human mortality that, in conjunction with a plausible belief, precipitates a collective quest for transcendence. Common examples include Virgin Mary "appearances," waves of claims and public discourse surrounding widespread reports of fairies in England prior to the twentieth century (Kirk 1815; Keightley 1882; Evans-Wentz 1909; Shepard 1984), and flying saucers since 1947 (Bartholomew 1989b, 1990a). Such myths arise as a result of a spiritual void left by the ascendancy of rationalism and secular humanism. A belief in extraterrestrial visitors is fostered by monolithic documentaries, movies, and publications, prompting scrutiny of the sky for "UFOs" (a proxy for extraterrestrial spacecraft) containing what prominent psychologist Carl Gustav Jung (1959) termed *technological angels.* Accounts of UFO occupants and fairies depict Otherworldly demigods capable of transcending natural laws and, thus, potentially elevating humans to their immortal realm (Bartholomew 1991b). They reflect similar folkloric, mythical, and religious themes camouflaged for contemporary acceptance (Bullard 1989).

Transcendence and magical, or supernatural, powers are an underlying theme in most wish fulfillments. Even observations of such imaginary or extinct creatures as Bigfoot and the Tasmanian "tiger," respectfully, once considered the sole domain of terrestrial zoology, have undergone a recent metamorphosis. Since the 1970s the power and function of UFOs have multiplied exponentially with the emergence of a new motif linking extraterrestrials with phantom animals. This association dramatically elevates the cogency of previously terrestrial creatures, paralleling the secularization of the Western collective unconscious. For example, Bigfoot's reported capabilities now rival those of extraterrestrials, fairies, and apparitions in terms of their power and function. This includes reports of its ability to exhibit transparency, vanish or materialize, communicate telepathically, alter shape, withstand motor vehicle impacts, and be impervious to bullets (Bartholomew 1991a). Even recent Tasmanian "tiger" sightings reflect similar Otherworldly elements, fostering popular folk theories that it possesses paranormal or extraterrestrial elements (Healy and Cropper 1994). The existence of phantom animals can also be viewed as an antiscientific symbol undermining secular humanism.

10. This could be either financial or symbolic in the form of time off or sick pay or to obtain a transfer to other, more enjoyable duties.

11. A similar historical example occurred among postal workers in Great Britain near the turn of the nineteenth century. In 1908 telegraphist's cramp was added to the list of diseases covered by the British Workman's Compensation Act on the recommendation of a physician who erroneously diagnosed it as a muscular failure resulting from rapid repetitive limb movements. By 1912 "up to 69 percent of the workforce were reporting symptoms and 30 percent of the workforce were reporting difficulties in manipulation, a situation which resembles that in the Australian Public Service today. Simultaneous prevalence studies on the European continent found only sporadic cases.

In the United States, 4 percent to 10 percent of telegraphic staff members were at the time reporting 'cramp symptoms'" (Lucire 1986, p. 324).

12. A similar iatrogenic epidemic of multiple personality disorder (MPD) occurred in the United States during the 1980s. The epidemic nature of behavior labeled *MPD* is typified by Putnam and colleagues (1986, p. 285), who remarked that "more cases of MPD have been reported within the last 5 years than in the preceding two centuries." Although many mental health professionals doubt that MPD is a clinical entity, clearly a multitude of disorders and behaviors were misdiagnosed as MPD (Thigpen and Cleckley 1984; Spanos 1996).

13. For a comprehensive list and discussion of over forty behaviors inappropriately identified as "epidemic hysteria," see Bartholomew (1990b).

14. Further exacerbating the confusion over the vague definition of "epidemic hysteria" are the interdisciplinary nature of the topic and the employment of diverse methods and assumptions in interpreting social delusions. Physicians typically write on singular cases of mass psychogenic illness they encounter (e.g., Tan 1963), whereas sociologists often discuss communitywide episodes involving false beliefs or perceptions, such as phantom windscreen pits (Medalia and Larsen 1958) or legendary creature sightings (Stewart 1989). Psychologists tend to focus on psychometric characteristics of those affected (e.g., Kerckhoff, Back, and Miller 1965), social psychologists have explored the influence of rumor and gossip (Shibutani 1966), and psychoanalytical approaches have been used to identify deep-seated subconscious psychic conflicts (e.g., Benaim, Horder, and Anderson 1973). Historians usually limit discussion to medieval dancing "manias" (e.g., Sigerist 1943), and anthropologists emphasize the cultural context of outbreaks and the position of subordinate females in repressive social structures (e.g., Ong 1987, 1988). Some folklorists have studied the influence of urban legends in precipitating mass delusions (Brunvand 1981), in addition to similarities between recurring folkloric genres (Sanarov 1981), whereas journalists have examined the mass media impact in perpetuating such mass phenomena (Johnson 1950; Strentz 1970). Finally, political scientists may employ the vernacular meaning to describe what they may view as overzealous or unsubstantiated adherence to an opinion that is unfounded (e.g., Selvin 1989).

15. The trademark of a database containing abstracts of medical articles.

16. Excluded from my definition as to what constitutes CCS but often erroneously described as CCS are spontaneous ecstasies arising within ritualized or institutionalized social environments. Goode (1992, p. 143) defines ecstatic collectives as "highly emotional states and trances, in which the dominant mood is positive, joyous, rapturous, even frenzied." This includes behavior at certain sporting events, such as emotional zeal associated with Brazilian soccer matches (Lever 1983), both charismatic (Massey, Brannon, and Riley 1981) and "primitive" (Robin 1981) religious groups, collective glossolalia (Samarin 1972; Stephen 1977), political rallies (Carr 1978), South American carnivals (DaMatta 1984), and rock music concerts (Teoh, Soewondo, and Sidharta 1975). Also excluded are clusters of individual traumatic neuroses, such as those reported in cinemagoers after viewing *The Exorcist* (Bozzuto 1975), and combat hysteria (Rickman 1941; Merskey 1979, pp. 37–44). "Sick building syndrome" among highrise office workers, which has become prevalent since the early 1980s and has a hysteri-

cal label (Brodsky 1983; Bardana and Montanaro 1986), is excluded from review because of the controversial nature of the diagnosis, which may be attributable in whole or part to polluted air (Ryan and Morrow 1992; Bauer et al. 1992). Finally, also excluded is a cluster of episodes characterized by epidemic malaise, emotional liability, depression, gastrointestinal upset, muscle aches, mild fever, and headache documented in primarily closed, socially cohesive populations in hospital and convent settings since 1934 that have been diagnosed as psychosocial in origin. Although most researchers argue that the symptoms in these hospitals and convents were elicited by an unidentified virus (Acheson 1959; Briggs and Levine 1994; Chester and Levine 1994), no causative agent has been conclusively identified. The origin of these outbreaks remains the subject of sordid medical debate since the publication of three *British Medical Journal* articles suggesting a hysterical etiology (McEvedy and Beard 1970a, 1970b; Anonymous 1970), and episodes have appeared under a variety of descriptive labels: benign myalgic encephalomyelitis (Daikos, Garzonis, and Paleologue 1959), epidemic neuromyasthenia (Shelokov et al. 1957; Poskanzer et al. 1957; Albrecht, Oliver, and Poskanzer 1964), Iceland Disease (White and Burtch 1954; Deisher 1957), and poliomyelitis-resembling (Gilliam 1938; Sigurdsson et al. 1950).

17. Malaysian newspapers often dispatch reporters directly to the scene of the episode and provide timely, voluminous, and highly detailed press coverage. This includes interviews with affected students, physicians, psychiatrists, school officials, and investigating government bodies in addition to follow-up accounts when episodes recur or have ceased, the specific number of students affected, and their ages.

18. Hysteria at School During Blackout, the *Star,* April 30, 1988.

19. Of course, Smelser's perspective is only one type of sociological approach. Although I could be accused of misrepresenting sociological explanations here by focusing on Smelser's somewhat dated functionalist paradigm, it continues to receive considerable attention among sociologists and social psychologists, as this perspective offers the only comprehensive, testable theory of collective behavior (Brown 1965, p. 713; Evans 1969; Quarantelli and Hundley 1971; Bartholomew 1989a). The sociological study of collective behavior is no longer dominated by this framework, which tends to pathologize deviance (Pakulski 1991, pp. 6–8). A strong critique of Smelser's overly deterministic approach comes from social constructionists analyzing the creation of deviance. One prominent area of study in this regard involves claims of satanic ritual child abuse (Richardson, Best, and Bromley 1991; Goode and Ben-Yehuda 1994; Nathan and Snedeker 1995).

20. I have taken care to use the term *folk beliefs* and avoided using *superstitions,* as most dictionaries define superstitions as involving a lack of logic and reasoning. Another culture's assumptions, and therefore the steps in reasoning, may differ from one's own. This suggests that to refer to another culture's beliefs as superstitions is ethnocentric.

21. For instance, physician Joel Nitzkin received a series of threatening telephone calls from belligerent parents (Nitzkin 1976; Roueche 1978), Wong and colleagues (1982) noted considerable public resentment to the "epidemic hysteria" label, and Cartter and colleagues (1989, p. 89) observed that "some parents insisted that we had accused their children of faking symptoms."

22. This list excludes the single case of mass pseudohysteria, as the students did not experience symptoms (and did not consider themselves to be ill), but they were "diagnosed" by their parents as ill.

23. I would also like to see how feminists could argue that spontaneous fainting in rapid succession of members of school marching bands is a form of female protest, as a fair number of males are also usually involved.

24. A notable exception to this pattern in the "epidemic hysteria" literature is Miller (1985, p. 103), who remarks that "where all or the majority of the victims were women, this fact alone is considered part of the proof that hysteria caused the affliction." Miller notes that in the famous case of the phantom gasser of Mattoon, Johnson (1945) used this exact argument. Johnson (1945, p. 186) states that "those who succumbed to the 'mental epidemic' were mostly women. . . . This supports the above analysis and puts the 'phantom anesthetist' of Mattoon, in some respects at least, into a familiar psychological pattern." As discussed in Chapter 4, in addition to the media defining women as the perceived targets of the "mad gasser," several newsmen reporting the story experienced headaches attributed to the gas aftereffects yet were not counted by Johnson as victims (Miller 1985).

25. Of course, it could also be argued that the young are subordinate to the old, and among youth, female participation in MPI episodes is overwhelmingly high.

26. Based on my Malay ethnographic fieldwork of male and female Malay children, females are widely believed to possess significantly weaker semangat than males. Also, ethnic Chinese and Indian Malaysians do not generally subscribe to the Malay theory of semangat.

27. Italics in original.

28. From a transcultural, transhistorical perspective, both of these groups of MPI outbreaks were labeled repressive even from within their historical and cultural environments, as will become evident shortly.

29. See the following Malaysian newspaper sources: 100 Pupils and Two Teachers Yet to Return, *New Straits Times,* July 10, 1987; Hysteria Students to Be Transferred, *Bernama,* May 20, 1985; Hysterical Pupils Take Schoolmates Hostage, *New Straits Times,* May 19, 1987, p. 1; Hysteria: Schoolgirls "confess," *New Straits Times,* May 21, 1987, p. 3; Hysteria Blamed on "Evil Spirits": School Head Wants the Ghosts to Go, *New Straits Times,* May 23, 1987, p. 7; Council to Meet Over Hysteria-Stricken Girls, *New Straits Times,* May 24, 1987, p. 4; Seven Girls Scream for Blood: Hysterical Outbursts Continue, *New Straits Times,* May 25, 1987, p. 4; Interview: Fatimah, "I Only Fulfilled My Parents Wishes," *New Straits Times,* May 31, 1987, p. 7; I Can't Believe It, Says Pupil, *New Straits Times,* May 31, 1987, p. 7; Transfer Plan for Girls Hit by Hysteria, *New Straits Times,* July 21, 1987; First Group of Hysteria Girls Sees Psychiatrist, *New Straits Times,* August 11, 1987; Hysteria: Second Batch Visits "Shrink," *New Straits Times,* August 13, 1987.

30. In this example the fine, often ambiguous demarcation between such terms as malingering, conversion, and dissociative disorders is evident. Gelder and colleagues (1994, p. 123) note that "some patients with dissociative (or conversion) disorder appear to add deliberate exaggeration to basic unconscious mechanisms." The Loudun episode appears to be one such case, as it involves obvious feigning (e.g., vomiting nail

parings, and so on) in conjunction with specific convulsions and abnormal movements that are characteristic features of repression-based mass motor conversion disorders recorded in transcultural, transhistorical settings for centuries (Madden 1857; Sirois 1974; Bartholomew and Sirois 1996).

31. Although some demonopath "victims" may have participated unconsciously in the form of conversion symptoms, part of these dramas typically included widespread deliberate deception and fraud. In 1566 des Enfans Trouves Hospital in Amsterdam, Holland, was the scene of collective convulsions, possession, and delirium. During their performances the "victims" reportedly vomited quantities of hair, cloth, thimbles, needles, pins, broken pottery, and glass (Madden 1857, pp. 253). Miraculous vomiting at a convent of demoniacs in Auxonne, France, during the mid-seventeenth century purportedly included bones, wax, pebbles, and living reptiles. Many "possessed" nuns claimed to have suffered anomalous lacerations from demonic forces or to have been levitated. Similar behaviors were reported among a group of possessed children during a witch accusation panic in Salem, Massachusetts, in 1692, as "nearly all of the children swore repeatedly that they had been pinched, choked and bitten, occasionally exhibiting marks of the bites or pinches on their arms" (Caulfield 1943, p. 793).

32. A voluminous literature exists on the events at Loudun, mostly in French. My analysis is based primarily on Madden (1857, pp. 278–344) and Huxley (1952).

33. This curious pattern is characteristic of numerous episodes of purported collective demonic possession in European nunneries during the period. Typical is the "epidemic" affecting virtually an entire community of sisters in a convent at Kintorp, near Strasburg, in 1552: "When one nun fell into a convulsive attack, all the others . . . who might be present, or within hearing of her cries, were instantly affected" (Madden 1857, p. 244). Perhaps the most famous example of this behavior occurred during the Salem witch trials of 1692. Caulfield (1943, p. 793) observes that of the ten young females affected by demonic attacks, the most convincing evidence occurred when the judges ordered the children to stare at the defendants, "whereupon they promptly went off into fits but, as a general rule, recovered as soon as the accused were made to touch them. This sort of evidence appears with monotonous regularity throughout the court records, and the apparent ease with which the children threw and recovered from their fits has been considered absolute proof that they were merely acting."

34. This is also true in occupational episodes, the results of which are summarized by Colligan and Murphy (1982, pp. 42–43).

7

Psychiatric Imperialism and the
Medicalization of Exotic Deviance

In learning about the other, about many "others," our conception of
humanity is enlarged and enriched. We gain insight into the plasticity of
human culture. We begin to see that our way of life is determined not so
much by nature but by culture and history. Only then can we see that our
way of life is just one of many possible ones. . . . In studying the other, we
begin to learn how to separate fact from fantasy . . . about humanity itself
(David Maybury-Lewis 1992, p. 8).

Psychiatry is an inexact science that uses ambiguous, Eurocentric diagnostic
criteria to label certain people as psychologically disturbed or mentally ill.
When it comes to determining what is acceptable behavior and what is not, a
fine and ever-changing boundary often tells us more about the social world of
the interpreter than the mental state of those being interpreted. Unfortunately,
the difference between which side of the line one stands on is typically the
result of who is holding the chalk and has the political power to draw the line.
Although contemporary global medical theory and practice are typified as a
culture and value-neutral process that objectively utilizes scientific methods to
uncover universal laws of human physiology, they contain a Eurocentric conceptual bias. Under the pretext of "neutral" scientific inquiry, professional
medical ideology has become a powerful agent of social control by usurping
both religious and legal authorities to become the most influential agency in
determining what constitutes illness and abnormality both transculturally and,
in terms of redefining past events, transhistorically.

Western medical bias is especially evident in psychiatry,[1] where practitioners rely almost exclusively on descriptive, ambiguous criteria in assessing the presence of mental illness or disorder. The "scientific" determination of the existence of psychological disturbance in any particular individual appears to be a relatively unproblematic process whereby culture- and value-free criteria are used to identify universal disease or disorder categories. However, constructs of disturbance or illness behaviors held by Eurocentric medical professionals typically mirror prevailing Eurocultural societal morals, values, beliefs, and assumptions, representing an insidious form of social control by upholding status quo social realities as scientific facts.

The placement of behaviors into psychological disturbance rubrics is subjective, interpretive, and predicated upon normality standards that change over time and space (i.e., geographically), reinforcing their existence as social constructions and political achievements rather than indisputable scientific facts. Realist or deterministic approaches to understanding deviance reflect the continued Western psychiatric commitment to a universalist disease model of mental disorder that emphasizes biological similarity and largely ignores sociocultural variations (see Marsella and White 1982, p. ix). Pursuit of this universalist approach, with its emphasis on the evaluation of actions per se, reduces and codifies the vast, complex matrix of human social experience into convenient, neat, narrow, Western-based categories of psychological disease or disorder.[2]

The relatively brief history of psychiatry is replete with instances where clinical observations of deviations in current social, cultural, political, and ethical standards of Eurocentric normality, rationality, and reality have received inappropriate pathological medical labels. These include illness designations for such deviant acts as prostitution, general violence, child abuse, homosexuality, political dissent, masturbation, polygamy, gambling, lying, and minority religious convictions. In this regard, psychiatry has much in common with religion and politics. Szasz (1974b, p. 95) notes that "psychiatry resembles religion rather than science, politics rather than medicine. In religion and politics we expect to find conflicting systems or ideologies. Broad consensus concerning the practical management of human affairs, and the ethical systems utilized in governing . . . are regarded merely as a measure of the political success of the dominant ideology." These words by Szasz are as poignant today as when they were written in 1974—indeed even more so, as each successive edition of *The Diagnostic and Statistical Manual of Mental Disorders* has grown thicker and thicker as more and more violations of contemporary Western norms and values are classified as psychological disturbances.

At the present rate it would not be beyond the bounds of imaginative license to envisage the publication of DSM-20 in the year 2100 as a ten-volume set.

Numerous examples of dubious disorder claims in the most recent publication of DSM-IV (APA 1994) appear to be moral and political judgments of the professional psychiatric community in the United States rather than part of any diagnostic nosology. For instance, if people deviate from contemporary Western norms of sexual intercourse frequency, they may be classified as having *hypoactive sex drive* (p. 496), or if they do not desire sexual relations the term is *sexual aversion disorder* (p. 499). Excessive participation in games of chance becomes *pathological gambling* under the general heading of "impulse-control disorders not elsewhere classified" (p. 615). The consistent exhibition of irritating behavior patterns is *antisocial personality disorder* (p. 645), and alcohol abuse or dependence is defined under "alcohol use disorders" (pp. 195–196).

The criterion for the presence of these "disorders" is a constellation of behaviors per se without thorough consideration of the social, cultural, and political circumstances under which the behavior in question became labeled a social problem. Homosexuality in Western society, for example, has been recently relabeled based on a vote after gender rights groups mustered sufficient support in U.S. society to remove this discriminatory psychiatric classification. Labeling gambling or substance abuse as a compulsive disorder or disease helps to remove the stigma and volition from those so labeled, and thus political pressure has not been excessively exerted for change. In fact, just the opposite has occurred despite considerable evidence questioning their illness/disorder status.

LATAH AS AN ADAPTIVE IDIOM

The medical/psychiatric model to account for the appearance of latah remains dominant in mainstream psychiatric theory and practice and, as discussed in Chapter 3, is portrayed as a culture-specific psychological disturbance in the most recent editions of diagnostic manuals published by both the World Health Organization (1993) and the American Psychiatric Association (1994). This model represents a form of neocolonialism, as evaluations are based on the exotic nature of the behavior per se without adequately assessing the context and meaning of the "disorder" from the cultural and historical perspective of the participants. Chapter 2 included an examination of varying degrees of latah (mild, intermediate, severe) in a Malay extended family, examining its logic and meaning for those affected and their relatives, which led to the conclusion that latah is purely a social idiom. When explicated from the social and cultural bedrock of Malay society, latah is best understood as a flexible, multifunctional idiom. Chapter 3 examined the history of latah, including the dubious circumstances under which it was identified and subsequently labeled a medical problem by the British colonial medical and political communities, reinforcing existing stereotypes of natives as physically, mentally, and culturally inferior.

We are now in a position to answer the questions raised in Chapter 1 regarding the pattern of latah behavior. An understanding of latah as a deviant social role can best account for its overall social, cultural, political, historical, and gender patterning. Politically, significant advantage was to be gained in successfully categorizing latah as a mimetic disorder within British-controlled colonial Malaya. It is conspicuous that the first recorded association of latah as a behavioral anomaly occurred during the 1860s, yet written records of latah without reference to disturbance or disease appear in traditional Malay texts as early as the fourteenth century. Winzeler (1995, p. 26) notes his puzzlement by the failure of several prominent Malayan writers of the early to mid-nineteenth century to mention latah. The successful attachment of a pathological label to latah was perpetrated in the name of science and theories of social Darwinism, which placed Malayo-Indonesians as socially and intellectually inferior to Europeans. The endemic presence of latah within this region justified the necessity of colonial custodial rule by the Dutch in the Netherlands Indies and the British in Malaya (and their accompanying capitalist exploitation), reinforcing the incapacity for self-rule. Indeed, the mimetic (and what some colonial psychiatrists termed monkeylike) features of latah implied that Malayo-Indonesians were innately suited to being followers. Another core feature of the latah literature holds that persons of high status, even within the Malayo-Indonesian world, rarely, if ever, latah. This underscores the point that those labeled as latah were composed of the powerless, without the capacity to change the deviance designations made by the powerful.

From a phenomenological standpoint that emphasizes the commonsense understandings of latah in everyday life, Malay folk beliefs held by latahs, their relatives, and society at large have never typified it as a disorder; nor do those engaging in latah, their relatives, or the community at large seek patienthood. Further, no special care is taken when latahs perform activities of a supposed potentially dangerous nature such as cradling babies or driving cars. This is consistent with the complete absence of a single credible firsthand legal, medical, historical, or journalistic record describing a latah-related death or serious injury. Only Westerners unfamiliar with the various social uses of latah express concern for the safety of onlookers. The frequency of latah at weddings, and placing young, vulnerable children at the front of these gatherings to better observe a latah exhibition, underscores its purely symbolic, harmless nature. If the latah performer was considered to be out of control, adults in the conservative Malayo-Indonesian cultural dynamic would not allow their children to be near those being teased; nor would the teasing of latahs, primarily confined to the oldest and hence most revered members of the community, be allowed in any form. In this regard, the latah idiom resembles baseball.

LATAH—THE GREAT MALAYSIAN PASTIME

Latah is the Western equivalent of a foreigner observing the occasional antics of North American major league baseball managers disputing umpiring decisions. Managers are renowned for kicking dirt on umpires; tossing bats, gloves, and other equipment onto the field; and knocking over watercoolers. Their most dramatic actions include appearing as if they are about to push or strike an umpire, only to be held back by fellow players, and placing their nose as close as possible to the umpire's face without touching. In reality, just lightly bumping an umpire would result in an automatic ejection and fine, and striking an umpire would likely result in a lifelong ban. U.S. and Canadian parents and children typically relish in these displays. Never have I observed parents shielding their children or refusing to take them to the ballpark again for fear that the manager might, in his seemingly uncontrollable fit of rage, strike someone in the stands.

The reason this does not occur is obvious to those familiar with traditional baseball conduct who expect managers to occasionally engage in such displays for many purposes. Often, he is trying to ensure that the next close call will be in his team's favor, reflecting a common folk reality among North American major league baseball coaches that such protestations are necessary. It may simply be an opportunity to release frustration during a losing streak. Sometimes a manager appears to be genuinely upset, and at other times he may be trying to inspire his team to perform better. On other occasions he will support the protestations of a close call by one of his players, even if he agrees with the umpiring decision. This is known in baseball circles as "protecting a player." On rare occasion he may debate an umpire as a stalling tactic to allow a "cold" pitcher time to warm up or if his team is trailing prior to reaching the 5½ innings mark and prolonged rain is forecast. In this latter instance, if the game is rained out it will be rescheduled. At other times a manager uses a close decision as an opportunity to engage in farce by playing to the crowd and offering his glasses to the umpire or pointing to a spot several feet from the foul line, implying that a ball ruled to have fallen in fair territory was actually foul by a wide margin. The manager, among the oldest and wisest team members, knows that an umpire almost never reverses his decision.

In this regard, like latah, the manager's actions have only a symbolic utility. And what if a foreigner were to ask me, "Why is that man running onto the field?" I doubt if I would go into any lengthy explanation. I'd probably just say, "He didn't like the call." Yet one could envisage this interaction between baseball managers and umpires being perceived literally by some foreigner psychiatrist as a transient Canadian-U.S. culture-bound syndrome affecting managers, triggered by the stress of a close umpiring decision. This has not occurred in part because of the global telecasting of baseball; the worldwide dominance of U.S. television, movies, and films; and the influence of U.S. psychiatrists in composing *DSM-IV.*

Latah is associated with and serves various functions for an array of different social groups, primarily females. Latah is associated with femininity, as it denotes a loss of self-control that is frowned on for Malayo-Indonesian males. Yet latah in males represents one of the most flexible, adaptive, creative aspects of this idiom, as it can denote transvestism, homosexuality, femininity, and, among Kelantanese silat practitioners, power and masculinity as their loss of control upon being startled reinforces their macho image. The dynamic, faddish nature of this idiom may explain Murphy's (1976, p. 11) bafflement with the complete absence of latah accounts in Malayo-Indonesia until about 1860; reports that latah had an epidemic character by the 1890s when it was very common and exhibited among those of both sexes and in centers of European settlement; its scarcity between 1900 and 1930, especially in areas of European settlement; and during the 1940s and 1950s its almost exclusive appearance among females and virtual absence from urban centers. Contemporary observations and reports of severe latah are almost exclusively confined to socially marginal, postmenopausal females within the Malayo-Indonesian cultural dynamic because their loss of control signifies their distress to others and allows them to speak or act more forthrightly than ordinarily would otherwise be tolerated in society.

Simons (1994, 1995) refers to the latah debate as "interminable," Winzeler (1995) uses the word "problematic," and Kenny (1990, p. 123) classes it among disputes that "are unresolved and are perhaps unresolvable." I do not share their pessimism. It is time to formulate testable research proposals before Malayo-Indonesian latah possibly disappears (as is apparently the case with miryachit) so that they or others can go into the field and potentially resolve this issue. One possible key to an unambiguous resolution of Malayo-Indonesian latah is to utilize more objective measures in evaluating patterned responses in latahs versus hyperstartlers. For example, hypothetically, if during their startle reactions hyperstartlers could be differentiated from nonhyperstartlers in their brain wave patterns, an electroencephalogram could be used to obtain readings from latah subjects during episodes, with the results compared to the readings of hyperstartlers. As hyperstartlers represent only a tiny portion of any population (1 in 2,000, as estimated by Thorne 1944), determining the presence of severe latah and hyperstartling in even a few latah subjects would tend to discredit purely social and culturalogical interpretations.

EPIDEMIC *KORO*:
THE LOGICAL CONSEQUENCE OF "EXOTIC" BELIEFS

Sporadic individual koro cases are conspicuously associated with the underlying presence of various psychosexual disturbances that require identification and treatment. These include sexual misconceptions and preoccupations about masturbation and nocturnal emissions, sexual indiscretions, perceived sexual inadequacies or excesses, and ignorance, inexperience, or insufficient confidence in sexual relationships. These factors are often, but not always, reinforced by social and cultural beliefs pertaining to sexuality. However, designating collective koro as exemplifying mass psychopathology is unsubstantiated and has a different symptom pattern from extremely rare singular koro. Individual koro typically persists for months or years in patients with psychosexual problems who exhibit unambiguous psychiatric disturbance. Large-scale collective delusion-type episodes are typified by the symptoms of anxiety, persisting for a few minutes to several days, and "victims" experience a complete "recovery" upon being convinced they are no longer in danger. The characteristic features of "epidemic" koro unambiguously meet the standard sociological definition of a collective social delusion. This designation may help to explain Jilek's (1986, p. 280) observation that koro is the only so-called culture-bound syndrome to occur in major epidemic form.

The medicalization of collective koro as a culture-specific variant of individual koro is based on narrow Western social realities and the fantastic, implausible contention that genitalia can shrink significantly and result in death. However, "reality" is socially constructed, and such convictions are plausible within societies experiencing episodes that have koro-related traditions, convictions, or rumors. Although no known history exists of epidemic koro in Thailand before 1976, when various cultural groups living within a specific region were affected during a major outbreak, social factors can account for the incident. The epidemic coincided with periods of socioeconomic upheaval and ethnic conflict with Vietnamese immigrants whereby those affected felt threatened and koro was attributed to the nefarious activities of these Vietnamese. In this instance the mass media was instrumental in legitimating and spreading rumors about these plausible koro-related folk devils.

My point is that a society need not have any direct koro-related beliefs for epidemic koro to occur.[3] Although this explanation may seem implausible to some Western-trained scientists removed from the sociocultural and political context of the 1976 Thai koro outbreak, similar episodes of collective delusion occur frequently in Western countries with no previous tradition of the imaginary threatening agent in question. The common thread in these "epidemics" is plausibility about the existence of the threat among the affected population. Prominent examples of social delusions occurring where no previous history was present among a particular people or region include extreme anxiety and misperceptions of rumor-related objects surrounding sightings of imaginary monoplanes in South Africa (Bartholomew 1989a), a three-legged monster in Illinois (Miller, Mieus, and Mathers 1978), phantom windshield pits in Seattle (Medalia and Larsen 1958), and nonexistent rockets over Sweden (Bartholomew 1993a).

In the case of mass koro, the widespread possession of such "deviant" social realities alters the perceptual orientations of many residents in the societies affected, increasing the likelihood that such people will redefine their ambiguous external sexual organs. Various physiological influences associated with external human genitalia may exacerbate this redefinition, such as cold, anxiety, and physical exertion. In collective koro, social, cultural, political, and community factors may need to be addressed to extinguish the contagion, including public reassurance from authority figures—such as community leaders, politicians, and health practitioners—as to the erroneous nature of any circulating koro-related rumors and the psychological origin of the epidemic. In extreme cases where patients are highly anxious and not comforted by reassurance, prescribing placebos or sedatives may be a practical alternative. Among Chinese patients who appear reluctant to accept conventional medical explanations for the outbreak, it may be effective to also suggest certain traditional remedies such as the consumption of herbal teas, abstinence from foods with excessive yin elements, or acupuncture, as such measures are widely held to be effective treatments and are deeply ingrained in traditional medical theories. Long-term prophylactic measures include public sex education and government-sponsored information campaigns that challenge traditional koro-related folk beliefs.

In summary, instead of assuming that "bizarre" koro-related folk realities help to initiate and shape a culture-specific form of mass psychopathology in affected societies, it is equally plausible that commonsense social and cultural understandings among "victims" of collective koro episodes could foster an absolute belief that their genitalia are shrinking. Further, anxiety precipitated by koro-related rumors can actually result in discernible penile or breast shrinkage, reinforcing folk beliefs. Although castration anxiety has been postulated as an explanation for the predominance of male victims, this does not explain cases among females. A plausible alternative explanation posits that the greater observable physiological plasticity of male genitalia renders males more vulnerable. Of course, exacerbating factors also exist among males in affected societies related to various sexual folk beliefs about semen loss and virility. When "epidemic" koro is explicated from its social, cultural, and cognitive bedrock and the political context of Western psychiatry, its present disorder status is dubious, and thus it should be withdrawn from the psychiatric literature.

MEDIEVAL DANCING MANIAS AS EXOTIC RITUAL

In Chapter 5 I examined episodes of tarantism and dancing mania supposedly predominant among females in Europe during the Middle Ages. Many contemporary medical and psychiatric historians note that these are the first recorded incidents of "epidemic hysteria," typifying them as culture-specific examples of mass psychogenic illness. This state of affairs only reinforces the status quo paradigm, which typifies "victims" as primarily innately susceptible abnormal females exhibiting cathartic reactions to accumulated "stress." Episodes are commonly considered to exemplify collective mental disturbances precipitated by unprecedented stresses such as sociopolitical upheaval in the aftermath of the Black Death, floods, famines, and crop failures. This depiction is typically founded on secondary sources. However, based on a series of translations of medieval European chronicles describing these events, typically firsthand, it is evident that contemporary depictions of "dancing manias" are inaccurate. This situation is likely an unconscious reflection of the assumptions, biases, and stereotypes of what until very recently have been the overwhelmingly male-dominated medical and psychiatric professions.

Medieval dancing mania episodes were not spontaneous but highly ritualized and pandemic. A significant portion of dancing mania participants were males, the appearance of whom allowed heathens to worship without fear of Christian sanction. Despite overwhelming contemporary claims to the contrary, a close examination of the period literature revealed that females were not overrepresented as participants. The symptoms of dancing mania and tarantism (visions, palpitations, headache, dizziness, fainting, and tremor) are predictable for any large population engaging in prolonged dancing, fasting, religious emotionalism, and excessive alcohol consumption. A large number of "dancers" were religious pilgrims from foreign countries and as such possessed unfamiliar customs and social realities often labeled abnormal or bizarre by local observers of the day. Present-day scholars almost unanimously agree that so-called dance manias were reactions to extreme stress. However, in examining the sociocultural circumstances, I have shown that a more plausible explanation is that participants were dancing during stressful times to receive divine assistance as opposed to general modern-day claims that the stress precipitated uncontrollable hysterical dancing. Such episodes were not random but occurred almost exclusively in the vicinity of religious shrines, with dancing and fasting in such settings intended to evoke divine cures or protection.

"EPIDEMIC HYSTERIA" AS MYTH: THE NEED FOR CAUTION

Chapter 6 cautioned researchers against regarding nearly any unconventional behavior pattern given a disorder label as a social construction. Chapter 6 examined reports of epidemic hysteria in school settings since the seventeenth century. Despite protestations by many feminists, who argue that the overrepresentation of female participants is a result of mental distress prompted by chauvinist oppression, the transcultural, transhistorical characteristic features of episodes strongly suggest the existence of a unitary psychiatric rubric involving the rapid spread of conversion symptoms. However, social and cultural factors can best account for the enigmatic clustering of reports and their almost exclusive confinement to females. Misogynist researchers continue to be unsuccessful in their attempts to implicate gender-specific biological factors that purportedly exacerbate abnormal personality traits and cathartic reactions to psychological stress. Such evaluations are based on culture-specific female stereotypes and their purported inherent susceptibility to mental disorder, failing to consider the global symbolic identity of females and gender differences in socialization.

THE PATTERN IN THE MEDICALIZATION
OF EXOTIC DEVIANCE

In their seminal study of the medicalization of deviance, Conrad and Schneider (1980) use a historical constructionist approach grounded in the labeling-interactionist perspective to analyze shifts in mainstream deviance designations in society in the United States, from moral and legal to medical domains ("from badness to sickness"). They outline a sequential five-stage model in the medicalization of deviance: "(1) definition of behavior as deviant; (2) prospecting: medical discovery; (3) claims-making: medical and nonmedical interests; (4) legitimacy: securing medical turf; and (5) institutionalization of a medical deviance designation" (p. 366). The present study utilizes a broadly similar theoretical approach, stressing the role of political and cultural factors that culminate in medicalized deviance designations in unfamiliar or exotic behaviors in non-Western societies/cultures or among Western peoples in distant history (from strangeness to illness). Expanding Conrad and Schneider's model to understand exotic deviance is applicable to understanding the Western construction of such culture-bound "syndromes" as latah and koro and strangeness among the Western historical "Other" (dancing mania).

Based on the case studies presented, a similar pattern to that of Conrad and Schneider (1980) is evident in the process of creating "exotic" deviance.

1. Definition of behavior as deviant—A "strange" and unfamiliar behavior pattern is observed and described. In their study of deviance in U.S. society, Conrad and Schneider (1980, p. 266) found that the deviant behaviors in question were typically defined as such prior to the advent of medical labels. In the present study, although the behavior of deviants was not defined as deviant before a medical label was applied, in each instance the deviant actions reinforced existing Eurocentric stereotypes of the gender or ethnic groups affected by the "illness." The erroneous depiction of female overrepresentation in medieval dancing manias within the medical, psychiatric, and historical literatures mirrors popular Eurocentric conceptions of the day of female vulnerability to emotionality and psychological disturbance that have globally existed since biblical times. A more contemporary example is the portrayal of females as innately susceptible to participate in "epidemic hysteria" as a cathartic reaction to stress per se. In both instances the social and cultural patterning of episodes was largely overlooked, and vogue normality codes were unproblematically superimposed on vague diagnostic criteria in explaining the behavior. Latah was identified and designated as an illness during the ascendancy of social and evolutionary Darwinism whereby Asians were portrayed as having an inferior societal structure and intellectual constitution relative to Europeans. The latter, incidentally, conveniently devised this schema, which placed them at the pinnacle of human evolution. "Epidemic" koro has been interpreted as psychological disturbance by Western scientists who have pathologized the physiological consequences of deviant social realities. It is, in essence, orientalism dressed up as science.

2. Prospecting: medical discovery—The behavior in question is at such variance with mainstream Western conceptualizations of normality, rationality, and reality that the deviance is deemed to signify psychological disturbance. In each of the "disorders" studied, scientific or folk theories about the genetic psychological predisposition of the gender or ethnic groups affected were assumed to be responsible for the deviance. The Eurocentric evaluators consist of Western scientific elites who assess the actions per se as bizarre or abnormal, separate from their social, cultural, or historical context and meaning.

Eurocentric professionals, particularly psychiatrists, describe these "disorders" in scientific periodicals and books, reifying their existence.

3. Claims making: medical and nonmedical interests—Organized groups with vested interests in creating a new deviance status for the strange or unfamiliar behavior, both medical and nonmedical, support scientists' attempts to portray the behavior as illness. In the case of latah, numerous statements by colonial scientists and political figures used the newly created mimetic psychiatric disorder as evidence that the Malay population could not adequately govern itself, thereby justifying paternalistic colonial rule and subsequent exploitation of the people and their resources. Portrayals of Asian peoples as susceptible to "epidemic" koro reinforce the contemporary Western notion of such peoples as inferior and parallel recent attempts to characterize their governments as engaging in human rights violations of universal ethical conduct codes (i.e., infanticide, taking political prisoners).

4. Legitimacy: securing medical turf—Unlike conventional deviance, where the new designation is actively challenged to varying degrees (e.g., homosexuality by the gay rights lobby, "masochistic personality disorder" among the feminist movement), virtually no resistance is offered by the deviants or groups representing them. This occurs because imperialistic Eurocentric medical hegemony has achieved almost global dominance within the scientific community. Although most Malays do not consider latah to be a disorder, they have passively accepted Western psychiatric relabeling of this behavior in pathological terms. Since the late nineteenth century, with the "discovery" of koro in various Asian countries, its status has changed from being considered a real disease by local medical practitioners to being accepted among medical communities as representing a psychological disturbance. The fact that "epidemics" of koro-related "psychological disturbance" can occur and are peculiar to certain Third World and "primitive" societies continues to reinforce stereotypes of Oriental peoples as somehow different from Westerners. The Western medical community erroneously assumes no rational person could believe his or her penis, testicles, breasts, ears, or nose was shrinking and that death may result. By elevating our own social realities as superior or somehow more valid, we unconsciously contribute to the characterization of such peoples as separate from us—"the Other." Assumptions regarding innate susceptibility in accounting for the female predominance among dancing mania and "epidemic hysteria" episodes have been supported by the medical community with nary a single voice of dissent until the 1970s. Although the impact of redefining individual hysteria as a female distress response to male oppression has gained considerable influence within the psychiatric/medical com-

munity, only a handful of researchers, academics, and scholars have discussed the possible role of social and cultural factors to account for female vulnerability to epidemic hysteria in medical or psychiatric journals and books.

5. Institutionalization of a deviance designation—The new deviance designations are institutionalized within Western medicine. Classic examples include the American Psychiatric Association's *Diagnostic and Statistical Manual of Mental Disorders* and the World Health Organization's *The ICD-10 Classification of Mental and Behavioural Disorders*. These two documents have enormous circulation and influence among psychiatric elites globally and represent the two "Bibles" of the Western psychiatric medical profession. Ironically, these documents reinforce the "new" deviance/illness status and are circulated globally under the guise of "science" and "truth." Such is the power of the present Eurocentric medical dominance that the new medicalization label is accepted even in universities within countries where the "strange" behavior was initially identified. Thus, through the Eurocentric university system, "local" scholars who become future scientists teach the new medical label as fact, further contributing to its legitimacy.

MEDICALIZING FOREIGN CULTURES
AND THE HISTORICAL WESTERN "OTHER"

Especially susceptible to unsubstantiated disease or disorder designations are behaviors in non-Western cultures, Western subcultures, or historical periods at variance with contemporary Eurocentric conceptions of normality, rationality, and reality. This study has examined the sociocultural context and meaning of several behaviors generally held to represent culture-specific forms of mental disturbance, arguing that they have been inappropriately classified using contemporary Western normality standards.

The underlying theme of this study holds that certain culture- and history-specific behavior patterns—namely latah, medieval dancing manias, and epidemic koro—have been misclassified as diseases or disorder entities. An alternative interpretation has been offered, an alternative sensitive to the events, circumstances, and social, cultural, historical, and political contexts of the persons involved, thereby challenging contemporary medical and psychiatric models by utilizing a historical phenomenological sociology of knowledge approach that emphasizes the environments under which these illness paradigms were constructed. Within the Western medical paradigm, mental illnesses or disorders are conceptualized as involuntary behaviors that result in personal pain to patients who exhibit universal symptoms that may vary in accordance with cultural beliefs. However, in each case study (with the exception of mass conversion reactions in schools), I have endeavored to demonstrate that the behaviors in question were volitional and governed by a set of local norms, values, and convictions insufficiently considered by the Western-trained investigators—investigators who have superimposed popular Western stereotypes about the behaviors of the people under scrutiny in creating and legitimizing unsubstantiated designations of mental disorder or disease. Of crucial importance is the reliance of most psychiatric evaluations on impressionistic criteria and clinical observations. Although compelling evidence supports the reality of mental illness or disorder, the social construction of latah, koro, and dance mania highlights the tendency of professional psychiatric ideology to reflect and reify prevailing Western social norms. This process legitimizes popular Western folk beliefs with medical designations while simultaneously discrediting non-Western folk explanations on the grounds that they have no scientific basis.

The present psychiatric designation of dancing manias, latah, and epidemic koro as "illnesses" is based on the exotic nature of the behaviors per se and is not likely to be redefined until political, as well as scientific, pressures are exerted. The most likely behavior to first be demedicalized is the dancing manias, as participants comprised the European historical "Other" exhibiting Christian conduct codes generally familiar to Eurocentric researchers. Redefining epidemic koro and latah as nonpathological entities will be greatly accelerated by articles in international refereed journals critiquing the ethnocentric nature of medical model designations and organized protests of scientists and laypersons in the countries affected.

Disease or disorder models of latah and epidemic koro are relics of a colonial past, have no verifiable scientific empirical support, and were originally formulated based on the strange nature of the beliefs per se, as defined by Western Caucasian male elites. They are an insidious form of neocolonialism that justifies the marginalization of foreign behaviors. They confirm that "strange" social realities and lifestyles precipitate bizarre mental disorders; that non-Western peoples cannot be trusted, as they are prone to irrationality, when in fact the behaviors are the rational outcomes of unfamiliar symbol systems and worldviews and are a testament to human imagination and creativity in perceiving and adapting to changes in myriad ways.

It is also important to exercise caution in using constructionist approaches, as they must be based on thorough social, cultural, and historical understandings of the behaviors in question. This is evident in Chapter 6 in the analysis of mass conversion reactions in schools, where predominantly male researchers continue to suggest that those typically affected are innately susceptible females, ignoring the social patterning of episodes. However, feminist efforts to explain away their existence ("epidemic hysteria") with such labels as purely protest and distress ignore the transcultural, transhistorical uniformity and presentation of symptoms. In other words, mass conversion reactions in schools do exist and meet the conventional medical definition of a syndrome, but the preponderance of female participation in such events is largely explainable using social and not biological explanations.

The examination of behaviors in this study misclassified as culture-specific hysterical disorders by contemporary Western standards of normality offers a lesson for future studies of history- or culture-bound psychiatric behavior patterns, particularly when the customs or beliefs of those evaluated differ significantly from those of the investigator. As in the past erroneous Western scientific treatment of sexual preference or masturbation as abnormal, illegal, or wrong, the caveat of imposing contemporary Eurocentric notions of mental disorder and normality to judge behavior in other cultures, subcultures, or historical eras risks potentially gross misunderstanding of the conduct under scrutiny and underestimates the human creative capacity. Western-trained social scientists harboring images of universal illness models that devalue the significance of local context and meaning are prone to perceive the unconventional as bizarre while the exotic becomes strange, diversity is viewed as perversity, creativity is mistaken for eccentricity, devoutness is seen as fanaticism, and the unusual is redefined as deviant with its pejorative and stigmatizing pathological connotations. Such erroneous labels are the result of social and psychiatric categories bound to Western social theory and practice. They are interpretations and evaluations and not culture- or value-free. However, they are typically presented as if they are an objective given.

The conception of these illness or disorder categories illustrates how too often the primary export of Eurocentric scientific ideologies, especially in the field of psychiatry, appears not to be theory or knowledge but "truth" and "reality," unconsciously imposed upon customs and beliefs that deviate from the norms and values of Western-trained investigators. In formulating future schemes of mental disease or disorder, researchers should thoroughly understand the extreme transcultural, transhistorical variation in human norms, values, customs, and beliefs.[4] They must also be acutely aware of the arbitrary nature of taxonomic construction and the temptation to reduce and codify the vast, complex matrix of human social experience into convenient categories of psychiatric disorder or disease, robbing us of our humanity. We must be ever mindful that the conception of scientific classification schemes is a complex social process and far from an objective, dispassionate, culture-free, value-neutral enterprise but is a highly subjective art form prone to shifts in political and social fashions.

OTHER INDIGENOUS KNOWLEDGE SYSTEMS

The Western model of science and medicine is typified within the global scientific community as the standard by which all other indigenous knowledge systems should be compared and assessed. Proponents of this Western knowledge model generally discredit adherence to indigenous knowledge systems as unscientific and irrational. However, one stream of relativizing argument (see Watson-Verran and Turnbull 1995) rejects the Western scientific enterprise as itself a form of local knowledge that should not be considered superior but equal to other indigenous knowledge systems, arguing that the general global adoption of the Western system is more an accident of history than the discovery and development of *the* one true and correct scientific system. I reject this argument. Although I have serious concerns over the failure of Western science and medicine to render accurate assessments as to the nature of the universe that often reflect Western social and cultural influences, this scientific model has produced unprecedented benefits for humanity. I do, however, support the Western model being more self-reflective and sensitive to each of the world's knowledge systems by making all practitioners thoroughly aware of the ethnographic record and past mistakes by investigators using the Western medical model (e.g., white supremacy, female inferiority, homosexuality as disease or disorder).

When assessing "exotic" deviance among non-Western peoples and the historical Other, investigators must be careful to avoid creating category fallacies by being schooled in cultural anthropology and thoroughly examining the history of the medical problem under scrutiny. This includes exploring the context and meaning of the deviant label as conceptualized among both the labeler and those being labeled. Kleinman (1980, p. 382) supports a similar integration of biomedical and ethnomedical models in an effort to "reshape the medical model to include social and cultural questions and methods."

FURTHER RESEARCH: THE NEED FOR
ETHNOGRAPHIC FAMILIARITY AND SELF-ASSESSMENT

It is hoped that this study will sensitize readers to more fully appreciate the wondrously broad spectrum and depth of the ethnographic record and culture-bound efforts by Eurocentric scientists to censor or amend this record by imposing their own moral superiority under the imperialistic guise of "neutral" science. In making such value judgments, we alienate ourselves from our common humanity and create the impression that only certain social groups can potentially engage in latah, koro, dancing manias, or conduct codes so foreign to those Western observers evaluating the behaviors that they appear unquestionably immoral or abnormal. The ethnographic record of human-kind will continue to expand as different peoples—both individually and in collectives—create new ways of adapting to their circumstances and under-standing the world.

Certainly, a future test of our scientific sophistication will be whether Western norms and values will continue to be superimposed under the guise of science without sufficiently evaluating the various contexts and meanings these behaviors have for the people or peoples concerned and whose best interest these designations serve. Although this is true for all knowledge systems in their various cultural settings, Western researchers have a special obligation because of the West's world domination. A greater knowledge and appreciation of the ethnographic record should heighten researcher tolerance and awareness of what Geertz (1973, p. 30) calls "the consultable record of what man has said." A thorough understanding of this record should help us to more fully comprehend the vast potentialities that exist for the expression of diverse beliefs, customs, norms, and values and to appreciate the meaning of being human—and different.

We also need to go beyond surface familiarity with other cultures and social realities, which have existed for centuries, and create through detailed study and awareness, genuine tolerance and respect for other social realities. This can be accomplished by subjecting our own worldviews, including the scientific, to continual scrutiny and see our Western culture and science as part of that record and not separate or superior to it. Given the preeminence of Western professional medical ideology and its influence, we have a responsibility to all of humanity to vigilantly scrutinize our assumptions about the world and its peoples by tearing down the insidious colonial vestiges that presently pervade psychiatry.

NOTES

1. Throughout this study I have been highly critical of Western ethnocentricity. Of course, Western cultures and people do not have a monopoly on ethnocentricity or such imperialistic projects as slavery and genocide, which are by-products of ethnocentric thinking. What makes the Western history of such activities pertinent is that because of accidents of history and circumstance, Western civilization has developed superior technological capabilities that have allowed it to achieve military and industrial dominance.

2. One example of the problems posed by ambiguous criteria in diagnosing psychiatric disease or disorder in a transcultural setting is *kuru*. This central nervous system disease is exclusively confined to South Fore, Papua New Guinea, and was once typified within mainstream psychiatry as a culture-specific hysterical disorder primarily affecting women, children, and on occasion, young men. It was subsequently discovered that the

cause is a slow-acting virus spread by touching human brains as they were being prepared for consumption (Lindenbaum 1979; Steadman and Merbs 1982).

3. Of course, indirectly folk realities such as those pertaining to semen loss may have contributed to but not initiated the koro epidemics in Thailand and India, but no evidence indicates an elaborate history of individual or mass koro in either country.

4. Scholars from all disciplines should closely study the ethnographic record of human diversity. Although this makes anthropologists well suited for decoding exotic symbol systems and seemingly strange behavior patterns generally unfamiliar to Western researchers, they are by no means immune to superimposing popular beliefs and stereotypes as scientific facts. For instance, Bartholomew (1993c) has challenged the American Anthropological Association's statement on ethics, claiming it is unethical, authoritarian, and ethnocentric, as it contains Eurocentric conceptualizations of ethics and morals unconsciously embedded in Western society and even imposed by scholars and scientists who assume they are an objective given or universal standard of behavior.

References

Abdul Rahman, T. (1987). "As I See It . . . Will the Hysteria Return?" *New Straits Times* (Malaysia), July 6.

Abdullah, J. (no date). *A Report of the Interview With the Female Teacher and Students at the Hishamuddin Secondary Islamic School, Klang.* Confidential Report to Pusat Islam: Author.

Abraham, J. J. (1912). Latah and Amok. *British Medical Journal* i:438–439.

Acheson, E. (1959). The Clinical Syndrome Variously Called Benign Myalgic Encephalomyelitis, Iceland Disease, and Epidemic Neuromyasthenia. *American Journal of Medicine* 26:569–595.

Ackerman, S. E. (1980). *Cultural Process in Malaysian Industrialization: A Study of Malay Women Factory Workers.* Ph.D. diss., University of California at San Diego. Ann Arbor: University Microfilms.

Ackerman, S. E., and Lee, R. L. (1978). Mass Hysteria and Spirit Possession in Urban Malaysia: A Case Study. *Journal of Sociology and Psychology* 1:24–35.

Adams, A.R.D. (1955). Latah and Amok. Pp. 1–9 in L. Horder (ed.), *The British Encyclopedia of Medical Practice.* London: Butterworth.

Adelman, F. (1955). Toward a Psycho-Cultural Interpretation of Latah. *Davidson Journal of Anthropology* 1:69–75.

Adeniran, R. A., and Jones, J. R. (1994). Koro: Culture-Bound Disorder or Universal Symptom? *British Journal of Psychiatry* 164:559–561.

Adomakoh, C. C. (1973). The Pattern of Epidemic Hysteria in a Girls' School in Ghana. *Ghana Medical Journal* 12:407–411.

Aemmer, F. (1893). *Eine Schulepidemie von Tremor Hystericus* [A School Epidemic of Hysterical Tremor]. Inaugural diss., Basel.

Ahluwalia, S. (1991). Currents in British Feminist Thought: The Study of Male Violence. *Critical Criminologist* 3(1):5–6, 12–14.

Akers, R. I. (1977). *Deviant Behavior: A Social Learning Approach* (2d ed.). Belmont, Calif.: Wadsworth.

Alatas, S. H. (1977). *The Myth of the Lazy Native.* London: Frank Cass.

Albrecht, R. M., Oliver, V., and Poskanzer, D. (1964). Epidemic Neuromyasthenia: Outbreak in a Convent in New York State. *Journal of the American Medical Association* 187:904–907.

Aldous, J. C., Ellam, G. A., Murray, V., and Pike, G. (1994). An Outbreak of Illness Among Schoolchildren in London: Toxic Poisoning Not Mass Hysteria. *Journal of Epidemiology and Community Health* 48:41–45.

Alloy, L., Acocella, J., and Bootzin, R. R. (1996). *Abnormal Psychology: Current Perspectives* (7th ed.). New York: McGraw-Hill.

American Psychiatric Association (APA). (1994). *Diagnostic and Statistical Manual of Mental Disorders* (4th ed.). Washington, D.C.: APA.

———. (1987). *Diagnostic and Statistical Manual of Mental Disorders* (3rd ed., rev.). Washington, D.C.: APA.

———. (1980). *Diagnostic and Statistical Manual of Mental Disorders* (3rd ed.) Washington, D.C.: APA.

———. (1968). *Diagnostic and Statistical Manual of Mental Disorders* (2d ed.). Washington, D.C.: APA.

———. (1952). *Diagnostic and Statistical Manual of Mental Disorders* (1st ed.). Washington, D.C.: APA.

Andelman, D. (1976a). Thai Junta Re-Examines Relations With Neighbor Nations and U.S. *New York Times,* October 18.

———. (1976b). Vietnam Accuses Thai Regime and Demands That It Free 800. *New York Times,* October 28:30.

———, D. (1976c). Campaign Grows Against Vietnamese in Thailand Region. *New York Times,* December 12:3.

Andersen, M. (1987). *Denying Difference: The Continuing Basis for Exclusion of Race and Gender in the Curriculum.* Memphis: Memphis State University, Center for Research on Women.

Anderson, D. N. (1990). Koro: The Genital Retraction Symptom After Stroke. *British Journal of Psychiatry* 157:142–144.

Ang, P. C., and Weller, M.P.I. (1984). Koro and Psychosis. *British Journal of Psychiatry* 145:335.

Anonymous. (1970). Epidemic Malaise. *British Medical Journal* i:1–2.

———. (1967). Tarantism, St. Paul, and the Spider. *Times Literary Supplement* (London), April 27:345–347.

———. (1966a). Editorial. *British Medical Journal* ii:1280.

———. (1966b). Two Schools Close in Tanzania Till Siege of Hysteria Ends. *New York Times,* May 25:36.

———. (1963a). *New York Times,* August 9:4.

———. (1963b). Laughing Malady a Puzzle in Africa. 1000 Along Lake Victoria Afflicted in 18 Months—Most Are Youngsters. Schools Close Down. *New York Times,* August 8:29.

———. (1949). Mars Raiders Caused Quito Panic; Mob Burns Radio Plant, Kills 15. *New York Times,* February 14:1, 7.

———. (1913). *London Daily Mirror,* February 26.

———. (1888). Psychic Disturbances in Russia. *Science* 11:178.

Appleby, L., and Forshaw, D. (1990). *Postgraduate Psychiatry.* Oxford: Heinemann Medical Books.

Araki, S., and Honma, T. (1986). Mass Psychogenic Systemic Illness in School Children in Relation to the Tokyo Photochemical Smog. *Archives of Environmental Health* 41:159–162.

Arbitman, R. (1975). Koro in a Caucasian. *Modern Medicine of Canada* 30(11):970–971.

Archer, D. (1985). Social Deviance. Pp. 743–804 in G. Lindzey and E. Aronson (eds.), *The Handbook of Social Psychology* (3rd ed.). New York: Random House.

Arieti, S., and Brody, E. B. (eds.) (1972). *American Handbook of Psychiatry, Vol. 3, Adult Clinical Psychiatry.* New York: Basic.

Arieti, S., and Meth, J. M. (1959). Rare, Unclassifiable, Collective, and Exotic Psychotic Syndromes. Pp. 546–563 in S. Arieti (ed.), *American Handbook of Psychiatry.* New York: Basic.

Armainguad, M. (1879). Recherches Cliniques sur l'hystérie; Relation d'une Petite Épidémie d'hystérie Observée à Bordeaux [Clinical Research on Hysteria and Its Relation to a Small Epidemic of Hysteria Observed in Bordeaux] *Memoire et Bulletin de la Societe de Medecine et Chirurgie de Bordeaux*:551–579.

Armstrong, D. (1996). Medical Sociology. Pp. 525–527 in A. Kuper and J. Kuper (eds.), *The Social Science Encyclopedia* (2d ed.). London: Routledge.

Aro, H., and Taipale, V. (1987). The Impact of Timing of Puberty on Psychosomatic Symptoms Among Fourteen- to Sixteen-Year-Old Finnish Girls. *Child Development* 58:261–268.

Asch, S. E. (1955). Opinions and Social Pressure. *Scientific American* 193:31–35.

Asher, H. (1979). Non-Psychoanalytic Approaches to National Socialism. *Psychohistory Review* 7(3):13–21.

Astbury, J. (1996). *Crazy for You: The Making of Woman's Madness.* Oxford: Oxford University Press.

Atkinson, P. (1995). *Medical Talk and Medical Work.* London: Sage.

Awerbuch, M. (1985). RSI or Kangaroo Paw? *Medical Journal of Australia* 142:376.

Baasher, T. (1963). The Influence of Culture on Psychiatric Manifestations. *Transcultural Psychiatric Research Review* 15:51–52.

Babington, P. (1859). Translator's Preface, Footnotes, and Appendix. Pp. xxiii–xxvi in J.F.C. Hecker (author), *Epidemics of the Middle Ages.* London: Trubner.

Backman, E. L. (1952). *Religious Dances in the Christian Church and in Popular Medicine* (trans. E. Classer). London: Allen and Unwin.

Baglivi, G. (1723). *The Practice of Physick.* London: A. Bell.

Bainbridge, W. S. (1987). Collective Behavior and Social Movements. Pp. 544–576 in R. Stark (ed.), *Sociology.* Belmont, Calif.: Wadsworth.

———. (1984). Religious Insanity in America: The Official Nineteenth-Century Theory. *Sociological Analysis* 45:223–240.

Baker, P., and Selvey, D. (1992). Malathio-Induced Epidemic Hysteria in an Elementary School. *Veterinary and Human Toxicology* 34:156–160.

Ballard, E. F. (1912). Comment on Amok and Latah. *British Medical Journal,* March 16:652.

Bardana, E. J., and Montanaro, A. (1986). Tight Building Syndrome. *Immunology and Allergy Practice* 8:74–88.

Barlow, D. H., and Durand, V. M. (1995). *Abnormal Psychology: An Integrative Approach.* Melbourne: Brooks/Cole.

Barnouw, V. (1975). *An Introduction to Anthropology, Vol. Two, Ethnology* (rev. ed.). Homewood, Ill.: Dorsey.

———. (1973). *An Introduction to Anthropology, Vol. Two, Ethnology.* Homewood, Ill.: Dorsey.

Barrett, K. (1978). Koro in a Londoner. Letter. *Lancet* 2:1319.

Bartholomew, R. E. (1998a). Dancing With Myths: The Misogynist Construction of Dancing Mania. *Feminism and Psychology* 8(2):173–183.

———. (1998b). The Importance of Historical Perspective: Remembering Colorado's UFO Mania of 1897. *Rocky Mountain Skeptic* 15 (January-February):1, 5–7.

———. (1998c). Before Roswell: The Meaning Behind the Crashed UFO Myth. *Skeptical Inquirer* 22(3):29–30, 59.

———. (1998d). The Great New Zealand Zeppelin Scare of 1909. *New Zealand Skeptic* 47 (autumn):1, 3–5.

———. (1998e). The Medicalization of Exotic Deviance: A Sociological Perspective on Epidemic Koro. *Transcultural Psychiatry* 35(1):5–38.

———. (1998f). The Oregon UFO Wave That Wasn't: The Importance of Press Skepticism in 1896–1897 Sightings. *Pro Facto: Newsletter of Oregonians for Rationality* 4(2):4–6.

———. (1997a). The Medicalization of the Exotic: Latah as a Colonialism-Bound Syndrome. *Deviant Behavior* 18:47–75.

———. (1997b). Epidemic Hysteria: A Dialogue With Francois Sirois. *Medical Principles and Practice* 6:38–44.

———. (1997c). The American Airship Hysteria of 1896–1897. Pp. 15–28 in K. Frazier, B. Karr, and J. Nickell (eds.), *The UFO Invasion.* Buffalo: Prometheus.

———. (1997d). Collective Delusions: A Skeptic's Guide. *Skeptical Inquirer* 21(3):29–33.

———. (1997e). Mass Hysteria. *British Journal of Psychiatry* 170:387–388.

———. (1997f). Mass Hysteria in Kentucky 100 Years Ago. *Kentucky Association of Science Educators and Skeptics* 10(2):1, 3, 6–7.

———. (1997g). A British Columbia–Manitoba Balloon Mystery of 1896–1897. *British Columbia Historical News* 30(4):27–29.

———. (1995a). Letter. The Idiom of Latah: Reply to Dr. Simons. *Journal of Nervous and Mental Disease* 183:184–185.

———. (1995b). Culture-Bound Syndromes as Fakery. *Skeptical Inquirer* 19(6):36–41.

———. (1994a). Tarantism, Dancing Mania, and Demonopathy: The Anthro-Political Aspects of "Mass Psychogenic Illness." *Psychological Medicine* 24:281–306.

———. (1994b). The Social Psychology of "Epidemic" Koro. *International Journal of Social Psychiatry* 40:44–60.

———. (1994c). Disease, Disorder, or Deception? Latah as Habit in a Malay Extended Family. *Journal of Nervous and Mental Disease* 182:331–338.

———. (1994d). When the Consequences of Beliefs Are Defined as Psychiatric Entities. *Journal of Developmental and Behavioral Pediatrics* 15(1):62–65.

———. (1993a). Redefining Epidemic Hysteria: An Example From Sweden. *Acta Psychiatrica Scandinavica* 88:178–182.

———. (1993b). *Miracle or Mass Delusion?: What Happened in Klang, Malaysia?* Study compiled for Pusat Islam, Prime Minister's Department, Kuala Lumpur, Malaysia.

————. (1993c). Whose Ethics? *Anthropology Newsletter* (American Anthropological Association) 34(7):2.

————. (1992a). A Brief History of "Mass Hysteria" in Australia. *Skeptic* (Australia) 12(1):23–26.

————. (1992b). Mutilation Mania—The Witch Craze Revisited: An Essay Review of an Alien Harvest. *Anthropology of Consciousness* 3(1–2):23–25.

————. (1991a). The Symbolic Significance of Modern Myths. *Skeptical Inquirer* 15:430–431.

————. (1991b). The Quest for Transcendence: An Ethnography of UFOs in America. *Anthropology of Consciousness* 2(1–2):1–12.

————. (1990a). The Airship Hysteria of 1896–1897. *Skeptical Inquirer* 14(2):171–181.

————. (1990b). Ethnocentricity and the Social Construction of "Mass Hysteria." *Culture, Medicine, and Psychiatry* 14(4):455–494.

————. (1989a). The South African Monoplane Hysteria: An Evaluation of the Usefulness of Smelser's Theory of Hysterical Beliefs. *Sociological Inquiry* 59(3):287–300.

————. (1989b). *UFOlore: A Social Psychological Study of a Modern Myth in the Making*. Stone Mountain, Ga.: Arcturus.

Bartholomew, R. E., and Bartholomew, P. B. (1991). Evaluating Bigfoot Videos as an Anthropology Teaching Aid. *Anthropology of Consciousness* 2(1–2):34–35.

Bartholomew, P. B., Bartholomew, R. E., Brann, W., and Hallenbeck, B. (1992). *Monsters of the Northwoods: An Investigation of Bigfoot Sightings in New York and Vermont*. Utica, N.Y.: North Country.

Bartholomew, R. E., Basterfield, K., and Howard, G. S. (1991). UFO Abductees and Contactees: Psychopathology or Fantasy Proneness? *Professional Psychology: Research and Practice* 22(3):215–222.

Bartholomew, R. E., and Cole, P. (1997). The Myth of Aboriginal Cannibalism: Using Urban Legends to Explore Australian Social Issues. *Teaching History: Journal of the History Teachers' Association of New South Wales* 31(3):25–27.

Bartholomew, R. E., and Gregory, J. (1996). "A Strange Epidemic": Notes on the First Detailed Documented Case of Epidemic Koro. *Transcultural Psychiatric Research Review* 33:365–366.

Bartholomew, R. E., and Howard, G. S. (1998). *UFOs and Alien Contact: Two Centuries of Mystery*. Buffalo: Prometheus.

Bartholomew, R. E., and Likely, M. (1998). Subsidising Australian Pseudoscience: Is Iridology Complementary Medicine or Witch Doctoring? *Australian and New Zealand Journal of Public Health* 22(1):163–164.

Bartholomew, R. E., and O'Dea, J. (1998). Religious Devoutness Construed as Pathology: The Myth of Religious Mania. *International Journal for the Psychology of Religion* 8(1):1–16.

Bartholomew, R. E., and Sirois, F. (1997). Occupational Mass Psychogenic Illness: Prevalence and Presentation Patterns. Mimeographed.

————. (1996). Epidemic Hysteria in Schools: An International and Historical Overview. *Educational Studies* 22(3):285–311.

Bartlett, J. (1992). *Familiar Quotations: A Collection of Passages, Phrases, and Proverbs Traced to Their Sources in Ancient and Modern Literature* (16th ed., rev. and ed. by J. Kaplan). Boston: Little, Brown.

Bartol, C. R. (1991). *Criminal Behavior: A Psychological Approach* (3rd ed.). Englewood Cliffs, N.J.: Prentice-Hall.

Bates, E. M. (1977). *Models of Madness.* St. Lucia: University of Queensland Press.

Bauer, R. M., Greve, K. W., Besch, E. L., Schramke, C. J., Crouch, J., Hicks, A., Ware, M. R., and Lyles, W. B. (1992). The Role of Psychological Factors in the Report of Building-Related Symptoms in Sick Building Syndrome. *Journal of Consulting and Clinical Psychology* 60(2):213–219.

Bayer, R. (1981). *Homosexuality and American Psychiatry: The Politics of Diagnosis.* New York: Basic.

Baynes, H. G. (1941). *Germany Possessed.* London: Jonathan Cape.

Beard, G. M. (1880a). Experiments With the "Jumpers" or "Jumping Frenchmen" of Maine. *Journal of Nervous and Mental Disease* 7:487–490.

———. (1880b). Experiments with the "Jumpers" of Maine. *Popular Science Monthly* 18:170–178.

———. (1878). Remarks Upon Jumpers, or Jumping Frenchmen. *Journal of Nervous and Mental Disease* 5:526.

Bebbington, E., Hopton, C., Lockett, H. I., and Madeley, R. J. (1980). From Experience: Epidemic Syncope in Jazz Bands. *Community Medicine* 2:302–307.

Becker, H. S. (1963). *Outsiders: Studies in the Sociology of Deviance.* New York: Free Press.

Bell, D. S. (1989a). Repetitive Strain Injury: An Iatrogenic Epidemic of Simulated Injury. *Medical Journal of Australia* 151:280–284.

———. (1989b). Repetitive Strain Injury: An Iatrogenic Epidemic. In Reply. *Medical Journal of Australia* 151:599–600.

Benaim, S., Horder, J., and Anderson, J. (1973). Hysterical Epidemic in a Classroom. *Psychological Medicine* 3:366–373.

Benedict, R. (1959 [1934]). Anthropology and the Abnormal. *Journal of General Psychology* 10(2):59–82. Reprinted as pp. 262–283 in M. Mead (ed.), *An Anthropologist at Work: Writings of Ruth Benedict.* Boston: Houghton Mifflin.

Bentham, J. (1789). *An Introduction to the Principles of Morals and Legislation.* London: Pickering.

Berger, P. L., and Luckmann, T. (1971 [1966]). *The Social Construction of Reality.* London: Allen Lane.

Berrios, G. E., and Morley, S. J. (1984). Korolike Symptoms in a Non-Chinese Subject. *British Journal of Psychiatry* 145:331–334.

Bliss, E. L. (1986). *Multiple Personality, Allied Disorders, and Hypnosis.* New York: Oxford University Press.

Blonk, J. C. (1895). Koro. *Geneeskundig Tijdschrift voor Nederlandsch-Indie* 35:562–563.

Bluglass, R. (1976). Malingering. Pp. 280–281 in S. Krauss (ed.), *Encyclopaedic Handbook of Medical Psychology.* London: Butterworth.

Blumer, H. (1971). Social Problems as Collective Behavior. *Social Problems* 18:298–306.

Boas, F. (1930). The Religion of the Kwakiutl Indians. *Columbia University Contributions to Anthropology* 10 (part 2). New York: Columbia University Press.

Bock, P. K. (1979). *Modern Cultural Anthropology: An Introduction.* New York: Alfred A. Knopf.

Bohn, T., and Gutman, J. S. (1989). The Civil Liberties of Religious Minorities. Pp. 239–253 in M. Galanter (ed.), *Cults and New Religious Movements: A Report of the American Psychiatric Association From the Committee on Psychiatry and Religion.* Washington, D.C.: APA.

Bokai, cited in Szegō, K. (1896). Uber die Imitationskrankheiten der Kinder [About the Imitative Illnesses of Children]. *Jahrbuch fur Kinderheilkunde* (Leipzig) 41:133–145.

Boling, L., and Brotman, C. (1975). A Fire-Setting Epidemic in a State Mental Health Center. *American Journal of Psychiatry* 132:946–950.

Bonfanti, L. (1977). *The Witchcraft Hysteria of 1692, Vol. 2.* Wakefield, Mass.: Pride.

Bordua, D. J. (1967). Recent Trends: Deviant Behavior and Social Control. *Annals of the American Academy of Political and Social Science* 369:149–163.

Boss, L. P. (1997). Epidemic Hysteria: A Review of the Published Literature. *Epidemiologic Reviews* 19(2):233–243.

Bourgeois, M. (1968). Un Koro Charentais (Transposition Ethnopsychiatrique). *Annales Medico-Psychologiques* (Paris) 126:749–751.

Bourguignon, E. (1979). *Psychological Anthropology: An Introduction to Human Nature and Cultural Differences.* New York: Holt, Rinehart, and Winston.

———. (1978). Spirit Possession and Altered States of Consciousness: The Evolution of an Inquiry. Pp. 477–515 in G. D. Spindler (ed.), *The Making of Psychological Anthropology.* Berkeley: University of California Press.

———. (1974). Culture and the Varieties of Consciousness. *An Addison-Wesley Module in Anthropology 47.* Reading, Mass.: Addison-Wesley.

Boxer, P. A. (1985). Occupational Mass Psychogenic Illness: History, Prevention, and Management. *Journal of Occupational Medicine* 27(12):867–872.

Bozzolo, G. (1894). Tosse Isterica Epidemica [Epidemic of Hysterical Coughing]. *Riforma Medica* 4:735–737.

Bozzuto, J. C. (1975). Cinematic Neurosis Following the Exorcist: Report of Four Cases. *Journal of Nervous and Mental Disease* 161:43–48.

Briggs, M. C., and Levine, P. H. (1994). A Comparative Review of Systemic and Neurological Symptomatology in 12 Outbreaks Collectively Described as Chronic Fatigue Syndrome, Epidemic Neuromyasthenia, and Myalgic Encephalomyelitis. *Clinical and Infectious Diseases* 18 (supplement 1):S32–42.

Brockington, I. F., Kelly, A., Hall, P., and Deakin, W. (1988). Premenstrual Relapse of Puerperal Psychosis. *Journal of Affective Disorder* 14(3):287–292.

Brodsky, C. M. (1983). Allergic to Everything: A Medical Subculture. *Psychosomatics* 24:731–742.

Bromberg, W. (1975). *From Shaman to Psychotherapist.* Chicago: Henry Regnery.

Bromley, D. G., and Shupe, A. (1989). Public Reaction Against New Religious Movements. Pp. 305–334 in M. Galanter (ed.), *Cults and New Religious Movements: A Report of the American Psychiatric Association From the Committee on Psychiatry and Religion.* Washington, D.C.: APA.

Brown, R. W. (1965). *Social Psychology.* New York: Free Press.

———. (1954). Mass Phenomena. Pp. 833–873 in G. Lindzey (ed.), *Handbook of Social Psychology, Vol. 2.* Cambridge: Addison-Wesley.

Brown, W. (1944). The Psychology of Modern Germany. *British Journal of Psychology* 34:43–59.

Brunvand, J. H. (1981). *The Vanishing Hitchhiker: American Urban Legends and Their Meanings.* New York: W. W. Norton.

Buckhout, R. (1980). Nearly 2,000 Witnesses Can Be Wrong. *Bulletin of the Psychonomic Society* 16:307–310.

Buckhout, R. (1974). Eyewitness Testimony. *Scientific American* 231(6):23–31.

Bulgatz, J. (1992). *Ponzi Schemes, Invaders From Mars, and More Extraordinary Popular Delusions and the Madness of Crowds.* New York: Harmony.

Bullard, T. E. (1994). Personal communication.

———. (1989). UFO Abduction Reports: The Supernatural Kidnap Narrative Returns in Technological Guise. *Journal of American Folklore* 102(404):147–170.

Bullough, V. (1976). *Sexual Variance in Society and History.* Chicago: University of Chicago Press.

Burnham, W. H. (1924). *The Normal Mind.* New York: D. Appleton-Century.

Bury, J. B. (1958). *History of the Later Roman Empire, Vol. 1.* London: Constable.

Cai, J. B. (1982). Five Case Reports of Suo-Yang Zhen. *Chinese Journal of Neuropsychiatry* 4:206.

Calhoun, D. W. (1976). *Persons-in-Groups.* New York: Harper and Row.

Calmeil, L. F. (1845). *De la Folie, Considérée Sous le Point de vue Pathologique, Philosophique, Historique et Judiciaire* [On the Crowd, Considerations on the Point of Pathology, Philosophy, History, and Justice]. Paris: Baillere.

Cantril, H. (1947 [1940]). *The Invasion From Mars: A Study in the Psychology of Panic.* Princeton, N.J.: Princeton University Press.

Caplan, P. (1985). *The Myth of Women's Masochism.* New York: Dutton.

Carr, W. (1978). *Hitler: A Study in Personality and Politics.* New York: St. Martin's.

Carson, R. C., Butcher, J. N., and Mineka, S. (1996). *Abnormal Psychology and Modern Life* (10th ed.). New York: HarperCollins.

Cartter, M. L., MsHar, P., and Burdo, H. (1989). The Epidemic Hysteria Dilemma. *American Journal of Diseases in Childhood* 143:89.

Cartwright, F. F., and Biddiss, M. D. (1972). *Disease and History.* New York: Thomas Y. Crowell.

Castel, R. (1985). Moral Treatment; Mental Therapy and Social Control in the Nineteenth Century. Pp. 246–266 in S. Cohen and A. Scull (eds.), *Social Control and the State.* Oxford: Blackwell.

Castellani, A., and Chalmers, A. J. (1919). *Manual of Tropical Medicine.* London: Bailliere, Tindall, and Cox.

Catanzaro, R. J. (1967). Psychiatric Aspects of Alcoholism. Pp. 31–45 in D. Pittman (ed.), *Alcoholism.* New York: Harper and Row.

Caulfield, E. (1943). Pediatric Aspects of the Salem Witchcraft Tragedy: A Lesson in Mental Health. *American Journal of Diseases of Children* 97:788–802.

Chait, L. R. (1986). Pre-Menstrual Syndrome and Our Sisters in Crime: A Feminist Dilemma. *Women's Rights Law Reporter* 9:267–293.

Chakraborty, A., Das, S., and Mukherji, A. (1983). Koro Epidemic in India. *Transcultural Psychiatric Research Review* 20:150–151.

Chamberlin, J. E., and Gilman, S. L. (1985). *Degeneration: The Dark Side of Progress.* New York: Columbia University Press.

Chapel, J. L. (1970). Latah, Myriachit, and Jumpers Revisited. *New York State Journal of Medicine* (September 1):2201–2204.

Chen, E. (1991). Drug-Induced Koro in a Non-Chinese Man. *British Journal of Psychiatry* 158:721.

Chen, P.C.Y. (1970). Indigenous Malay Psychotherapy. *Tropical and Geographical Medicine* 22:409.

Chester, A. C., and Levine, P. H. (1994). Concurrent Sick Building Syndrome and Chronic Fatigue Syndrome: Epidemic Neuromyasthenia Revisited. *Clinical and Infectious Diseases* 18 (supplement 1):S43–48.

Chew, P. K. (1978). How to Handle Hysterical Factory Workers. *Occupational Health and Safety* 47(6):50–53.

Chiu, T., Tong J., and Schmidt, K. (1972). A Clinical Survey of Latah in Sarawak, Malaysia. *Psychological Medicine* 2:155–165.

Chowdhury, A. N. (1992). Psychopathosexuality in Koro Patients. *Journal of the Indian Academy of Applied Psychology* 18(1–2):57–60.

———. (1989a). Penile Perception of Koro Patients. *Acta Psychiatrica Scandinavica* 80:183–186.

———. (1989b). Dysmorphic Penis Image Perception: The Root of Koro Vulnerability. *Acta Psychiatrica Scandinavica* 80:518–520.

Chowdhury, A. N., and Bagchi, D. J. (1993). Koro in Heroin Withdrawal. *Journal of Psychoactive Drugs* 25(3):257–258.

Chowdhury, A. N., and Bera, N. K. (1994). Koro Following Cannabis Smoking: Two Case Reports. *Addiction* 89(8):1017–1020.

Christophersen, E. (ed.). (1946). *Results of the Norwegian Scientific Expedition in Tristan da Cunha 1937–1938.* Oslo: Norwegian Government.

Cirillo, D. (1770). A Letter to Dr. William Watson, F.R.S., Giving Some Account of the Manna Tree and the Tarantula. *Philosophical Transactions of the Royal Society* (London) 60:233–238.

Clammer, J. (1983). The Straits Chinese in Melaka. Pp. 156–173 in K. S. Sandhu and P. Wheatley (eds.), *Melaka: The Transformation of a Malay Capital City c. 1400–1980, Vol. II.* Kuala Lumpur: Oxford University Press.

Clark, R. (1984). *The Survival of Charles Darwin.* New York: Random House.

Clarke, A. C. (1980). *Voices From the Sky.* New York: Pocket Books.

Clarke, W. C. (1973). Temporary Madness as Theatre: Wild-Man Behaviour in New Guinea. *Oceania* 43(3):198–214.

Clifford, H. (1898). *Studies in Brown Humanity.* London: Grant Richards.

Clinard, M. B., and Meier, R. F. (1995). *Sociology of Deviant Behavior* (9th ed.). New York: Harcourt Brace College Publishers.

———. (1992). *Sociology of Deviant Behavior* (8th ed.). New York: Harcourt Brace Jovanovich.

Cochrane, R. (1983). *The Social Creation of Mental Illness.* London: Longman.

Cockerham, W. C. (1981). *Sociology of Mental Disorder.* Englewood Cliffs, N.J.: Prentice-Hall.

Cohen, S., Tennenbaum, S. Y., Teitelbaum, A., and Durst, R. (1995). The Koro (Genital Retraction) Syndrome and Its Association With Fertility: A Case Report. *Journal of Urology* 153(2):427–428.

Cohn, N. (1957). *The Pursuit of the Millennium.* Fair Lawn, N.J.: Essential.

Cole, T. B. (1990). Pattern of Transmission of Epidemic Hysteria in a School. *Epidemiology* 1:212–218.

Coleman, J. C. (1976). *Abnormal Psychology and Modern Life.* Glenview, Ill.: Scott, Foresman.

Colligan, M. J. (1978). *An Investigation of Apparent Mass Psychogenic Illness in an Electronics Plant.* Unpublished National Institute for Occupational Safety and Health Report.

Colligan, M. J., and Murphy, L. R. (1982). A Review of Mass Psychogenic Illness in Work Settings. Pp. 33–52 in M. Colligan, J. Pennebaker, and L. Murphy (eds.), *Mass Psychogenic Illness: A Social Psychological Analysis.* Hillsdale, N.J.: Lawrence Erlbaum.

Colligan, M. J., Pennebaker, J. W., and Murphy, L. R. (1982). Overview of Mass Psychogenic Illness: Hysteria Revisited? Pp. 1–3 in M. Colligan, J. Pennebaker, and L. Murphy (eds.), *Mass Psychogenic Illness: A Social Psychological Analysis.* Hillsdale, N.J.: Lawrence Erlbaum.

Colligan, M. J., and Urtes, M. A. (1978). *An Investigation of Apparent Mass Psychogenic Illness in an Electronics Plant.* Unpublished National Institute for Occupational Safety and Health Report.

Colligan, M. J., Urtes, M. A., Wisseman, C., Rosensteel, R. E., Anania, T. L., and Hornung, R. W. (1979). An Investigation of Apparent Mass Psychogenic Illness in an Electronics Plant. *Journal of Behavioral Medicine* 2:297–309.

Colson, A. C. (1971). The Perception of Abnormality in a Malay Village. Pp. 88–100 in N. Wagner and E. S. Tan (eds.), *Psychological Problems and Treatment in Malaysia.* Kuala Lumpur: University of Malaya Press.

Comfort, A. (1967). *The Anxiety Makers: Some Curious Preoccupations of the Medical Profession.* London: Nelson.

Conner, J. W. (1975). Social and Psychological Reality of European Witchcraft Beliefs. *Psychiatry* 38:366–380.

Conrad, P. (1979). Types of Medical Social Control. *Sociology of Health and Illness* 1(1) (June):1–11.

————. (1975). The Discovery of Hyperkinesis: Notes on the Medicalization of Deviant Behavior. *Social Problems* 23:12–21.

Conrad, P., and Schneider, J. W. (1980). *Deviance and Medicalization: From Badness to Sickness.* St. Louis: C. V. Mosby.

Constable, P. J. (1979). Koro in Hertfordshire. *Lancet* 1:163.

Cornish, J. (1814). On a Convulsive Epidemic in Cornwall, Caused by a Religious Excitement. *Medical and Physical Journal* 31:373–379.

Coughlan, J. E. (1997). Personal communication, October 20.

Cremona, A. (1981). Another Case of Koro in a Briton. Letter. *British Journal of Psychiatry* 138:180.

Curra, J. (1994). *Understanding Social Deviance: From the Near Side to the Outer Limits.* New York: HarperCollins.

Czaplicka, M. (1914). *Aboriginal Siberia.* Oxford: Clarendon.

Daikos, G. K., Garzonis, S., and Paleologue, A. (1959). Benign Myalgic Encephalomyelitis: An Outbreak in a Nurses' School in Athens. *Lancet* 1:693–696.

Dajer, A. (1990). St. Vitus's Dance. *Discover* 11(3):86, 88, 90.

Dalton, J. J. (1980). *The Cattle Mutilators.* New York: Manor.

DaMatta, R. (1984). Carnival in Multiple Planes. Pp. 210–258 in J.J. MacAloon (ed.), *Rite, Drama, Spectacle, Festival.* Philadelphia: ISHI.

Darnton, R. (1984). *The Great Cat Massacre and Other Episodes in French Cultural History.* New York: Basic.

Davidson, A. (1867). Choreomania: An Historical Sketch, With Some Account of an Epidemic Observed in Madagascar. *Edinburgh Medical Journal* 13:124–136.

Davis, L. (1987). Battered Women: The Transformation of a Social Problem. *Social Work* 32:306–311.

Davis, N. J. (1972). Labeling Theory and Deviance Research: A Critique and Reconsideration. *Sociological Quarterly* 13:447–474.

Dawood, N. J. (trans.) (1977). *The Koran.* Harmondsworth, Middlesex: Penguin.

Davy, R. B. (1880). "St. Vitus" Dance and Kindred Affection; The Recent Epidemic at the Ursulin Convent in Brown County, Ohio; A Sketch of the Historic Disease. *Cincinnati Lancet and Clinic* 4:440–445, 467–473.

de Certeau, M. (1970). *La Possession de Loudun* [The Possession of Loudun]. Julliard: Collection Archives.

de Leo, D., Mauro, P., and Pellegrini, C. (1989). An Organic Triggering Factor in Koro Syndrome? A Case Report. *European Journal of Psychiatry* 3(2):77–81.

de Martino, E. (1966). *La Terre du Remords* [The Land of Self-Affliction] (trans. from Italian by Claude Poncet). Paris: Gallimard.

Deisher, J. B. (1957). Benign Myalgic Encephalomyelitis (Iceland Disease) in Alaska. *Northwest Medicine* 56:1451–1456.

Desenclos, J. C., Gardner, H., and Horan, M. (1992). Mass Sociogenic Illness in a Youth Center. *Revue d'Epidemiologie et de Sante Publique* (Paris) 40:201–208.

Despine, P. (1875). *De la Folie au Point de vue Philosophique ou Specialement Psychologique Etudiee chez le malade et chez l'homme en Sante* [Madness From the Philosophical Viewpoint, in Particular a Psychological Study of a Sick Person in Relation to a Healthy Person]. Paris: F. Savy.

Deutsch, A. (1967). *The Mentally Ill in America.* New York: Columbia University Press.

Deva, M. P. (1990). *Psychiatry: A Brief Outline of Clinical Psychological Medicine.* Selangor, Malaysia: Ophir Medical Specialists.

Devan, G. S., and Hong, O. S. (1987). Koro and Schizophrenia in Singapore. *British Journal of Psychiatry* 150:106–107.

Devereux, G. (1980). *Basic Problems of Ethnopsychiatry* (trans. B. M. Gulati and G. Devereux). Chicago: University of Chicago Press.

Dhadphale, M., and Shaikh, S. P. (1983). Epidemic Hysteria in a Zambian School: "The Mysterious Madness of Mwinilunga." *British Journal of Psychiatry* 142:85–88.

Dobash, R. E., and Dobash, R. P. (1992). *Women, Violence, and Social Change.* New York: Routledge.

Douglas, J. D. (ed.). (1972). *Research on Deviance.* New York: Random House.

Dow, T. W., and Silver, D. A. (1973). A Drug-Induced Koro Symptom. *Journal of the Florida Medical Association* 60:32–33.

Downes, D. (1979). Praxis Makes Perfect: A Critique of Critical Criminology. Pp. 1–16 in D. Downes and P. Rock (eds.), *Deviant Interpretations.* Oxford: Martin Robertson.

Dubnikov, E. I. (1927). Manifestations Collectives d'hysterie Traumatique durant la guerre civile [Collective Manifestations of Hysterical Trauma During the Civil War]. *Vrach. Dielo* 10:595–599.

236

REFERENCES

Duke, M. P., and Nowicki, S. (1986). *Abnormal Psychology: A New Look.* New York: Holt, Rinehart, and Winston.

Dumont, J. (1988). The Tasaday, Which and Whose? Toward the Political Economy of an Ethnographic Sign. *Cultural Anthropology* 3:261–275.

Dumville, B. (1908). Should the French System of Moral Instruction Be Introduced Into England. Pp. 116–117 in M. E. Sadler (ed.), *Moral Instruction and Training in Schools: Report of an International Inquiry, Vol. 2.* London: Longmans, Green.

Durst, R., and Rosca-Rebaudengo, R. P. (1988). Koro Secondary to a Tumour of the Corpus Callosum. *British Journal of Psychiatry* 153:251–254.

Duster, T. (1970). *The Legislation of Morality.* New York: Free Press.

Dutta, H., Phookan, R., and Das, P. D. (1982). The Koro Epidemic in Lower Assam. *Indian Journal of Psychiatry* 24:370–374.

Eastwell, H. D. (1979). A Pica Epidemic: A Price for Sedentarism Among Australian Ex-Hunter-Gatherers. *Psychiatry* 42:264–273.

———. (1976). Associative Illness Among Aboriginals. *Australian and New Zealand Journal of Psychiatry* 10:89–94.

Ebrahim, G. J. (1968). Mass Hysteria in School Children, Notes on Three Outbreaks in East Africa. *Clinical Pediatrics* 7:437–438.

Echols, J. M., and Shadily, H. (eds.). (1968). *An Indonesian-English Dictionary.* Ithaca, N.Y.: Cornell University Press.

Ede, A. (1976). Koro in an Anglo-Saxon Canadian. *Canadian Psychiatric Association Journal* 21:389–392.

Edwards, A. (1988). *Regulation and Repression: The Study of Social Control.* Sydney: Allen and Unwin.

Edwards, J. G. (1970). The Koro Pattern of Depersonalization in an American Schizophrenic Patient. *American Journal of Psychiatry* 126(8):1171–1173.

Edwards, J. W. (1984). Indigenous Koro, a Genital Retraction Syndrome of Insular Southeast Asia: A Critical Review. *Culture, Medicine, and Psychiatry* 8:1–24.

Ehrenreich, B., and English, D. (1978). *For Her Own Good: 150 Years of the Experts' Advice to Women.* Garden City, N.Y.: Anchor.

Einstadter, W., and Henry, S. (1995). *Criminological Theory: An Analysis of Its Underlying Assumptions.* Sydney: Harcourt Brace College Publishers.

Elkins, G. E., Gamino, L. A., and Rynearson, R. R. (1988). Mass Psychogenic Illness, Trance States, and Suggestion. *American Journal of Clinical Hypnosis* 30:267–275.

Ellis, W. G. (1897). Latah, a Mental Malady of the Malays. *Journal of Mental Science* 43:32–40.

———. (1893). The Amok of the Malays. *Journal of Mental Science* 39:325–338.

Emsley, R. A. (1985). Koro in Non-Chinese Subject. Letter. *British Journal of Psychiatry* 146:102.

Endicott, K. (1970). *An Analysis of Malay Magic.* Oxford: Clarendon.

Epstein, J. (1995). *Altered Conditions: Disease, Medicine, and Storytelling.* New York: Routledge.

Evans, H. (1984). *Visions, Apparitions, Alien Visitors.* Wellingborough: Aquarian.

Evans, R. R. (1969). Theoretical Viewpoints in Collective Behavior. Pp. 1–18 in R. Evans (ed.), *Readings in Collective Behavior.* Chicago: Rand McNally.

Evans-Wentz, W. Y. (1909). *The Fairy Faith in Celtic Countries, Its Psychological Origin and Nature.* Rennes, France: Oberthur.

Eysenck, H. J. (1977). *Crime and Personality.* London: Routledge and Kegan Paul.

Eysenck, H. J., and Gudjonsson, G. H. (1989). *The Causes and Cures of Criminality.* New York: Plenum.

Faguet, R. A., and Faguet, K. F. (1982). La Folie a Deux. Pp. 1–14 in C.T.H. Friedmann and R. A. Faguet (eds.), *Extraordinary Disorders of Human Behavior.* New York: Plenum.

Faust, H. S., and Brilliant, L. B. (1981). Is the Diagnosis of "Mass Hysteria" an Excuse for Incomplete Investigation of Low-Level Environmental Contamination? *Journal of Occupational Medicine* 23:22–26.

Fenwick, P.B.C. (1990). Automatism, Medicine, and the Law. *Psychological Medicine Monograph,* supplement 17. Cambridge: Cambridge University Press.

Ferguson, D. (1987). RSI: Putting the Epidemic to Rest. *Medical Journal of Australia* 147:213.

———. (1971). An Australian Study of Telegraphist's Cramp. *British Journal of Industrial Medicine* 28:280–285.

Fernando, S. (1991). *Mental Health, Race, and Culture.* Hampshire: Macmillan Education.

———. (1988). *Race and Culture in Psychiatry.* London: Croom Helm.

Festinger, L. (1950). Informal Social Communications. *Psychological Review* 57:271–280.

Figueroa, M. (1979). (Related) in Epidemic Hysteria (editorial). *British Medical Journal* ii:409.

Fingarette, H. (1988). *Heavy Drinking: The Myth of Alcoholism as a Disease.* Berkeley: University of California Press.

Fishbain, D. A., Barsky, S., and Goldberg, M. (1989). "Koro" (Genital Retraction Syndrome): Psychotherapeutic Interventions. *American Journal of Psychotherapy* 43(1):87–91.

Fitzgerald, R. (1923). A Thesis on Two Tropical Neuroses (Amok and Latah) Peculiar to the Malays. Pp. 148–160 in *Far Eastern Association of Tropical Medicine, Transactions of the Fifth Biennial Congress.* Singapore.

Fletcher, W. (1908). Latah and Crime. *Lancet* (July 25) 2:254–255.

Folland, D. S. (1975). *Suspect Toluene Exposure at a Boot Factory.* Internal Report from the Tennessee Department of Health.

Forbes, H. O. (1885). *A Naturalist's Wanderings in the Eastern Archipelago.* New York: Harper.

Ford, C. S., and Beach, F. A. (1951). *Patterns of Sexual Behaviour.* New York: Harper and Row.

Forrester, R. M. (1979). Epidemic Hysteria—Divide and Conquer. *British Medical Journal* 2 (September 15):669.

Forsyth, J.R.L. (1989). "Repetitive Strain Injury": An Iatrogenic Epidemic. *Medical Journal of Australia* 151:598.

Fournial, H. (1892). *Essai sur la Psychologie des Foules: Considerations Medico-Judiciaires sur les Responsabilites Collectives* [Essay on the Philosophy of Crowds: Medico-Judicial Considerations on Group Responsibilities]. Paris: G. Masson.

Frankel, S. (1976). Mass Hysteria in the New Guinea Highlands: A Telefomin Outbreak and Its Relationship to Other New Guinea Hysterical Reactions. *Oceania* 47:105–133.

Freedman, A. M., and Kaplan, H. I. (1967). Psychiatric Disorders Not in Standard Nomenclature. Pp. 1150–1168 in *Comprehensive Textbook of Psychiatry.* Baltimore: Williams and Wilkins.

Freidson, E. (1988). *Professional Powers: A Study of the Institutionalization of Formal Knowledge.* Chicago: University of Chicago Press.

———. (1970). *Profession of Medicine.* New York: Dodd and Mead.

Freud, S. (1975 [1923]). A Seventeenth-Century Demonological Neurosis. Pp. 67–105 in *The Standard Edition of the Complete Psychological Works of Sigmund Freud, Vol. 19 (1923–1925).* London: Hogarth.

———. (1975 [1915]). The Unconscious. Pp. 161–215 In *The Standard Edition of the Complete Psychological Works of Sigmund Freud, Vol. 14 (1914–1916).* London: Hogarth.

Friedmann, M. (1901). *Uber Wahnideen im Volkerleben* [About Delusions and Folk Life]. Wiesbaden.

Friel, J. P. (ed.). (1982). *Dorland's Illustrated Medical Dictionary* (26th ed.). Philadelphia: W. B. Saunders.

Fulcher, G. (1975). Schizophrenia: A Sociologist's View of Psychiatrists' Views. Pp. 75–91 in A. R. Edwards and P. R. Wilson (eds.), *Social Deviance in Australia.* Melbourne: Cheshire.

Gaither, C. C., and Cavazos-Gaither, A. E. (1996). *Statistically Speaking: A Dictionary of Quotations.* London: Institute of Physics.

Galanter, M. (1989). Cults and New Religious Movements. Pp. 25–40 in M. Galanter (ed.), *Cults and New Religious Movements: A Report of the American Psychiatric Association From the Committee on Psychiatry and Religion.* Washington, D.C.: APA.

Gallini, C. (1988). *La Ballerina Variopinta: Une Festa Guarigione in Sardegna* [The Multicolored Dancer: A Healing Festival in Sardinia]. Naples: Liguori.

Galloway, D. J. (1924). On Amok. Pp. 162–171. In *Transactions of the Fifth Biennial Congress Held at Singapore 1923.* Far Eastern Association of Tropical Medicine. London: John Bale, Sons and Danielson.

———. (1922). A Contribution to the Study of "Latah." *Journal of the Straits Branch of the Royal Asiatic Society* 85:140–150.

Gamino, L. A., Elkins, G. R., and Hackney, K. U. (1989). Emergency Management of Mass Psychogenic Illness. *Psychosomatics* 3(4):446–449.

Garber, P. M. (1989). Tulipmania. *Journal of Political Economy* 97:535–560.

Gardner, M. (1984). Cruel Deception in the Philippines. *Discover* 8.

Gardner, R. A. (1991). *Sex Abuse Hysteria: Salem Witch Trials Revisited.* Cresskill, N.J.: Creative Therapeutics.

Garfinkel, H. (1967). *Studies in Ethnomethodology.* Englewood Cliffs, N.J.: Prentice-Hall.

Garnier, S. (1895). *Barbe Buvee, en Religion, Soeur Sainte-Colombe et la Pretendue Possession des Ursulines d'Auxonne* [Barbe Buvee and Religion, Sister Columbe and the Feigned Possession of the Ursulines at Auxonne]. Paris: Felix Alcan.

Garrison, F. H. (1913). *An Introduction to the History of Medicine.* Philadelphia: W. B. Saunders.

Garton, S. (1988). *Medicine and Madness: A Social History of Insanity in New South Wales, 1880–1940.* Kensington: New South Wales University Press.

Geertz, C. (1983). *Local Knowledge: Further Essays in Interpretive Anthropology.* New York: Basic.

———. (1973). *The Interpretation of Cultures.* New York: Basic.

Geertz, H. (1968). Latah in Java: A Theoretical Paradox. *Indonesia* 3:93–104.

Gelder, M., Gath, D., and Mayou, R. (1994). *Concise Oxford Textbook of Psychiatry.* Oxford: Oxford University Press.

Genik, Y. A. (1898). Deuxieme Epidemic d'hysterie dans le comte de Podolsk (Government of Moscow) [A Second Hysterical Epidemic in the County of Podolsk] *Nevrol. Vestnik, Kanzan* 6(4):146–159.

Gerlach, A. (1995). Castration Anxiety and Oral Envy in Sexual Relations: Analytic Studies With Ethnological Observations. *Psyche Stuttg* 49(9–10):965–988.

Gerrard, P. (1904). Hypnotism and Latah. *Dublin Journal of Medical Science* 118:13–17.

Gibbons, D. C., and Jones, J. F. (1975). *The Study of Deviance: Perspectives and Problems.* Englewood Cliffs, N.J.: Prentice-Hall.

Gibbons, D. C. (1968). *Society, Crime, and Criminal Careers.* London: Prentice-Hall.

Gibbs, J. P. (1966). Conceptions of Deviant Behaviour: The Old and the New. *Pacific Sociological Review* 9:9–14.

Gilbert, A. N. (1975). Doctor, Patient, and Onanist Diseases in the Nineteenth Century. *Journal of the History of Medicine and Allied Science* 30(3):217–234.

Gilles de la Tourette, G. (1884). Jumping, Latah, and Miryachit. *Archives de Neurologie* (Paris) 8:68–74.

Gilliam, A. G. (1938). Epidemiologic Study of an Epidemic, Diagnosed as Poliomyelitis, Occurring Among the Personnel of the Los Angeles County General Hospital During the Summer of 1934. Pp. 1–90 in *Bulletin 240.* Washington, D.C.: U.S. Public Health Service Division of Infectious Diseases, National Institutes of Health.

Gilmour, A. (1902). Latah Among South African Natives. *Scottish Medical Journal* 10:18–20.

Gimlette, J. D. (1915). *Malay Poisons and Charm Cures.* London: Oxford University Press.

———. (1901). Notes on a Case of Amok. *Journal of Tropical Medicine* 4:195–199.

———. (1897). Remarks on the Etiology, Symptoms, and Treatment of Latah, With a Report of Two Cases. *British Medical Journal* 2:455–457.

Gimlette, J. D., and Thompson, H. W. (eds.). (1971 [1939]). *A Dictionary of Malayan Medicine.* Kuala Lumpur: Oxford University Press.

Gittelson, N. L., and Levine, S. (1966). Subjective Ideas of Sexual Change in Male Schizophrenics. *British Journal of Psychiatry* 112:1171–1173.

Gloyne, H. F. (1950). Tarantism: Mass Hysterical Reaction to Spider Bite in the Middle Ages. *American Imago* 7:29–42.

Glueck, S., and Glueck, E. (1974). *Of Delinquency and Crime: A Panorama of Years of Search and Research.* Springfield, Ill.: Charles C. Thomas.

———. (1956). *Physique and Delinquency.* New York: Harper.

Goetz, P. W. (ed.). (1986). Droit du seigneur. P. 610 in *The New Encyclopedia Britannica, Vol. 10* (15th ed.). Chicago: University of Chicago Press.

Goffman, E. (1961). *Asylums.* Garden City, N.Y.: Anchor.

Goh, K. T. (1987). Epidemiological Enquiries Into a School Outbreak of an Unusual Illness. *International Journal of Epidemiology* 16(2):265–270.

Goldberg, E. L. (1973). Crowd Hysteria in a Junior High School. *Journal of School Health* 43:362–366.

Goldenson, R. M. (1970). Pp. 752–754 in *The Encyclopedia of Human Behavior: Psychology, Psychiatry, and Mental Health, Vol. 2.* Garden City, N.Y.: Doubleday.

Goldsmith, M. F. (1989). Physicians With Georgia on Their Minds. *Journal of the American Medical Association* 262:603–604.

Goleman, D. (1985). New Psychiatric Syndromes Spur Protests. *New York Times,* November 19:C-1, 16.

Goode, E. (1992). *Collective Behavior.* New York: Harcourt Brace Jovanovich.

———. (1978). *Deviant Behavior: An Interactionist Approach.* Englewood Cliffs, N.J.: Prentice-Hall.

Goode, E., and Ben-Yehuda, N. (1994). *Moral Panics: The Social Construction of Deviance.* Oxford: Blackwell.

Gordon, B. L. (1959). *Medieval and Renaissance Medicine.* New York: Philosophical Library.

Gordon, R. A. (1971). Letters. *Science* 171:957.

Goshen, C. E. (1967). *Documentary History of Psychiatry.* London: Vision.

Gove, P. B. (ed.). (1972). *Webster's Seventh New Collegiate Dictionary.* Springfield, Mass.: G. and C. Merriam.

Greenberg, D. F. (1988). *The Construction of Homosexuality.* Chicago: University of Chicago Press.

Gruenberg, E. M. (1957) Socially Shared Psychopathology. Pp. 201–229 in A. H. Leighton, J. Clausen, and R. Wilson (eds.), *Explorations in Social Psychiatry.* London: Tavistock.

Gusfield, J. R. (1980). Foreword. Pp. v–x in P. Conrad and J. Schneider (eds.), *Deviance and Medicalization: From Badness to Sickness.* St. Louis: C. V. Mosby.

———. (1963). *Symbolic Crusade: Status Politics and the American Temperance Movement.* Urbana: University of Illinois Press.

Guthrie, D. (1960). *A History of Medicine.* New York: Thomas Nelson and Sons.

Gutman, J. (1977). Constitutional and Legal Aspects of Deprogramming. Pp. 208–215 in H. W. Richardson (comp.), *Deprogramming: Documenting the Issue.* New York: American Civil Liberties Union and Toronto School of Theology.

Gwee, A. L. (1968). Koro—Its Origin and Nature as a Disease Entity. *Singapore Medical Journal* 9(1):3–6.

———. (1963). Koro—a Cultural Disease. *Singapore Medical Journal* 4:119–122.

Gwee, A. H., Lee, Y. K., Tham, N. B., Chee, K. H., Chew, W., Ngui, P., Wong, Y. C., Lau, C. W., and Tsee, C. K. [commonly referred to as the "Koro Study Team"]. (1969). The Koro "Epidemic" in Singapore. *Singapore Medical Journal* 10(4):234–242.

Gwee, A. H., and Ransome, G. A. (1973). Neurological Disorders in Singapore. Pp. 283–298 in J. D. Spillane (ed.), *Tropical Neurology.* London: Oxford University Press.

Hafez, A. (1985). The Role of the Press and the Medical Community in an Epidemic of Mysterious Gas Poisoning in the Jordan West Bank. *American Journal of Psychiatry* 142:833–837.

Hagenbach, E. (1893). Chorea-epidemie [Epidemic Chorea]. *Kor-Blatt f Schweit Arzte* (Basel) 23:631–632.

Haggard, H. W. (1934). *The Doctor in History.* New Haven: Yale University Press.

Hall, E. M., and Johnson, J. V. (1989). A Case Study of Stress and Mass Psychogenic Illness in Industrial Workers. *Journal of Occupational Medicine* 31(3):243–250.

Hall, W., and Morrow, L. (1988). Repetition Strain Injury: An Australian Epidemic of Upper Limb Pain. *Social Science and Medicine* 27:645–649.

Hall-Williams, J. E. (1982). *Criminology and Criminal Justice.* London: Butterworth.

Hallowell, A. I. (1934). Culture and Mental Disease. *Journal of Abnormal and Social Psychology* 29:1–9.

Hamilton, A. (1943). *Exploring the Dangerous Trades: The Autobiography of Alice Hamilton.* Boston: Little, Brown.

Hammond, W. A. (1884). Miryachit: A Newly Described Disease of the Nervous System and Its Analogs. *New York Medical Journal* 39:191–192.

Haralambos, M., van Krieken, R., Smith, P., and Holborn, M. (1996). *Sociology: Themes and Perspectives.* Melbourne: Addison Wesley Longman.

Hardison, J. (1980). Are the Jumping Frenchmen of Maine Goosey? *Journal of the American Medical Association* 244:70.

Hare, E. H. (1962). Masturbatory Insanity: The History of an Idea. *Journal of Mental Science* 108:1–25.

Hare, R. D., and Connolly, J. F. (1987). Perceptual Asymmetries and Information Processing in Psychopaths. Pp. 218–238 in S. Mednick, T. Moffitt, and S. Stack. (eds.), *The Causes of Crime: New Biological Approaches.* Cambridge: Cambridge University Press.

Harrington, J. A. (1982). Epidemic Psychosis. Letter. *British Journal of Psychiatry* 141:98–99.

Harris, R. (1985). Murder Under Hypnosis in the Case of Gabrielle Bompard: Psychiatry in the Courtroom in Paris. Pp. 197–241 in R. Porter and M. Shepherd (eds.), *The Anatomy of Madness: Essays in the History of Psychiatry, Vol. 2.* London: Tavistock.

Haviland, W. A. (1987). *Cultural Anthropology.* New York: Holt, Rinehart, and Winston.

Hawkins, R., and Tiedeman, G. (1975). *The Creation of Deviance: Interpersonal and Organizational Determinants.* Columbus, Ohio: Charles E. Merrill.

Hawley, R. M., and Owen, J. H. (1988). Koro: Its Presentation in an Elderly Male. *International Journal of Geriatric Psychiatry* 3(1):69–72.

Healy, T., and Cropper, P. (1994). *Out of the Shadows: Mystery Animals of Australia.* Chippendale: Ironbark.

Hecker, J.F.C. (1970 [1837]). *The Dancing Mania of the Middle Ages* (trans. B. Babington). New York: B. Franklin.

———. (1844). *Epidemics of the Middle Ages* (trans. from German by B. Babington). London: Sydenham Society.

Heinsohn, G., and Steiger, O. (1982). The Elimination of Medieval Birth Control and the Witch Trials of Modern Times. *International Journal of Women's Studies* 5(3):193–214.

Helvie, C. (1968). An Epidemic of Hysteria in a High School. *Journal of School Health* 38:505–509.

Hensyl, W. R. (ed.) (1982). *Stedman's Medical Dictionary* (25th ed.). Baltimore: Williams and Wilkins.

Hes, J. P., and Nassi, G. (1977). Koro in a Yemenite and a Georgian Jewish Immigrant. *Confinia Psychiatrica* (Basel) 20:180–184.

Hicks, R. (1990). Police Pursuit of Satanic Crime Part II: The Satanic Conspiracy and Urban Legends. *Skeptical Inquirer* 14:378–389.

Hilgard, E. R. (1977). *Divided Consciousness: Multiple Controls in Human Thought and Action.* New York: John Wiley.

Hill, P., Murray, R., and Thorley, A. (1986). *Essentials of Postgraduate Psychiatry.* London: Grune and Stratton.

Hines, T. (1988). *Pseudoscience and the Paranormal: A Critical Examination of the Evidence.* Buffalo: Prometheus.

Hirsch, A. (1883). *Handbook of Geographical and Historical Pathology.* London: New Sydenham Society.

Hirt, L. (1893). Eine Epidemie von Hysterischen Krampfen in einer Schleisischen Dorfschule [An Epidemic of Hysterical Cramp in a Village School in Schleisischen]. *Zeitschrift fur Schulgesundheitspflege* 6:225–229 (summary of an article by L. Hirt in the *Berliner Klinische Wochenschrift*).

———. (1892). Eine Epidemie von Hysterischen Krampfen in einer Dorfschule [An Epidemic of Hysterical Cramp in a Village School]. *Berliner Klinische Wochenschrift* 29:1271–1274.

Hobson, B. M. (1987). *Uneasy Virtue: The Politics of Prostitution and the American Reform Tradition.* New York: Basic.

Holden, T. J. (1987). Koro Syndrome Associated With Alcohol-Induced Systemic Disease in a Zulu. *British Journal of Psychiatry* 151:695–697.

Hopkins, A. (1990). The Social Recognition of Repetition Strain Injuries: An Australian/American Comparison. *Social Science and Medicine* 30:365–372.

Horne, E. (1974). *Javanese-English Dictionary.* New Haven: Yale University Press.

Hotopf, M., and Mullen, R. (1992). Koro and Capgras Syndrome in a Non-Chinese Subject. *British Journal of Psychiatry* 161:577.

Howard, R., and Ford, R. (1992). From the Jumping Frenchmen of Maine to Post-Traumatic Stress Disorder: The Startle Response in Neuropsychiatry. *Psychological Medicine* 22:695–707.

Howe, L. M. (producer). (1980). "A Strange Harvest." Television documentary premiering on KMGH, Channel 7, Denver, Colo., May 25.

Howells, K. (1984). Introduction. Pp. 1–4 in K. Howells (ed.), *The Psychology of Sexual Diversity.* Oxford: Basil Blackwell.

Howells, W. (1986). *The Heathens.* Salem, Wisc.: Sheffield.

Hunter, L. (1989). "Repetitive Strain Injury": An Iatrogenic Epidemic. *Medical Journal of Australia* 151:598.

Hunter, R., and Macalpine, I. (1963). *Three Hundred Years of Psychiatry: 1535–1860.* London: Oxford University Press.

Huxley, A. (1952). *The Devils of Loudun.* New York: Harper and Brothers.

Hyde, J. K. (1973). *Society and Politics in Medieval Italy: The Evolution of the Civil Life, 1000–1350.* New York: St. Martin's.

Hyman, R. (1985). A Critical Historical Overview of Parapsychology. Pp. 3–96 in P. Kurtz (ed.), *A Skeptic's Handbook of Parapsychology.* Buffalo: Prometheus.

Ifabumuyi, O. I., and Rwegellera, G. G. (1979). Koro in a Nigerian Male Patient: A Case Report. *African Journal of Psychiatry* 5:103–105.

Ikeda, Y. (1966). An Epidemic of Emotional Disturbance Among Leprosarium Nurses. *Psychiatry* 23:152–164.

Ilechukwu, S.T.C. (1992). Magical Penis Loss in Nigeria: Report of a Recent Epidemic of a Koro-Like Syndrome. *Transcultural Psychiatric Research Review* 29:91–108.

———. (1988). Letter From S.T.C. Ilechukwu, M.D. (Lagos, Nigeria), Which Describes Interesting Korolike Syndromes in Nigeria. *Transcultural Psychiatric Research Review* 25:310–314.

Illich, I. (1976). *Limits to Medicine: Medical Nemesis.* London: Marion Boyars.

Indriastuti, L. (1995). Latah, Dalam Perspektif Sociobudaya—Dengan Fokus Khusus: Peninjauan dari Budaya Jawa [Latah From a Sociocultural Perspective, With a Particular Focus Based on a Survey From Javanese Culture]. *Indonesian Psychiatric Quarterly* 28(1):87–101.

Inglis, B. (1990). *Trance: A Natural History of Altered States of Mind.* London: Paladin.

———. (1965). *A Brief History of Medicine.* London: Weidenfeld and Nicolson.

Iten, O. (1986). Die Tasaday: Ein Philippinischer Steinzeit Schwindel [The Tasaday: A Philippine Stone Age Swindle]. *Neue Zurcher Zeitung* (Zurich) April 12–13:77–79.

Jacobs, N. (1965). The Phantom Slasher of Taipei: Mass Hysteria in a Non-Western Society. *Social Problems* 12:318–328.

Jacobs, P. A., Bunton, M., Melville, M. M., Brittain, R. P., and McClemont, W. F. (1965). Aggressive Behavior, Mental Subnormality, and the XYX Male. *Nature* 208:1351.

Jaspers, K. (1968). General Psychopathology (trans. from German by J. Hoenig and M. W. Hamilton). Chicago: University of Chicago Press.

Jenner, J. (1991). A Successfully Treated Dutch Case of Latah. *Journal of Nervous and Mental Disease* 179:636–637.

———. (1990). Latah as Coping: A Case Study Offering a New Paradox to Solve the Old One. *International Journal of Social Psychiatry* 36:194–199.

Jilek, W. G. (1986). Epidemics of "Genital Shrinking" (koro): Historical Review and Report of a Recent Outbreak in Southern China. *Curare* 9:269–282.

———. (1985). The Metamorphosis of "Culture-Bound" Syndromes. *Social Science and Medicine* 21(2):205–210.

Jilek, W. G., and Jilek-Aall, L. (1977a). A Koro Epidemic in Thailand. *Transcultural Psychiatric Research Review* 14:56–59.

———. (1977b). Mass Hysteria With Koro Symptoms in Thailand. *Schweizer Archive Neurologie Neurochirurgie un Psychiatrie* 120(2):257–259.

Johnson, D. B. (1950). *Flying Saucers—Fact or Fiction?* Master's thesis, University of California Journalism Dept., Los Angeles.

Johnson, D. M. (1945). The "Phantom Anesthetist" of Mattoon: A Field Study of Mass Hysteria. *Journal of Abnormal Psychology* 40:175–186.

Johnson, H. (1908). Moral Instruction and Training in France. Pp. 1–50 in M. E. Sadler (ed.), *Moral Instruction and Training in Schools: Report of an International Inquiry, Vol. 2.* London: Longmans, Green.

Jones, A.H.M. (1984). *The Decline of the Ancient World.* London: Longman.

Jung, C. G. (1959). *Flying Saucers: A Modern Myth of Things Seen in the Sky.* New York: Harcourt Brace and World.

Kagan, J. (1969). *Personality Development.* New York: Harcourt Brace Jovanovich.

Kagwa, B. H. (1964). The Problem of Mass Hysteria in East Africa. *East African Medical Journal* 41:560–566.

Kapferer, B. (1983). *A Celebration of Demons: Exorcism and the Aesthetics of Healing in Sri Lanka*. Bloomington: Indiana University Press.

Kaplan, H. I., and Sadock, B. J. (eds.). (1985). *Comprehensive Textbook of Psychiatry, Vol. 2*. Baltimore: Williams and Wilkins.

Katner, W. (1956). Das Ratsel des Tarentismus. Eine Atiologie der Italienischen Tanzkrankheit [The Mystery of Tarantism: An Etiology of Italian Dancing Illness]. *Nova Acta Leopoldina* (n.s. 18, no. 124). Leipzig: Barth.

Keesing, R. M. (1989). Exotic Readings of Cultural Texts. *Current Anthropology* 30(4):459–469.

Keightley, T. (1882). *The Fairy Mythology*. London: Longman.

Kempe, C. H., Silverman, F. N., Steele, B. F., Droegemueller, W., and Silver, H. K. (1962). The Battered Child Syndrome. *Journal of the American Medical Association* 181:107–112.

Kendall, E. M., and Jenkins, P. L. (1987). Koro in an American Man. *American Journal of Psychiatry* 144(12):1621.

Kendell, R. E., and Zealley, A. K. (eds.). (1993). *Companion to Psychiatric Studies* (5th ed.). London: Churchill Livingstone.

Kenny, M. (1990). Latah: The Logic of Fear. Pp. 123–141 in W. J. Karim (ed.), *The Emotions of Culture—a Malay Perspective*. Singapore: Oxford University Press.

———. (1985). Paradox Lost: The Latah Problem Revisited. Pp. 63–76 in R. Simons and C. Hughes (eds.), *The Culture-Bound Syndromes*. Dordrecht: D. Reidel.

———. (1978). Latah: The Symbolism of a Putative Mental Disorder. *Culture, Medicine, and Psychiatry* 2:209–231.

Kerckhoff, A. C. (1982). A Social Psychological View of Mass Psychogenic Illness. Pp. 199–215 in M. Colligan, J. Pennebaker, and L. Murphy (eds.), *Mass Psychogenic Illness: A Social Psychological Analysis*. Hillsdale, N.J.: Lawrence Erlbaum.

Kerckhoff, A. C., Back, K. W., and Miller, N. (1965). Sociometric Patterns in Hysterical Contagion. *Sociometry* 28:2–15.

Kessler, C. (1977). Conflict and Sovereignty in Kelantanese Malay Spirit Seances. Pp. 295–329 in V. Crapanzano and V. Garrison (eds.), *Case Studies in Spirit Possession*. New York: Cambridge University Press.

Kiev, A. (1972). *Transcultural Psychiatry*. New York: Free Press.

Kinsey, A. C., Pomeroy, W. B., and Martin, C. E. (1948). *Sexual Behavior in the Human Male*. Philadelphia: W. B. Saunders.

Kinsey, A. C., Pomeroy, W. B., Martin, C. E., and Gebhard, P. H. (1953). *Sexual Behavior in the Human Female*. Philadelphia: W. B. Saunders.

Kirk, R. (1815). *The Secret Commonwealth of Elves, Fauns, and Fairies*. London: Longman.

Kirmayer, L. J. (1992). From the Witches' Hammer to the Oedipus Complex: Castration Anxiety in Western Society. *Transcultural Psychiatric Research Review* 29:133–158.

Kitsuse, J. I., and Spector, M. (1975). Social Problems and Deviance: Some Parallel Issues. *Social Problems* 22:584–595.

Klein, D. F. (1993). False Suffocation Alarms, Spontaneous Panics, and Related Conditions: An Integrative Hypothesis. *Archives of General Psychiatry* 50:306–317.

Kleinman, A. (1988). *Rethinking Psychiatry: From Cultural Category to Personal Experience*. New York: Free Press.

———. (1987). Culture and Clinical Reality: Commentary on Culture-Bound Syndromes and International Disease Classifications. *Culture, Medicine, and Psychiatry* 11:49–52.

———. (1980). *Patients and Healers in the Context of Culture.* Berkeley: University of California Press.

———. (1977). Depression, Somatization, and the "New Cross-Cultural Psychiatry." *Social Science and Medicine* 11:3–10.

Kline, N. (1963). Psychiatry in Indonesia. *American Journal of Psychiatry* 119:809–815.

Knight, J. A., Friedman, T. I., and Sulianti, J. (1965). Epidemic Hysteria: A Field Study. *American Journal of Public Health* 55:858–865.

Kobler, F. (1948). Description of an Acute Castration Fear, Based on Superstition. *Psychoanalytical Review* 35:285–289.

Kosa, J. (1970). Entrepreneurship and Charisma in the Medical Profession. *Social Science and Medicine* 4:25–40.

Kren, G. (1978–1979). Psychohistory and the Holocaust. *Journal of Psychohistory* 6:409–417.

Kraepelin, E. (1883). *Psychiatrie* [Psychiatry]. Leipzig: Barth.

Krug, S. (1992). Mass Illness at an Intermediate School: Toxic Fumes or Epidemic Hysteria? *Pediatric Emergency Care* 8:280–282.

Kruse, L. (1986). Conceptions of Crowds and Crowding. Pp. 117–142 in C. Graumann and S. Moscovici (eds.), *Changing Conceptions of Crowd Mind and Behavior.* New York: R. R. Donnelley.

Kumar, R. (1994). Postnatal Mental Illness: A Transcultural Perspective. *Social Psychiatry and Psychiatric Epidemiology* 29(6):250–264.

Kunkle, E. C. (1967). The "Jumpers" of Maine: A Reappraisal. *Archives of Internal Medicine* 119:355–358.

Kurtz, P. (1985). Spiritualists, Mediums, and Psychics: Some Evidence of Fraud. Pp. 177–223 in P. Kurtz (ed.), *A Skeptic's Handbook of Parapsychology.* Buffalo: Prometheus.

Kutchins, H., and Kirk, S. A. (1989). DSM-III-R: The Conflict Over New Psychiatric Diagnoses. *Health and Social Work* 14(2):91–101.

———. (1988). The Business of Diagnosis: DSM-III and Clinical Social Work. *Social Work* 33:215–220.

Lader, M. (1977). *Psychiatry on Trial.* Harmondsworth: Penguin.

Laing, R. D. (1965). *The Divided Self.* Baltimore: Penguin.

Lajonchere, C., Nortz, M., and Finger, S. (1996). Gilles de la Tourette and the Discovery of Tourette Syndrome. *Archives of Neurology* 53:567–574.

Landis, C., and Hunt, W. A. (1939). *The Startle Pattern.* New York: Farrar and Rhinehart.

Landrigan, P. J., and Miller, B. (1983). The Arjenyattah Epidemic: Home Interview Data and Toxicological Aspects. *Lancet* 2:1474–1476.

Lang, K., and Lang, G. E. (1961). *Collective Dynamics.* New York: Thomas Y. Crowell.

Langness, L. L. (1967). Hysterical Psychosis: The Cross-Cultural Evidence. *American Journal of Psychiatry* 124:143–152.

———. (1965). Hysterical Psychosis in the New Guinea Highlands: A Bena Bena Example. *Psychiatry* 28:258–277.

Lapierre, Y. D. (1972). Koro in a French Canadian. *Journal of the Canadian Psychiatric Association* 17:333–334.

Lapp, R. E. (1965). *The New Priesthood: The Scientific Elite and the Uses of Power.* New York: Harper and Row.

Laquer, L. (1888). Uber eine chorea-epidemie [An Epidemic of Chorea]. *Deutsche Medizinische Wochenschrift* (Leipzig) 14:1045–1046.

Lattas, A. (1992). Hysteria, Anthropological Disclosure, and the Concept of the Unconscious: Cargo Cults and the Scientisation of Race and Colonial Power. *Oceania* 63(1):1–14.

LeBon, G. (1896). *La Psychologie des Foules* [The Psychology of Crowds] (2d ed.). Paris: Felix Alcan.

Lee, R. L. (1981). Structure and Anti-Structure in the Culture-Bound Syndromes: The Malay Case. *Culture, Medicine, and Psychiatry* 5:233–248.

Lee, R. L., and Ackerman, S. E. (1980). The Sociocultural Dynamics of Mass Hysteria: A Case Study of Social Conflict in West Malaysia. *Psychiatry* 43:78–88.

Lefebvre, G. (1954). *Etudes sur la Revolution Francaise* [Studies on the French Revolution]. Paris: PUF.

Legendre, J. (1936). A Propos du Koro: Une Curieuse Epidemie [On Koro: A Curious Epidemic]. *La Presse Medicale* (Paris): 1534.

Lehmann, H. E. (1967). Psychiatric Disorders Not in Standard Nomenclature. Pp. 1150–1168 in A. Freeman and H. Kaplan (eds.), *Comprehensive Textbook of Psychiatry.* Baltimore: Williams and Wilkins.

Leuch (1896). Eine Sogenannte Chorea-Epidemie in der Schule [A So-Called Chorea Epidemic in the School]. *Kor Blatt f Schweit Aerzte* (Basel) 26:465–476.

Lever, J. (1983). *Soccer Madness.* Chicago: University of Chicago Press.

Levine, R. J. (1977). Epidemic Faintness and Syncope in a School Marching Band. *Journal of the American Medical Association* 238(22):2373–2376.

Levine, R. J., Sexton, D. J., Romm, F. J., Wood, B. T., and Kaiser, J. (1974). An Outbreak of Psychosomatic Illness at a Rural Elementary School. *Lancet* 2:1500–1503.

Levine, S. V. (1989). Life in the Cults. Pp. 95–107 in M. Galanter (ed.), *Cults and New Religious Movements: A Report of the American Psychiatric Association From the Committee on Psychiatry and Religion.* Washington, D.C.: APA.

Lewis, D. (1986). A Study of 15 Convicted Murderers Shows That All Had Once Suffered Head Injuries. *New York Times,* June 3:22.

Lewis, I. M. (1991). The Spider and the Pangolin. *Man* (n.s.) 12(3):513–525.

———. (1971). *Ecstatic Religion.* Harmondsworth: Penguin.

Lidz, T. (1963). Hysteria. Pp. 818–826 in A. Deutsch and H. Fishman (eds.), *The Encyclopedia of Mental Health, Vol. 3.* New York: Franklin Watts.

Lindenbaum, S. (1979). *Kuru Sorcery: Disease and Danger in the New Guinea Highlands.* Palo Alto: Mayfield.

Linsky, A. S., Colby, J. P., and Straus, M. A. (1987). Social Stress, Normative Constraints, and Alcohol Problems in American States. *Social Science and Medicine* 24:875–883.

———. (1986). Drinking Norms and Alcohol-Related Problems in the United States. *Journal of Studies on Alcohol* 47:384–393.

Linton, R. (1956). *Culture and Mental Disorders.* Springfield: C. C. Thomas.

Little, C. B. (1995). *Deviance and Social Control: Theory, Research, and Social Policy.* Itasca, Ill.: F. E. Peacock.

Littlewood, R., and Lipsedge, L. M. (1987). The Butterfly and the Serpent: Culture, Psychopathology, and Biomedicine. *Culture, Medicine, and Psychiatry* 11:289–335.

———. (1985). Culture-Bound Syndromes. Pp. 105–142 in K. Granville-Grossman (ed.), *Recent Advances in Clinical Psychiatry.* London: Churchill Livingstone.

Lock, M. (1988). New Japanese Mythologies: Faltering Discipline and the Ailing Housewife. *American Ethnologist* 15(1):43–61.

Logan, J. R. (1849). Five Days in Naning. *Journal of the Indian Archipelago and Eastern Asia* 3:24–41.

Lombroso, C. (1911). *Crime, Its Causes and Remedies* (trans. H. P. Horton). Boston: Little, Brown.

Loredan, J. (1912). *Un Grand Proces de Sorcellerie au XVIIe siecle, L'Abbe Gaufridy et Madeleine de Demandolx (1600–1670)* [The Grand Process of Witchcraft in the Seventeenth Century, L'Abbe Gaufridy and Madeleine de Demandolx (1600–1670)]. Paris: Perrin et Cie.

Lucire, Y. (1986). Neurosis in the Workplace. *Medical Journal of Australia* 145:323–327.

Lyons, H. A., and Potter, P. E. (1970). Communicated Hysteria—an Episode in a Secondary School. *Journal of the Irish Medical Association* 63:377–379.

Mackay, C. (1852). *Memoirs of Extraordinary Popular Delusions and the Madness of Crowds, Vol. 2.* London: Office of the National Illustrated Library.

MacKenzie, J. M. (1995). *Orientalism: History, Theory, and the Arts.* Manchester: Manchester University Press.

MacNalty, A. S. (ed.). (1961). *The British Medical Dictionary.* London: Caxton.

Madden, R. R. (1857). *Phantasmata or Illusions and Fanaticisms of Protean Forms Productive of Great Evils.* London: T. C. Newby.

Magalini, S. I., and Scrascia, E. (1981). *The Dictionary of Medical Syndromes.* Philadelphia: J. B. Lippincott.

Malinick, C., Flaherty, J. A., and Jobe, T. (1985). Koro: How Culturally Specific? *International Journal of Social Psychiatry* 31(1):67–73.

Mann, J., and Rosenblatt, W. (1979). Collective Stress Syndrome. Letter. *Journal of the American Medical Association* 242(1):27.

Manson, P., and Manson-Bahr, P. (1972). Section X: Neurological Diseases. Pp. 721–726 in *Manson's Tropical Diseases* (17th ed.). Baltimore: Williams and Wilkins.

Manson-Bahr, P. H. (1983). *Manson's Tropical Diseases* (18th ed.). Eastbourne: Cassel.

———. (1966). Kuru, Latah, Running Amok, and Koro. Pp. 575–578 in *Manson's Tropical Diseases* (16th ed.). London.

Marano, L. (1982). Windigo Psychosis: The Anatomy of an Emic-Etic Confusion. *Current Anthropology* 23(4):385–412.

Markush, R. E. (1973). Mental Epidemics: A Review of the Old to Prepare for the New. *Public Health Reviews* 4(2):353–442.

Marsella, A. J., and White, G. M. (1982). *Cultural Conceptions of Mental Health and Therapy.* Dordrecht: D. Riedel.

Massad, C. M., Hubbard, M., and Newtson, D. (1979). Selective Perception of Events. *Journal of Experimental Social Psychology* 15:513–532.

Massey, E. W., Brannon, W. L., Jr., and Riley, T. L. (1981). The "Jerks": Mass Hysteria or Epilepsy? *Southern Medical Journal* 74(5):607–609.

Matza, D. (1969). *Becoming Deviant.* Englewood Cliffs, N.J.: Prentice-Hall.

Mausner, J. S., and Gezon, H. M. (1967). Report on a Phantom Epidemic of Gonorrhea. *American Journal of Epidemiology* 85:320–331.

Maybury-Lewis, D. (1992). *Millennium: Tribal Wisdom and the Modern World.* New York: Viking.

Mayer-Gross, W., Slater, E., and Roth, M. (1963). *Clinical Psychiatry.* London: Cassell.

McArthur, T. (ed.). (1992). *The Oxford Companion to the English Language.* Oxford: Oxford University Press.

McCloy, J. F., and Miller, R. (1976). *The Jersey Devil.* Wallingford, Penn.: Middle Atlantic Press.

McEvedy, C. P., and Beard, A. W. (1970a). Royal Free Epidemic: A Reconsideration. *British Medical Journal* i:7–11.

———. (1970b). Concept of Benign Myalgic Encephalomyelitis. *British Medical Journal* 1:11–15.

McEvedy, C. P., Griffith, A., and Hall, T. (1966). Two School Epidemics. *British Medical Journal* ii:1300–1302.

McHugh, J. N. (1959). *Hantu Hantu: An Account of Ghost Belief in Modern Malaya.* Singapore: Eastern Universities Press.

McLeod, L. (1865). *Madagascar and Its People.* London: Longman.

McNair, J. (1972 [1878]). *Perak and the Malays.* Kuala Lumpur: Oxford University Press.

Medalia, N. Z., and Larsen, O. N. (1958). Diffusion and Belief in a Collective Delusion. *Sociological Review* 23:180–186.

Menezes, S. B. (1992). A Case of Koro and Folie a Deux in a Shona Family. Letter. *South African Medical Journal* 82(6):483.

Merskey, H. (1979). *The Analysis of Hysteria.* London: Bailliere Tindall.

Merton, R. (1938). Social Structure and Anomie. *American Sociological Review* 3:672–683.

Meth, J. M. (1974). Exotic Psychiatric Syndromes. Pp. 723–739 in S. Arieti and E. Brody (eds.), *American Handbook of Psychiatry, Vol. 3.* New York: Basic.

Meyer, R. G., and Salmon, P. (1988). *Abnormal Psychology.* Boston: Allyn and Bacon.

Meyerson, A. T. (1989). *Conditions Not Attributable to a Mental Disorder.* Pp. 1396–1399 in H. Kaplan and B. Sadock (eds.), *Comprehensive Textbook of Psychiatry.* Baltimore: Williams and Wilkins.

Micale, M. S. (1995). *Approaching Hysteria: Disease and Its Interpretations.* Princeton, N.J.: Princeton University Press.

———. (1994a). Introduction: Reflections on Psychiatry and Its Histories. Pp. 3–36 in M. S. Micale and R. Porter (eds.), *Discovering the History of Psychiatry.* Oxford: Oxford University Press.

———. (1994b). Henri F. Ellenberger: The History of Psychiatry as the History of the Unconscious. Pp. 112–134 in M. S. Micale and R. Porter (eds.), *Discovering the History of Psychiatry.* Oxford: Oxford University Press.

Michaux, L., Lemperiere, T., and Juredieu, C. (1952). Considérations Psychpathologiquessur une Épidémie d'hystérie Convulsive dans un Internat Professionnel [Considerations of an Epidemic of Convulsive Hysteria in a Boarding School]. *Archives Françaises Pédiatrie* (Paris) 9:987–990.

Michelmore, P. (1962). *Einstein: Profile of the Man.* New York: Dodd, Mead.

Miles, D. (1996). Personal communication, May 1 (senior lecturer, Anthropology Department, James Cook University).

Miller, D. L. (1985). *Introduction to Collective Behavior.* Belmont, Calif.: Wadsworth.

Miller, D. L., Mieus, K. J., and Mathers, R. A. (1978). A Critical Examination of the Social Contagion Image of Collective Behavior: The Case of the Enfield Monster. *Sociological Quarterly* 19:129–140.

Miller, E. (1988). Hysteria. Pp. 245–267 in E. Miller and P. J. Cooper (eds.), *Adult Abnormal Psychology.* London: Churchill Livingstone.

———. (1987). Hysteria: Its Nature and Explanation. *British Journal of Clinical Psychology* 26:163–173.

Millon, T. (1969). *Modern Psychopathology: A Biosocial Approach to Maladaptive Learning and Functioning.* Philadelphia: W. B. Saunders.

Millon, T., and Millon, R. (1974). *Abnormal Behavior and Personality: A Biosocial Learning Approach.* Philadelphia: W. B. Saunders.

Mills, C. W. (1956). *The Power Elite.* New York: Oxford University Press.

Mo, K. M. (1991). Sociocultural Aspects of a Koro Epidemic in Southern China. Paper presented at the International Symposium on Cultural Psychiatry in Budapest, Hungary, August 26–28.

Modai, I., Munitz, H., and Aizenberg, D. (1986). Koro in an Israeli Male. *British Journal of Psychiatry* 149:503–505.

Modan, B., Tirosh, M., Weissenberg, E., Acker, C., Swartz, T., Coston, C., Donagi, A., Revach, M., and Vettorazzi, G. (1983). The Arjenyattah Epidemic. *Lancet* 2:1472–1476.

Moffat, M. E. (1982). Epidemic Hysteria in a Montreal Train Station. *Pediatrics* 70:308–310.

Mohr, P. D. (1980). From Demoniac Possession to Mystery Gases. *World Medicine* 15:17–19.

Mohr, P., and Bond, M. J. (1982). Epidemic Blindness. *British Medical Journal* 284:961–962.

Molema, S. M. (1963 [1920]). *The Bantu Past and Present.* Cape Town: C. Struik.

Monter, W. E. (1976). *Witchcraft in France and Switzerland.* Ithaca, N.Y.: Cornell University Press.

Montgomery, J. D. (1908). The Education of Girls in Germany: Its Methods of Moral Instruction and Training. Pp. 231–241 in M. E. Sadler (ed.), *Moral Instruction and Training in Schools: Report of an International Inquiry, Vol. 2.* London: Longmans, Green.

Mora, G. (1963). A Historical and Socio-Psychiatric Appraisal of Tarantism. *Bulletin of the History of Medicine* 37:417–439.

Morris, T. (1976). *Deviance and Control: The Secular Heresy.* London: Hutchinson.

Moss, P. D., and McEvedy, C. P. (1966). An Epidemic of Overbreathing Among Schoolgirls. *British Medical Journal* ii:1295–1300.

Muhangi, J. R. (1973). Mass Hysteria in an Ankole School. *East African Medical Journal* 50:304–309.

Muluka, E. A., Dhadphale, M., and Mwita, J. (1985). Family Hysteria in a Kenyan Setting. *Journal of Nervous and Mental Diseases* 173:249–252.

Mun, C. I. (1968). Epidemic Koro in Singapore. Letter. *British Medical Journal* i (March 9):640–641.

Murphy, H.B.M. (1986). The Koro Epidemic in Hainan Island. Paper presented at the Regional Conference of the World Psychiatric Association's Transcultural Psychiatry Section, Beijing, China, August 17–31.

———. (1976). Notes for a Theory on Latah. Pp. 3–21 in W. P. Lebra (ed.), *Culture-Bound Syndromes, Ethnopsychiatry, and Alternate Therapies.* Honolulu: East-West Center.

———. (1973). History and Evolution of Syndromes: The Striking Case of Latah and Amok. Pp. 33–55 in M. Hammer, K. Salzinger, and S. Sutton (eds.), *Psychopathology.* New York: Wiley.

Mutibwa, P. M. (1974). *The Malagasy and the Europeans: Madagascar's Foreign Relations, 1861–1895.* London: Longman.

Naish, J. M. (1979). Problems of Deception in Medical Practice. *Lancet* 2:139–142.

Nandi, D. N., and Banerjee, G. (1986). A Psycho-Analytical Study of Koro. *Samiksa* 40(3):94–104.

Nandi, D., Banerjee, G., Bera, S., Nandi, S., and Nandi, P. (1985). Contagious Hysteria in a West Bengal Village. *American Journal of Psychotherapy* 39:247–252.

Nasuruddin, M. G. (1990). Dancing to Ecstasy on the Hobby Horse. Pp. 142–158 in W. J. Karim (ed.), *The Emotions of Culture—a Malay Perspective.* Singapore: Oxford University Press.

Nathan, D., and Snedeker, M. (1995). *Satan's Silence: Ritual Abuse and the Making of a Modern American Witch Hunt.* New York: Basic.

Neale, R. (1884). Miryachit or Lata. *British Medical Journal* i:884.

Neugebauer, R. (1978). Treatment of the Mentally Ill in Medieval and Early Modern England: A Reappraisal. *Journal of the History of the Behavioral Sciences* 14:158–169.

Newman, P. L. (1964). "Wild Man" Behavior in a New Guinea Highlands Community. *American Anthropologist* 66:1–19.

Ng, B. (1997). History of Koro in Singapore. *Singapore Medical Journal* 38(8):356–357.

Ng, B., and Kua, E. (1996). Koro in Ancient Chinese History. *History of Psychiatry* 7:563–570.

Ngui, P. W. (1969). The Koro Epidemic in Singapore. *Australian and New Zealand Journal of Psychiatry* 3:263–266.

Nitzkin, J. L. (1976). Epidemic Transient Situational Disturbance in an Elementary School. *Journal of the Florida Medical Association* 63:357–359.

Nolen, W. (1974). *Healing: A Doctor in Search of a Miracle.* New York: Random House.

Norman, E. H. (1945). Mass Hysteria in Japan. *Far Eastern Survey* 14(6):65–70.

Norris, W. (1849). Sentence of Death Upon a Malay Convicted of Running Amuck. *Journal of the Indian Archipelago and Eastern Asia* 3:460–463.

Notosusanto, N. (1961). *Rasa Sajange* [Feeling Sajange]. Jakarta: P. T. Pembangun.

Nyberg, F., Lindstrom, L. H., and Terenius, L. (1988). Reduced Beta-Casein Levels in Milk Samples From Patients With Postpartum Psychosis. *Biological Psychiatry* 23(2):115–122.

O'Brien, H. A. (1883). Latah. *Journal of the Straits Branch of the Royal Asiatic Society* 2:143–153.

O'Donnell, B., Elliot, T. J., and Huibonhoa, C. (1980). An Outbreak of Illness in a Rural School. *Journal of the Irish Medical Association* 73:300–302.

Ohnuki-Tierney, E. (1985). Shamans and Imu: Among Two Ainu Groups: Toward a Cross-Cultural Model of Interpretation. Pp. 91–110 in R. Simons and C. Hughes (eds.), *The Culture-Bound Syndromes.* Dordrecht: D. Reidel.

Olczak, P., Donnerstein, E., Hershberger, T., and Kahn, I. (1971). Group Hysteria and the MMPI. *Psychological Reports* 28:413–414.

Oliver, C. (1981). *The Discovery of Humanity.* New York: Harper and Row.

Olkinuora, M. (1984). Psychogenic Epidemics and Work. *Scandinavian Journal of Work, Environment, and Health* 10(6):501–515.

Olson, G. (1980). Schmitt Urges Federal Mutilation Probe. *Rio Grande Sun,* April 17.

Olson, W. C. (1928). Account of a Fainting Epidemic in a High School. *Psychology Clinic* (Philadelphia) 18:34–38.

Ong, A. (1988). The Production of Possession: Spirits and the Multinational Corporation in Malaysia. *American Ethnologist* 15(1):28–42.

———. (1987). *Spirits of Resistance and Capitalist Discipline: Factory Women in Malaysia.* Albany: State University of New York Press.

Opler, M. K. (1967). *Culture and Psychiatry.* New York: Atherton.

Ormerod, J. A. (1912). *System of Medicine, Vol. 8* (2d ed.). London: Allbutt and Rolleston.

Oyebode, F., Jamieson, M. J., and Davison, K. (1986). Koro—a Psychophysiological Dysfunction. *British Journal of Psychiatry* 148:212–214.

Paicheler, G. (1988). *The Psychology of Social Influence* (trans. A. St. James-Emler and N. Emler). Cambridge: Cambridge University Press.

Pakulski, J. (1991). *Social Movements: The Politics of Moral Protest.* Melbourne: Longman Cheshire.

Palmer (1892). Psychische seuche in der Sbersten Slasse einer Sadchenschule [A Psychic Epidemic in the First Class of a Girls' School]. *Zentralblatt fur Nervenheilkunde und Psychiatrie* 3:301–308.

Parigi, S., and Biagiotti, F. (1956). Su di una Epidemia di Isterismo [On an Epidemic of Hysteria]. *Rassegna de Studi Psichiatrici* (Siena) 45:1112–1114.

Park, A. (1986). Tasmanian Tiger: Extinct or Merely Elusive? *Australian Geographic* 1:66–83.

Parsons, T. (1955). Family Structure and the Socialization of the Child. Pp. 35–131 in T. Parsons and R. F. Bales (eds.), *Family, Socialization, and the Interaction Process.* New York: Free Press.

———. (1951). *The Social System.* New York: Free Press.

Patrick, E. (1971). Emotional Stresses in University Students. Pp. 81–87 in N. N. Wagner and E. S. Tan (eds.), *Psychological Problems and Treatment in Malaysia.* Kuala Lumpur: University of Malaya Press.

Peele, S. (1986). The Implications and Limitations of Genetic Models of Alcoholism and Other Addictions. *Journal of Studies on Alcohol* 47:63–73.

Penrose, L. S. (1952). *On the Objective Study of Crowd Behavior.* London: H. K. Lewis.

Persinger, M., and Derr, J. (1989). Geophysical Variables and Behavior: LIV. Zeitoun (Egypt) Apparitions of the Virgin Mary as Tectonic Strain-Induced Luminosities. *Perceptual and Motor Skills* 68:123–128.

Pfeiffer, P. H. (1964). Mass Hysteria Masquerading as Food Poisoning. *Journal of the Maine Medical Association* 55:27.

Pfeiffer, W. (1968). New Research Findings Regarding Latah. *Transcultural Psychiatric Research Review* 5:34–38.

Pfohl, S. J. (1977). The Discovery of Child Abuse. *Social Problems* 24:310–323.

Philen, R. M., Kilbourn, E. M., and McKinley, T. W. (1989), Mass Sociogenic Illness by Proxy: Parentally Reported in an Elementary School. *Lancet* 2:1372–1376.

Phoon, W. H. (1982). Outbreaks of Mass Hysteria at Workplaces in Singapore. Pp. 21–33 in M. Colligan, J. Pennebaker, and L. Murphy (eds.), *Mass Psychogenic Illness: A Social Psychological Analysis*. Hillsdale, N.J.: Lawrence Erlbaum.

Pick, D. (1989). *Faces of Degeneration*. Cambridge: Cambridge University Press.

Pino, E., and Wittermans, T. (eds.). (1963). *Kamus Inggeris* [English Dictionary]. Groningen: J. B. Wolters.

Pitts, J. R. (1968). Social Control: The Concept. Pp. 381–396 in D. Sills (ed.), *International Encyclopedia of the Social Sciences, Vol. 14*. New York: Macmillan and Free Press.

Plummer, K. (1984). Sexual Diversity: A Sociological Perspective. Pp. 219–253 in K. Howells (ed.), *The Psychology of Sexual Diversity*. Oxford: Basil Blackwell.

———. (1979). Misunderstanding Labelling Perspectives. Pp. 85–121 in D. Downes and P. Rock (eds.), *Deviant Interpretations*. Oxford: Martin Robertson.

Polk, L. D. (1974). Mass Hysteria in an Elementary School. *Clinical Pediatrics* 13:1013–1014.

Pollock, G., and Clayton, T. M. (1964). Epidemic Collapse: A Mysterious Outbreak in Three Coventry Schools. *British Medical Journal* ii:1625–1627.

Pool, J. H., Walton, J. N., Brewis, E. G., Uldall, P. R., Wright, A. E., and Gardner, P. S. (1961). Benign Myalgic Encephalomyelitis in Newcastle Upon Tyne. *Lancet* 1:733–737.

Porter, R. (1987). *A Social History of Medicine: Stories of the Insane*. London: Weidenfeld and Nicolson.

Poskanzer, D. C., Henderson, D. A., Kunkle, C. E., Kalter, S. S., Clement, W. B., and Bond, J. D. (1957). Epidemic Neuromyasthenia: An Outbreak in Punta Gorda, Florida. *New England Journal of Medicine* 257:356–364.

Post, S. G. (1992). DSM-III-R and Religion. *Social Science and Medicine* 35(1):81–90.

Prince, R. (1992a). Koro and the Fox Spirit on Hainan Island (China). *Transcultural Psychiatric Research Review* 29:119–132.

———. (1992b). A Symposium on the Vulnerable Male: Cultural Variations on the Castration Theme. *Transcultural Psychiatric Research Review* 29:87–90.

Prince, R., and Tcheng-Laroche, F. (1987). Culture-Bound Syndromes and International Disease Classifications. *Culture, Medicine, and Psychiatry* 11:3–19.

Prins, H. (1990). *Bizarre Behaviours: Boundaries of Psychiatric Disorder*. London: Routledge.

Proctor, R. (1988). *Racial Hygiene: Medicine Under the Nazis*. Cambridge: Harvard University Press.

Pullela, S. (1986). An Outbreak of Epidemic Hysteria: An Illustrative Case Study. *Irish Journal of Psychiatry* 7(1):9–11.

Puranik, A., and Dunn, J. (1995). Koro Presenting After Prostatectomy in an Elderly Man. *British Journal of Urology* 75(1):108–109.

Putnam, F. W., Guroff, J. J., Silberman, E. K., Barban, L., and Post, R. M. (1986). The Clinical Phenomenology of Multiple Personality: Review of 100 Recent Cases. *Journal of Clinical Psychiatry* 47:285–293.

Quarantelli, E. L., and Hundley, J. R. (1971). A Test of Some Propositions About Crowd Formation and Behavior. Pp. 538–554 in R. Evans (ed.), *Readings in Collective Behavior.* Chicago: Rand McNally.

Rabinovitch, R. (1965). An Exaggerated Startle Reflex Resembling a Kicking Horse. Letter. *Canadian Medical Association Journal* 93:130.

Rack, P. (1982). *Race, Culture, and Mental Disorder.* London: Tavistock.

Rado, S. (1963). Fighting Narcotic Bondage and Other Forms of Narcotic Disorders. *Comprehensive Psychiatry* 4:160–167.

Randi, J. (1987). *The Faith Healers.* Buffalo: Prometheus.

———. (1986). Be Healed in the Name of God! An Expose of the Reverend W. V. Grant. *Free Inquiry* 6(2):8–19.

Rankin, A. M., and Philip, P. J. (1963). An Epidemic of Laughing in the Buboka District of Tanganyika. *Central African Journal of Medicine* 9:167–170.

Raschka, L. B. (1976). Lynching: A Psychiatrist's View. *Canadian Psychiatric Association Journal* 21(8):577–580.

Raven, T. (1886). Retraction of the Penis. *Lancet* 2:250.

Rawnsley, K., and Loudon, J. B. (1964). Epidemiology of Mental Disorder in a Closed Community. *British Journal of Psychiatry* 110:830–839.

Reay, M. (1965). Mushroom Madness and Collective Hysteria. *Australian Territories* 5(1):18–28.

Redlich, F. C., and Freedman, D. X. (1966). *The Theory and Practice of Psychiatry.* New York: Basic.

Regnard, M., and Simon, J. (1877). Sur une Épidémie de Contracture des Extrémités Observée à Gentilly [On an Epidemic of Limb Contracture Observed in Gentilly]. *Comptes Rendus des Seances de la Societe de Biologie* (Paris) 3:344–347, 350–353.

Reig-y-Casco, J. (1881). Los Convulsionarios de Santa Crosia [The Convulsionnaires of Santa Crosia]. *Siglo Medico* (Madrid) 28:584–587.

Rembold, S. (1893). Acute Psychiche Contagion in Einer Madchenschule [Acute Psychic Contagion in a Girls' School]. *Berliner Klinische Wochenschrift* 30:662–663.

Resner, G., and Hartog, J. (1970). Concepts and Terminology of Mental Disorder Among Malays. *Journal of Cross-Cultural Psychology* 1:369–381.

Richards, A. (1981). *An Iban-English Dictionary.* Oxford: Clarendon.

Richardson, J. T., Best, J., and Bromley, D. G. (eds.) (1991). *The Satanism Scare.* New York: Aldine de Gruyter.

Richardson, M. (1984). Comments. *Current Anthropology* 25:275.

Rickman, J. (1941). A Case of Hysteria: Theory and Practice in Two Wars. *Lancet* 1:785–786.

Ridington, R. (1988). Knowledge, Power, and the Individual in Subarctic Hunting Societies. *American Anthropologist* 90(1):98–111.

Rin, H. (1965). A Study of the Aetiology of Koro in Respect to the Chinese Concept of Illness. *International Journal of Social Psychiatry* 11:7–13.

Roach Anleu, S. L. (1995). *Deviance, Conformity, and Control.* Melbourne: Longman.

Roback, H. B., Roback, E., and LaBarbera, J. D. (1984). Epidemic Grieving at a Birthday Party: A Case of Mass Hysteria. *Journal of Developmental and Behavioral Pediatrics* 5:86–89.

Robbins, T. (1980). The Fact Pattern Behind the Deprogramming Controversy. *Review of Law and Social Change* 9(1):73–90.

Robbins, T., and Anthony, D. (1982). Deprogramming, Brainwashing, and the Medicalization of Deviant Religious Groups. *Social Problems* 29(3):283–297.

Robertson, F. (1806). Account of a Singular Convulsive Affection Which Prevails in the State of Tennessee. *Philadelphia Medical and Physical Journal* 2:86–95.

Robin, R. (1981). Revival Movement Hysteria in the Southern Highlands of Papua New Guinea. *Journal for the Scientific Study of Religion* 20(2):150–163.

Robinson, P., Szewczyk, M., Haddy, L., Jones, P., and Harvey, W. (1984). Outbreak of Itching and Rash. *Archives of Internal Medicine* 144:159–162.

Rockney, R. M., and Lemke, T. (1992). Casualties from a Junior High School During the Persian Gulf War: Toxic Poisoning or Mass Hysteria? *Journal of Developmental and Behavioral Pediatrics* 13:339–342.

Rodwin, M. A. (1993). *Medicine, Money, and Morals: Physicians' Conflicts of Interest.* Oxford: Oxford University Press.

Rosecrance, J. (1985). Compulsive Gambling and the Medicalization of Deviance. *Social Problems* 32 (3):275–284.

Rosen, G. (1968). *Madness in Society.* London: Routledge and Kegan Paul.

———. (1962). Psychopathology in the Social Process: Dance Frenzies, Demonic Possession, Revival Movements, and Similar So-Called Psychic Epidemics. An Interpretation. *Bulletin of the History of Medicine* 36:13–44. Paper presented at the Fielding H. Garrison Lecture at the 34th annual meeting of the American Association for the History of Medicine, Chicago, Ill., May 18, 1961.

Rosenhan, D. L. (1973). On Being Sane in Insane Places. *Science* 179 (January):250–258.

Rosenthal, D. (1970). *Genetic Theory and Abnormal Behavior.* New York: McGraw-Hill.

Ross, D. F., Read, J. D., and Toglia, M. P. (1994). *Adult Eyewitness Testimony: Current Trends and Developments.* Cambridge: Cambridge University Press.

Roueche, B. (1978). *New Yorker* (August 21) (interview with Dr. Joel Nitzkin).

Rubin, R. T. (1982). Koro (Shook Yang): A Culture-Bound Psychogenic Syndrome. Pp. 155–172 in C.T.H. Friedmann and R. A. Faguet (eds.), *Extraordinary Disorders of Human Behavior.* New York: Plenum.

Rubington, E., and Weinberg, M. S. (1973). *Deviance: The Interactionist Perspective* (2d ed.). New York: Macmillan.

Ruiz, M. T., and Lopez, J. M. (1988). Mass Hysteria in a Secondary School. *International Journal of Epidemiology* 17:475–476.

Rush, B. (1962 [1812]). *Medical Inquiries and Observations Upon the Diseases of the Mind* (facsimile of the Philadelphia 1812 ed.). New York: Hafner.

Russell, D. (1995). *Women, Madness, and Medicine.* Cambridge: Polity.

Russell, J. F. (1979). Tarantism. *Medical History* 23:404–425.

Rust, F. (1969). *Dance in Society: An Analysis of the Relationship Between the Social Dance and Society in England From the Middle Ages to the Present Day.* London: Routledge and Kegan Paul.

Ryan, C. M., and Morrow, L. A. (1992). Dysfunctional Buildings or Dysfunctional People: An Examination of the Sick Building Syndrome and Allied Disorders. *Journal of Consulting and Clinical Psychology* 60:220–224.

Sachdev, P. S. (1985). Koro Epidemic in North-East India. *Australian and New Zealand Journal of Psychiatry* 19:433–438.

Sachdev, P. S., and Shukla, A. (1982). Epidemic Koro Syndrome in India. *Lancet* 2:1161.

Said, E. W. (1978). *Orientalism.* London: Routledge and Kegan Paul.

Sainte-Hilaire, M. H., Sainte-Hilaire, J. M., and Granger, L. (1986). Jumping Frenchmen of Maine. *Neurology* 36:1269–1271.

Samarin, W. J. (1972). *Tongues of Men and Angels.* New York: Macmillan.

Sanarov, V. I. (1981). On the Nature and Origin of Flying Saucers and Little Green Men. *Current Anthropology* 22:163–167.

Sandyk, R. (1992). Postpartum Psychosis and the Pineal Gland. *International Journal of Neuroscience* 62(1–2):101–105.

Sapir, E. (1932). Cultural Anthropology and Psychiatry. *Journal of Abnormal and Social Psychology* 27:229–242.

Sargent, M., and Cooper, M. (eds.). (1962). *The Outline of Music.* New York: Arco.

Schadewaldt, H. (1971). Musik und Medizin [Music and Medicine]. *Arztliche Praxis* 23:1846–1851, 1894–1897.

Schafer, S. (1976). *Introduction to Criminology.* Reston, Va.: Reston.

Schatalow, N. (1891). Zur Frage von der Epidemischen Histerie [On the Question of Epidemic Hysteria]. *Neurologische Centralblatt* 10:405.

Scheff, T. J. (1966). *Being Mentally Ill.* Chicago: Aldine.

Scher, M. (1987). Koro in a Native-Born Citizen of the U.S. *International Journal of Social Psychiatry* 33(1):42–45.

Schmidgall-Tellings, A., and Stevens, A. M. (1981). *Contemporary Indonesian-English Dictionary.* Athens: Ohio University Press.

Schmidt, C. G. (1984). The Group-Fantasy Origin of AIDS. *Journal of Psychohistory* 12(1):37–78.

Schneider, J. W., and Conrad, P. (1980). The Medical Control of Deviance: Contests and Consequences. *Research in the Sociology of Health Care* 1:1–53.

Schoedel, J. (1906). Uber Induzierte Krankheiten [On Induced Illness]. *Jahrbuch fur Kinderheilkunde* 14:521–528.

Schoeneman, T. J. (1984). The Mentally Ill Witch in Textbooks of Abnormal Psychology: Current Status and Implications of a Fallacy. *Professional Psychology: Research and Practice* 15(3):299–314.

Schuler, E. A., and Parenton, V. J. (1943). A Recent Epidemic of Hysteria in a Louisiana High School. *Journal of Social Psychology* 17:221–235.

Schumacher, J. (1940). *Die Seelischen Volkskrankheiten im Deutschen Mittelalter und ihre Darstellungen in der Bildenden Kunst* [Mental Epidemics in the Middle Ages and Their Representation in the Graphic Arts]. Berlin: Junker and Dunnhaupt.

Schur, E. M. (1971). *Labeling Deviant Behavior.* New York: Harper and Row.

Schutte, P. (1906). Eine neue form Hysterischer Zustande bei Schulkindern [A New Form of Hysterical Conditions in Schoolchildren]. *Muenchener Medizinsche Wochenschrift* 53:1763–1764.

Schutz, A. (1967 [1932]). *The Phenomenology of the Social World.* Evanston: Northwestern University Press.

Scott, J. C. (1985). *Weapons of the Weak.* New Haven: Yale University Press.

Seeligmuller, A. (1876). Uber Epidemisches Auftreten von Hysterischen Zustanden [An Epidemic Manifestation of Hysterical Conditions]. *Allgemeine Zeitschrift fur Psychiatrie* (Berlin) 33:510–528.

Selden, B. S. (1989). Adolescent Epidemic Hysteria Presenting as a Mass Casualty, Toxic Exposure Incident. *Annals of Emergency Medicine* 18(8):892–895.

Selvadurai, S. (1985). *Problems of Residential Students in a Secondary Technical School.* Master's thesis, University of Malaya, Kuala Lumpur.

Selvin, D. F. (1989). An Exercise in Hysteria: San Francisco's Red Raids of 1934. *Pacific Historical Review* 58(3):361–374.

Serao, F. (1750). *Idem, Della Tarantula Ovvero Falangio di Puglia* [Madness of the Tarantula Harvest Spider From Apulia]. Naples.

Shapiro, H. L. (1936). *The Heritage of the Bounty.* London: Simon and Schuster.

Sharrod, H. L. (1985). RSI, Kangaroo Paw, or What? *Medical Journal of Australia* 142:376.

Sheldon, W. H., Hartl, E. M., and McDermott, E. (1949). *Varieties of Delinquent Youth: An Introduction to Constitutional Psychiatry.* New York: Harper and Row.

Sheldon, W. H., Stevens, S. S., and Tucker, W. B. (1940). *Varieties of Human Physique.* New York: Harper and Row.

Shelokov, A., Habel, K., Verder, E., and Welsh, W. (1957). Epidemic Neuromyasthenia: An Outbreak of Poliomyelitis-Like Illness in Student Nurses. *New England Journal of Medicine* 257:345–355.

Shepard, L. (1984). Letter from Leslie Shepard, former president of the now defunct Fairy Investigation Society, based in the United Kingdom.

Shepard, R. D., and Kroes, W. H. (1975). *Report of an Investigation at the James Plant.* Internal document prepared for the National Institute for Occupational Safety and Health, Cincinnati, Ohio.

Shibutani, T. (1966). *Improvised News.* Indianapolis: Bobbs-Merrill.

Shirokogoroff, M. (1935). *The Psychomental Complex of the Tungus.* London: Trubner.

Showalter, E. (1991). *The Female Malady: Women, Madness, and English Culture, 1830–1980.* London: Virago.

Shukla, G. D., and Mishra, D. N. (1981). Koro-like Syndrome: A Case Report. *Indian Journal of Psychiatry* 23:96–97.

Shweder, R. A. (1984). Anthropology's Romantic Rebellion Against the Enlightenment, or There's More to Thinking Than Reason and Evidence. Pp. 27–66 in R. A. Shweder and R. A. LeVine (eds.), *Culture Theory: Essays on Mind, Self, and Emotion.* New York: Cambridge University Press.

Shweder, R. A., and Bourne, E. J. (1984). Does the Concept of the Person Vary Cross-Culturally? Pp. 158–199 in R. A. Shweder and Robert A. LeVine (eds.), *Culture Theory: Essays on Mind, Self, and Emotion.* New York: Cambridge University Press.

Siegler, M., and Osmond, H. (1974). *Models of Madness, Models of Medicine.* New York: Macmillan.

Sieveking, P. (1993). Fear and Loathing in France. *Fortean Times* 67:47.

Sigerist, H. E. (1943). *Civilization and Disease.* Ithaca, N.Y.: Cornell University Press.

———, (ed.). (1941). *Four Treatises of Theophrastus von Hohenheim called Paracelsus.* Baltimore: Johns Hopkins University Press.

Sighele, S. (1892). *La Foule Criminelle, Essai de Psychologie Collective* [The Criminal Crowd, Essay on Group Psychology] (trans. from Italian by P. Vigny). Paris: Felix Alcan.

Sigurdsson, B. J., Sigurjonsson, J., Sigurdsson, J., Thorkelsson, J., and Gudmundsson, K. (1950). Disease Epidemic in Iceland Simulating Poliomyelitis. *American Journal of Hygiene* 52:222–238.

Sim, M. (1981). *Guide to Psychiatry* (4th ed.). New York: Churchhill Livingstone.

Simmel, E. (ed.). (1946). *Anti-Semitism.* New York: International Universities Press.

Simon, B. (1978). *Mind and Madness in Ancient Greece: The Classical Roots of Modern Psychiatry.* London: Cornell University Press.

Simons, R. C. (1996). *Boo!—Culture, Experience, and the Startle Reflex.* New York: Oxford University Press.

———. (1995). Of Sticks and Stones. *Journal of Nervous and Mental Disease* 183:185–186.

———. (1994). Commentary: The Interminable Debate on the Nature of Latah. *Journal of Nervous and Mental Disease* 182:339–341.

———. (1987). A Feasible and Timely Enterprise: Commentary on "Culture-Bound Syndromes and International Disease Classifications" by Raymond Prince and Francoise Tcheng-Laroche. *Culture, Medicine, and Psychiatry* 11:21–28.

———. (1985a). The Resolution of the Latah Paradox. Pp. 43–62 in R. C. Simons and C. C. Hughes (eds.), *The Culture-Bound Syndromes.* Dordrecht: D. Reidel.

———. (1985b). Introduction: The Genital Retraction Taxon. Pp. 151–153 in R. C. Simons and C. C. Hughes (eds.), *The Culture-Bound Syndromes.* Dordrecht: D. Reidel.

———. (1985c). Latah II—Problems With a Purely Symbolic Interpretation. Pp. 77–89 in R. C. Simons and C. C. Hughes (eds.), *The Culture-Bound Syndromes.* Dordrecht: D. Reidel.

———. (1985d). Introduction: The Startle Matching Taxon. Pp. 41–42 in R. C. Simons and C. C. Hughes (eds.), *The Culture-Bound Syndromes.* Dordrecht: D. Reidel.

———. (1980). The Resolution of the Latah Paradox. *Journal of Nervous and Mental Disease* 168:195–206.

Simons, R. C., and Hughes, C. C. (eds.). (1985). *The Culture-Bound Syndromes.* Dordrecht: D. Reidel.

Simpson, J. A., and Weiner, E.S.C. (eds.). (1989a). *The Oxford English Dictionary, Vol. 7.* Oxford: Clarendon.

———. (1989b). *The Oxford English Dictionary, Vol. 8.* Oxford: Clarendon.

Singer, C., and Underwood, E. A. (1962). *A Short History of Medicine.* Oxford: Clarendon.

Singer, J. E., Baum, C. S., Baum, A., and Thew, B. D. (1982). Mass Psychogenic Illness: The Case for Social Comparison. Pp. 155–169 in M. Colligan, J. Pennebaker, and L. Murphy (eds.), *Mass Psychogenic Illness: A Social Psychological Analysis.* Hillsdale, N.J.: Lawrence Erlbaum.

Sinks, T., Kerndt, P. R., and Wallingford, K. M. (1989). Two Episodes of Acute Illness in a Machine Shop. *American Journal of Public Health* (79):1024–1028.

Sirois, F. (1982). Perspectives on Epidemic Hysteria. Pp. 217–236 in M. Colligan, J. Pennebaker, and L. Murphy (eds.), *Mass Psychogenic Illness: A Social Psychological Analysis.* Hillsdale, N.J.: Lawrence Erlbaum.

———. (1975). A Propos de la Frequence des Epidemies d'hysterie [On the Frequency of Epidemic Hysteria]. *Union Medicale du Canada* (Montreal) 104:121–123.

———. (1974). Epidemic Hysteria. *Acta Psychiatrica Scandinavica Supplementum* 252:7–46.

Skeat, W. W. (1900). *Malay Magic.* London: Macmillan.

Skultans, V. (1979). *English Madness: Ideas on Insanity, 1580–1890.* London: Routledge and Kegan Paul.

———. (1975). *Madness and Morals: Ideas on Insanity in the Nineteenth Century.* London: Routledge and Kegan Paul.

Slater, E. (1965). Diagnosis of "Hysteria." *British Medical Journal* 1:1395–1399.

Slot, J. A. (1935). Koro in Zuid-Celebes [Koro in Sulawesi]. *Geneeskundig Tijdschrift voor Nederlandsch-Indie* 75:811–820.

Small, G., and Borus, J. (1983). Outbreak of Illness in a School Chorus. Toxic Poisoning or Mass Hysteria? *New England Journal of Medicine* 308:632–635.

Small, G. W., and Nicholi, A. M. (1982). Mass Hysteria Among Student Performers: Early Loss as a Predisposing Factor. *Archives of General Psychiatry* 39:721–724.

Small, G. W., Propper, M. W., Randolph, E. T., and Eth, S. (1991). Mass Hysteria Among Student Performers: Social Relationship as a Symptom Predictor. *American Journal of Psychiatry* 148:1200–1205.

Smart, C. (1990). Feminist Approaches to Criminology, or Postmodern Woman Meets Atavistic Man. Pp. 70–84 in L. Gelsthorpe and A. Morris (eds.), *Feminist Perspectives in Criminology.* Milton Keynes, Eng.: Open University Press.

Smelser, N. J. (1962). *Theory of Collective Behavior.* Englewood Cliffs, N.J.: Prentice-Hall.

Smith, F. (1976). *Cattle Mutilations: The Unthinkable Truth.* Cedar Mesa, Colo.: Freeland.

Smith, H.C.T., and Eastham, E. J. (1973). Outbreak of Abdominal Pain. *Lancet* 2:956–959.

Smith, M., Colligan, M., and Hurrell, J. (1978). Three Incidents of Industrial Mass Psychogenic Illness. *Journal of Occupational Medicine* 20:339–400.

Smith-Rosenberg, C. (1972). The Hysterical Woman: Sex Roles and Role Conflict in Nineteenth-Century America. *Social Research* 39(4):652–678.

Smyth, M. G., and Dean, C. (1992). Capgras and Koro. *British Journal of Psychiatry* 161:121–123.

Spanos, N. P. (1996). *Multiple Identities and False Memories: A Sociocognitive Perspective.* Washington, D.C.: APA.

———. (1978). Witchcraft in Histories of Psychiatry: A Critical Analysis and an Alternative Conceptualization. *Psychological Bulletin* 85:417–439.

Spiller, G. (1908a). Moral Education in the Boys' Schools of Germany. Pp. 213–230 in M. E. Sadler (ed.), *Moral Instruction and Training in Schools: Report of an International Inquiry, Vol. 2.* London: Longmans, Green.

———. (1908b). An Educational Democracy: Moral Instruction and Training in the Schools of Switzerland. Pp. 196–206 in M. E. Sadler (ed.), *Moral Instruction and Training in Schools: Report of an International Inquiry, Volume 2.* London: Longmans, Green.

Sponsel, L. E. (1990). Ultraprimitive Pacifists: The Tasaday as a Symbol of Peace. *Anthropology Today* 6(1):3–5.

Spores, J. C. (1988). *Running Amok: An Historical Inquiry.* Ohio University, Monographs in International Studies, Southeast Asia Series, no. 82.

———. (1976). *Running Amok: A Sociological Analysis.* Ph.D. diss., University of Michigan. Ann Arbor: University Microfilms.

Stahl, S. M. (1982). Illness as an Emergent Norm, or Doing What Comes Naturally. Pp. 183–198 in M. Colligan, J. Pennebaker, and L. Murphy (eds.), *Mass Psychogenic Illness: A Social Psychological Analysis.* Hillsdale, N.J.: Lawrence Erlbaum.

Stahl, S. M., and Lebedun, M. (1974). Mystery Gas: An Analysis of Mass Hysteria. *Journal of Health and Social Behavior* 15:44–50.

Steadman, L. B., and Merbs, C. F. (1982). Kuru and Cannibalism? *American Anthropologist* 84(3):611–627.

Stephen, M. (1977). *Cargo Cult Hysteria: Symptoms of Despair or Technique of Ecstasy?* Occasional paper no. 1. Research Centre for Southwest Pacific Studies, La Trobe University, Bundoora, Victoria, Australia.

Sterling, W. (1936). Epidemia dzieciecej histeri religijnej [Epidemic of Infantile Religious Hysteria]. *Warsz Czas Lek* 13:728–731, 749–752.

Stevens, H. (1965). "Jumping Frenchmen of Maine" (Myriachit). *Archives of Neurology* 12:311–314.

———. (1964). Jumping Frenchmen of Maine. *Transactions of the American Neurological Association* 89:65–67.

Stewart, J. R. (1989). Sasquatch Sightings in South Dakota: An Analysis of an Episode of Collective Delusion. Pp. 287–304 in G. Zollschan, J. Schumaker, and G. Walsh (eds.), *Exploring the Paranormal.* Bridport, Eng.: Prism.

———. (1977). Cattle Mutilations: An Episode of Collective Delusion *Skeptical Inquirer* (formerly the *Zetetic*) 1(2):55–66.

Strentz, H. J. (1970). *A Survey of Press Coverage of Unidentified Flying Objects, 1947–1966.* Ph.D. diss., Northwestern University, Department of Journalism.

Stricklin, A., Sewell, M., and Austas, C. (1990). Objective Measurements of Personality Variables in Epidemic Neuromyasthenia Patients. *South African Medical Journal of Epidemiology* 132:1120–1129.

Strong, R. P. (1945). Diseases of Rare Occurrence or of Doubtful Origin. Pp. 1129–1146 in *Sitt's Diagnosis, Prevention, and Treatment of Tropical Diseases* (7th ed.). London: H. K. Lewis.

Sumner, W. G. (1906). *Folkways: A Study of the Sociological Importance of Usages, Manners, Customs, Mores, and Morals.* New York: Ginn.

Suwanlert, S., and Coates, D. (1979). Epidemic Koro in Thailand—Clinical and Social Aspects. Abstract of the report by F. R. Fenton appearing in *Transcultural Psychiatric Research Review* 16:64–66.

Swettenham, F. (1963 [1895]). *Malay Sketches.* London: John Lane.

———. (1900). *The Real Malay: Pen Pictures.* London: John Lane.

Szasz, T. S. (1994). *Cruel Compassion: Psychiatric Control of Society's Unwanted.* New York: John Wiley and Sons.

———. (1990). *Sex by Prescription.* Syracuse: Syracuse University Press.

———. (1987). *Insanity: The Idea and Its Consequences.* New York: John Wiley and Sons.

———. (1979). *The Theology of Medicine: The Political-Philosophical Foundations of Medical Ethics.* Oxford: Oxford University Press.

———. (1974a). *Law, Liberty, and Psychiatry: An Inquiry Into the Social Uses of Mental Health Practices.* London: Routledge and Kegan Paul.

———. (1974b). *The Myth of Mental Illness.* New York: Harper and Row.

———. (1970). *The Manufacture of Madness.* New York: Delta.

Szegō, K. (1896). Uber die Imitationskrankheiten der Kinder [On the Imitative Illness of Children]. *Jahrbuch fur Kinderheilkunde* (Leipzig) 41:133–145.

Tam, Y. K., Tsoi, M. M., Kwong, G. B., and Wong, S. W. (1982). Psychological Epidemic in Hong Kong, Part 2, Psychological and Physiological Characteristics of Children Who Were Affected. *Acta Psychiatrica Scandinavica* 65:437–449.

Tan, E. S. (1980). Culture-Bound Syndromes Among Overseas Chinese. Pp. 371–386 in A. Kleinman and T. Y. Lin (eds.), *Normal and Abnormal Behavior in Chinese Culture.* Boston: Reidel.

———. (1972). Prospects for Psychiatric Research in a Multiracial Developing Community—West Malaysia. Pp. 3–12 in W. P. Lebra (ed.), *Transcultural Research in Mental Health. Vol. 2 of Mental Health Research in Asia and the Pacific.* Honolulu: University Press of Hawaii.

———. (1963). Epidemic Hysteria. *Medical Journal of Malaya* 18:72–76.

Tarde, G. (1901). *L'Opinion et la Foule* [The Opinion of the Crowd]. Paris: Felix Alcan.

Tavris, C. (1993). *The Mismeasure of Woman.* New York: Touchstone.

Taylor, B. W., and Werbicki, J. E. (1993). A Case of Mass Hysteria Involving Nineteen Schoolchildren. *Pediatric Emergency Care* 9:216–217.

Taylor, R. (1979). *Medicine Out of Control: The Anatomy of a Malignant Technology.* Melbourne: Sun.

Teoh, J. I. (1972). The Changing Psychopathology of Amok. *Psychiatry* 35:345–351.

Teoh, J. I., Soewondo, S., and Sidharta, M. (1975). Epidemic Hysteria in Malaysia: An Illustrative Episode. *Psychiatry* 8(3):258–268.

Teoh, J. I., and Tan, E. S. (1976). An Outbreak of Epidemic Hysteria in West Malaysia. Pp. 32–43 in W. P. Lebra (ed.), *Culture-Bound Syndromes, Ethnopsychiatry, and Alternate Therapies, Vol. 4 of Mental Health Research in Asia and the Pacific.* Honolulu: University Press of Hawaii.

Teoh, J., and Yeoh, K. (1973). Cultural Conflict in Transition: Epidemic Hysteria and Social Sanction. *Australian and New Zealand Journal of Psychiatry* 7:283–295.

Thase, M. E., Reynolds, C. F., and Jennings, J. R. (1988). Nocturnal Penile Tumescence Is Diminished in Depressed Men. *Biological Psychiatry* 24:33–46.

Theopold (1955). Induzierte Amplexus neural bei Madchen einer Schulklasse [Induced Neural Amplexus in Girls in a School Class]. *Monatsschrift fur Kinderheilkunde* 103.

Thigpen, C. H., and Cleckley, H. M. (1984). On the Incidence of Multiple Personality Disorder. *International Journal of Clinical and Experimental Hypnosis* 32:63–66.

Thio, A. (1988). *Deviant Behavior* (3rd ed.). New York: Harper and Row.

Thomas, A., and Sillen, S. (1972). *Racism and Psychiatry.* New York: Brunner/Mazel.

Thomas, C. L. (ed.). (1989). *Taber's Cyclopedic Medical Dictionary* (17th ed.). Philadelphia: F. A. Davis.

Thomas, K. (1971). *Religion and the Decline of Magic.* London: Weidenfeld and Nicolson.

Thomas, W. I. (1932). *The Child in America.* New York: Alfred Knopf.

———. (1923). *The Unadjusted Girl.* Boston: Little, Brown.

Thorne, F. C. (1944). Startle Neurosis. *American Journal of Psychiatry* 101:105–109.

Thornton, J. B. (1885). Some Curious Facts Concerning the "Jumpers." *Medical Record* (New York) 28:713.

Toibin, C. (1985). *Moving Statues in Ireland: Seeing Is Believing.* County Laois, Erie: Pilgram.

Tong, R. (1989). *Feminist Thought: A Comprehensive Introduction.* Boulder: Westview.

Torrey, E. F. (1986). *Witch Doctors and Psychiatrists: The Common Roots of Psychotherapy and Its Future.* Northvale, N.J.: Jason Aronson.

Trethowan, W., and Sims, A.C.P. (1983). *Psychiatry.* London: Bailliere Tindall.

Trimble, J. E., and Medicine, B. (1976). Development of Theoretical Models and Levels of Interpretation in Mental Health. Pp. 161–200 in J. Westermeyer (ed.), *Anthropology and Mental Health: Setting a New Course.* The Hague: Mouton.

Troup, F. (1972). *South Africa: An Historical Introduction.* London: Eyre Methuen.

Troyer, R. J., and Markle, G. E. (1982). Creating Deviance Rules: A Macroscopic Model. *Sociological Quarterly* 23:157–169.

Truper, J. (1908). Zur Frage der Schulerselbstmorde [On the Question of School Illness]. *Zeitschrift fur Kinderforschung* 143:75–86.

Tseng, W. S., and McDermott, J. F., Jr. (1981). *Culture, Mind, and Therapy: An Introduction to Cultural Psychiatry.* New York: Brunner/Mazel.

Tseng, W. S., and Hsu, J. (1980). Minor Psychological Disturbances of Everyday Life. Pp. 61–97, in H. C. Triandis and J. G. Draguns (eds.), *Handbook of Cross-Cultural Psychology, Vol. 6, Psychopathology.* Boston: Allyn and Bacon.

Tseng, W. S., Mo, K. M., Hsu, J., Li, L. S., Ou, L. W., Chen, G. Q., and Jiang, D. W. (1988). A Sociocultural Study of Koro Epidemics in Guangdong, China. *American Journal of Psychiatry* 145(12):1538–1543.

———. (1987). A Socio-Cultural and Clinical Study of a Koro (Genital Retraction Panic Disorder) Epidemic in Guangdong, China. Paper presented at the Conference of the Society for the Study of Psychiatry and Culture, Quebec City, Canada, September 16–19.

Tseng, W. S., Mo, K. M., Li, L. S., Chen, G. Q., Ou, L. W., and Zheng, H. B. (1992). Koro Epidemics in Guangdong, China: A Questionnaire Survey. *Journal of Nervous and Mental Disease* 180(2):117–123.

Tumin, M. M., and Feldman, A. S. (1955). The Miracle at Sabana Grande. *Public Opinion Quarterly* 19:124–139.

Turnbull, A. (1771). Letter From Mr. Turnbull to Archibald Menzies of Kildares, Esq., Dated From Delphos, Concerning Italy, the Alleged Effects of the Bite of the Tarantula, the Grecian Antiquities. Pp. 100–115 in *Essays and Observations Physical and Literary.* Edinburgh: Balfour.

Turner, B. S. (1987). *Medical Power and Social Knowledge.* London: Sage.

Turner, R. H., and Killian, L. M. (1987). *Collective Behavior* (3rd ed.). Englewood Cliffs, N.J.: Prentice-Hall.

Turner, V. (1974). *Dramas, Fields, and Metaphors: Symbolic Action in Human Society.* Ithaca, N.Y.: Cornell University Press.

———. (1969). *The Ritual Process: Structure and Anti-Structure.* Harmondsworth: Penguin.

Turnier, L., and Chouinard, G. (1990). Effet Anti-Koro d'un Antidepresseur Tricyclique [Anti-Koro Effect of a Tricyclic Antidepressant]. *Canadian Journal of Psychiatry* 35(4):331–333.

Uchimura, Y. (1935). "Imu": A Malady of the Ainu. *Lancet* (June 1):1272–1273.

Ungerleider, J. T., and Wellisch, D. K. (1989). Deprogramming (Involuntary Departure), Coercion, and Cults. Pp. 239–253 in M. Galanter (ed.), *Cults and New Religious Movements: A Report of the American Psychiatric Association From the Committee on Psychiatry and Religion.* Washington, D.C.: APA.

Ussher, J. (1991). *Women's Madness: Misogyny or Mental Illness?* Hemel Hempstead: Harvester Wheatsheaf.

Van Brero, P.C.Z. (1897). Koro, eine Eigenthümliche Zwangsvorstellung [Koro, a Strange Imaginary Compulsion]. *Allgemeine Zeitschaft fur Psychiatrie* 53:569–573.

———. (1896). Einiges uber die Geisteskrankheiten der Bevolkerung des Malayischen Archipels [Some of the Mental Illnesses of the People of the Malay Archipelago]. *Allgemeine Zeitschrift fur Psychiatrie und ihre Grenzgebiete* 53:25–33.

———. (1895). Latah. *Journal of Mental Science* 41:537–538.

Van Leent, F. J. (1867). Contributions a la Geographie Medicale [Contributions on Medical Geography]. *Archives de Medecine Navale* 8:172–173.

Van Loon, F.H.G. (1931) Die Bedeutung Ur-instinctiver Phaenomene bei "Primitiven" und in der Kulturgesellschaft (The Significance of Ultimate Instinctive Phenomena Among Primitive and Highly Civilized Peoples). *Zeitschrift fuer Voelkerpsychologie und Soziologie* 7:21–33.

———. (1928). Protopathic-Instinctive Phenomena in Normal and Pathological Malay Life. *British Journal of Medical Psychology* 8:264–276.

———. (1927). Amok and Lattah. *Journal of Abnormal and Social Psychology* 21:434–444.

———. (1924). Latah, a Psychoneurosis of the Malay Races. Pp. 305–321. *Mededeelingen van den Burgerlijken Geneeskundigen Dienst in Nederlandsch-Indie.* Report of the Dutch-Indian Medical Service, Foreign Edition, part 4.

Van Wulfften-Palthe, P. M. (1936). Psychiatry and Neurology in the Tropics. Pp. 525–547 in C. de Langen and A. Lichtenstein (eds.), *Clinical Textbook of Tropical Medicine.* Batavia: G. Kolff.

———. (1935). Koro. Eine Merkwuerdige Angsthysterie (Koro: An Unusual Type of Anxiety). *Internationale Zeitschrift fuer Psychoanalyse* 21:248–257.

———. (1933). Psychiatry and Neurology in the Tropics. *Malayan Medical Journal* 8:133–139.

Vatz, R. E., and Weinberg, L. S. (1994). The Rhetorical Paradigm in Psychiatric History: Thomas Szasz and the Myth of Mental Illness. Pp. 311–330 in M. Micale and R. Porter (eds.), *Discovering the History of Psychiatry.* Oxford: Oxford University Press.

Victor, J. S. (1992). Telephone interview with Robert E. Bartholomew on radio station WWSC, 217 Dix Ave., Glens Falls, N.Y.

———. (1990). The Spread of Satanic-Cult Rumors. *Skeptical Inquirer* 14(3):287–291.

———. (1989). A Rumor-Panic About a Dangerous Satanic Cult in Western New York. *New York Folklore* 15:23–49.

Vinogradov, S., and Csernansky, J. G. (1990). Postpartum Psychosis With Abnormal Movements: Dopamine Supersensitivity Unmasked by Withdrawal of Endogenous Estrogens? *Journal of Clinical Psychiatry* 51(9):363–366.

Vittorio, L. (1963). *Religions of the Oppressed: A Study of Modern Messianic Cults.* New York: Alfred Knopf.

Von Holwede (1898). Eine Epidemie von hysterischen Zufallen in einer Burgerschule zu Braunschweig [Hysterical Cases in a Citizens' School in Brunswick]. *Jahrbuch fur Kinderheilkunde* (Leipzig), n.f. 48:229–234.

Vorstman, A. H. (1897). "Koro" in Westerafdeeling van Borneo ["Koro" in the Western Part of Borneo]. *Geneeskundig Tijdschrift voor Nederlandsch-Indie* 37:499–505.

Voss, H. L. (1979). The Medicalization of Deviance: A Critical Assessment. *Sociological Forum* 2(1):21–36.

Waldenberg, S. (1981). Koro. *Canadian Journal of Psychiatry* 26:140–141.

Wallace, A.F.C. (1963). Mass Hysteria. Pp. 990–997 in A. Deutsch and H. Fishman (eds.), *The Encyclopedia of Mental Health, Vol. 3.* New York: Franklin Watts.

Walters, G. D. (1992). A Meta-Analysis of the Gene-Crime Relationship. *Criminology* 30:595–613.

Walther, H. (1984). *Hitler.* Greenwich, Conn.: Bison.

Walton, J., Beeson, P., and Scott, R. (eds.). (1986). *The Oxford Companion to Medicine, Vol. 1.* Oxford: Oxford University Press.

Washburn, S. L. (1951). Review of W. H. Sheldon, Varieties of Delinquent Youth. *American Anthropologist* 53:561.

Wason, S., and Bausher, J. (1983). Epidemic Mass Hysteria. *Lancet* 2 (September 24):731–732.

Watson, N. (1982). An Outbreak of Hysterical Paraplegia. *Paraplegia* 3:154–157.

Watson-Verran, H., and Turnbull, D. (1995). Science and Other Indigenous Knowledge Systems. Pp. 115–139 in S. Jasanoff, G. Markle, J. Petersen, and T. Pinch (eds.), *Handbook of Science and Technology Studies.* Thousand Oaks, Calif.: Sage.

Weintraub, M. I. (1983). *Hysterical Conversion Reactions: A Clinical Guide to Diagnosis and Treatment.* Lancaster, UK: MTP.

Wessely, S. (1987). Mass Hysteria: Two Syndromes? *Psychological Medicine* 17:109–120.

Wheeler, L. (1966). Toward a Theory of Behavior Contagion. *Psychological Review* 73:179–192.

White, D. N., and Burtch, R. B. (1954). Iceland Disease: A New Infection Simulating Acute Anterior Poliomyelitis. *Neurology* 4:506–516.

Wichmann, R. (1890). Eine sogenannte veitstanzepidemie in Wildbad [A So-Called Epidemic of Saint Vitus Dance in Wildbad]. *Deutsche Medizinische Wochenschrift* (Leipzig) 16:632–636, 659–663.

Wiedner, D. (1962). *A History of Africa South of the Sahara.* New York: Vintage.

Wilkinson, R. J., Coope, A. E., and Mohamed, M. (1961). *An Abridged Malay-English Dictionary.* London: Macmillan.

Willis, E. (1983). *Medical Dominance: The Division of Labour in Australian Health Care.* Sydney: Allen and Unwin.

Willson, M. (1989). Two Films About Truth and Falsehood. *Anthropology Today* 5(5):17–18.

Wilson, S. A. (1940). Motor Neuroses, the Tics. Pp. 1629–1637 in *Neurology.* London: Butterworth.

Wilson, S. C., and Barber, T. X. (1983). The Fantasy-Prone Personality: For Understanding Imagery, Hypnosis, and Parapsychological Phenomena. Pp. 340–387 in A. A. Sheikh (ed.), *Imagery: Current Theory, Research, and Application.* New York: Wiley.

———. (1981). Vivid Fantasy and Hallucinatory Abilities in the Life Histories of Excellent Hypnotic Subjects ("Somnambules"): Preliminary Report With Female Subjects. Pp. 133–149 in E. Klinger (ed.), *Imagery, Vol. 2, Concepts, Results, and Applications.* New York: Plenum.

Wing, J. K. (1978). *Reasoning About Madness.* Oxford: Oxford University Press.

Winzeler, R. L. (1995). *Latah in Southeast Asia: The History and Ethnography of a Culture-Bound Syndrome.* Cambridge: Cambridge University Press.

———. (1984). The Study of Malayan Latah. *Indonesia* 37:77–104.

Wittstock, B., Rozental, L., and Henn, C. (1991). Mass Phenomena at a Black South African Primary School. *Hospital and Community Psychiatry* 42:851–853.

Wolfgang, M. E. (1972). Cesare Lombroso, 1835–1909. Pp. 232–291 in H. Mannheim (ed.), *Pioneers in Criminology.* Montclair, N.J.: Patterson Smith.

Wong, S. W., Kwong, B., Tam, Y. K., and Tsoi, M. M. (1982). Psychological Epidemic in Hong Kong. *Acta Psychiatrica Scandinavica* 65:421–436.

World Health Organization (1993). *The ICD-10 Classification of Mental and Behavioural Disorders: Diagnostic Criteria for Research.* Geneva: World Health Organization.

Yandell, D. W. (1882). Epidemic Convulsions. *Brain* 4:339–350.

Yap, P. M. (1967). The Culture-Bound Reactive Syndromes. *Australian and New Zealand Journal of Psychiatry* 1:172–179.

———. (1965). Koro—a Culture-Bound Depersonalization Syndrome. *British Journal of Psychiatry* 111:43–50.

———. (1962). Words and Things in Comparative Psychiatry, With Special Reference to Exotic Psychoses. *Acta Psychiatrica Scandinavica* 38:163–169.

———. (1952). The Latah Reaction: Its Pathodynamics and Nosological Position. *Journal of Mental Science* 98:516–564.

———. (1951). Mental Disease Peculiar to Certain Cultures: A Survey of Comparative Psychiatry. *Journal of Mental Science* 97:313–337.

Yassa, R. (1980). A Sociopsychiatric Study of an Egyptian Phenomenon. *American Journal of Psychotherapy* 34:246–251.

Yassi, A., Weeks, J. L., Samson, K., and Raber, M. B. (1989). Epidemic of "Shocks" in Telephone Operators: Lessons for the Medical Community. *Canadian Medical Association Journal* 140:816–820.

Zimbardo, P. G. (1972). Pathology of Imprisonment. *Society* 9:4–8.

Zola, I. (1972). Medicine as an Institution of Social Control. *Sociological Review* 20:487–503.

MALAYSIAN PRESS SOURCES (in Tables 6.1 and 6.2)

These are Malaysian accounts from reliable press sources based on the author's firsthand examination of the newspaper archives of the *New Straits Times* and the *Star.* This section includes an additional report from the *New York Times.*

1. Ramalingam, A. Mystery Attack of Fits and Seizures. *Straits Times,* November 19, 1966.

2. Four-Man Medical Team Visits School: Student Describes Mystery Ghost. *Straits Times,* November 21, 1966, p. 11.

3. Hysteria Breaks Out in Another School in Pahang. *Straits Times,* April 30, 1971, p. 10.

4. Peace Offering Brings School "in Hysterics" Back to Normal. *Straits Times,* May 1, 1971, p. 20.

5. "Hysteria" Pupils Out of Hospital. *Straits Times,* May 7, 1971, p. 21.

6. A Mass Hysteria Puts an End to First Aid Course. *Straits Times,* April 5, 1972, p. 17.

7. Two Girls Warded for Hysteria Leave Hospital. *Straits Times,* April 6, 1972, p. 4.

8. Mass Hysteria Hits School Kuah. *Star,* March 27, 1978.
9. Hysteria at Girls' School. *New Straits Times,* May 18, 1982.
10. School Hit by Mass Hysteria. *New Straits Times,* September 9, 1982.
11. Hysterical Schoolgirls Cause Panic. *Echo,* September 9, 1982.
12. Hysteria Probe. *Bernama,* September 10, 1982.
13. Omar, A. Mass Hysteria in Two Johore Schools. *New Straits Times,* September 21, 1982.
14. "Pontianak" Hysteria. *New Straits Times,* September 21, 1983.
15. Veera, R. V. Soccer Women Fall Foul to Hysterical Fits. *New Straits Times,* August 10, 1983.
16. School Closes After Thirteen Become Hysterical. *Bernama,* August 22, 1983.
17. School Hit by Hysteria. *Bernama,* August 26, 1983.
18. Sekolah ditutup kerana 15 murid sakit histeria [School Closed Because Fifteen Students Had Hysteria Disease]. *Berita Harian,* August 29, 1983.
19. Fifteen Pupils Hit by Mystery Itch. *New Straits Times,* June 6, 1984.
20. Bomoh to the Aid of Hysteria-Stricken Pupils. *New Straits Times,* May 22, 1984.
21. Three in Hospital After Bouts of Hysteria. *New Straits Times,* February 22, 1986.
22. 9 pelajar diserang histeria [Nine Students Stricken With Hysteria]. *Utusan,* February 22, 1986.
23. Sembilan pelajar diserang histeria [Nine Students Stricken With Hysteria]. *Berita Harian,* February 22, 1986.
24. Department Probes Hysteria Outbreak. *New Straits Times,* September 4, 1987.
25. Eleven Hit by Hysteria. *Malay Mail,* September 23, 1987.
26. Hysteria Hits Twenty-three Students. *Bernama,* October 1, 1987.
27. Hysteria at School During Blackout. *Star,* April 30, 1988.
28. Laughing Malady Puzzle in Africa. 1,000 Along Lake Victoria Afflicted in 18 Months—Most Are Youngsters. Schools Close Down. *New York Times,* August 8, 1963, p. 29.
29. Tan, S. Fifty Girls in School Hit by Strange Hysteria. *Straits Times,* March 26, 1971, pp. 1, 24.
30. Tan, S. Girls Hit Again by Hysteria. *Straits Times,* March 27, 1971, p. 15.
31. Tan, S. Hostel Hysterics: 250 Pupils Boycott Classes. *New Straits Times,* March 13, 1973, p. 18.
32. Hysteria Attacks Shut Down Trade School. *New Straits Times,* March 16, 1973, p. 6.
33. New Hostel for Al-Ulum Girls. *Malay Mail,* July 21, 1981.
34. Vijian, K. Hysteria Hits Estate Classes. *New Straits Times,* June 26, 1982.
35. Estate School Spirit on the Prowl Again. *New Straits Times,* August 17, 1982.
36. More Pupils Affected by Hysteria. *Bernama,* October 26, 1986.
37. 12 lagi murid perempuan diserang histeria [Twelve More Female Students Stricken With Hysteria]. *Utusan,* October 26, 1986.
38. Seventeen Bahu Pupils Hit by Hysteria. *Bernama,* October 22, 1986.
39. Rachel, A. Probing Hysteria Cases in Two Schools. *New Straits Times,* July 4, 1986.
40. Rachel, A. Probing Hysteria Cases in Two Schools. *New Straits Times,* July 4, 1986 (second, separate episode from previous citation).
41. 12 lagi murid perempaun diserang histeria [Twelve More Female Students Stricken With Hysteria]. *Utusan,* October 26, 1986.

42. More Pupils Affected by Hysteria. *Bernama,* October 26, 1986.

43. Hysteria Students "cured." *New Straits Times,* July 21, 1987.

44. Hysteria Hits Sixteen Pupils of Residential School. *New Straits Times,* August 25, 1987.

45. Hysteria Hit School Closed for Two Days. *New Straits Times,* July 8, 1987.

46. Outbreak of Hysteria Caused by a Bomoh. *New Straits Times,* July 9, 1987.

47. Students Still Hysterical. *New Straits Times,* July 10, 1987.

48. 100 Pupils and Two Teachers Yet to Return. *New Straits Times,* July 10, 1987.

49. Hysteria Students to Be Transferred. *Bernama,* May 20, 1985.

50. Hysterical Pupils Take Schoolmates Hostage. *New Straits Times,* May 19, 1987, p. 1.

51. Hysteria: Schoolgirls "Confess." *New Straits Times,* May 21, 1987, p. 3.

52. Hysteria Blamed on "Evil Spirits": School Head Wants the Ghosts to Go. *New Straits Times,* May 23, 1987, p. 7.

53. Council to Meet Over Hysteria-Stricken Girls. *New Straits Times,* May 24, 1987, p. 4.

54. Seven Girls Scream for Blood: Hysterical Outbursts Continue. *New Straits Times,* May 25, 1987, p. 4.

55. Interview: Fatimah, "I Only Fulfilled My Parents' Wishes." *New Straits Times,* May 31, 1987, p. 7.

56. I Can't Believe It, Says Pupil. *New Straits Times,* May 31, 1987, p. 7.

57. Transfer Plan for Girls Hit by Hysteria. *New Straits Times,* July 21, 1987.

58. First Group of Hysteria Girls Sees Psychiatrist. *New Straits Times,* August 11, 1987.

59. Hysteria: Second Batch Visits "Shrink." *New Straits Times,* August 13, 1987.

60. Parents of "Hysteria" Girls Agree to Transfer. *New Straits Times,* July 24, 1987.

61. Girls Turn Hysterical After Forest Outing. *New Straits Times,* June 12, 1989.

62. Hysterics Over "Spirit of the Coin." *New Straits Times,* June 17, 1989.

63. Students Hit by Hysteria. *New Straits Times,* February 24, 1989.

64. 100 Factory and College Girls in Hysterical Drama. *New Straits Times,* September 18, 1991.

65. Wahab, A., and Jamaludin, F. Hysterical Fifteen Get More Time. *New Straits Times,* September 27, 1991.

66. Hysteria in Three Schools Under Control. *New Straits Times,* September 29, 1991.

67. Hysteria Hits Thirty More Students. *New Straits Times,* October 1, 1991.

68. Jamaludin, F. "Haunted" School Bans Newsmen. *New Straits Times,* October 3, 1991.

69. Klang Pupils in a Frenzy: Hysteria Hits School. *Malay Mail,* July 20, 1993.

70. De Paul, V. Mass Hysteria in Sentul Girls' School. *Malay Mail,* January 28, 1994, p. 12.

71. Vasudevan, V. More Pupils Hit by Hysteria. *Malay Mail,* July 29, 1994.

Index